Analytical Transport Economics

TRANSPORT ECONOMICS, MANAGEMENT AND POLICY

General Editor: Kenneth Button, *Professor of Public Policy, Institute of Public Policy, George Mason University, USA*

Transport is a critical input for economic development and for optimizing social and political interaction. Recent years have seen significant new developments in the way that transport is perceived by private industry and governments, and in the way academics look at it.

The aim of this series is to provide original material and up-to-date synthesis of the state of modern transport analysis. The coverage embraces all conventional modes of transport but also includes contributions from important related fields such as urban and regional planning and telecommunications where they interface with transport. The books draw from many disciplines and some cross disciplinary boundaries. They are concerned with economics, planning, sociology, geography, management science, psychology and public policy. They are intended to help improve the understanding of transport, the policy needs of the most economically advanced countries and the problems of resource-poor developing economies. The authors come from around the world and will represent some of the outstanding young scholars as well as established names.

Titles in the series include:

Air Transport Networks
Theory and Policy Implications
Kenneth Button and Roger R. Stough

Analytical Transport Economics
An International Perspective
Edited by Jacob B. Polak and Arnold Heertje

Analytical Transport Economics

An International Perspective

Edited by

Jacob B. Polak

*Professor of Transport Economics, University of Groningen,
The Netherlands*

and

Arnold Heertje

*Professor of Economics, University of Amsterdam,
The Netherlands*

TRANSPORT ECONOMICS, MANAGEMENT AND POLICY

Edward Elgar

Cheltenham, UK • Northampton, MA, USA

Published by
Edward Elgar Publishing Limited
The Lypiatts
15 Lansdown Road
Cheltenham
Glos GL50 2JA
UK

Edward Elgar Publishing, Inc.
William Pratt House
9 Dewey Court
Northampton
Massachusetts 01060
USA

A catalogue record for this book is available from the British Library

Library of Congress Cataloguing in Publication Data

Analytical transport economics : an international perspective / edited by Jacob B. Polak, Arnold Heertje.
    Includes bibliographical references and index.
    1. Transportation. 2. Transportation and state. I. Polak, J.B. II. Heertje, Arnold, 1934– III. Title.

HE151 .A366 2001
388–dc21

00–033171

MIX
Paper from
responsible sources
FSC   FSC® C013604
www.fsc.org

ISBN   978 1 84542 626 2 (Hardback)
        978 1 84064 816 4 (Paperback)

Printed and bound by CPI Group (UK) Ltd, Croydon, CR0 4YY

This book was made possible, in part, by the support of
the Schiphol Group, The Netherlands.

Contents

Figures

Tables

Editor biographies

Arnold Heertje studied economics at the University of Amsterdam, The Netherlands, where he also obtained his PhD (cum laude). In 1964, he became Professor of Economics in the Faculty of Law of the same university, until his retirement in 1999. He has written books and articles on the economics of technical change, oligopoly, welfare economics, Schumpeterian economics and the history of economic thought. He is the editor of several books which deal with international economic problems and are written by scholars of international repute. He was President of the J.A. Schumpeter Society during 1986–88. In 1997, he was appointed Professor in the History of Economic Thought at the University of Amsterdam.

Jacob B. Polak also studied economics at the University of Amsterdam, The Netherlands. Until his retirement a few years ago, he was a Senior Lecturer in Transport Economics at the University of Amsterdam and Professor in the same field at the University of Groningen, The Netherlands. He has been the editor or principal co-editor of a number of books, on the subjects of general transport economics, transport policy and transport for elderly and handicapped persons. He is Chairman of the Transport Committee of the Social and Economic Council of The Netherlands and has been Chairman of the Benelux Interuniversity Association of Transport Economists. He also is a member of a number of editorial or editorial advisory boards of transport journals.

Contributors

Monika Bąk studied economics at the University of Gdansk, Poland, where she obtained her PhD in 1996. Her present position is (PhD) Tutor at the Department of Comparative Analysis of Transportation Systems. She works in the fields of the economics of transport, transport policy and the theory of European integration (especially of transport).

Herbert Baum studied economics at the universities of Berlin and Cologne. He has been Professor of Economics at the Federal Armed Forces University in Hamburg, and at the universities of Bochum and of Essen. Presently he is Professor of Economics and Director of the Institute for Transport Economics at the University of Cologne, Germany. He is a member of the Advisory Board of the Ministry of Transport of the Federal Republic of Germany and of the Airport Commission of the same Ministry. He furthermore functions as an expert for the European Conference of Ministers of Transport (ECMT) in Paris.

Jan Burnewicz studied economics at the University of Gdansk, Poland, where he also obtained his PhD. He is Professor of Comparative Analysis of Transportation Systems, heading the department of this name, and presently also is Dean of the Faculty of Economics at the University of Gdansk. His work is in the fields of the economics of transport, the theory of European integration (especially of transport), simulation of economic decision making with the help of informatics, investment decisions and the theory of competitive strategy.

Kenneth J. Button is Professor of Public Policy at the Institute of Public Policy, George Mason University, USA. Prior to this he was Counsellor in the Advisory Unit to the Secretary General of the Organization for Economic Cooperation and Development (OECD) in Paris, where he directed work on International Aviation. At that time, he was also Professor of Applied Economics and Transport at Loughborough University, UK, and VSB Visiting Professor of Transport and the Environment at the Tinbergen Institute in Amsterdam, The Netherlands. He is the author of a great number of books and articles.

Manfred M. Fischer is Professor of Geography and Head of the Department of Economic and Social Geography at the Vienna University of Economics and Business Administration. He studied mathematics and geography at the university of Erlangen-Nürnberg, Germany. Since obtaining his PhD in 1975, Professor Fischer has visited many European and American universities as visiting professor, scholar or external examiner. He has published widely in the leading journals in the fields. He serves on the editorial boards of many distinguished international geography and regional science journals and has acted as Chairman of the International Geographical Union (IGU) Commission on Mathematical Models since 1988.

Ken Gwilliam is principal transport economist with the World Bank, Washington, DC, where he authored the 1996 World Bank Transport Sector Policy paper. He has been involved in transport project and policy design and evaluation in many countries. From 1967 to 1988 he was Professor of Transport Economics and Director of the Institute for Transport Studies at the University of Leeds, UK and from 1989 to 1992 was Professor of Economics of Transport and Logistics at Erasmus University, Rotterdam, The Netherlands. Other major activities have included appointments as Director of the British National Bus Company, as Adviser to the British House of Commons Transport Committee, and as Director General of Transport for the European Economic Community (EEC). For ten years, he was joint editor of the *Journal of Transport Economics and Policy*.

Jan Owen Jansson holds a PhD in economics from Stockholm School of Economics. He is Professor of Transport Economics at Linköping University, Sweden and is a member of the Scientific Council of the Statens Instit för Kommunikationsanalys (Swedish National Institute for Communication Analysis: SIKA) of the Ministry of Transport in Sweden. Commissions abroad include work for the New Zealand Ministry of Transport and for Zim Navigation Co. (Israel). The main research projects in which he has been engaged had to do with cost–benefit analysis of transport infrastructure, urban transport and land-use policy, and pricing policy for transport infrastructure and services. He has also published several books and many articles on transport economics.

Sergio R. Jara-Díaz is Professor of Transport Economics at the Civil Engineering Department, Universidad de Chile. He holds several degrees, including a PhD and an MSc from the Massachusetts Institute of Technology (MIT), USA. His research includes multi-output transport cost functions, users' behaviour, welfare measures, value of time and public transport pricing. He has been a member of the Editorial Board of *Transportation Research B*, President of the Chilean Society of Transport Engineers, and Visiting Professor at MIT for three terms. He has published more than forty research articles in books and refereed journals.

Martin J.H. Mogridge has been a transport and planning consultant specializing in policy development for large cities since 1978. He has worked at the Greater London Council, at the Centre for Environmental Studies (London), and from 1978 to 1993 also held a part-time position as an associate senior researcher at University College London. Until his sudden death in early 2000, he was working on forecasting the spatial development of the rapidly growing population of London.

Peter Nijkamp studied econometrics at Erasmus University, Rotterdam, The Netherlands, where he also obtained his PhD (cum laude). Since 1975, he has been Professor in Regional and Urban Economics and in Economic Geography at the Free University, Amsterdam. His main research interests cover plan evaluation, multicriteria analysis, regional and urban planning, transport systems analysis, mathematical modelling, technological innovation, and resource management. In recent years he has focused his research in particular on quantitative methods for policy analysis, as well as on behavioural analysis of economic subjects. In all these fields, he has published various books and numerous articles. He has been an adviser to several Dutch ministries, employers' organizations, private institutions, the Commission of the European Union, the Organization for Economic Cooperation and Development (OECD), the European Conference of Ministers of Transport (ECMT) and many other institutions. Furthermore he is past-president of the Regional Science Association International, Chairman of the Network on European Communications and Transport Activity Research (NECTAR), Chairman of the Dutch Social Science Council, a member of the Board of the Royal Dutch Academy of Science and Chairman of the new research school, TRAIL (a collaborative initiative of the Erasmus University Rotterdam and Delft Technical University).

Emile Quinet is Professor at the Ecole Nationale des Ponts et Chaussées in Paris and at the Ecole Polytechnique Féderale de Lausanne, Switzerland; he is also a part-time adviser to the Ministry of Transport in France, as a member of the Conseil Général des Ponts et Chaussées. He works mainly in the fields of public services economics and especially transport; his main publications are related to environment, infrastructure and regulation. He works as an expert to governments and international organizations and is a member of the editorial board of several international journals.

Piet Rietveld studied econometrics at Erasmus University, Rotterdam, The Netherlands. He holds a PhD in regional economics from the Free University, Amsterdam where he is currently Professor of Transport Economics. Over the past fifteen years he has worked on various topics in the fields of transport economics and regional economics, including: the impact of transport infrastructure on spatial development, the social feasibility of transport policies, multicriteria analysis and policy evaluation in transport planning, barrier effects of borders on transport and communication, and regional dimensions of development problems in developing countries.

Werner Rothengatter studied industrial engineering at the University of Karlsruhe, Germany, where he obtained his PhD and finished his habilitation (2nd PhD). His special fields of research are forecasting and assessment for the transport infrastructure, system dynamics in transport, regulation and pricing policy as well as transport and the environment. He presently is Professor of Economics at the University of Karlsruhe, Germany. He has published a large number of journal articles and several books. Furthermore, he is a member of the Scientific Advisory Board of the German Ministry of Transport, Construction and Housing and participates in a number of national and international research associations, among which is the World Congress on Transport Research (WCTR), where he is Chairman of the Scientific Committee and Member of the Steering Committee. He also is a member of a number of editorial advisory boards of transport journals.

Wolfgang H. Schulz studied economics at the University of Bochum, Germany. Since 1990, he has been research assistant at the Institute for Transport Economics at the University of Cologne, where he obtained his doctorate in 1994. His main research areas are focused on monitoring and assessing of infrastructure investment, the deregulation of transport markets and modelling the effects of transport.

Preface

For over half a century, with great regularity books have appeared that give an introduction to transport economics. Each of these has its own qualities. Not many, however, have an international character in both dealing with issues of interest to an international audience and being written by a combined international authorship. This is what is particular for the present book.

The book first appeared under the title *European Transport Economics*, at the occasion of the fortieth anniversary of the European Conference of Ministers of Transport (ECMT), in 1993. That edition has now been revised. A few chapters had lost their usefulness and were, therefore, omitted. A number of completely new chapters, such as those on transport in transitional economies and on transport in developing economies, were added. Most of the other chapters were thoroughly revised and updated by their authors. In the eyes of the editors, the result was a new book, and not merely a revised edition of the earlier book. This is expressed by the changed title, *Analytical Transport Economics: An International Perspective*. One may wonder why 'Analytical' and not just 'Transport Economics'. Adding the word 'Analytical' reflects the opinion of the editors that transport economics is a fully-fledged part of the discipline of economics, with a theoretical analysis of its own, and neither a body of descriptive detail nor just some tool for solving practical transport problems. The latter statement should not be misunderstood, however, as the theoretical insights developed by transport economics can be of great help in finding solutions for the many transport problems that beset all kinds of economies.

Although there is some variation in the degree of complexity and in the use of formal, mathematical, analysis between the various chapters, the book will on the whole be found to be most useful to advanced students. The word 'students' should here be taken in a wide sense. It includes both those still studying at a university or comparable institution and those who have their studies behind them and want to refresh their knowledge of the subject.

It is a very sad circumstance indeed, that one of the authors, Dr Martin J.H. Mogridge did not live to see the publication of the present book. He died suddenly on 29 February 2000. Dr Mogridge was an outstanding expert in the problems of urban transport, and particularly those in London. He published widely on this subject. We are highly grateful that Dr Mogridge was willing to contribute to our book. We are convinced that for many years to come readers of the book will reap the benefits from his very thorough knowledge of the subject of urban transport.

This Preface is the place for the editors to express their gratitude to the management of Schiphol Airport (N.V. Luchthaven Schiphol), The Netherlands, for having contributed to the realization of this project.

Some who have done their work behind the scenes should also be named here. In particular, we are very grateful to Mrs E. Dokter-Parchow, who was very involved in the organizational and secretarial tasks connected with the publishing of this book, and to Mr K. Versélewel de Witt Hamer, formerly assistant in the Faculty of Economics, University of Groningen, The Netherlands, who, without having the title, enthusiastically undertook the tasks of an assistant editor of the book.

Jacob B. Polak
Arnold Heertje

PART I

Introduction

1. A perspective of transport economics

Jacob B. Polak[*]

1 AIM AND CONTENTS OF THIS CHAPTER

The aim of the present chapter is twofold: first to introduce the reader to the field of transport economics and second, to introduce the reader to the other chapters of this book.

The first part, dealing with the introduction to the field of transport economics, is approached by means of a number of steps. The first step consists of finding an answer to the basic question why it is even necessary to have transport economics as a distinct field within economics (Section 2).

Once the answer to this question has been given, we then consider what place transport economics holds within the whole of economics (Section 3). Next, we examine the question of what fields from economics may be found in transport economics (Section 4). While this question is of a theoretical nature, it is followed by a brief historical sketch of transport economics. In this, the main fields from economics around which transport economics has so far actually developed are identified (Section 5).

Introducing the reader to the further contents of the book – the second part of the aim of the chapter – is done by means of three sections, of increasing detail as far as the book's contents are concerned. Thus, first, and in very general terms, the scope of the book is elucidated (Section 6). After this, the main fields covered by the book are reviewed and commented upon (Section 7). The final section of the chapter (Section 8) contains summaries of all other chapters, which are intended as a preview of each of the chapters. By this the reader may be better able to choose, if so desired, a path through the book different from the one chosen by the editors.

2 WHY TRANSPORT ECONOMICS?

Today, no one would doubt that 'transport' is something to be studied by economics. In earlier periods of its development, however, as will presently be set out, it was not at all clear that 'transport' was within the scope of economics.

[*] The author wishes to thank Professors Arnold Heertje and Jan Oosterhaven and Mr Ken Versélewel de Witt Hamer for their valuable comments on an earlier draft of this chapter.

2.1 Value

As is generally known, Adam Smith was of the opinion that the 'value' of an object is determined by its cost of production or, more specifically, by the cost of labour sacrificed. Not all labour was considered by Smith as 'productive', or contributing to value. Thus, in the eyes of Smith, 'the labour of the manufacturer fixes and realises itself in some particular subject or vendible commodity'. Smith thought quite differently of the labour of the 'menial servant'. This is because, according to Smith, the services of such a person 'generally perish in the very instant of their performance, and seldom leave any trace or value behind them' (Smith, 1776/1964).[1] Not much imagination is required in order to see that for Smith labour sacrificed in bringing about 'transport' would have been in much the same category as the services of the menial servant, equally 'not leaving any trace behind it' – and therefore not of any value either.[2]

This situation, where transport could only be seen as something outside the scope of economics, changed fundamentally about a century after Adam Smith. This may appear as follows. By the 1870s, a view of what causes 'value' quite different from that held by Adam Smith and his followers conquered the stage. Now it was judged that commodities have value when people, to use a formulation by Menger (1871), depend on them for the satisfaction of their wants.[3] If a distance exists between households and the objects these households demand, either as an input for production or for purposes of consumption, doing away with this distance by transferring a person representing a given household towards the object demanded or vice versa – 'transporting' either of these – clearly is something people depend on for the 'satisfaction of their wants'.

From the foregoing it follows that only with the views of Menger (and others; the subjectivists) replacing those held by the objectivists (Smith and his adherents) has it became possible to conceive of 'transport' as an economic category.

2.2 Space

If it is accepted that a study of transport falls within the scope of economics, this in itself does not call for a separate field within economics for the study of transport. For this to be the case, transport in some respect would have to be different from all other commodities, such as grain or machines for road building. For a long time during the history of economics, the grounds for seeing transport in such a way were lacking. In the oft-quoted words of Isard (1956): most of economic theory confined itself to 'a wonderland of no spatial dimensions'.[4] On the other hand, Isard stressed that all economic behaviour should be seen as taking place in space.

'Space' implies 'the separation of economic activities by distance and the organisation of the economy into distinct areas, such as towns and regions' (Vickerman, 1980, p. 1). In a more formal manner, 'space' has been defined as a relation on a set of objects (Gattrell, 1983). The 'objects' may be anything belonging to a well-defined set. In the context of economics, the elements of the set would be households, or the objects demanded by households. An immediate consequence of taking account of space is that the definition of any particular commodity consists not only of its physical and time characteristics, but also of its spatial characteristics.

One might rightfully remark that on a higher level of abstraction any distinction between the various dimensions of a commodity, in particular its physical and its spatial characteristics, would fall away. In principle, this may be true. The fact is, however, that Isard's 'wonderland of no spatial dimensions' is still very much present in economic reasoning.[5] Thus, a definition of a commodity is still mostly limited to its physical and time characteristics. As long as this situation continues to exist, a very strong case remains for making special room in economics for the study of all spatial subjects, among which is transport.

3 TRANSPORT ECONOMICS AND OTHER ECONOMICS

Above it has been argued that transport economics is entitled to a distinct place of its own. The relationship of transport economics to other parts of economics will now be examined. To this end, the following questions will be considered in turn:

1. How can the relation of transport economics to general economics be characterized?
2. Is transport economics of a theoretical or of a practical nature?
3. What is the place of transport economics within spatial economics?

3.1 Transport Economics and General Economics

The definitions of transport and of transport economics given above imply a definition of the relationship of transport economics to general economic theory. For a proper understanding of what transport economics is it may still be useful, however, to see whether anything more general about this relationship can be said.

As one may see from any academic curriculum, the discipline of economics has grown to consist of a great many specializations – or subsets of general economic theory. The particular relationship to general economic theory of any given specialization is determined, as will be clear, by the way the set of phenomena that is studied by general economic theory is narrowed down in order to obtain the specialized field in question. Thus, one may study 'trade' in general, but also limit oneself to trade between countries, which leads one to the theory of international economic relations. To give another example, one may study certain phenomena in an economy without specifying the level of development of that economy. On the other hand, one finds that certain assumptions are being made about the level of development, of which the theory of development economics is an instance.

In the same way, it is possible to single out one particular type of commodity – or element from the set of all types of commodities – and study the behaviour of economic subjects with regard only to that type of commodity. This, apparently, is the criterion that defines the relationship of transport economics to economic theory in general. In this, transport economics is in one class with subjects like health economics, insurance economics, the economics of art and agricultural economics.

3.2   Theoretical Analysis or Practical Instrument?

In the argument above, it is implied that transport economics consists of theoretical analysis. One sometimes comes across a different view, however. Transport economics then is seen as a form of what is called 'applied economics'. If one consults a dictionary, for the word 'applied, one may find a definition like: 'put to practical use as opposed to being theoretical' (*The Concise Oxford Dictionary*, 1999). It is true that the theoretical analysis given by transport economics may be used for shedding light on the solution of practical problems. In this, however, transport economics is not different from any other part of economics, such as microeconomics, macroeconomics, monetary theory or welfare theory.[6] It would, therefore, certainly be wrong to identify transport economics with the 'putting to practical use' of economic theory. The character of transport economics is that of theoretical analysis as much as any other part of economics.

As an illustration of the theoretical character of transport economics, attention may be drawn to certain illuminating statements by the great historian of economic analysis, Schumpeter (1954). It may be considered very significant that Schumpeter, when surveying the development of general economics from 1870 onwards, had already taken care to examine the contribution by fields such as international trade, public finance, labour economics, agricultural economics and railroad economics (Schumpeter chose to call these 'the applied fields').[7]

Schumpeter's position with regard to fields like those mentioned becomes very clear from a remark he made concerning 'railroad economics'. After having stated that 'any decent theory of cost and price ought to be able to make valuable contributions to railroad economics', Schumpeter went on to say: 'and railroad economics ought to be able to repay the service by offering to general theory interesting special patterns and problems' (Schumpeter, 1954, p. 948).

What Schumpeter said about 'railroad economics' may be considered as exemplary, that is, may be extended to all other subjects that Schumpeter would have called 'applied fields', including, in particular, transport economics. What may be concluded from this illustration is that any repayment – in the Schumpeterian sense – to general economic theory by fields like those mentioned by Schumpeter can logically only be thought of if these fields themselves are of a theoretical nature.

It may, finally, be noted that contributions to general economic theory by transport economics are not, as may easily be imagined, limited to railway economics or to what Schumpeter said about this. Several other important instances of such contributions may be cited.[8]

3.3 Transport Economics and Spatial Economics

Above it has been argued that as soon as space is introduced into economics, then transport presents itself to economics as an object of study. Transport economics, therefore, may clearly be seen as part of that field within economics that studies the consequences of space for the behaviour of economic subjects – spatial economics. With this, however, the relationship between transport economics and the more encompassing subject of spatial economics has been described only partly. The relationship between the two will be examined further in what follows.

For the sake of exposition, let the simple case be considered of two households, A and B, located at different points in space. Suppose that one of these two households, say A, wants to enter into an economic relationship with the other household, B. A solution for A to the problem of its being spatially separated from B would be resorting to transport – of goods and/or of persons from and/or to B, as the case may be. In order to be in equilibrium, A will have to determine what is the optimum amount of transport (in the simplest case, given the quantities to be transported: the optimum number of movements; the 'optimum' may be measured by whatever standard). For A, resorting to transport would not do away with what might be called the 'underlying cause' of its having to resort to transport, that is, its spatial separation from B as such. Given this separation, every time A wants to renew its economic relationship with B transport would again be necessary. An alternative solution, however, exists for A. Clearly, it could also decide to change its location in space and move closer to B.

The important point here is that if this latter possibility is taken into account, for A to be in an overall – spatial – equilibrium, it is not enough to choose its optimum amount of transport, but it will also have to choose an optimal change in its location. Choosing an optimum amount of transport, in other words, appears to be only a partial solution to the spatial equilibrium of A (compare van den Bergh, 1997).

It need not be said that reality is much more complex than the (two-household) example used here. The conclusions regarding the relative roles of transport and of locational changes, however, would remain fundamentally the same for a situation of any number of households larger than two.

In the foregoing, transport has been treated as fully complementary with locational changes. Something more needs to be said about this, however. In non-spatial economics, a distinction is usually made between a short- and a long-run equilibrium of any given household; such a distinction can also be made with respect to its spatial equilibrium. The short run then is defined as that period of time where all locations necessarily are fixed. The only possible changes in the short run by definition are changes in the amount of transport. The long run, by contrast, is defined as that period of time where all locations can also be varied.

With regard to the initial question of the relationship between transport economics and overall spatial economics it may now be concluded that, from the point of view of a spatial equilibrium, transport economics deals only with short-run equilibria. Spatial economics as a whole also extends to long-run equilibria.

4   'PROBLEMS TACKLED'

It has been noted by Button (1993, p. 2) that: 'The scope of each of the sub-disciplines within economics (for example, agricultural economics, development economics, public sector economics, etc.) is determined not by particular schools or philosophies but rather by the type of subject matter examined and the problems tackled'. The general question of the 'type of subject matter' has been dealt with above, and it may now be seen, in more detail, what are the 'problems tackled', or fields analysed, in transport economics.

To begin with, a number of authors see transport economics (mostly) as a specialized field of microeconomics.[9] Such a view of transport economics, it may be said, may have been valid during a certain – perhaps even long – period of time. Now, however, it is contradicted by the facts in many ways. This will become clear from the (brief) remarks on the historical development of the subject below as well as from the further contents of this book (in particular Chapters 8, 12 and 13, on transport infrastructure and regional development, on transport in economies in transition and on the role of transport in developing economies, respectively).

Further, logically, there is absolutely no need to conceive of transport economics as having to do with only one – or whatever limited number – out of the many fields of economics. It had already been observed many years ago (for instance, Napp-Zinn, 1948, 1968) – and the same applies to all other specializations of economics that focus on one particular type of commodity – that transport economics cuts across all other (non-sectoral) fields of economics. One may note that this is implied by the nature of transport economics as having as its object of study one particular class of commodities out of the total set of classes of commodities. Transport economics, in other words, in principle may encompass all subjects one normally finds in the curriculum of the economics department of a university. This is with the (logical) exception of monetary subjects and of subjects dealing with other single classes of commodities than transport.

What problem fields have actually come to make up the subject of transport economics over time will be set out briefly in the following section.

5   A LITTLE HISTORY

The history of transport economics overall has not received much attention from the practitioners of the subject.[10] Two notable exceptions are Munby (1968) and Button (1993).[11]

The following may be seen as a brief indication of the main problem fields around which transport economics has been structured.

1. *Theory of the relationship between transport and economic development*
    Munby (1968, p. 8) has stated that the 'wide influence of transport on almost all aspects of life has long been generally known to economists and others' from Adam Smith onwards. Indeed, the subject of the influence of transport on economic development has already been studied by eighteenth- and nineteenth-century writers. In addition to Adam Smith (1776), the main early contributors to this field have been authors such as List (1838) and Knies (1853).[12] What originally was the study of economic development as a very broad field, in more recent times has evolved into a number of distinct specializations within economics, for example, the theories of economic growth, of regional economics and of development economics. This development on the level of economics in general is mirrored in transport economics.

2. *Microeconomics*   It is mostly agreed that for a long time transport economics was dominated by the study of problems of microeconomics (see, for instance, Button, 1993). For a large part, these were problems of what today would be called problems of producer behaviour and of

competition. The expansion of the railways in the second half of the nineteenth century stimulated interest in these problems. As railways grew into monopolies, problems of monopoly pricing received special attention.[13] In later years, the analysis of competition, originally limited to railways, was extended to other branches of transport.[14] Consumer behaviour was a subject long neglected in transport economics. However, it developed slowly out of post-Second World War planning studies, for which travel forecasts were an important input.

3. *Welfare theory*   Welfare theory has been connected with transport problems at least since Dupuit, whose contribution was twofold. First, he developed a measure for the utility of public works (Dupuit, 1844). This, as is generally recognized, was the basis for what today is known as 'cost–benefit analysis'. Second, he analysed the problem of the optimum use of infrastructure (Dupuit, 1849).

   As has been pointed out by a number of authors (for instance, Thomson, 1974; Button, 1993), the place of welfare theory in the study of transport was considerably expanded at a much later date, in the second half of the twentieth century.[15] One may think here of the problem of the external effects of transport and, somewhat later, also of that of the (welfare) effects of various liberalizing measures (deregulation, privatization) for transport.[16] It also deserves to be mentioned, however, that from the 1960s onwards various studies of a welfare-theoretical nature appeared, relating to the subject of infrastructure (for example: Walters, 1961, 1968; Allais et al., 1965; Malcor, 1970; Oort, 1960, 1970).

4. *Macroeconomics*   It is not customary to associate transport economics with macroeconomics. Nevertheless, attention should be drawn to the fact that during the 1960s a number of studies, by German authors, appeared in which transport was considered in relation to problems of a macroeconomic nature. Examples are the dependence of transport volumes on cyclical development and the relationship between transport investment and national economic development.[17] More recently, Gwilliam (1998) likewise has pointed out that transport economics also implies the study of macroeconomic problems.

5. *Business economics*   Like macroeconomics, the study of transport from the point of view of business economics is also not generally considered part of transport economics. Nevertheless, the many studies in this field that have appeared since at least the 1960s, especially by German-language economists, witness the importance of this subject for transport.[18] In addition to the 'classical' business economics approach to transport it should be noted that in more recent years – from the 1970s onwards – the study of transport as part of the field of business logistics has been greatly developed (see also Rakowski, 1976).

6   SCOPE OF THE BOOK

'Transport economics' is, as will have become clear from the previous section, a very wide subject. It would be virtually impossible to cover the whole of this field and the book does not pretend to do this. One limitation in particular is that, in the book, transport is approached from the perspective of general economics. Because of its specialized nature and (mostly) different approach, problems of business economics are not included.

This also is the place to pay attention to the word 'analytical' in the title of the book. As discussed in the previous section, some see transport economics and similar fields merely as 'applications' of economic theory. For others, description weighs heavily in their approach to transport economics. By using the word 'analytical' in the title, the editors want to express that they have let themselves be guided by their view of transport economics as a domain of theoretical analysis.

7   STRUCTURE OF THE BOOK

The book is divided into five parts. Part I consists of this, introductory, chapter. The other parts are: Households and markets in transport (Part II), Infrastructure (Part III), Policy (Part IV) and Some special cases (Part V). This structure is based principally on the distinction between the analysis of private and that of public households.

It is not unusual for treatises on transport economics to follow a different logic. That is, the main distinction made is that between problems connected with the output of the 'mobile' means of production and those connected with the spatially fixed ones, or transport and infrastructure services. Which of the two logics is to be preferred? The distinction between mobile and spatially fixed means of production is of a technical nature. As such, there is no use for it in an economic context. One might object, however, that transport services in the main are provided by private households and infrastructure services by public households. Then, the two types of distinctions would coincide and consequently it makes no difference whether the one or the other is used.

It may be true that in certain periods and/or for certain institutional settings a 'division of labour' between private and public households applies, such as in the latter case. This certainly cannot be considered as a general rule, however. It is for this reason that preference is given here to a structure based on the distinction between private and public households, which fits in with general economic analysis.

Based on the above, in Part II the behaviour of private households – demand, supply and their confrontation in the transport market – is analysed. Parts III and IV both have as their object the behaviour of governments and other public authorities. The distinction between these last two parts coincides with the two main groups of instruments that public authorities may use in order to influence the economic process. One group consists of the ownership of certain means of production. This is dealt with in Part III, where it is in particular assumed that the spatially fixed means of production for transport – infrastructure – are owned by the public authorities. The second group of instruments to be used by public authorities consists of the direct compulsion of private households, or regulation, regardless of whether these households are producers or consumers of transport. This, in the main, is the subject of Part IV.

It might be thought that not much scope remains for an analysis of transport policy, since in recent years transport deregulation and privatization have much diminished the role of government as an active player. Any decision on the part of a public authority, whether to intervene in the economic process or not, affects the allocation of scarce resources. This is why there will always be a need for an analysis of transport policy, whatever the actual behaviour of the public authorities.

Finally, Part V (special cases) considers a number of problem areas concerning transport that present themselves if certain implicit assumptions of standard economic theory are relaxed. The exact nature of these assumptions will be explained, together with the review of the individual chapters concerned, in the next section.

8   THE INDIVIDUAL CHAPTERS

Following the discussion on the different parts of this book, the scope will now be narrowed down to the individual chapters. It will be recalled that the purpose of this is to assist the reader in making a choice as to the chapters to be read and the order in which to read them.

Chapter 2 ('Transport production and the analysis of industry structure') first sets out the theory of the production of transport. From this, it moves on to an analysis of the structure of the transport industry. The chapter combines a theoretical treatment with an overview of results from empirical work. The theoretical analysis first considers the concept of transport production. The mathematical formulation clearly brings out what familiar concepts like 'output' and 'production function' come to look like if the existence of space is taken into account.

Next, short-run decision rules for the transport operator are identified, regarding frequencies, routes, speeds and vehicle loads, which concern the efficient combinations of inputs for a given structure and size of output. This technical optimum is linked with the cost function. At this point, the spatial character of transport once more becomes apparent. The spatial character inevitably leads to the treatment of transport as a multi-output activity, each pair of origins and destinations being a single output of the transport firm. Treating transport as a multi-output activity logically leads to a multi-output cost function, which is presented as a fundamental tool for the analysis of economies of scale and of scope. Such an analysis is instrumental for understanding what can be seen as the optimal industry structure. Finally, in this part of the chapter, some reflections are presented on the concepts of aggregate output and the 'cost' of aggregate output. The ambiguity of these two concepts is shown and it is argued that the analysis of the structure of the transport industry is made much more complicated by this ambiguity. After this theoretical analysis, an extensive review of empirical work concerning transport cost functions follows. In particular, the different functional forms of cost functions that have been used are discussed. Furthermore, the problem of the proper specification of output is considered. In conclusion, problems in the estimation of scale and of scope economies when output aggregates are used are discussed.

Chapter 3 ('Travel demand') deals with the demand for the transport of persons (passenger transport). The chapter explicitly does not deal with the demand for the transport of goods. This is because the latter type of demand is exercised by producers (demand for inputs to production processes). Demand for inputs is the subject of the theory of the firm and as such falls within the scope of the previous chapter. Chapter 3 first makes clear that after the Second World War, in the context of large-scale planning exercises, especially for urban areas, the need arose for making forecasts of travel demand. The chapter reviews the developments in travel demand modelling over the past three decades. Although travel demand models may have their origin in transport planning, in present-day research the emphasis in the main is analytical in character, and this also applies in this chapter.

Three main approaches of travel demand modelling are reviewed, based on: aggregate flows, microeconomics and activity analysis. The accent is on the second of these, which can be seen as the present-day, 'mainstream', approach. Attention is also paid to the measurement of travel choice, notably the functional form of choice models and the way data may be obtained. Lastly, the approach that focuses on the relationship between activities and travel is set out. The chapter concludes by stating that the two modern approaches, microeconomic and activity-based analyses of travel demand, both have much to offer. It is therefore recommended that a major effort be devoted to further integrating these two, in themselves very different, approaches.

'Cost' in Chapters 2 and 3 has been taken as cost that is fully borne by the household that gives rise to these costs ('internal' cost). Chapter 4 ('External effects of transport') considers costs caused to third parties. First, the concept of external effects is clarified. This clarification consists of a discussion, and also modelling, of the two very differing approaches of this concept as advanced by Pigou on the one hand and by Coase on the other. Following this discussion of the concept of externalities in general, an extensive theoretical treatment is given of the external effects of transport. Most space is devoted here to the valuation of the external costs of accidents and of the environment. These may indeed be considered as the most complicated and controversial topics. Also in this chapter, the theoretical analysis is followed by a review of empirical findings. In this, attention is given not only to monetary values found, but also to procedures used in the estimation of values. Finally, the chapter considers how transport policy may react to the existence of external effects. Within this context, particular attention is paid to the possibilities of an internalization policy.

Chapter 5 ('Imperfect competition in transport markets') examines the functioning of transport markets. Before summarizing the chapter, a comment will be made regarding the role of transport markets. Part of the activity of moving goods or persons, that is to say all such activity that is 'on own account', by definition does not appear in transport markets. This phenomenon should not be seen as anything peculiar. 'Transport on own account' is merely a special case of an economic agent performing a particular task when he could also choose to hire (the services of) another (specialized) firm. The important point here is that although part of the activity of moving goods or persons takes places outside transport markets, this part nevertheless is not without influence on what is going on in these markets. Any household – producer or consumer – demanding the movement of goods or persons is able to switch from hire and reward transport to transport on own account, and vice versa. Transport firms operating in the market, therefore, will constantly have to take into account the possibility of an alternative existing for those demanding transport.

In Chapter 5, two main parts may be distinguished. First, the main characteristics of transport markets are examined: 'the profuseness' of transport markets (compare the multi-output character of transport pointed out in Chapter 2); the way transport markets are interrelated; and the transparency of these markets – the last two in comparison with what is commonly assumed in economic textbooks.

In the second place, the chapter gives an exposition of how transport markets operate. In this context two different problems are considered. The first of these is the nature of competition in transport markets. The second one, less commonly found in an analysis of transport markets but to be judged of equal importance, is the stability of these markets. The chapter points to the practical significance of knowledge about the stability of transport markets, that is, for strategies to be followed by transport firms as well as by governments.

Chapters, 6, 7 and 8 deal with transport infrastructure. First the question may be asked what makes transport infrastructure different from many other capital goods that are sometimes reckoned to belong to a nation's infrastructure, such as schools and hospitals? Its spatial character is common to other infrastructures such as those for the distribution of energy (electricity and gas) and for telecommunications. This may also be expressed by stating that its nature is that of a network, consisting of links and nodes. Infrastructure is one of the inputs of the transport firm (it briefly appears as such in Chapter 2). A further question therefore is why a separate treatment of this input is needed. Transport infrastructure bears certain characteristics that are those of a public good. Therefore, the answer to the question is that fields other than the theory of the firm will have to be invoked, notably welfare theory and the theory of public finance.

In addition, because of technical and organizational innovations, in the real world the (semi-)public good character of transport infrastructure is gradually disappearing. This may lead to transport infrastructure eventually becoming a subject only for the theory of the firm. Two of the three chapters in this book in which infrastructure is examined are closely related: Chapters 6 ('Transport infrastructure: the investment problem'), and 7 ('Transport infrastructure: the problem of optimum use'), both consider optimum problems. In Chapter 6, that problem is the optimum size of infrastructural facilities (long-run problem), and in Chapter 7 it is the optimum use of such a facility – the capacity of infrastructure figures as given (short-run problem).

In its opening paragraphs, Chapter 6 lays the groundwork for the analysis of each of the problems mentioned. It discusses the concept of 'transport infrastructure', the main characteristics of the production function of infrastructure and a number of developments in postwar Western Europe with regard to the road network, the latter being the principal component of transport infrastructure. The experience in Western Europe is likely to apply also to many other parts of the world. In the analysis of the investment problem, the emphasis is put on two types of modifications of 'classical' cost–benefit analysis (for the latter, the reader is advised to consult one of the many textbooks on this subject). The first of these modifications concerns the case of long-distance travel. It consists of the introduction of an alternative to investing in roads, namely, investing in railways or in airlines. The second modification is the exact opposite of the one just mentioned. Here all travel is assumed to take place over relatively short distances (the case of urban transport).

As is well known, welfare theory states that the optimum use of some capital good is obtained if a price is set that equals marginal cost. Against this background, Chapter 7 considers the case of the optimum use of infrastructure. Two main questions are raised here. The first of these concerns the concept of the cost of the use of infrastructure. It is pointed out that in the case of transport this cost consists not only of the cost to the producer, but also of the cost to the user – in the form of his travel time. Next, these two categories of cost are analysed. For user costs, it is also demonstrated how these could be calculated in the particular case where users are not able to access a given infrastructural facility. For this case, the parking market is used as an example.

The second question raised in this chapter, which is evidently of great practical importance, is whether a price equal to marginal cost will be able to cover the capital cost of infrastructural facilities. This issue is considered for a number of different cases. The argument so far has considered only transport system internal costs (cost to the producer and cost to users). The question remains, therefore, how users should be charged for costs caused by them to third parties (transport system external costs). This issue is shown to bring with it problems of its own and is, therefore, dealt with separately. The chapter closes with a number of options for policy that may be derived from the analysis presented.

Now let the case of transport infrastructure as an input for the transport firm be considered again. If the price or the quality of this input changes, this will, in principle, provoke a reaction from the transport firm (the firm may, for instance, change the quantity of transport services it supplies). This reaction may be called a 'direct' effect of the change in the price or quality of infrastructure. However, other households in the economy may experience an effect from the change concerned. This will be the case when other households are 'linked' – either as suppliers or as customers – to the transport firm. The effects for the other households are usually called 'indirect' effects. These indirect effects of transport infrastructure are the subject of Chapter 8 ('Transport infrastructure and regional development'). Here we can note that the analysis of the indirect effects of transport infrastructure is the area where transport economics intersects with regional economics.

Chapter 8 reviews models that express the influence of transport infrastructure on economic activity outside the transport sector. To this end, first, with the help of interregional trade theory, a theoretical foundation is laid for the further analysis of the problem. After this, two different interpretations of the significance of transport infrastructure for regional development are discussed: in the first of these, the impact of transport infrastructure on the productivity of firms is the relevant parameter; in the second interpretation, this parameter consists of changes in the location of economic activity that are a consequence of an increase in productivity. A review is given of a number of different methods that have been developed for the measurement of these kinds of changes. Finally, the chapter shows that a generalization may be obtained of the relationship between transport infrastructure and regional development. This generalization consists of integrating the two separate approaches discussed earlier – the productivity and the locational approaches – into one single model.

In Section 7, it was stated that government may influence the economic process either through ownership of the means of production or by means of regulation. While the former situation applied to Chapters 6 and 7, Chapters 9

('Transport policy') and 10 ('Transport policy in the European Union') (Part IV of the book), mostly deal with the latter.

The main theme of Chapter 9 is the future function of the public authorities *vis-à-vis* the transport sector in view of the fact that interference in transport by these authorities in many parts of the Western world has much diminished. Against the background of – often strong – opinions to the contrary, an examination is made first as to whether markets at least in principle can guarantee an efficient provision with transport, and then as to how far deregulation has progressed and what is known about the effects of deregulation on the performance of transport markets. Furthermore, attention is drawn to the close connection between the supply of infrastructure services and that of transport services. The options are considered for organizing the supply of infrastructure services in such a way that this supply is neutral with respect to the supply of transport services. A further task for the public authorities would be to ensure the full harmonization of competitive conditions. It is next pointed out that firms, whether acting as suppliers of transport services or of services of infrastructure, could develop a dominant position for themselves in the market. This is yet another case where action on the part of the government would be required, in the form of competition policy. Finally, it is argued that there are many more instances – such as curtailing the growth of transport, taking care of the internalization of the costs of external effects and safeguarding a minimum provision standard for transport services – where government will remain actively involved in the transport sector.

Chapter 10 may be seen as complementary to the preceding chapter in that it focuses on the particular case of transport policy in a supranational context. The European Union, the most developed instance of an economic union in the real world so far, here serves as a concrete example. First, two important issues connected with the formation of an EU transport policy are considered. These issues are, first, the gains from trade for nations forming an economic union as a result of an improvement in the availability of transport and, second, the impact of having a common transport policy on a number of problems. Some of the problems examined relate to matters of substance while others may be seen as boundary conditions for the decision-making process. Among the first are matters of regulation and ownership and of the internalization of external costs. In the latter category may be reckoned the complexity of EU transport policy and the problem of transition from an initial configuration to a fully liberalized transport market. A second theme of the chapter is the development of EU transport policy over time. The whole of the period during which this development took place is divided into two different periods, one before and one after the creation of the Single European Market in 1992. As developments before this date may mainly be seen as being of historical significance, the accent, understandably, is on developments after 1992. The treatment is very comprehensive, in the sense that it spans all modes of 'inland' as well as of 'intercontinental' transport.

In Section 7, it was stated that a number of specific fields in the study of transport may be distinguished if certain assumptions of standard economic theory are relaxed. A first such assumption is that at no time are there any physical limitations to the space that may be used for economic activity, including transport. As soon as this -- mostly implicit -- assumption is relaxed, circumstances that are commonly met with in urban transport may be studied. This particular situation is the subject of Chapter 11 ('Urban transport'). The dominating thesis of this chapter is that, although theoretical knowledge about optimal pricing and optimal investment in urban transport is much developed, not a great deal of this can be found in actual decision making for urban transport. In order to help remedy this situation, the chapter analyses the progress of modelling, since its beginning in the 1960s, in the case of London. It is shown that during the whole of this period the scope of the models, from an economic point of view, is constantly widened, which in the chapter serves as the basis for distinguishing a number of different stages in this development. After the overview of the evolution during past years, and by way of conclusion for the chapter, a number of future developments are pointed out -- concerning population, employment, the environment and accidents -- that will call for the further elaboration of urban transport models.

As with Chapter 11, the subject of Chapter 12 ('Transport in economies in transition') also arises from relaxing a particular assumption in standard economic theory. This is the (implicit) assumption that no change will produce itself in the mechanism for the allocation of scarce resources in the economy. If this assumption is relaxed, it becomes possible to study a transitional economy, such as the formerly centrally planned Central and Eastern European (CEE) economies. In a first, theoretical, part, Chapter 12 familiarizes the reader with the main problems of the transformation of the CEE economies in general. After this, the attention is focused on the transition process in the transport sector. Here, two questions are raised: first whether all elements that may be said to determine the structure of the transport sector are of equal importance for the transition process; and second, what conditions have to be fulfilled for a successful outcome of the transition process. The relevant conditions are distinguished according to whether they relate to the formerly centrally directed countries themselves ('internal' conditions) or to the surrounding, 'Western', market economies ('external' conditions). Internal conditions are those connected to financial, legal and social factors, while external conditions are those concerned with the differences between the CEE countries and the countries belonging to the European Union. In a second section, the chapter examines actual changes due to the transformation process within the CEE countries' transport sector. Particular areas discussed are demand for and supply of transport, transport markets and transport infrastructure. The chapter concludes with an analysis of two particular topics, both of great practical relevance, namely the influence of the concept of trans-European networks on CEE infrastructure policy and the evolution of the sources of finance for infrastructure.

The third and final instance in the book of removing an assumption of standard economic theory concerns the level of scarcity of resources. The common assumption is that no long-run ('structural') extreme scarcity of resources reigns; removing this assumption creates the possibility of studying the situation of a developing economy. Transport in developing economies is the subject of Chapter 13 ('The new economics of sustainable transport in developing countries'), which reviews the options for improving the performance of the transport sector in developing economies. The argument is set against the background of the concept of 'sustainability'. It is maintained that this concept should be taken in a wider sense than merely that of the environmental aspect of economic activity. It appears that the trend towards a larger involvement of the private sector in the supply of transport discussed in earlier chapters (see in particular Chapters 9 and 10) also manifests itself in developing countries. Both national and international authorities, it is contended, will have to take care to protect themselves from both market and regulatory failures. The chapter next considers issues in developing countries with regard to three particular areas of transport. Thus, for the road sector, attention is given to the very crucial problems of obtaining finance for road maintenance and of the involvement of the private sector in the supply and the financing of road infrastructure services. With regard to rail transport a number of problems are considered that centre mostly around the question of privatization. Third, attention is drawn to the problem of the frequent operational failure of urban public transport, which appears to haunt developing countries. The chapter closes with a consideration of the highly important question of how, in developing countries, private and public sector interests in the transport sector may be reconciled.

NOTES

1. Book II, Chapter III, 'Of the accumulation of capital, or of productive and unproductive labour', 1964 edition: vol. 1, p. 295.
2. The conflict may be noted between Smith's view of the concept of transport on what one might term a micro level and that on a more macro level (transport as one of the determining factors for the size of the market and through this of the extent of the division of labour).

   It may further be remarked that it has taken a very long time for the objectivist view of the concept of value to disappear completely from economics. An indication of this is that, nearly a century and a half after Adam Smith, Marshall (1919, p. 423) speaks of the 'transport industries' as undertaking 'nothing more than the mere movement of persons and things from one place to another' – it is as if one hears the echo of Smith.

It is, of course, no surprise that, the same as with Smith, a conflict also exists with Marshall between a 'micro' and a 'macro' view of the concept of transport (the transport industries have 'constituted one of the most important activities of man in every stage of advanced civilization', Marshall, 1919, p. 423).

3. '[D]er Wert (ist) die Bedeutung, welche concrete Güter oder Güterquantitäten für uns dadurch erlangen, das wir in der Befriedigung unsere Bedürfnisse von der Verfügung über dieselben abhängig zu sein uns bewusst sind' (value is the significance concrete commodities or quantities of commodities obtain for us because we are aware we depend on these for the satisfaction of our wants), Menger (1871, p. 78).
4. In full, Isard's words are: 'But actually he confines himself to "a wonderland of no spatial dimensions"'. 'He' here is J.R. Hicks, in *Value and Capital* (1939). Isard's criticism overall was directed towards the 'Anglo-Saxon tradition'.

    See also Blaug (1997, p. 596): 'Indeed it is not too much to say that the whole of mainstream economics was until about 1950 effectively confined to the analysis of an economic world without spatial dimensions'.
5. Compare Blaug (1997, pp. 611–12): '[the] neglect of spatial economics by mainstream economists ... largely continues to this day'.
6. For the case where transport economics is used to help in solving practical problems the term 'applied transport economics' could be used, as has been done, for instance by Button and Pearman (1985). Some authors (for instance, Thomson, 1974; de Rus and Nash, 1997) describe transport economics as being an 'application of economic theory'. Their way of treatment leaves little doubt that these authors view transport economics as a theoretical and not as a practical subject. Because of the apparent possible confusion about its real character it seems better, however, completely to avoid words like 'application' and 'applied' in relation to transport economics.
7. Schumpeter (1954, Part IV, Ch. 6, Section 6), 'Railroads, public utilities, "trusts", and cartels'.
8. The following instances are given by Button (1993, p. 1): 'the development of the notion of consumers' surplus by French economists/engineers such as Dupuit, in the 1840's, the refinement of cost allocation models by US economists such as Clark and Taussig in the early part of this century, the refinement of the marginal cost pricing principle to improve the charging of rail service'. Button further points out that transport problems 'have encouraged work on applied econometrics (for example the development of discrete choice models in consumer theory and refinements to flexible form cost functions)'.

    A few additional comments may be made here. The transport context, first, of Dupuit's derivation of the notion of consumers' surplus appears from the fact that for Dupuit consumers' surplus served for determining the benefits of roads, bridges and canals. In the same vein, discrete choice models were developed initially in order to be able to explain the choice by an individual between different modes of transport (see, for instance, McFadden, 1973).

    Two further examples may be added to those given by Button: (1) the development of monopoly theory as the result of an analysis of monopoly pricing in the particular situation of railways (Marshall, 1919); (2) the equality of price to marginal cost as one of the conditions for a welfare maximum, developed initially as the basis for a system of optimal tolls for the use of infrastructure (see, for instance, Oort, 1960, 1970; Walters, 1961, 1968; Allais et al., 1965; Malcor, 1970).
9. Button (1993, p. 2): 'The main tools of the transport economist are taken directly from the kitbag of standard microeconomic theory', to which he adds, however, 'that the actual implements used by transport economists have changed significantly over the years'. De Rus and Nash (1997, p. 1): 'In many aspects transport economics is simply the application of microeconomic principles and methods to an economic activity consisting of the movement of freight and passengers'.
10. This circumstance may be attributed to the fact that transport economics as a generally recognized specialization within economics, with its own academic chairs, does not date back, at the moment of writing, much more than about forty years.
11. A useful building block for a more detailed insight in developments from the mid-1960s onwards is the analysis of papers that have appeared in the *Journal of Transport Economics and Policy* during the first thirty years (1967–97) of its existence (Starkie, 1999).

12. It is possible, as Munby (1968, p. 8) does, to consider both the contribution by Smith (about the relationship between transport and the size of the market) and that by List (about the 'developmental aspects of railway promotion in the nineteenth century') as instances of the analysis of 'the wide influence of transport on almost all aspects of life'.

It may nevertheless be remarked that Smith's treatment formed part of his theory of value and distribution, while List's was a quite different, one might say more 'modern', angle (compare the following words by List: 'Früher hatte ich die Wichtigkeit der Transportmittel nur gekannt, wie sie von der *Wertetheorie* gelehrt wird; ich hatte nur den Effekt der Transportanstalten im einzelnen beobachtet und nur mit Rücksicht auf die Erweiterung des Marktes und Verminderung des Preises der materiellen Güter. Jetzt erst fing ich an, sie aus dem Gesichtspunkt der Theorie der produktiven Kräfte und in ihrer *Gesamtwirkung als Nationaltransportsystem*, folglich nach ihrem Einflusz auf das ganze geistige und politische Leben, den geselligen Verkehr, die Produktivkraft und die Macht der Nationen zu betrachten' ('Earlier, I had only known the importance of the means of transport as it is being taught by the theory of value; I had only looked at the effect of transport facilities in isolation and only with regard to the enlargement of the market and the lowering of the price of material goods. Only now I started to consider it from the point of view of the theory of productive forces and in its overall effect as a national transport system, consequently according to its influence on the whole of spiritual and political life, on social relations, productive force and the might of nations), List (1838, quoted in Rehbein et al., 1989, p. 54). Schumpeter, it may parenthetically be noted, discusses List's 'doctrine of "productive forces"' but does not mention his views on the particular role of transport (see Schumpeter, 1954, p. 505).

13. To this field, to quote Munby, 'Edgeworth and Pigou made notable contributions' (Munby, 1968, p. 15). Munby's references are: F.Y. Edgeworth (1925), *Papers Relating to Political Economy*, vol. 1, London: Macmillan, pp. 172–91; A.C. Pigou (1932), *The Economics of Welfare*, 4th edn, Part II, Chapter XVIII, 'The special problem of railway rates', London etc.: Macmillan (chapter 13 of *Wealth and Welfare*, 1912).

14. Here in particular Marshall should be mentioned. His analysis of transport, in *Industry and Trade* (1919), covered road transport, shipping, railways and inland waterway transport. That at the time railways were still very much the dominant mode appears from the fact that Marshall's discussion of these occupies nearly two-thirds of the space he devoted to transport in this book.

15. Compare Thomson (1974, pp. 12–13): 'transport is now treated as a branch of welfare economics in which market economics play a secondary role rather than a branch of market economics with welfare implications'. Thomson even concludes from this that 'The subject ... has changed out of all recognition'. Further, Button (1993, p. 3), who states that the interest in matters of organization, competion and charging 'has ... more recently been supplemented by concern with the wider welfare and spatial implications of transport. Greater emphasis is now placed on the environmental and distributional effects of transport'.

16. Some authors (de Wit and van Gent, 1996; Gwilliam, 1998) have pointed out that privatization and deregulation, as these have taken place in many countries during the last decades of the twentieth century, have again brought the attention on microeconomics to the fore.

17. Funck (1961); John (1966); Kuhlmann (1965); Gleiszner (1967); and Meyer (1971).

18. Napp-Zinn (1948, p. 21): 'dasz ... die Kenntnis der betriebswirtschaftlichen Verhältnisse der einzelnen Verkehrszweige kaum zu entbehren ist' (that ... knowledge of the conditions of the single modes of transport from the point of view of business economics can hardly be missed); and Aberle (1997, p. v), who does not mention Napp-Zinn: 'Ein Buch, das sich mit der Vielzahl der für die Verkehrswirtschaftrelevanten Fragen befaszt und ein Überblick über die aktuellen Entwicklungen zu geben versucht, musz aufgrund der Problemstellungen sowohl betriebswirtschaftlich wie auch volkswirtschaftlich ausgerichtet sein' (A book that deals with the many questions that are of relevance for the transport sector ... will, because of the nature of these questions, have to approach these both from the point of view of business economics and of that of general economics).

These statements are witnessed by, for example, the following studies: Illetschko (1959); Lechner (1960); Böttger (s.a./1968); Diederich (1977); Brauer (1979); and Aberle (1997), Part III: 'Leistungsstrukturen, Kostenstrukturen und Preisbildung in der Verkehrswirtschaft'

(The structure of production, the structure of cost and pricing in the transport sector), Part V: 'Verkehrswirtschaft und Logistik' (Transport and logistics).

REFERENCES

Aberle, G. (1997), *Transportwirtschaft* (Transport economics), Zweite Auflage, Munich: Oldenbourg.
Allais, M., M. Del Viscovo, L. Duquesne de la Vinelle, C.J. Oort and H. St. Seidenfus (1965), *Options de la politique tarifaire dans les transports* (Options in transport tariff policy), Studies, Transport series, no. 1, Luxemburg: Office des Publications Officielles des Communautés Européennes.
Blaug, M. (1997), *Economic Theory in Retrospect*, 5th edn, Cambridge: Cambridge University Press.
Böttger, W. (s.a./1968), *Kosten und Kostenrechnung bei Güterverkehrsbetrieben* (Cost and cost accounting in goods transport enterprises), Düsseldorf: Fischer.
Brauer, K.M. (1979), *Betriebswirtschaftslehre des Verkehrs* (Business economics theory of transport), Berlin: Duncker & Humblot.
Button, K.J. (1993), *Transport Economics*, 2nd edn, Aldershot, UK: Edward Elgar.
Button, K.J. and A.D. Pearman (1985), *Applied Transport Economics. A Practical Case Studies Approach*, New York etc.: Gordon & Breach.
De Bernardi, M. (1933), *Jules Dupuit, De l'utilité et de sa mesure, écrits choisis et republiés par ...*, Turin: La riforma sociale (Collezione di scritti inediti o rari di economisti).
de Rus, G. and C. Nash (1997), *Recent Developments in Transport Economics*, Aldershot: Ashgate.
de Wit, J. and H. van Gent (1996), *Economie en Transport* (Economics and transport), Utrecht: Lemma.
Diederich, H. (1977), *Verkehrsbetriebslehre* (Business economics and transport), Wiesbaden: Gabler.
Dupuit, A.J.E.E. (1844), 'De la mesure de l'utilité des travaux publics', in De Bernardi (ed.), (1933) (English translation: 'On the measurement of the utility of public works', in Munby (ed.) (1968), pp. 19–57).
Dupuit, A.J.E.E. (1849), 'De l'influence des péages sur l'utilité des voies de communication' (On the influence of tolls on the utility of transport infrastructure), in De Bernardi (ed.) (1933).
Edgeworth, F.Y. (1925), *Papers Relating to Political Economy*, vol. 1, London: Macmillan.
Funck, R. (1961), *Verkehr und volkswirtschaftliche Gesamtrechnung* (Transport and national accounting), Göttingen: Vandenhoeck & Ruprecht.
Gattrell, A.C. (1983), *Distance and Space: A Geographical Perspective*, Oxford: Clarendon.
Gleiszner, E. (1967), *Transportelastizität und wirtschaftliche Entwicklung. Ein internationaler Vergleich* (Transport elasticity and economic development. An international comparison), München: Duncker & Humblot.
Gwilliam, K.M. (1998), 'Differentiation in Transport Economics', in J.B. Polak (ed.), *Differentiatie in de vervoerseconomie* (Differentiation in transport economics), limited edn, Groningen: Stichting Ruimtelijke Economie Groningen, pp. 59–68. This same text in Dutch ('Vervoerseconomie als gedifferentieerd vakgebied') in edition for the general public, pp. 1–12.

Hicks, J.R. (1939; 2nd edn: 1946), *Value and Capital: An Inquiry into some Fundamental Principles of Economic Theory*, Oxford: Clarendon.

Illetschko, L.L. (1959), *Betriebswirtschaftliche Probleme der Verkehrswirtschaft* (Problems of business economics of the transport sector), Wiesbaden: Gabler.

Isard, W. (1956), *Location and Space-Economy. A General Theory Relating to Industrial Location, Market Areas, Land Use, Trade, and Urban Structure*, Cambridge, MA: MIT.

John, G. (1966), *Die Verkehrsinvestitionen in der Bundesrepublik Deutschland und ihr Einflusz auf die Wirtschaftsentwicklung* (Transport investment in the Federal Republic of Germany and its influence on economic development), Berlin: Duncker & Humblot.

Knies, K. (1853), *Die Eisenbahnen und ihre Wirkungen* (The railways and their repercussions), Braunschweig: Schwetschke.

Kuhlmann, F. (1965), *Die Abhängigkeit des Verkehrsaufkommens von der konjonkturellen Entwicklung* (The dependence of the volume of transport on cyclical development), Göttingen: Vandenhoeck & Ruprecht.

Lechner, K. (1960), *Betriebswirtschaftslehre und Verkehrswissenschaft (Versuch einer Abgrenzung)* (Business economics and transport economics (An attempt at demarcation)), Wien: Springer.

List, F. (1838), *Das deutsche National-Transport-System in volks- und staatswirthschaftlicher Beziehung* (The German national transport system in relation to the national and the state economy), Altona/Leipzig: Hammerich; Reprint Transpress, Berlin, 1988.

Malcor, R. (1970), *Problèmes posés par l'application pratique d'une tarification pour l'utilisation des infrastructures routières / rapport établi sur demande de la Commission des Communautés européennes par René Malcor* (Problems posed by the practical application of a tarification for the use of road infrastructure / report drawn up at the request of the Commission of the European Communities by René Malcor), Studies, Transport series, no. 2, Luxemburg: Office des Publications Officielles des Communautés Européennes.

Marshall, A. (1919), *Industry and Trade: A Study of Industrial Technique and Business Organisation and of Their Influences on the Conditions of Various Classes and Nations*, London: Macmillan.

McFadden, D. (1973), 'Conditional logit analysis of qualitative choice behavior', in P. Zarembka, *Frontiers in Econometrics*, New York and London: Academic Press.

Menger, C. (1871), *Grundsätze der Volkswirthschaftslehre*, Wien: Braumöller (see also: C. Menger, 1933–1936, *The Collected Works of Carl Menger*, London: London School of Economics and Political Science, Series of reprints of scarce tracts in economic and political science; no. 17–20).

Meyer, G. (1971), *Verkehrssektor und Zuliefererindustrien – eine interindustrielle Verflechtungsanalyse* (The transport sector and its supplying industries – an analysis of interindustrial intertwining), Göttingen: Vandenhoeck & Ruprecht.

Munby, D. (ed.), (1968), *Transport*, Harmondsworth: Penguin.

Napp-Zinn, A.F. (1968), *Verkehrswissenschaft* (Transport Science), Heidelberg: Quelle & Meyer (Chapter referred to originally published in *Zeitschrift für Verkehrswissenschaft*, **20** (1), 1948).

Oort, C.J. (1960), *Het marginalisme als basis voor de prijsvorming in het vervoerwezen; een analyse* (Marginalism as a basis for pricing in transport; an analysis), Rotterdam: Stichting Verkeerswetenschappelijk Centrum.

Oort, C.J. (1970), *The Economic Regulation of the Road Transport Industry*, Washington,
    DC: International Bank for Reconstruction and Development.
Pigou, A.C. (1932), *The Economics of Welfare*, 4th edn, London etc.: Macmillan.
Rakowski, J.P. (1976), *Transportation Economics. A Guide to Information Sources*,
    Detroit: Gale Research.
Rehbein, E., G. Fabiunke and H. Wehner (1989), *Friedrich List – Leben und Werk*
    (Friedrich List – life and works), Berlin: Transpress.
Schumpeter, J.A. (1954), *History of Economic Analysis*, ed. E.B. Schumpeter, 8th
    printing 1972, London: Allen & Unwin.
Smith, A. (1776), *The Wealth of Nations*, Reprinted 1964, New York: Dent.
Starkie, D. (1999), *Transport Economics and Policy. 30 Years of Classified Abstracts*,
    Rochester: St Andrews.
Thomson, J.M. (1974), *Modern Transport Economics*, Harmondsworth: Penguin.
van den Bergh, J.C.J.M. (1997), 'Economy wide effects of freight transport in a spatial
    general equilibrium setting', *International Journal of Transport Economics*, **24** (1),
    101–21.
Vickerman, R.W. (1980), *Spatial Economic Behaviour. The Microeconomic Foundations
    of Urban and Transport Economics*, London etc.: Macmillan.
Walters, A.A. (1961), 'The theory and measurement of private and social cost of highway
    congestion', *Econometrica*, **29**, 676–99.
Walters, A.A. (1968), *The Economics of Road User Charges*, Washington, DC: Inter-
    national Bank for Reconstruction and Development.

PART II

Households and markets in transport

2. Transport production and the analysis of industry structure

Sergio R. Jara-Díaz*

1 INTRODUCTION

As transport activities mean displacements of individuals and goods in both time and space, the analysis of transport production involves the assignment of resources to generate trips among many different points in space during many different periods. As a consequence, the microeonomic analysis of transport production is far from a simple extension of the theory of the firm. In this chapter we present the underpinnings of a microeconomic theory of the transport firm, with particular emphasis on the nature of the technical relations between inputs and outputs (production or transformation function) and the use of the cost function as a tool to obtain valuable information for the design of transport policies (for example, pricing, regulation).

The chapter is sequentially organized, beginning with the notion of transport production, including the definition of transport output, the role of space, the idea of operating rules and the concept of scale, all of which are illustrated using simple cyclical systems (Section 2). Then the cost function and its properties regarding the calculation of marginal costs, economies of scale and economies of scope, are presented and explained within the context of transport systems analysis (Section 3). A synthesis of the empirical work using transport cost functions is offered, with special emphasis on the adequate treatment of output in its specification, and on the difficulties with the prevailing approach of analysing industry structure, including recently improved procedures to calculate economies correctly and a discussion on network density versus economies of scope (Section 4). The closing section (5) contains a synthesis and directions for research.

2 TRANSPORT PRODUCTION

In essence, the production of goods and services can be synthetically described using the concepts of inputs, outputs and technology. Inputs have to be acquired

* This research was partially funded by Fondecyt, Chile. The collaboration of C. Cortés is appreciated.

by the firm in order to be combined – within the boundaries of process-specific rules – in order to produce outputs. For a given level of outputs, the firm has to choose type and amount of inputs, as well as a subset of combination rules. All feasible input combinations define the technology.

In the case of transport, the firm has to use vehicles, terminals, rights-of-way, energy, labour and so on, to produce movements – freight and/or passenger – from many origins to many destinations during many different periods. Thus, the output of a transport firm is a vector

$$Y = \left\{ y_{ij}^{kt} \right\} \in R^{KxNxT} \tag{2.1}$$

where each component y_{ij}^{kt} represents the flow of type k moved from origin i to destination j (O–D pair ij), within period t, for example, passengers from Paris to Frankfurt during a specific weekend (K, N and T are the number of flow types, the number of O–D pairs, and the number of time periods considered in Y, respectively).

For a given set of flows in Y, the firm has to make a number of choices: number and capacity of vehicles (fleet size), design of the rights-of-way (location, flow capacity), design of terminals (location, loading–unloading capacity), route structure (that is, how vehicles would flow on the network), vehicle frequencies and so on. Some of these decisions involve choosing the characteristics of inputs, and some are related to their use, that is, with the form in which inputs are combined to accommodate the flow vector. We shall call these latter types of choices 'operating decisions'.

For a given type of transport firm (for example, interurban bus) some of the decisions related to the acquisition of inputs are constrained, because of the existence of common infrastructure (for example, the road system) or the rigidity of input markets (for example, fleet size). On the other hand, operating decisions are generally made within the boundaries of existing inputs. As a simple example, consider an O–D system with three nodes, a single period and a single flow type (see Figure 2.1).

For a given set of flows $\{y_{ij}\}$, the appropriate combination of inputs and operating rules would depend on many factors. If, in Figure 2.1, nodes 1, 2 and 3 represent distant cities (airports), then three possible air route structures are (a), (b) and (c). These route structures should be analysed in parallel with aircraft size and frequency in order to make the most convenient choice of routes and if this were either a road or a railway system, the physical structure of the road network would constrain the choice of routes and schedules. Moreover, for a given fleet size (including vehicle capacity), scheduling would be the only decision to make.

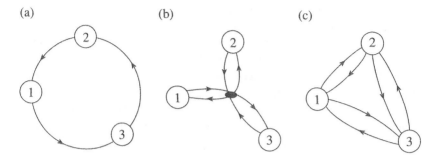

Figure 2.1   Possible route structures for a simple O–D system

The technical relation between inputs and outputs is summarized through the concept of a transformation or production function. Let us give an example using the simplest possible case, that is a single O–D pair, single product, single period (Gálvez, 1978; Jara-Díaz, 1982b). Let Y be the flow from O to D. If k is load size, B is fleet size, $t(k)$ is travel time as a function of load size and μ is loading–unloading speed, then

$$Y \equiv \frac{Bk}{t(k) + 2\dfrac{k}{\mu} + t(0)}. \tag{2.2}$$

For a given B and μ, one can find the value of k that maximizes Y, k^*. It can easily be proved that k^* would be given by vehicle capacity K, provided the effect of k on travel time is small. Therefore

$$Y \leq \frac{BK}{t(K) + 2\dfrac{K}{\mu} + t(0)} = h(B, K, \mu) \tag{2.3}$$

where $h(B, K, \mu)$ is the production function which gives the maximum flow for a given value and characteristics of the inputs: B, K and μ. Which combination should be chosen for a *given* value of Y, would depend on the relative prices of vehicles and loading–unloading capacity. In this simple cyclical system, the input choice, their feasible combinations and the operating rule can be clearly distinguished.

Thus, depending on the characteristics of the particular transport system, the transport firm could adjust inputs and operating rules according to the different levels of Y. This concept remains when Y is a vector. The simplest possible version of a multi-output transport firm is one serving a backhaul system with two nodes (1 and 2) and two flows (y_{12} and y_{21}) of a single product during a single period (Gálvez, 1978; Jara-Díaz, 1982b). Let us assume for simplicity that the firm operates the same fleet to move both flows. Then vehicle frequency in both directions is the same, and given by the maximum necessary, which in turn depends upon the relative flows; let us assume $y_{12} \geq y_{21}$. Then the technical optimum requires the vehicles in the $1 \to 2$ direction, to be fully loaded, and frequency will be given by

$$f = \frac{y_{12}}{K} \tag{2.4}$$

and the load size in the opposite direction, k_{21}, will be

$$k_{21} = \frac{y_{21}}{f} = \frac{y_{21}}{y_{12}} K. \tag{2.5}$$

The fleet size needed, B, has to be equal to f times cycle time t_c which, under our simplifying assumption, is given by

$$t_c = t_{12}(K) + \frac{2K}{\mu} + \frac{2}{\mu} \frac{y_{21}}{y_{12}} K + t_{21}(k_{21}). \tag{2.6}$$

Just for the sake of simplicity, let us see the case characterized by vehicle speed v independent of load size and potentially different route distances d_{ij} in each direction. Then using equations (2.4) and (2.6), the equality $B = f t_c$ can be turned into

$$BK = y_{12}\left(\frac{d_{12}}{v} + 2\frac{K}{\mu} + \frac{d_{21}}{v}\right) + 2\frac{K}{\mu} y_{21}. \tag{2.7}$$

As this is valid for $y_{12} \geq y_{21}$, and there is a symmetric expression for $y_{21} \geq y_{12}$, the general result for the technical relation among flows and inputs is

$$y_{ij} = \frac{\mu(d_{12} + d_{21})B}{2} - \left(\frac{d_{12} + d_{21}}{2Kv} + 1\right)y_{ji}, \forall y_{ji} \geq y_{ij}. \tag{2.8}$$

It is fairly simple to show that the graphical representation of the backhaul system in the output space looks like Figure 2.2. Equation (2.8) represents the production or transformation function of the system, and the shaded area in the figure represents all the vectors (y_{12}, y_{21}) that can be produced with a given fleet B, and capacities μ and K, but only the boundary represents optimal usage. This boundary is the production possibility frontier, whose symmetry is derived from the assumption of load independence of speed.

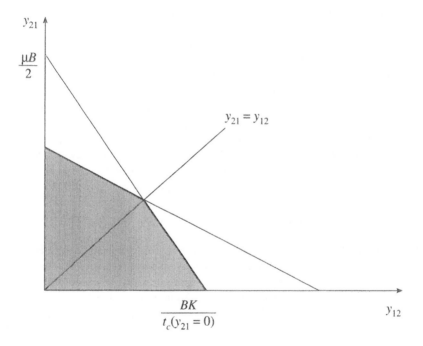

Figure 2.2   The backhaul system

Both the cyclical and backhaul systems are illustrative of the idea of technical feasibility and optimality. One of the most important conceptual points is the distinction between inputs, as fleet or loading–unloading capacities, and operating rules, as frequency, speed or vehicle load. The former is related to things that have to be acquired and the latter are ways to combine the former to produce flows. Roles and relations are clear.

In complex systems, the technical relations cannot be obtained in such an explicit form as in equations (2.3) and (2.8), but they can be envisaged as a sort of 'specialized black box' which includes a number of analytical relations dealing with networks, itineraries, routes, frequencies and so on, trying to aim at the best possible use of resources: fleet, terminals and rights-of-way. This general idea helps us to understand the kernel of transport production; changes in the flow vector Y potentially induce changes in input usage as well as in route structures and operating rules in general. It may well be that some of the inputs cannot be adjusted, which means that some other inputs will have to be changed in combination with different operating rules. A good example is the restructuring of routes and itineraries for a given fleet of buses facing a change in the passenger volumes in different O–D pairs.

To conclude this general idea of transport production, let us introduce an important technical concept that can be examined directly from the transformation function: the concept of scale economies. The relevant question is by how much can output be expanded if all inputs are expanded by the same proportion. In the single-output case represented by equation (2.3), a local expansion of vehicle capacity (BK through K) and loading–unloading capacity (μ) would allow Y to be increased by the same proportion if speed was unrelated to K; note that in this example the right-of-way input is assumed to be exogenous to the firm. In the two-outputs case represented by Figure 2.2, a similar expansion of inputs moves the production possibility frontier away from the origin, but the 'how much can output be expanded' question becomes ambiguous, as nothing has been said about output combinations. If the concept of scale economies is forced to deal with proportional expansions of output, it is clear that, again, (y_{12}, y_{21}) can be expanded by the same proportion as inputs (same condition as in the earlier case).

In general, if $F(X, Y) \geq 0$ represents the transformation function (that is all technically feasible combinations of inputs and outputs) where X is the input vector and equality represents technical optimality, the (multi-output) degree of scale economies, S, is defined as the maximum proportional expansion of Y, $\lambda^S Y$, after an expansion of X by λX (Panzar and Willig, 1977). Analytically,

$$F(\lambda X, \lambda^S Y) = 0 \tag{2.9}$$

which means than in the previous examples S takes the value of one, usually called constant returns to scale. A value of S greater or smaller than one is called increasing or decreasing returns to scale, respectively.

3 TRANSPORT COST FUNCTIONS: THE THEORY

3.1 Basic Definitions and Properties

Technical analysis is not enough to understand the choice of inputs combination by the firm. The question is which of the combinations in the technical frontier is the most convenient to produce a given output Y. The answer is given by one of the most interesting tools in the microeconomics of production: the cost function, which requires input prices to be introduced into the picture. Formally, the cost function $C(w,Y)$ gives the minimum expenditure necessary to produce output Y at given factor prices w. It corresponds to the solution of

$$\min_{X} \sum_{i} w_i x_i, \text{ subject to } F(X,Y) \geq 0. \tag{2.10}$$

The solution for each input x_i is a conditional demand function $x_i^*(w, Y)$ which represents the optimum amount of input. Then the cost function is

$$C(w,Y) \equiv \sum_{i} w_i x_i^*(w,Y). \tag{2.11}$$

If some inputs x_j are fixed at a level $\bar{x}_j$, then the short-run cost function is defined as $C(w_v, \bar{X}, Y)$, where $\bar{X}$ is a vector containing fixed inputs and w_v is a vector containing variable input prices. The optimization process represented by equations (2.10) and (2.11) is exactly the same.

Out of the many properties of the cost function, five are particularly relevant for a basic analysis and discussion of production in general and of transport in particular. First, the derivative property or Sheppard's Lemma, which states that the derivative of the cost function $C(w, Y)$ with respect to each factor input price w_i equals the cost-minimizing amount of $x_i(w, Y)$, that is $x_i^*(w, Y)$. Analytically,

$$\frac{\partial C(w,Y)}{\partial w_i} \equiv x_i^*(w,Y) \tag{2.12}$$

and is very helpful in estimating and interpreting a cost function. Second, the marginal cost specific to product i, m_i, is simply

$$m_i = \frac{\partial C(w,Y)}{\partial y_i}. \tag{2.13}$$

Next, the (multi-output) degree of scale economies which has been defined on the technology can be shown (Panzar and Willig, 1977) to be obtainable from the cost functions as

$$S = \frac{C(w,Y)}{\sum_i y_i \dfrac{\partial C}{\partial y_i}} = \frac{1}{\sum_i \eta_i}, \tag{2.14}$$

where η_i is the cost elasticity with respect to output i.

Fourth, the degree of economies of scope relative to a subset R, SC_R can be calculated (Baumol et al., 1982) as

$$SC_R \frac{1}{C(Y)}\left[C(Y_R) + C(Y_{M-R}) - C(Y)\right], \tag{2.15}$$

where Y_R represents vector Y with $y_i = 0$, $\forall i \notin R \subset M$, with M being the set of all products (we have suppressed w for simplicity). Thus, a positive SC_R – the existence of economies of scope – means that it is cheaper to produce Y with a single firm than to split production into two orthogonal subsets R and $M - R$.

Finally, a cost function is said to be subadditive for a particular output vector Y when Y can be produced more cheaply by a single firm than by any combination of smaller firms (Baumol et al., 1982, p. 170). Therefore, a cost function is subadditive if

$$\sum_i C(Y^i) \geq C(Y) \quad \forall\{Y^i\} / \sum_i Y^i = Y \tag{2.16}$$

which is the multi-output notion of natural monopoly. Under this set of definitions and properties, it is very clear that both $S > 1$ and $SC_R > 0$ favour subadditivity, but neither guarantees its presence by itself.

3.2 Scale and Scope in Transport Production

With product defined as in equation (2.1) and the notion of scale synthesized in equation (2.9), scale analysis in transport should be conceptually clear. It refers to the behaviour of costs as flows in all markets served by a firm expand proportionally. In order to emphasize space, let us create an example using the O–D structure depicted in Figure 2.1 relative to non-perishable cargo. Imagine that distances i–j are relatively short, that flows y_{ij} and y_{ji} are unbalanced, and that the sum of flows clockwise is approximately equal to the sum of flows counterclockwise. It may well be that for relatively low volumes, a route structure like (a), with complete vehicle cycles involving a homogeneous fleet, is the least-cost answer. Imagine output expands proportionally; the firm could accommodate that expansion by increasing frequency (enlarging fleet) and/or using larger vehicles. For further expansions, the hub-and-spoke structure like (b) could well become the best answer, making the hub a transfer point and involving vehicles of different sizes. It might be the case that direct services as in (c) happen to be the least-cost structure for individually large enough flows. If there are scale advantages in loading–unloading activities and in vehicle size, it is very likely that through appropriate scheduling and rerouting, total cost will increase less than proportionally with increases in the flow vector, at least up to a certain scale.

Regarding scope, again Figure 2.1 will prove very helpful. If the six flows are divided into subsets $\{y_{12}, y_{23}, y_{31}\}$ and $\{y_{21}, y_{13}, y_{32}\}$, very possibly the sum of the costs of assigning each subset to a different firm will be greater than the cost of moving all six flows with one firm. The case is not that clear when the partition is $\{y_{12}, y_{21}\}, \{y_{13}, y_{31}, y_{23}, y_{32}\}$. In general, the partition of the flow vector could be made in terms of flow type (for example, passengers and freight), periods (for example, weekends and weekdays) or O–D pairs, as we have done in the example. In this latter case we would talk about economies of spatial scope, when they exist.

In order to provide a specific analytical example, let us use the simple backhaul system technically described in Section 2.2 to obtain and analyse the corresponding cost function (see Figure 2.3). The system represented by equation (2.8) can be used to get the number of vehicles as a function of product, $B(y_{12}, y_{21})$. On the other hand, the number of loading–unloading sites, L, is given by $2(y_{12} + y_{21})/\mu$. Without affecting the conceptual analysis, we can hold d, v, k and μ constant such that inclusive prices for vehicles (P_B) and sites (P_L) can be defined, that is, prices that encompass rent, labour and energy (fuel) necessary to operate one vehicle and one site, respectively. Replacing all variables, the multi-output cost function is given by

$$C(y_{12}, y_{21}) = C_0 + y_{ij}\left[P_B\left(\frac{d_{12} + d_{21}}{vK} + \frac{2}{\mu}\right) + \frac{2P_L}{\mu}\right] + y_{ji}\frac{2}{\mu}(P_B + P_L) \qquad y_{ij} > y_{ji}$$

(2.17)

where C_0 represents costs that are associated with the right-of-way.[1] This is graphically represented in Figure 2.2.

Although equation (2.17) has been obtained using highly simplifying assumptions, it represents a fairly transparent cost function for the simplest possible multi-output transport system. Its importance becomes apparent when it is used to analyse scale, scope and aggregate output. If the degree of economies of scale is calculated using (2.14), it is quite easy to show that $S = 1$ for $C_0 = 0$, which we can name the 'lorry' case, as lorries (or buses) do not pay a fixed cost

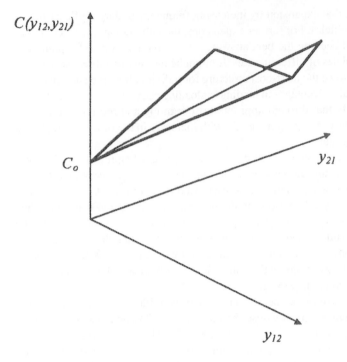

Figure 2.3   Transport cost function of the backhaul system

for road infrastructure. On the other hand, scope analysis can be done for the only partition possible in this case (that is, assigning each of the flows in the backhaul system to different firms). After elementary calculations we get

$$C(y_{12},0)+C(0,y_{21})-C(y_{12},y_{21})=C_0+P_B\frac{d_{12}+d_{21}}{vK}y_{ji}\quad \forall y_{ij}\geq y_{ji}$$

$$(2.18)$$

which is positive even if C_0 is nil. This shows that, under the assumptions made, it is fleet utilization that causes the existence of economies of scope. Thus, if $C_0 = 0$, we have constant returns (a case for competition or deregulation) and economies of scope. These latter would cause incentives for merging if two firms are operating, each in one direction. The conclusion is that, as far as costs of production are concerned, competition would be desirable, with each firm operating both markets. It is relevant to mention here that, in their pioneering work on hedonic cost functions, Spady and Friedlaender (1978) verbally explained merging among trucking firms serving different routes when a regulatory regime that had exercised restrictions on routes is dismantled. However, that phenomenon was said to reflect 'economies of density and utilization', which cannot be derived from their cost function specification. With a well-defined output, it is directly explainable as economies of (spatial) scope. This leads to the third interesting aspect that can be explored using this simple example: output aggregation.

Aggregates such as passenger- (or ton-) kilometres (*TK*) have been used as a basic or synthetic unit to describe transport output both in general and within the context of empirically estimated cost functions. However, since the late 1970s, its ambiguity began to be addressed, raising the issues of network shape and fleet utilization, as described in the preceding paragraph. The simplified cost function of the backhaul system can be used to explore the adequacy of the *TK* index as a representation of transport output.

First we have to recognize that *TK* is indeed a function of the true output as defined in (2.1). In the backhaul system,

$$TK = y_{12}d_{12} + y_{21}d_{21}. \qquad (2.19)$$

On the other hand, (2.17) can be used to represent the combinations of y_{12} and y_{21} that yield the same expenditure C_i. The resulting iso-cost locus can be shown in the output space as we have done in Figure 2.4, where cost increases with the distance from the origin. The popular 'output' *TK* can be shown in the same space using equation (2.19) as a straight line with a negative slope that depends on the relative value of d_{12} and d_{21}. As evident, all flow combinations within the straight line yield the same value for *TK*. We have represented as TK_0 the case of $d_{12} > d_{21}$; as the corresponding line intersects many iso-cost curves, TK_0 cannot be associated with a single minimum cost figure. It should be noted that this ambiguity remains even if both distances are equal (as represented by TK_1). On the other hand, every pair (y_{12}, y_{21}) corresponds to a single-cost value, unambiguously.

The ambiguity of aggregate output is a key aspect in the analysis of industry structure in transport activities by means of a cost function. We have shown that, even in a simple system like the backhaul service developed in this section, an association between expenses C and output *TK* might yield completely erroneous conclusions. In terms of scale analysis, an expansion of *TK* by λ corresponds to many possible flow combinations, as shown by equation (2.19).

In terms of scope, the pairs $(0, y_{21})$ and $(y_{12}, 0)$ get reflected as $y_{21} d_{21}$ and $y_{12} d_{12}$, respectively, when converted into *TK* units. Thus, scope 'turns' into scale, provoking an extremely confusing panorama when trying to obtain conclusions on industry structure.

For synthesis, transport production is a multi-output process where the concepts of scale and scope are very useful for the analysis of industry structure,

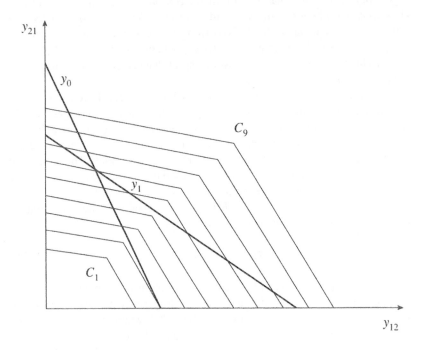

Figure 2.4   Cost ambiguity of aggregate output

provided they are properly applied. The degree of economies of scale reflects the behaviour of cost as all flows (for example, in every O–D pair) expand proportionally. The degree of economies of scope examines the convenience of partitioning transport services into two mutually exclusive subsets; depending on the type of partition, we shall refer to economies of spatial scope, commodity scope, or time scope, whenever the cost of producing the whole set is less than the sum of costs for the partition. Diseconomies of scope reflect the opposite. Within this context, the use of aggregates to describe transport output distorts the analysis of scale and reduces (and sometimes destroys) the possibility of analysing scope. However, transport systems produce passenger and/or commodity trips over many O–D pairs, which makes reduced output description a key issue in empirical studies.

3.3   Transport Output and the Estimation of Cost Functions

Obtaining an adequate representation of either $C(w,Y)$ or $C(w, \bar{X}, Y)$ – the long-run and the short-run cost functions, respectively – is not a simple task in transport activities. As evident, the general idea is to construct a reliable statistical relation between expenses as the dependent variable, and output, input prices and fixed factors as explanatory variables. The statistical data is composed of a series of observations, each one relating production to cost. This series can be fed by the evolution of a single transport firm in time, by the activity of many firms within a period (cross-section), or by observations of many firms during many periods (pool).

The case of a time series is, conceptually speaking, the most transparent one; product (as defined in equation (2.1)) is quite precise, as well as factors of production. Let us consider the case of a firm moving a single type of commodity (or passengers) among many points in space during homogeneous periods, and imagine potential observations that include services from two to six O–D pairs as depicted in Figure 2.5. If all observations were associated with an O–D system like (a), output would be a two-dimensional vector. Output would be a six-dimensional vector if *all* observations were related to movements like those represented in (c). How to represent output if observations included all three cases? The answer is straightforward: the output vector should have six components and some of them will be nil for observations including flows as in (a) or (b). Formally,

$$y = \{y_{12}, y_{21}, y_{13}, y_{31}, y_{23}, y_{32}\}$$
$$y^a = \{y^a_{12}, y^a_{21}, 0, 0, 0, 0\}$$
$$y^b = \{y^b_{12}, y^b_{21}, 0, 0, y^b_{23}, y^b_{32}\}$$

where y^n_{ij} corresponds to actual flow in O–D pair ij for observation (period) n. The case is very similar if observations correspond to transport firms operating on the same spatial setting.

(a)   (b)   (c)

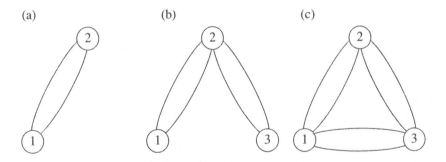

Figure 2.5   Transport output in a three-nodes system

On the other hand, observations of firms serving different O–D systems correspond, in fact, to different products. This does make a difference regarding other production processes observed through a cross-section, as the optimal combination of resources to produce a given amount of an output bundle (say shoes, bags and belts) at given input prices is likely to be equal across firms if all of them have access to the same technology. But the optimal combination of vehicles, terminals and rights-of-way (by means of routes, frequencies and load sizes) will depend upon the characteristics of the underlying physical network and the actual configuration of each O–D system. Nevertheless, it is true that an external observer (transport analyst) should be able to obtain some information regarding cost structure from observations of different transport firms performing similar services on different spatial settings (for example, interurban rail, urban transit, international flights and so on). But this requires a careful analysis in order to make the correct inferences on policy and industry structure.

Thus, transport output description within the context of the estimation of cost functions implies a challenge in at least two dimensions. First, when output is well defined, the number of components is usually huge and certainly unmanageable in detail for statistical purposes. Second, cross-sectional observations usually involve different products. How to aggregate flow components and how to introduce product equivalency or homogeneity across different systems are indeed problems to solve; neither, however, changes the strict definitions of scale and scope which are unambiguous with a well-defined transport output.

4 TRANSPORT COST FUNCTIONS: THE EMPIRICAL WORK

4.1 Functional Form

The estimation of cost functions for different transport industries has been the preferred tool for the analysis of industry structure, regulation, technical change, productivity and so on. Within the period 1970–97, the empirical work on transport cost functions has experienced a series of improvements. Perhaps the most evident is the use of flexible forms for the functional specification of the function, the translog form being the most popular one (see Christensen et al., 1973). In order to understand this form analytically, it is useful to view first another flexible specification called the quadratic. Conceptually, the quadratic corresponds to a second-order Taylor expansion of $C(w,Y)$ around a point (w^0,Y^0), which is usually the mean of input prices ($\overline{w}_i$) and flows ($\overline{y}_i$) in the data set. Analytically, the stochastic expression for the quadratic cost function is

$$C(w,Y) = A_0 + \sum_{i=1}^{n} A_i\left(w_i - \overline{w}_i\right) + \sum_{i=1}^{m} C_j\left(y_j - \overline{y}_j\right)$$

$$+ \frac{1}{2}\sum_{i=1}^{n}\sum_{j=1}^{n} A_{ij}\left(w_i - \overline{w}_i\right)\left(w_j - \overline{w}_j\right)$$

$$+ \frac{1}{2}\sum_{i=1}^{n}\sum_{j=1}^{m} B_{ij}\left(w_i - \overline{w}_i\right)\left(y_j - \overline{y}_j\right)$$

$$+ \frac{1}{2}\sum_{i=1}^{m}\sum_{j=1}^{n} C_{ij}\left(y_i - \overline{y}_i\right)\left(y_j - \overline{y}_j\right) + \varepsilon, \tag{2.20}$$

where the system considers n inputs and m outputs; ε is the error term. The translog form is analogous to equation (2.20) with $C(w, Y)$, w_i and y_i in logs. Both forms are flexible in the sense that no a priori functions are postulated either for technology or for costs.

Each of these flexible forms has its own advantages. The translog facilitates the analysis of the properties corresponding to the underlying technology (that is, homogeneity, separability, scale economies and non-joint production) by means of relatively simple tests on the adequate set of parameter estimates.[2] Its first-order coefficients are the cost elasticities of output calculated at the mean, and their summation yields an estimate of the inverse of S as shown in equation (2.14). Further, this form makes it easy to impose homogeneity of degree one in factor prices.

On the other hand, the plain quadratic form is extremely adequate to directly obtain marginal costs evaluated at the mean of observations, C_i, and the elements of the Hessian C_{ij}, which are essential for analysing subadditivity. In addition, equation (2.20) is well defined for zero output levels (while the translog is not); this not only represents an advantage for the estimation process, but also allows for the calculation of economies of scope, which involve output vectors with some zero components. Nevertheless, adequate transformations of output (for example, Box–Cox) allow for nil values of output using the translog form as well.

One of the shortcomings of flexible forms is the fairly high number of coefficients to be estimated, which requires a substantially larger number of observations for statistical relevance of the estimated function. However, the application of Sheppard's Lemma to equation (2.20) generates as many additional equations as factor prices included, involving part of the coefficients from the original equation. Thus, inputting some usually available information (factor usage, factor expenditure or factor cost share),[3] the number of 'observations' can be multiplied, generating a system of equations, which increases the efficiency in parameter estimation. This problem is particularly relevant in transport analysis, because the usually high dimension of Y is further magnified by squared and interaction terms. This makes output aggregation an extremely important aspect: it is required to make estimation feasible in most real systems, but it should not distort the analysis, thus obtaining irrelevant or misleading results.

4.2 Output Aggregates

Aggregation of output over any dimension (commodity, time or space) involves losing information associated with the transport processes generated by the system in reference, as illustrated earlier in the backhaul system. As is evident, spatial aggregation destroys information on the geographical context of the origin–destination system in which a transport system operates. Aggregation of output over time may cause distortions when estimating cost functions if periods of distinctive mean flows are averaged. Finally, commodity aggregation may affect cost estimation since the (minimum) cost of moving the same aggregate weight or volume will generally depend on the composition of that output.

In summary, the loss of information due to aggregation over any dimension may cause serious problems of coefficient interpretation when estimating a cost function. The bulk of the empirical work, however, has not been developed with full awareness of the problem. Most reported transport cost functions use a basic output aggregate (for example, ton-kilometres or total passenger trips) together with other 'output' variables or, as called in the literature, 'output characteristics'. In other words, we do not find efforts to construct appropriate aggregates from disaggregated information on output.[4] The usual procedure is to add other aggregates that should somehow control for the ambiguity of the single-output index.

Thus, seasonal and 'traffic condition' dummies are in fact trying to capture the effect of the implicit time aggregation on costs. Similarly, variables such as traffic mix or insurance value try to grasp commodity aggregation. The first effort to somehow counterbalance spatial aggregation was the use of mean haul length as part of output description within a 'hedonic' treatment (Spady and Friedlaender, 1978). In the last twenty years, the literature on transport cost functions includes an enormous variety of output descriptions. Unfortunately, this has not led yet to a universally accepted form of output treatment, mainly due to an implicit reluctance to try to understand transport technology, which is a fairly complex construct as suggested at the beginning of the chapter. In order to clarify this, let us use the synthesis presented in Table 2.1, where we have included studies covering more than twenty years of evaluation.[5]

Table 2.1   Output description in transport cost functions

	Modes	Output	Attribute
Berechman (1983)	Bus	REV	–
Berechman (1987) Berechman and Giuliano (1984)	Bus	VK, PAS	–
Ying (1990) Ying and Keeler (1991)	Lorries	RTK	ALH, %LTL, AL, AS, IN
Caves et al. (1984) Gillen et al. (1990) Windle (1991)	Air	RPK Scheduled services RTK Charter services	ALH, LF, NC
Daughety et al. (1985) Friedlaender and Bruce (1985) Kim (1987) (*) Spady and Friedlaender (1978) Wang and Friedlaender (1984)	Lorries	TK	ALH, AS, AL, %LTL, IN CU (*)
Gagné (1990)	Lorries	TK and N	ALH, AS, CU, IN
Caves et al. (1980, 1981, 1985)	Rail	TK PK	ALH, ATL
Filippini and Maggi (1992) Formby et al. (1990) Keeler and Formby (1994) Tauchen et al. (1983) Koshal and Koshal (1989) Braeutigam et al. (1980) Keaton (1990)	Air Bus Lorries Railways	SK VK LCK	LF, ALH, TD, NC
Harmatuck (1981, 1985, 1991)	Lorries	NTL NLTL	ALH, AS (TL), AS (LTL)

Key

TK:	ton-kilometres	ALH:	average length of haul (freight)
PK:	passenger-kilometres	ATL:	average trip length (passengers)
PAS:	passengers-trips	% LTL:	percentage of less-than-truckload services
RTK:	revenue ton-kilometres of cost	AL:	average load
RPK:	revenue pax-kilometres	AS:	average shipment size
REV:	revenue per pax-kilometre	IN:	average cargo loss-and-damage insurance per
VK:	vehicle-kilometres		dollar
SK:	seat-kilometres hub, etc.)	LF:	load factor
LCK:	loaded car-kilometres	CU:	capacity utilization
N:	number of shipments	TD:	traffic density
NTL:	number of truckload shipments	NC:	network characteristics (for example, points
NLTL:	number of less-than-truckload shipments		served

From the table we can verify that in addition to full aggregation of flows (for example, passengers) or distance-weighted flows (for example, ton-kilometres), the list of accompanying variables is varied: average load, average trip length, percentage of less-than-truckload services, number of shipments, average shipment size and so on. It is important to note that these variables are sometimes called outputs, sometimes output characteristics, and sometimes quality dimensions. The most sophisticated variables appeared during the 1980s, and they are related to network shape and size. And here we have a new source of confusion: network as infrastructure (that is, a fixed factor associated with the rights-of-way) and network as route structure, which is an endogenous, operating decision for many modes or transport systems (for example, the cyclical system or the hub-and-spoke in Figure 2.1).

4.3 Scale and Scope from Aggregates

Whenever a cost function is specified in terms of one or more output aggregates, the analyst obtains a series of coefficients that can be given a microeconomic interpretation by simple association with properties (2.13) or (2.14). If the function is a translog-around-the-mean, first-order coefficients are 'output' elasticities, and the inverse of their sum could be offered as an estimate of the degree of scale economies. This is a procedure that has frequently been applied in the literature with some qualifications. Just as an example, Caves et al. (1985) included passenger-kilometres, ton-kilometres, average length of haul (freight) and average trip length (passengers) in their translog specification, and then calculated the degree of scale economies in various ways, always using the cost elasticities (obtained directly from the coefficients). Cost elasticities for ton- and passenger-kilometres were always used, but the average-distance elasticities were left out in one of the measures of $\tilde{S}$ and included in the other. The reason offered was that ton- or passenger-kilometres might increase due to either more or longer trips. In fact, a coefficient of 0.5 on the elasticity of the average trip distance variables was suggested as a compromise. An increase in the mean distance travelled necessarily requires that flows in the more distant O–D pairs have to increase more than flows in the relatively closer ones, and this violates the condition for scale analysis which relates to proportional expansions of output. Failure to look at S properly is in fact the main cause of ambiguity in this example. As we have said, S is related to proportional expansions within the vector of flows Y, and not directly to changes in ton- or passenger-kilometres. And when all flows increase by a factor of λ, then average distance remains constant, which means that their elasticities should always be left out.

The fact that aggregates make the calculation of S obscure was highlighted by Gagné (1990) and by Ying (1992). Both observed that aggregates are usually interrelated, for example, ton-kilometres is equal to total flow times average length of haul, a fact that had not been taken into account when making calculations of S. Our view is different: we should look at the behaviour of $C(w,Y)$ as the basic flow variables increase, but this operates through the aggregates. Let $\tilde{Y}$ be the vector of aggregates with components $\tilde{y}$ (for example, ton-kilometres, total flow, less-than-truckload movements, and so on). The key fact is that most of these $\tilde{y}_j$ s are implicit constructs from the components of Y. This is evident in the case of ton-kilometres (equation 2.19) or total flow (for example, total passengers in a period) which is simply the summation over all y_i. Thus, if $\tilde{y}_j$ is an implicit function of Y, then the estimated $\tilde{C}(w,\tilde{Y})$ is an implicit representation $\hat{C}$ of $C(w, Y)$ because (Jara-Díaz and Cortés, 1996)

$$\tilde{C}\left(w,\tilde{Y}\right) \equiv \tilde{C}\left[w,\tilde{Y}(Y)\right] \equiv \hat{C}(w,Y). \tag{2.21}$$

Then the correct calculation of an estimate $\hat{S}$ for S can be obtained through direct application of equation (2.14) using the y_is as arguments. It can be easily shown (Jara-Díaz and Cortés, 1996) that

$$\hat{S} = \left[\sum_i \frac{\partial \hat{y}}{\partial y C_i} \frac{C}{y_i}\right]^{-1} = \left[\sum_j \alpha_j \tilde{\eta}_j\right]^{-1} \tag{2.22}$$

where $\tilde{\eta}$ is the cost elasticity associated with aggregate j in $\tilde{C}$, and

$$\alpha_j = \sum_i \frac{\partial \tilde{y}_j}{\partial y_i} \frac{y_i}{\tilde{y}_j}. \tag{2.23}$$

In summary, the correct estimate is not necessarily equal to the inverse of the sum of the aggregate's elasticities, $\tilde{\eta}$, unless the α_js are all equal to one.

The procedure to use $\tilde{C}$ correctly rests upon the relation between the $\tilde{y}_j$s and the y_is. But, according to equation (2.22), this applies to all arguments of $\tilde{C}$ which are functions of Y, no matter what they are called (that is, characteristics, attributes or outputs). Thus, equation (2.23) provides a test for the inclusion of any aggregate elasticity in the calculation of $\hat{S}$. Just as an example, we show here the coefficients α_j which correspond to a ton-kilometres variable (TK) and an average length of haul variable (ALH). To make it explicit this requires that

$$TK = \sum_i y_i d_i \tag{2.24}$$

and

$$ALH = \left(\sum_i y_i d_i \right) \Big/ \sum_i y_i. \qquad (2.25)$$

From this, one can easily show that α_{TM} is equal to one and α_{ALH} is nil. Therefore, the elasticity of TK should be used always in the calculation of $\hat{S}$, and the elasticity of ALH should never be used. These are simple cases to illustrate how to proceed with a $\tilde{C}(w,\tilde{Y})$ function. A fairly complete analysis of nearly all forms of output description and their role in the calculation of $\hat{S}$ is contained in Jara-Díaz and Cortés (1996). It is relevant to note that the a_js are not necessarily equal to either zero or one.

To illustrate the point, consider the case of an output index, which is in fact related to transport supply, like vehicle-kilometres. The relation between this index and the flow vector is dependent on the manner in which frequency and average load are adapted following an increase in the flows. It can be shown that a pure frequency adjustment makes $\alpha_j = 1$ and a pure load adjustment (which has a limit) makes $\alpha_j = 0$; most cases would be in between, making $0 \le \alpha_j \le 1$.

Before moving into scope analysis, it is useful to introduce a concept that has been in the transport economics literature since the late 1970s: economies of density. This concept coincides with the notion of scale economies, except for the fact that the physical network is held constant (originally, it was either total track or road length that was held constant). In the literature, the degree of economies of density (ED) has always been calculated from a $\tilde{C}(w,\tilde{Y},\bar{X})$ type cost function, including some index or variable representing either the network as a fixed factor (for, example track length) or a network 'characteristic' related to operations (for example, number of points served). The usual procedure (which is actually nearly a definition) is to calculate ED as the inverse of the sum of all cost elasticities except those related to the network. An estimate of S, on the other hand, would include all elasticities. Again, failure to think in terms of Y prevents the true analysis from surfacing. The key issue is whether the O–D system varies or not with the variable representing network shape or operations, because if it does, the associated elasticity is not related to flow expansions but to the addition of new flows. And this is not related to scale but to scope analysis.

The best example of what we have exposed in the previous paragraph is the number of points served, PS, a variable that is usually part of the output description in the analysis of the airline industry. Is a variation of PS related to scale? If PS increases by one, the number of O–D pairs can increase up to two times PS, because the new point is a potential new destination for PS origins, and a potential new origin for PS destinations. In other words, a change in PS

means a change in the number of O–D pairs which, by definition, is a matter of scope. This is an issue in the transport economics literature that has only recently been addressed (Jara-Díaz et al., 1997).

Finally, transport cost functions using output aggregates do allow for some type of scope analysis whenever the value of the aggregates can be recovered when some of the components of Y go to zero. Trivially, this can be done when, for instance, we have passenger and freight movements distinctly represented; in this case, the presence of economies of scope between both type of services simply requires making each aggregate at a time zero, and calculating SC as in (2.15).

5   SYNTHESIS

In this chapter we have presented the main concepts of a microeconomic framework for the analysis of transport production and industry structure. The theory of transport production involves two key aspects: transport output, which is a vector of flows with many dimensions, and operating rules, which are the forms of input combinations to produce a flow vector. The main elements here are frequency, load size, route structure and so on, which are operating decisions. On the other hand, fleet size, vehicle capacity, loading–unloading capacity, rights-of-way design, and so on, are decisions related to input acquisition. Both types of decisions are related, but the former are taken within the boundaries of the latter.

Thus, the theory of multi-output production provides the appropriate framework for the study of transport industries, where the analysis of both scale *and* scope economies is necessary for an assessment of the optimal industry structure. This is done through the estimation of transport cost functions. However, we have shown that attempts to simplify matters by using output aggregates introduces a non-negligible degree of ambiguity. Economies of scale are clearly defined on the original output description, as the concept examines the behaviour of costs since all flows in all O–D pairs expand in the same proportion, but this clean interpretation is darkened by aggregation. Since output is usually a vector of huge dimensions, the empirical literature shows a variety of aggregate output indices that, placed in groups of three or four, are used for the estimation of cost functions in an effort to capture the complexity of transport services. We have summarized here a method to calculate correctly the degree of scale economies from such transport cost functions, which is based upon the recognition of aggregates as constructs from the original flow components.

Economies of scope are difficult to analyse from the transport cost functions reported in the literature, unless distinct aggregate output variables are used for different movement types (for example, passenger-km and ton-km). The main cause of the problem, as has been explained in Section 4, is that making some of the flows zero has an unknown impact on the value of each aggregate. This is further complicated when the transport cost function includes 'network' variables (which *are* important in an aggregate analysis), because their variation implies a variation in the number of O–D pairs; thus, scope becomes somehow related to scalar variables. This is indeed a topic for further research.

NOTES

1. A complete analytical derivation of cost functions for both the simple cyclical system (equation 2.7) and the backhaul system (equation 2.8) can be found in Jara-Díaz (1982b).
2. For a condensed overview of the technical analysis based upon the coefficients obtained from the translog specification of $C(w, Y)$, see Spady and Friedlaender (1978).
3. Sheppard's Lemma states that $[\partial C(w, y)] / \partial w_i = X_i$; this can be manipulated to obtain either w_i $(\partial C / \partial w_i)$ (factor expenditure) or $w_i \partial C / C \partial w_i$ (factor share). This third form is particularly appropriate when using the translog form.
4. Possible exceptions are two pieces on output aggregation published by the author (Jara-Díaz et al., 1991, 1992).
5. Note that this is not intended as a review of techniques and results. The reader might want to look at two fairly complete studies: the period 1970–80 is reviewed in detail in Jara-Díaz (1982a); the remainder is analysed by Oum and Waters (1996).

REFERENCES

Baumol, W.J., J.C. Panzar and R.D. Willig (1982), *Contestable Markets and the Theory of Industry Structure*, New York: Harcourt Brace Jovanovich.

Berechman, J. (1983), 'Costs, economies of scale and factor demand in bus transport', *Journal of Transport Economics and Policy*, **17**, 7–24.

Berechman, J. (1987), 'Cost structure and production technology in transit', *Regional Science and Urban Economics*, **17**, 519–34.

Berechman, J. and G. Giuliano (1984), 'Analysis of the cost structure of an urban bus transit property', *Regional Science and Urban Economics*, **17**, 519–34.

Braeutigam, R.R., A.F. Daughety and M.A. Turnquist (1980), 'The estimation of a hybrid cost function for a railroad firm', *Review of Economics and Statistics*, **62**, 394–402.

Caves, D.W., L.R. Christensen and J.A. Swanson (1980), 'Productivity in U.S. railroads, 1951–1974', *Bell Journal of Economics*, **11**, 166–81.

Caves, D.W., L.R. Christensen and J.A. Swanson (1981), 'Productivity growth, scale economies, and capacity utilisation in U.S. railroads, 1955–74', *American Economic Review*, **71**, 994–1002.

Caves, D.W., L.R. Christensen and M.W. Tretheway (1984), 'Economies of density versus economies of scale: why trunk and local service airline costs differ', *Rand Journal of Economics*, **15**, 471–89.

Caves, D.W., L.R. Christensen, M.W. Tretheway and R.J. Windle (1985), 'Network effects and the measurement of returns to scale and density for U.S. railroads', in Daughety (ed.), pp. 97–120.

Christensen, L.R., D.W. Jorgenson and L.J. Lau (1973), 'Transcendental logarithmic production frontiers', *Review of Economics and Statistics*, **55**, 28–45.

Daughety, A.F. (ed.) (1985), *Analytical Studies in Transport Economics*, Cambridge: Cambridge University Press.

Daughety, A.F., F.D. Nelson and W.R. Vigdor (1985), 'An econometric analysis of the cost and production structure of the trucking industry', in Daughety (ed.), pp. 65–95.

Filippini, M. and R. Maggi (1992), 'The cost structure of the Swiss private railways', *International Journal of Transport Economics*, **19**, 307–27.

Formby, J.P., P.D. Thistle and J.P. Keeler (1990), 'Costs under regulation and deregulation: the case of US passenger airlines', *Economic Record*, **66**, 308–21.

Friedlaender, A.F. and S.S. Bruce (1985), 'Augmentation effects and technical change in the regulated trucking industry, 1974–1979', in Daughety (ed.), pp. 29–62.

Gagné, R. (1990), 'On the relevant elasticity estimates for cost structure analyses of the trucking industry', *Review of Economics and Statistics*, **72**, 160–64.

Gálvez, T. (1978), *Análisis de operaciones en Sistemas de Transporte* (Operations analysis in transport systems), Publicación ST-INV/04/78, Santiago de Chile: Universidad de Chile, Departamento de Obras Civiles.

Gillen, D.W., T.H. Oum and M.W. Tretheway (1990), 'Airline cost structure and policy implications', *Journal of Transport Economics and Policy*, **24**, 9–34.

Harmatuck, D.J. (1981), 'A motor carrier joint cost function', *Journal of Transport Economics and Policy*, **21**, 135–52.

Harmatuck, D.J. (1985), 'Short run motor carrier cost function for five large common carriers', *Logistics and Transportation Review*, **21**, 217–37.

Harmatuck, D.J. (1991), 'Economies of scale and scope in the motor carrier industry', *Journal of Transport Economics and Policy*, **25**, 135–51.

Jara-Díaz, S.R. (1982a), 'The estimation of transport cost functions: a methodological review', *Transport Reviews*, **2**, 257–78.

Jara-Díaz, S.R. (1982b), 'Transportation product, transportation function and cost functions', *Transportation Science*, **16**, 522–39.

Jara-Díaz, S. and C. Cortés (1996), 'On the calculation of scale economies from transport cost functions', *Journal of Transport Economics and Policy*, **30**, 157–70.

Jara-Díaz, S., C. Cortés and F. Ponce (1997), 'Número de puntos servidos y economías de diversidad espacial en funciones de costo en transporte aéreo' (Number of points served and economies of spatial scope in air transport cost functions), *Actas del Octavo Congreso Chileno de Ingeniería de Transporte*, Santiago, Chile: Universidad Católica de Chile, pp. 133–45.

Jara-Díaz, S.R., P. Donoso and J. Araneda (1991), 'Best partial flow aggregation in transportation cost functions', *Transportation Research B*, **25**, 329–39.

Jara-Díaz, S.R., P. Donoso and J. Araneda (1992), 'Estimation of marginal transport costs using the flow aggregation function approach', *Journal of Transport Economics and Policy*, **26**, 35–48.

Keaton, M.H. (1990), 'Economies of density and service levels on U.S. railroads: an experimental analysis', *Logistics and Transportation Review*, **26**, 211–27.

Keeler, J. and F. Formby (1994), 'Cost economies and consolidation in the U.S. airline industry', *International Journal of Transport Economics*, **21**, 21–45.

Kim, M. (1987), 'Multilateral relative efficiency levels in regional Canadian trucking', *Logistics and Transportation Review*, **23**, 155–72.

Koshal, R.K. and M. Koshal (1989), 'Economies of scale of state road transport industry in India', *International Journal of Transport Economics*, **16**, 165–72.

Oum, T.H. and W.G. Waters II (1996), 'A survey of recent developments in transportation cost function research', *Logistics and Transportation Review*, **32**, 423–62.

Panzar, J.C. and R.D. Willig (1977), 'Economies of scale in multioutput production', *Quarterly Journal of Economics*, **91**, August, 481–92.

Spady, R. and A.F. Friedlaender (1978), 'Hedonic cost functions for the regulated trucking industry', *Bell Journal of Economics*, **9**, 159–79.

Tauchen, H., F.D. Fravel and G. Gilbert (1983), 'Cost structure in the intercity bus industry', *Journal of Transport Economics and Policy*, **17**, 25–47.

Wang Chiang, S.J. and A.F. Friedlaender (1984), 'Output aggregation, network effects, and the measurement of trucking technology', *Review of Economics and Statistics*, **66**, 267–76.

Windle, R.J. (1991), 'The world's airlines', *Journal of Transport Economics and Policy*, **25**, 31–49.

Ying, J.S. (1990), 'The inefficiency of regulating a competitive industry: productivity gains in trucking following reform', *Review of Economics and Statistics*, **72**, 191–201.

Ying, J.S. (1992), 'On calculating cost elasticities', *Logistics and Transportation Review*, **28**, 231–5.

Ying, J.S. and T.E. Keeler (1991), 'Pricing in a deregulated environment: the motor carrier experience', *Rand Journal of Economics*, **22**, 264–72.

3. Travel demand

Manfred M. Fischer

1 INTRODUCTION

Transport planning is basically concerned with the establishment of a stable relationship between the demand for, and the supply of traffic infrastructure and transport services. In the recent past and in the current situation, the relationship between supply and demand has been somewhat one-sided in many European countries in the sense that (commodity and person) transport growth and demand for transport services have outstripped both investment outlay and institutional ability to deal with the complexity of the problems attached to the renewal and expansion of transport infrastructure. This strong contrast between traffic growth and infrastructure investments since the 1970s has resulted in transport bottlenecks in many countries and regions (see Nijkamp et al., 1990).

In this chapter, focus is laid on passenger transport or travel demand. The legacy of more than three decades of travel demand analysis is a large, rather diverse and often disparate body of information. No longer is research into travel demand to be focused narrowly on the theme of forecasting; the need for understanding travel behaviour itself has become a prominent theme. This broader debate has resulted in a flux of new ideas, methodologies and techniques which were stimulating to transport researchers, but might have frustrated transport practitioners seeking to identify the state-of-the-art in the field.

This contribution is concerned primarily with passenger travel models and especially with those applied within an urban context. Various aspects relating to the development of travel demand models are discussed and some views on outstanding research issues are offered. The discussion will be at a relatively general level, and while the material is wide-ranging, it is inevitably selective. In structuring the discussion it is convenient to refer to three broad classes of models which characterize the development and progression in the field:

1. the traditional four-stage transport models associated with the large urban transport studies (UTS) and characterized by an aggregate and descriptive use of data;

2. the microeconomic approach of travel choice behaviour underpinned with random utility theory and emphasizing explanation of behaviour at the level of the individual; and
3. the activity-orientated approach based on more holistic research styles and viewing travel behaviour as daily or multi-day patterns of behaviour, related to and derived from differences in life styles and activity participation among the population.

Accordingly, the chapter is divided into three major parts. Section 2 considers the more traditional research style of the aggregate four-stage approach, while in Section 3 more recent theoretical issues and research requirements relating to the microeconomic approach are analysed. Activity-based studies emerged in the 1980s as a challenge to the established travel demand techniques. Major aspects of the conceptual foundation and methodological developments of the activity-based approach are discussed in Section 4. In the final section, some research and development priorities for the future are sketched.

2   THE TRADITIONAL FOUR-STAGE TRANSPORT APPROACH

In this aggregate approach, the focus is on zones as generators of travel and as destinations for travel. Such a focus is appropriate for the kind of large-scale, long-range transport planning which dominated planning in the past.

2.1   The Demand Forecasting Process

Most large-scale travel demand studies in an urban context – not only in the 1960s and 1970s, but also in current planning practice – are built around the classical four-stage travel demand forecasting process outlined in Figure 3.1 (for more details see, for example, Sheppard, 1986). Basically they rely on the following passenger demand model approach (see Williams and Ortuzar, 1979):

$$T(k, i, j, m, r) = G_i^k T_{ij}^k M_{ij}^{km} R_{ij}^{kmr}, \qquad (3.1)$$

where G_i^k is the total number of trips made by persons of type k generated in zone i, T_{ij}^k is that proportion attracted to zone j, M_{ij}^{km} denotes the proportion of T_{ij}^k associated with mode m (for example, car, bus, rail), while the route share R_{ij}^{kmr} is similarly defined. The four quantities $G_i^k, T_{ij}^k, M_{ij}^{km}$ and R_{ij}^{kmr} correspond to the four stages of demand forecasting: trip generation, trip distribution, mode choice and network assignment, designed to predict traffic flows on links of a transport network from knowledge of land use, car ownership, economic, population and travel conditions.

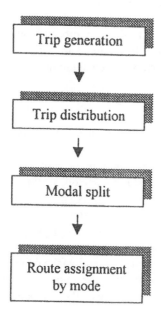

Figure 3.1   Four-stage model of the demand forecasting process

Trip generation

Trip generation is the first submodel of the conventional four-stage model sequence. Trip generation models attempt to predict the total quantity of travel, that is G_i^k, measured in terms of the number of trips of a certain kind (usually home-based work trips) leaving a zone i during a fixed period of time (usually peak or off-peak hours) and based upon attributes of that zone. Two types of methodologies, linear regression and category analysis, are generally used for modelling the generation of trips.

Trip generation models may be criticized due to several limitations. The most severe one is their evident inability to predict the hidden demand which is released by transport improvements. The interrelation between the transport system and land-use patterns is not captured in this type of model.

Trip distribution

Trip distribution models link the origin and destination ends of the trip generated by the trip generation model. That is, a trip destination model predicts how many trips made by persons of type k and originating in zone i ($i = 1, \dots , n$)

will terminate in zone j ($j = 1, \dots, n$), that is T_{ij}^k. A variety of trip distribution models have been proposed, including classical gravity models, intervening opportunity models and entropy models (see, for example, Wilson, 1969, 1970). No matter how different these models are, they all contain three basic elements to model the distribution of trips: the number of trips generated by a zone i of origin, the degree to which the *in situ* characteristics of a particular zone j of destination attracts trip makers, and the inhibiting effect of separation (distance, generalized costs).[1]

Modal split

Modal split or mode choice is concerned with the prediction of the number of trips from each origin to each destination which will use each transport mode. Thus, the objective of modal split or mode choice analysis is the prediction of M_{ij}^{km}, the number of trips made by persons of type k from i to j by mode m, given a prediction of the number of trips T_{ij}^k. Mode selection is usually seen as a choice between just two broad categories: private cars (and trucks) on the one side, and public transport on the other. Certain groups of travellers can be virtually eliminated before considering modal split. Passengers who cannot afford or cannot drive a car must generally take public transport. Thus, the first step in modal split is to identify the public-transport-captive fraction of population of each zone and to allocate these subpopulations to the one mode which they use.

Two basic model types have been used to predict M_{ij}^{km} modal split and mode choice models, where the former term refers to aggregate and the latter to disaggregate model forms. The core of disaggregated logit-type choice models (see Section 2.6) in the context of mode choice modelling is accepted practice today. The modal split stage of the travel forecasting model provides useful information for transport policy in general and in particular for decisions such as, for example, whether to invest in a new subway system; whether to implement an exclusive high-occupancy-vehicle lane for buses and/or car pools; and so on.

Trip assignment

The final step in the conventional four-stage model sequence is generally referred to as trip or traffic assignment (route choice). The rationale behind trip assignment is based on the assumption that all trips between zones follow the 'best' route, best being defined in terms of travel time or generalized cost. It is implicitly assumed that travellers are sufficiently familiar with the network for making their optimal route choice, an assumption which is quite reasonable for work and shopping trips, but questionable for recreational trips. Network assignment models (such as all-or-nothing assignment, multipath assignment and constrained assignment) contain two components: a tree-building process for searching out the 'best' route for each interzonal movement in a network and a procedure for allocating the interzonal modal trip volume among the paths.

2.2 Criticisms of the Approach

Many conceptual, methodological and technical problems have been identified in the aggregate four-stage sequential approach. One is the absence of any feedback between the various stages of the travel demand forecasting process. The submodels are applied in a uni-directional way. Errors in submodels are compounded in any forward linkage.

More significantly, the traditional research style of large-scale modelling has been strongly criticized in academia in the 1970s as:

- descriptive rather than explanatory in nature;
- theoretically deficient and in particular lacking in a behavioural rationale;
- subject to ecological fallacies and aggregation biases;
- policy insensitive and unresponsive to exploratory new policies in the context of transport system management, and
- expensive to develop and operate.

At the same time, aggregate models have been improved considerably by introducing household- and individual-based category analysis for trip generation, incorporating the generalized cost concept (with micro parameters) within the entropy maximizing-based trip distribution stage, integrating disaggregate logit-type models in the context of mode choice and interrelating the stages of the travel demand forecasting process. The SELNEC transport model developed by Wilson et al. (1969) and its descendants are prominent examples of aggregate models which anticipated elements of the disaggregate modelling philosophy and are free from some of the above-mentioned criticisms. Thus, in many respects the distinction between aggregate and disaggregate models is becoming blurred (see Williams and Ortuzar, 1982).

There is no doubt now that travel demand models, whether aggregate or disaggregate, should be based on a well-specified behavioural representation of the travel decision process. It is possible to develop aggregate travel demand models derived from a realistic representation of travel decision making at the micro level. Thus, the clearest remaining distinctive feature between the two classes of travel demand models is the level of data analysis. Each model type has a distinct role to play in transport planning and policy (see Jones, 1983). Aggregate models provide important insights into the working of the (urban) transport system as a whole and are appropriate for the sort of large-scale, long-range transport planning while disaggregate models can provide insights into the nature of the travel decision process and are more suited for the type of transport planning and policy which has became more important since the late 1970s, the finer-scaled, shorter time frame and low-capital cost planning epitomized by transport system management (see Hanson and Schwab, 1986).

3   THE MICROECONOMIC APPROACH OF TRAVEL CHOICE

The disaggregate approach takes individuals or households rather than zones as the units of observation and analysis. There are three major reasons for shifting the focus of research away from zones to individuals or households. The first is related to theory building and derives from the desire to explain how and why traffic-flow patterns emerge. There is now consensus that the decision-making unit is the appropriate level at which to build travel choice theory. The second refers to the potential of increased policy sensitivity at a much finer scale of analysis. The third is more technical in nature and relates to the potential for a greater statistical efficiency of data requirements (see Hanson and Schwab, 1986).

The specific focus in this section is on the random utility-based discrete choice approach of travel choice behaviour which has proved a great stimulus to the promotion of disaggregate travel choice models. Its essential conceptual contribution lies in its explicit treatment of the processes, making perfect predictions of travel choice behaviour unattainable. Before progressing to the choice-theoretic framework we first introduce some basic notions, such as travel choice behaviour, and characterize the travel decision process in some detail.

3.1   The Travel Decision-making Process

The need to travel arises at the level of the individual and at this level choices about travel are important. The term individual choice refers to the selection decision by an individual between commodities which are discrete in nature, such as, for example, mode of travel to use. Travel behaviour is reflected, among other things, by pre-trip decisions consisting of destination, mode, route and departure time choices, and *en route* decisions which may consist of decisions such as diversion of alternative routes or rescheduling of intended trips (see Khattak, 1991). Figure 3.2 describes the decision-making problem with which the traveller is faced in a simplified manner. According to this framework, travel choice is principally concerned with two givens:

1. the individual in question with his subjective needs, travel experience, preferences, perceptions and attitudes, influenced by both the socio-

demographic environment in which the individual lives (including, for example, his household, car ownership, age and other individual characteristics) and the normative environment (including the set of norms and values derived from society), and

2. the physical environment (including the built-up surroundings, the transport network infrastructure and so on) determining the objective travel opportunities and their characteristics.

The decision-making process itself is seen as consisting of the formation of perceptions and cognitive representations of travel opportunities and their char-

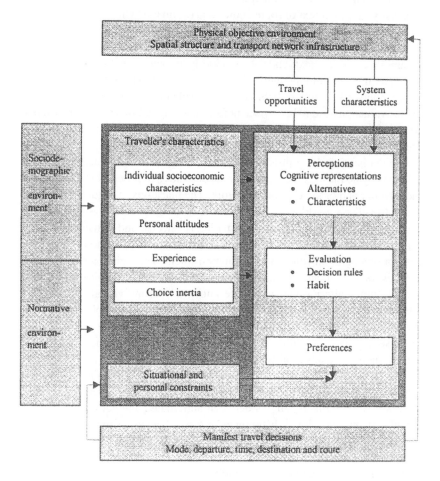

Figure 3.2 Decision-making process: a simplified view

acteristics, and attitude formation (that is, learned predispositions to respond to a situation in a consistent way) (see Golledge and Stimson, 1987; Bovy and Stern, 1990). In route choice contexts – in contrast to other travel choices – the set of choice opportunities may be quite extensive and complex. The traveller has only limited knowledge (cognition) of all the opportunities available. Cognition is associated with his experiences and the manner of acquiring information. There is a growing body of literature confirming the widely held view that in travel choice contexts individuals act under restricted knowledge of alternatives and their attribute values. The traveller may have – to a certain degree – a distorted image (cognitive representation) of the actual situation. There may be constraints which preclude certain alternatives, especially in the context of route choice and destination choice behaviour (see Bovy and Stern, 1990).

The perceived choice options are likely to be evaluated consciously in unfamiliar choice contexts and subconsciously in routine contexts. For example, travellers may get into the habit of taking a certain mode and route through a familiar network. Inertia or habit may play a role in so far as certain thresholds in the evaluation need to be crossed before changing (attitudes towards) routine behaviour. Situational and personal constraints along with preferences determine observable choices then.

The decision-making process outlined in Figure 3.2 indicates that travel choice is by no means a direct and simple derivative of observable attributes of the traveller and of the transport network. The black box in Figure 3.2, the so-called traveller's world, may be considered as a complicated system of filters through which choice-relevant information is selected and transformed. Two types of filters are of central importance in the choice process: perception/cognition filters and evaluation filters. Through perception filters the universal set of choice options is narrowed into feasible choice sets, that is, sets of choice alternatives which are known to the individual and actively considered in the choice process. The individual receives a certain cognition of the existence of choice options and a certain perception of the characteristics of these alternatives while through evaluation filters these perceptions are transformed into a desirability (utility) scale (Bovy and Stern, 1990).

The decision-making problem is also characterized by dynamic components. Perception/cognition filters as well as attitudes are likely to change via learning processes due to discrepancies between anticipated and actual experience. Finally, strong individual differences in travel behaviour may occur which cannot be easily derived from observable personal characteristics such as sex or age. This diversity is caused by the filter functions (perception, cognition and evaluation), which differ from individual to individual.

3.2 The Discrete Choice Framework and Random Utility Choice Models

Classical travel choice theory explains individual behaviour as the outcome of a two-step recursive process. First, exogenous forces pose a travel choice problem, that is, an individual decision maker and an associated choice set. Then, with the choice set well defined, the decision maker chooses among the available travel options. In general, research on travel choice theory has focused on the second stage of the decision process, the characterization of classes of decision rules, formalization of choice set structure and analysis of the attributes of the outcome when decision rules of a given class are applied to choice sets of a specified structure.

Random utility choice theory is based upon the hypothesis of preference (utility) maximization which postulates that the distribution of demands in a population is the result of individual preference (utility) maximization, with preferences influenced by unobservable variables. Utilities are treated as random variables, not to reflect a lack of rationality of the decision maker, but to reflect a lack of information concerning the characteristics of alternatives and decision makers on the part of the observer/researcher.

Basic concepts and conceptual considerations

Figure 3.3 illustrates the general strategy adopted by the microeconomic approach to accommodate various aspects of the travel decision-making process characterized in Figure 3.2. The approach requires four primary ingredients:

1. a population I of decision makers i which may be partitioned into population segments $s = 1, \ldots, S$ defined by some socioeconomic descriptors;
2. objects of travel choice (such as routes, modes, destinations or times of travel) and a set A_s of travel options available to i (known as choice set definition);
3. decision-relevant characteristics z_{ia} of both the decision maker i and alternative a, and
4. a decision rule for combining them.

The hypothesis of random preference (utility) maximization plays a key role in modelling the travel decision-making process and assumes that there exists a mathematical function U, called (indirect) utility function, such that decision maker i prefers travel option a to option a' if and only if $U(z_{ia}) = U_{ia}$ (the value of the utility function corresponding to the attributes of the pair (i, a) exceeds $U(z_{ia'}) = U_{ia'}$ (the value of the utility function corresponding to (i, a')). In other

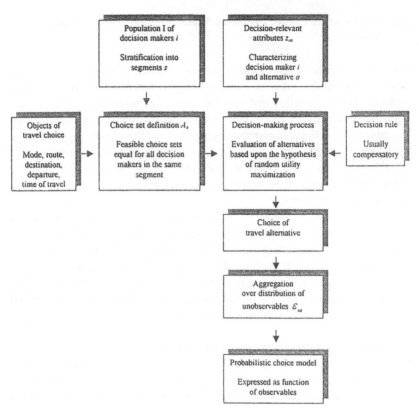

Figure 3.3　Major elements of the microeconomic random utility-based approach

words, decision makers are assumed always to choose the utility-maximizing alternatives, that is

$$U(z_{ia}) > U(z_{ia'}), \text{ for all } a' = \neq a, a' \in A_s. \tag{3.2}$$

It is generally recognized that not all the attributes characterizing the decision makers and the alternatives which are relevant to choices among travel alternatives are known to the researcher, and that it is usually not feasible to measure or observe the values of all the known attributes. Moreover, there may be unobserved taste variations in a population (segment) influencing measurement errors (see Horowitz, 1986; Ben-Akiva and Lerman, 1985; Fischer and Nijkamp, 1985).

In random utility travel choice models, these inherent uncertainties are dealt with by random utility functions of the following form

$$U_{ia} = U [f_1(x_{ia}), f_2(x_{ia}), f_3(\varepsilon_{ia})] \tag{3.3}$$

where U_{ia} is the overall utility (or preference) of alternative a, $U(\cdot)$ denotes the utility function (for the s-th population segment), $f_1(x_{ia})$ is the function measuring the average (systematic) taste of decision makers within s, $f_2(x_{ia})$ a random function representing the idiosyncratic variations in taste (random taste variation), and $f_3(\varepsilon_{ia})$ a random disturbance term capturing the effects of unobserved, but decision-relevant attributes of both the decision makers and the alternatives. x_{ia} is a vector of observed characteristics of the pair (i, a). In applications it has generally been assumed that the utility values (for example, for alternative a) may be expressed as

$$U_{ia} = x_{ia}\beta + (x_{ia}\delta_i + \zeta_{ia}) = v_{ia} + \varepsilon_{ia} \tag{3.4}$$

where the first term, v_{ia}, at the right side of (3.4) is referred to as the systematic (deterministic) component of utility, while the second term, ε_{ia}, denotes the random component. This component consists of two parts. ζ_{ia} is a random disturbance term capturing the effects of unobserved attributes of the decision maker and the choice alternatives, while $x_{ia}\delta_i$ represents the idiosyncratic tastes of i. β is a vector of the deterministic component of utility and δ_i the taste variation parameter vector. This linear-in-the-parameters and additive form is not as restrictive as it might look at the first glance, as non-linearities and non-additivities may be readily accommodated.

In typical travel choice applications, observed attributes of decision makers might include automobile ownership, income and household size. Unobserved attributes of individuals might relate to social status (except income), occupation, health and schedule commitments affecting travel choices. Observed characteristics of alternatives typically involve travel times and costs, and employment and population levels, if the alternatives are locations. Unobserved attributes of alternatives typically include reliability and comfort, if the travel options are modes, and the prices, quality and variety of available goods and services if the alternatives are locations (see Horowitz, 1983).

Random utility travel choice models specify the probability p_{ia} that a randomly selected travel decision maker i chooses alternative $a \in A_s$:

$$p_{ia} = \text{prob } (u_{ia} > u_{ia'}, \text{ for all } a' \neq a, a' \in A_s) \tag{3.5}$$

conditional on the matrix $x_i = (x_{ia}, a \in A_s)$ of observed attributes characterizing i's choice problem and an unknown parameter vector θ including parameters of the utility function U (that is β and δ_i) and parameters of the distribution F

of the random components $e_i = (\varepsilon_{ia}, a \in A_s)$. The choice probabilities are assumed to fulfil the conditions that they are non-negative, sum to one, and depend only on the measured attributes of travel options and individual characteristics.

Functional forms

The primary issues in selecting a functional form for the choice probabilities in (3.5) are computational practicability and flexibility in representing patterns of similarity across travel options. Three major classes of concrete functional forms for random utility travel choice models may be distinguished. These are logit models based on the work of Luce (1959), probit models based on the work of Thurstone (1927), and elimination models based on the work of Tversky (1972a, b) (see McFadden, 1981 for more details). Figure 3.4 outlines these classes as well as their most important members.

By far the best-known functional form, the multinomial logit (MNL) allows easy computation and interpretation, but has a very restrictive pattern of inter-alternative substitution

$$p_{ia} = \exp(x_{ia}\beta) / \sum_{a' \in A} \exp(x_{ia'}\beta) \tag{3.6}$$

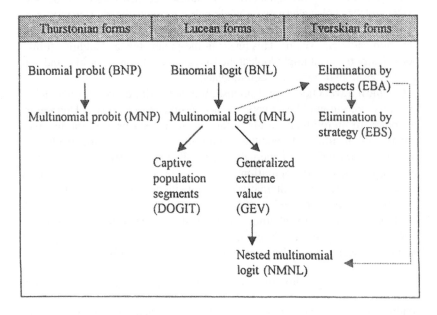

Source: McFadden (1981).

Figure 3.4   Three major classes of functional forms

derived from the assumption that the random terms ε_i are independently and identically (IID) distributed with the Gumbel Type I extreme value distribution. In the MNL, no allowance is made for random taste variation. The values of the parameter vector must be estimated by fitting the model to data consisting of observations of the choices and measurements of the attributes for a random sample of decision makers. Usually the maximum likelihood procedure is used for this purpose. The most significant feature of MNL is the independence of irrelevant alternatives (IIA) property – a property which implies that the relative choice probability of any two alternatives depends exclusively on their systematic components – and can give rise to somewhat odd and erroneous predictions when the travel options are clear substitutes for each other.

Because of its simplicity, the MNL model form has been a primary focus of attempts at functional generalizations to transcend the limitations inherent in the IIA property of MNL. The most general ones are Thurstonian forms which can be derived by assuming the errors to have a multivariate normal distribution (see Hausman and Wise, 1978). These model forms allow the random components of the travel options to be correlated, to have unequal variances, and also permit random taste variation to be incorporated across decision makers. For binary choice this yields the binomial probit model (BNP). The primary difficulty in applying the multinomial probit model (MNP) is the lack of practical, accurate procedures for approximating the choice probabilities when the number of alternatives is large, as is usually the case in destination and route choice contexts.

The most promising and widely adopted generalization of the MNL form is the nested multinomial logit (NMNL) model which can be obtained as a special case of the generalized extreme value (GEV) model form by choosing appropriate values of the parameter of the GEV distribution (see, for example, Sobel, 1980; Ben-Akiva and Lerman, 1985). To illustrate the NMNL model, a simple journey-to-work mode-choice context may be considered as displayed in Figure 3.5 in which four travel options are distinguished: drive alone, shared ride, metro and bus. Using the MNL model, one would treat the four modes as distinctly independent alternatives and assume that each individual selects one particular mode following a simultaneous evaluation of all four. In contrast, using the NMNL model one would treat the trip decision process as a recursive sequential choice structure where results of the decision on the lower decision level feed into that of the higher level. The NMNL form has the advantage of retaining the desirable computational and other characteristics of the MNL model, embodies more general properties of cross-substitution, but is less general than Thurstonian forms.

All the functional forms considered so far belong to the family of compensatory choice models assuming that the travel decision-making process is compensatory in nature, in other words that individuals 'trade off' attributes of

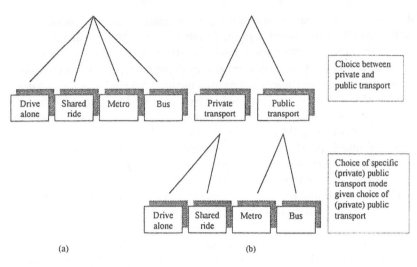

Figure 3.5   Alternative decision structures and model forms for a simple travel-to-work mode choice example: (a) the MNL form; (b) the NMNL form

the travel options in the decision process. Non-compensatory models employ other decision rules. The most prominent examples are the elimination-by-aspects (EBA) models (see Figure 3.4) where lexicographic and satisfaction rules are combined (see, for example, Recker and Golob, 1979). Choice is viewed as a process in which the attributes are hierarchically ranked by the importance associated to them, and alternatives are eliminated from the choice set until a single alternative remains.

These models, however, are more complicated than the MNL model and require considerable a priori information. Thus, empirical practice confines itself to the exclusively used Lucean forms in general and the MNL model in particular. Their domain of applicability has been steadily extended from binary mode choice to simultaneous choices over complex choice sets in a destination or route choice context (see, for example, Kern et al., 1984; Borgers and Timmermans, 1986).

Revealed versus stated choice models
Traditionally, travel choice models have been based on data obtained by direct observation of travel behaviour or in surveys asking for actual travel behaviour (that is, revealed (preference) data). Such data, however, have some limitations which restrict their general suitability. First, it might be difficult to obtain sufficient variation in the revealed preference data to analyse all variables of interest. Second, there may be strong correlations between explanatory variables

of interest (especially travel time and cost) which makes it difficult to estimate model parameters reflecting the proper trade-off ratios. Third, the revealed preference data approach cannot be used in a direct way to evaluate demand under conditions which do not yet exist (such as new forms of public transport, new regulations affecting the use of cars and so on). In view of these problems, the use of stated (preference) or experimental data became an attractive option in travel demand analysis (see Louvière and Hensher, 1982, Kroes and Sheldon, 1988).

Stated (preference) data relate to observations of choices made by individuals in laboratory choice experiments carried out in hypothetical environments. A key feature of the stated data approach is that individuals are exposed to a set of choice experiments generated by some controlled experimental design procedure (for example, full or fractional factorial design) so that the independent variables can be made truly independent. A crucial issue in the design is the definition of the variables (factors) of interest and the values (levels) of the factors which need to be evaluated by the respondents. The last few years have seen an increasing attention devoted to computer integrative procedures to increase the reliability of the behavioural responses of the respondents.

Choice models based on revealed data are termed revealed choice models, while choice models based on stated data are called stated choice models. Revealed and stated choice models have complementary advantages and disadvantages. Revealed ones have high external validity in the sense that they are calibrated to real data. This advantage, however, may be considerably diluted by the difficulty of defining the choice set in destination and route choice contexts, and by the concern about the accuracy of the data actually used in making the choice. Stated choice models have several advantages over the revealed choice models in analysing travel behaviour. The most important one refers to the controlled nature of the choice experiments which allows greater freedom in defining travel choice contexts, alternatives and attributes as well as direct comparison with the responses across individuals. With these advantages comes the liability that the success of the stated preference approach largely depends on the consistency of the hypothetical alternatives and the corresponding sets of attributes with their perception in actual choice situations (see Wardman, 1988). Stated choice models are being employed increasingly in academic studies (especially in destination and route choice contexts) and in policy analysis to analyse how people would adjust their behaviour under radically different alternative futures (for example, new forms of public transport, new regulations affecting the use of cars, and so on).

3.3 Range of Applications of Random Utility Models

Revealed and stated choice models have found an increasing range of application in travel demand analysis in the past two decades. They have been used simply to replace the forecasting components of aggregate models. But often inflexibility in the large-scale aggregate frameworks has restricted the benefits obtained. Most success has been found in specialized policy analysis. For example, car pooling has been studied by Ben-Akiva and Atherton (1977), the elasticity of gasoline taxes, parking taxes, transit fares and housing taxes to finance public transport by Anas (1982) and the effectiveness of ride-sharing incentiveness on work trips to reduce congestion and air pollution by Brownstone and Golob (1992).

The early applications were confined to mode choice in the urban area for work trips. The choice of mode for travel to work has been analysed extensively, using different types of data from widely differing urban areas (see, for example, Domencich and McFadden, 1975; Ben-Akiva and Lerman, 1985). Initially satisfied with identifying those attributes characterizing the system and/or individual which significantly affected one's choice decision, transport researchers have since broadened their scope to include virtually every aspect of an individual's choice of travel mode. Consequently, considerable efforts have been devoted to the valuation of traveller's time, uni- and multidimensional procedures for obtaining an index of vehicle safety, comfort and other qualitative aspects, procedures which attempt to minimize aggregation biases, due to spatial or socioeconomic groupings and so on. These and other issues have been analysed both in isolation and together with related individual decisions such as trip purpose, time of day of travel, frequency of travel and residential and employment location choice.

Although still dominated by mode choice studies, the application of discrete choice models now includes departure time (see, for example, Abkowits, 1981; Brownstone and Small, 1989), route choice (see, for example, Bovy and Stern, 1990), automobile ownership and use (see, for example, Hensher et al., 1989), travel frequency (see, for example, Domencich and McFadden, 1975), multi-destination travel or trip chaining (see Horowitz, 1979). Most of the studies assume trip decisions are being made independently. However, some also explore relationships between decisions, such as, for example, between mode, destination and frequency (see Domencich and McFadden, 1975); mode destination and trip chaining (see Horowitz, 1980); frequency, mode, destination and time of day of travel (see Charles River Associates, 1967), shopping mode and destination choice (see Ben-Akiva and Lerman, 1985).

Work has also progressed on applying discrete choice models to intercity travel demand situations. Thus, Koppelman and Hirsch (1989) have developed an intercity travel demand model representing trip frequency, trip destination, mode and service class choice in the form of a nested decision structure.

Changes in the transport system are likely to have significant effects not only on travel decisions, but also on travel-related choices such as car ownership, employment and residential location. In turn, these decisions may have a significant impact on travel demand, since travel decisions of an individual are constrained by fixed employment and residential location as well as by fixed automobile ownership or availability. Thus, a fully successful travel demand model has to take into account the structural relationships between these decisions which directly or indirectly influence trip-making behaviour (see Domencich and McFadden, 1975). There are good reasons to assume that the longer-run mobility-related choices are intertwined with the short-run travel choices while within each of both bundles of decisions a simultaneous structure may be assumed. Figure 3.6 illustrates one possible choice hierarchy in a travel and mobility-related context. Until the nature of the interactions between transport services, travel and travel-related decisions is better understood, there is little hope that travel choice models will provide reliable tools for long-term policy analysis.

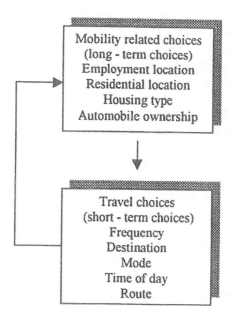

Source: Ben-Akiva and Lerman (1979, p. 669).

Figure 3.6   A simple hierarchy of travel and travel-related choices

With the exception of mode choice modelling, most transport applications of random utility models have been carried out by individuals who are either mainly engaged in or closely associated with travel choice behaviour analysis.

The ability of discrete choice models to represent broad ranges of travel choices and policies has not yet been fully exploited in transport planning practice.

3.4 Criticisms and Limitations of Travel Choice Models

The random utility travel choice models represent an important advance over other operational modelling approaches and reflect an increasing awareness of the need to understand a wide range of travel and travel-related decisions. There has been much research and experience with random utility travel choice models during the last two decades. Strengths and weaknesses of the particular forms of models have been increasingly well understood.

In the past decade, various objections and criticisms have been directed at currently implemented probabilistic travel choice models. These have generally focused on limitations of the variants of the MNL model and have generated a whole range of extensions, generalizations and new approaches. More specifically, some of the objects of attention have been related to the incorporation of taste variability in a population, the investigation of alternative individual decision rules, the treatment of similar travel options in choice contexts, the incorporation of time-varying exogenous explanatory variables, unobserved variables with a general serial correlation structure and complex structural interrelationships among decisions taken at different times and so on (see, for example, Fischer and Nijkamp, 1987).

A serious shortcoming of the discrete choice approach is the use of single trips as the basic unit of analysis, despite the widely recognized fact that travel is a derived demand. That is, demand for travel is derived from needs and desires to participate in various activities in space and time. Most operational travel choice models ignore the relationship between activities and travel, and, thus, are unable to provide meaningful information about how changes in the activities themselves may affect individuals' travel behaviour (see Recker et al., 1983). In this context, studies of behaviour within an integrated activity–travel framework are of particular importance (see Section 4).

A second major problem associated with current travel choice theory is its failure to consider explicitly the mechanism generating choice problems. Little work has been done up to now on relaxing the assumption of homogeneous choice sets, on identifying systematic differences in the choice sets of individuals, specifying variables which define the individual's choice set, and on modelling endogenous choice set formation for appropriate types of individuals. Closely related is the problem of the proper specification of the individual's choice set, a problem far from trivial because meaningful choices can only be made from known and evaluated travel options. Although environmental, informational, personal and situational constraints delineate the set of feasible travel options to an individual, the models fail to identify these options which are perceived and actually considered by the individuals.

Applications of travel choice models have generally assumed that information about travel alternatives available to the decision maker is exogenous and subject to systematic inaccuracies. This classic assumption, however, is unrealistic. Individuals' information is not only imperfect, but also dependent on experience with the transport system and on information-gathering activities (see Manski, 1981). The integration of the dynamic relation between information and travel choice moves one away from the current cross-sectional to a dynamic framework where effects of experience, time-discounted preferences, learning processes, habit persistence and so on become central issues.

Finally, it has been argued that the underpinning theory, involving a perfectly discriminating rational man, endowed with complete information, is unacceptable for analysing travel behaviour (see, for example, Burnett and Hanson, 1982). Indeed, it is not too difficult to find examples of travel-related situations in which the utility-maximization principle does not seem to apply, at least without some substantial conceptual modifications.

4 THE ACTIVITY-BASED APPROACH

Activity-based studies began to emerge in the 1980s as a challenge to the established travel demand techniques. The replacement of the trip-based view by a broader, more holistic framework in which travel is analysed as daily or multi-day patterns of behaviour is considered by many scholars to be essential for a deeper understanding of travel behaviour. The growing interest in this approach has been reflected in an increase in the number of studies undertaken in the recent past (for comprehensive overviews, see Kitamura, 1988; Jones, 1990; Axhausen and Gärling, 1992; Ettema and Timmermans, 1997) and in the wide range of issues which have been addressed by an activity orientation point of view. The rationale underlying the activity-based approach is that of understanding complex behaviour, and as such, the focus has turned towards the explanation of travel behaviour rather than its prediction.

4.1 Conceptual Foundation and Major Characteristics

The major conceptual foundations of the activity-based approach can be traced back to two major schools of thought:

1. the time geographic or Lund perspective resulting from attempts to develop a model of society in which constraints can be formulated in physical terms (see Hägerstrand, 1970), and

2. the transductive or Chapel Hill perspective which conceives activities in terms of the individual and his physiologically regulated and learned behaviour (see Chapin, 1974).

The two perspectives are complementary in nature. The Lund group paid specific attention to understanding the operation of constraints (such as capability, coupling and authority constraints) on travel behaviour in space and time, while the Chapel Hill group focused primarily on individuals' preferences, assessing the relative significance of role and personal factors preconditioning individuals to particular patterns, and the relative importance of motivations and other attitudinal factors affecting predisposition to act.[2]

Much of the activity-based work is descriptive rather than theoretical in nature and relates to a wide range of issues including activity patterns and rhythms of individuals and households, the scheduling of activities in time and space, the importance of space–time and other constraints on activity behaviour, interactions among persons (both intra- and inter-household), relationships between activity and travel choices, detailed timing and the duration of activities and travel, routine travel behaviour and so on. Despite the wide diversity of the studies, they share a common philosophical ground – not so much a clear common theoretical or methodological orientation – which results from their interest in patterns, linkages, trip timing and constraints.

Although difficult to characterize simply, the following characteristics may be considered to be of central importance (see Jones et al., 1983, 1990 and Jones, 1991):

1. The approach emphasizes the need to consider travel within a broader context through the pattern or sequence of activities, undertaken by individuals at various locations in space during a period of time (a day, week or month). The way in which the concept of activity patterns has been operationalized differs greatly from study to study.
2. Activities are undertaken to satisfy basic needs (for example, sleeping, eating), institutional requirements (for example, school, work), role commitments (for example, child care, shopping) and personal preferences (for example, specific leisure activities).
3. There are various degrees of constraint on when activities can be undertaken, for how long, where and with whom. Special emphasis is laid on spatial, temporal and interpersonal constraints and linkages.
4. Emphasis is laid on decision making in a household context, taking into account relationships and interactions among household members.
5. Travel is explicitly treated as a derived demand, representing a space-shifting mechanism by which people move around space to take part in a succession of non-travel activities at different points in time and space. Thus, travel

results from activity participation and trip making. Individual trips are manifestations of activity needs and motivations, given perceptions of opportunities and constraints (see Golob, 1985).

6. The observed daily activity and travel patterns are viewed as outcomes of a – widely routinized – activity scheduling and rescheduling process in which obligatory and discretional activities are fitted into an available period of time, given perceptions of opportunities and subject to various constraints due to physiological factors, institutional requirements, norms and rules of society and family life.

The activity-based approach provides a more realistic, but also a more complex view of travel behaviour than does the microeconomic approach. The emphasis on complexity has deepened our qualitative understanding of travel decision processes, options and constraints, but also inhibited the development of a more comprehensive and rigorous theoretical framework and analytical methodologies up to now.

4.2 Methodological Developments

Several methodological developments have been motivated by or developed from the activity-based approach which have been fundamental to activity-based research and have made important contributions to other approaches to travel behaviour research, covering aspects of survey data collection, analysis and modelling. The following discussion is based largely on Jones et al. (1990); see also Kitamura (1988) for more details.

Survey data collection
The data requirements of the new approach are very demanding, reflecting the need for more comprehensive data on travel and activity patterns. These requirements have motivated the development of computer-based survey techniques (for example, the Household Activity and Travel Simulator (HATS) and the IGOR techniques) based on the use of interactive measurement and/or gaming simulations to obtain travel preference and response data in the context of daily or weekly activity patterns and to identify the types of constraints within which travel-activity patterns are formed (see Jones, 1991, for more details).

Analysis of complex travel-activity behaviour
An important issue in the analysis of travel-activity patterns refers to the development of methods which can be used to measure and analyse travel as a complex phenomenon by incorporating relevant linkages and interactions. Two general approaches to measuring travel patterns can be identified. The first – the one usually adopted – decomposes the pattern into dimensions (such as

timing, location, mode of travel, activity sequencing) and generates measures for each of the dimensions. The second approach attempts to treat the patterns as a whole in the form of a multidimensional space representation, to analyse the structure of the travel-activity patterns by means of classification procedures and to identify the relationships between travel-activity behaviour and hypothesized determinants of that behaviour. A prominent example is given in the work of Koppelman and Pas (1985). This approach involves defining a set of indicators that adequately characterize the travel patterns; this in itself involves considerable difficulty since activity and travel patterns evolve in a multidimensional space comprising time, location, activity type, duration, trip attributes such as mode of travel, and other factors.

Quantitative modelling of travel behaviour
Research on activity-based travel has made an important contribution to applied travel behaviour modelling in two ways. First, and more successfully, insights obtained by activity-orientated studies have stimulated economists to refine and improve the specifications of existing random utility choice models. Second, but less significant up to now, there have been some first steps towards developing acitivity-based models (see Jones et al., 1990).

Studies using travel choice models have integrated the results of activity-based work in several ways:

1. by incorporating new types of explanatory variables, for example, socio-demographic variables representing role, life cycle and life style, which have been identified to be significant determinants of daily travel-activity behaviour;
2. by integrating temporal, spatial and transport constraints, and explicitly treating interdependencies (for example, car availability at the intra-household level or inter-household interdependencies through ride sharing) via NMNL model forms; and
3. by developing travel choice models with new kinds of dependent variables, such as the duration of travel.

There have been several attempts at modelling activity participation, timing and duration with econometric tools developed for modelling single trip decisions. Practical illustrations are van der Hoorn (1983) and Kawakami and Isobe's (1990) one-day travel-activity scheduling model for workers. There have also been efforts to develop more comprehensive activity-based models of activity scheduling based on combinatorial programming or computer simulation (see Recker et al., 1986b; Gärling et al., 1986). They typically assume that the individual plans beforehand and predetermines his or her entire daily schedule of activities and trips through a simultaneous decision concerned with the daily schedule as a whole. Since the travel-activity pattern evolves within a multidimensional space and thus the decision process is characterized by multidimensional aspects, the operational formulation of the decision process is far from easy and involves discrete choices of activities and location as well as continuous allocation of time and financial resources.

Examples include CARLA (Combinatorial Algorithm for Rescheduling Lists of Activities; see Jones et al., 1983) and the STARCHILD (Simulation of Travel/Activity Response to Complex Household Interactive Logistics Decisions; see Recker et al., 1983, 1986a, b) model system which capture several important aspects of how people schedule their activities and represent a progression from a less to a more realistic conceptualization (for an overview, see Axhausen and Gärling, 1992). CARLA is focused more on the choice set generation process, while the STARCHILD model system extends the generation process to include activity/travel pattern choice in a constrained environment.

4.3 Shortcomings and Research Problems

The emphasis on patterns, constraints and linkages of activity and travel behaviour provides a more realistic, but also more complex view than do the trip-based approaches. Even though the progress to date is impressive, the activity-based approach still lacks a clear methodological orientation and a unified theoretical framework. There is an urgent need to develop a more comprehensive theoretical framework that can be used to predict the likely consequences of policy measures on activity participation, scheduling, mode, destination and route choice. This is indispensable to the formulation and implementation of the policies needed to cope with the problems of managing traffic demand in the face of the serious threats of traffic congestion and environmental pollution (see Borgers et al., 1997).

Development of such a theoretical framework requires the integration of concepts from several disciplines: psychology (perception of constraints, nature of activity participation needs, identification of attitudes, motivation and emotions for activity participation and travel), sociology (life style, life cycle and roles, interdependencies in social networks), geography (understanding of spatial aspects of travel and activity participation, nature of spatial cognition and spatial behaviour, acquisition of spatial knowledge, links between travel and residential mobility); and economics (role of time and money in activity participation and travel, utility derived from activity participation) (see also Jones et al., 1990). Equally important is a more explicit treatment of dynamic processes. Up to now, activity-based studies tend to take dynamic effects into account only implicitly by looking at life-cycle stages and transitions.

5   OUTLOOK

The issues addressed in travel demand research have clearly broadened very considerably over the years. At the same time, new innovative approaches have emerged. In spite of the progress made, we are still far away from understanding travel behaviour or from the development of sound theory underpinning travel demand.

Future research and development priorities should concentrate on two major directions. The first is to consolidate and make more widely available existing activity-orientated and choice-theoretic modelling technologies to the practitioner-orientated environment and to demonstrate their usefulness in the policy area. Both the discrete choice and the activity-based approaches to travel choice modelling offer a rich potential. The second priority is to improve our theories, refine the methods and integrate different strands of theoretical contributions. One major challenge will be to reconcile the activity-based and the choice-theoretic approaches, which differ widely in vocabulary and philosophy. Considering the power of discrete choice models on the one side and the limited activity modelling work to date on the other, it certainly seems appropriate to devote major future efforts to generalizing and refining rather than to discarding random utility-based travel choice models. One obvious strategy is to define choice sets, constraints and explanatory variables in a more refined way.

Equally important is the need to shift the focus away from the dominating static to a more explicit dynamic perspective, from static cross-section to panel data sources, especially in a rapidly changing policy world. Static methods might provide biased forecasts of, for example, traffic growth, even if the estimates of input variables are correct, and may lead to wrong policy implications (see Goodwin et al., 1990; Meurs, 1991). Methodologies and statistical techniques already exist to cope dynamically with discrete and continuous choices, aggregate and disaggregate data. The emphasis should be on the nature of behavioural adjustment processes inherent in travel choices, leads, lags, thresholds and uncertainties in travel decision making. The further development of dynamic concepts in travel demand analysis is crucial for the derivation of better and more reliable policy instruments.

If the ultimate goal is not only to develop better travel demand research tools, in the form of more powerful models and analysis software, but also to assist the transport planning and policy-making process, then the integration of travel demand models and Geographic Information Systems (GIS) technology is an obvious, challenging and promising research topic for the future.[3] The challenge is to really merge and combine travel demand modelling and GIS, rather than just using them together.

NOTES

1. 'Generalized cost' besides the money cost of transport also includes the time cost and furthermore 'quality' characteristics such as the reliability, punctuality and 'comfort' of a given transport service. In symbols, generalized cost may be expressed as: $G = m + ht + qs$, where: m is money cost, h is the value of time, t is time spent in transport, q is a quality index, and s is the unitary value of quality.
2. *Capability constraints* circumscribe activity participation by demanding the allocation of large portions of time to physiological necessities such as sleeping, eating and personal care.

    Coupling constraints: most of our activities are performed in conjunction with other people, either singly or in organizations such as, for example, business firms, public institutions, schools and shops. Coupling constraints create bundles of activities at particular locations. The coordination of human activities in time and space through the operation of coupling constraints is a major cause of some of the highly regular temporal and spatial patterns characteristic of modern societies.

    Authority constraints impose limited access to either space or time locations.
3. In general, a GIS may be defined as a computer-based information system which attempts to capture, store, manipulate, analyse and display spatially referenced and associated tabular attribute data, for solving complex research, planning and management problems. Such a system will normally embody a database of spatially referenced data, appropriate software components encompassing procedures for the interrelated transactions from input via storage and retrieval, and the adhering manipulation and spatial analysis facilities to output, and associated hardware components including high-resolution graphic displays, large-scale electronic storage devices which are organized and interfaced in an efficient and effective manner to allow rapid data storage, retrieval and management capabilities and facilitate the analysis (see Fischer and Nijkamp, 1993, for more details).

REFERENCES

Abkowits, M.D. (1981), 'Understanding the effect of transit service reliability on work-travel behaviour', *Transportation Research Record*, 794, 33–41.

Anas, A. (1982), *Residential Location Markets and Urban Transportation. Economic Theory, Econometrics, and Policy Analysis with Discrete Choice Models*, New York: Academic Press.

Axhausen, K.W. and T. Gärling (1992), 'Activity-based approaches to travel analysis: conceptual frameworks, models and research problems', *Transport Reviews*, **12**, 323–41.

Ben-Akiva, M. and T.J. Atherton (1977), 'Methodology for short-range travel demand predictions: analysis of car pooling incentives', *Journal of Transport Economics and Policy*, **11**, 224–61.

Ben-Akiva, M. and S. Lerman (1979), 'Disaggregate travel and mobility choice models and measures of accessibility', in D.A. Hensher and P.R. Stopher (eds), *Behavioral Travel Modelling*, London: Croom Helm, pp. 654–79.

Ben-Akiva, M. and S.R. Lerman (1985), *Discrete Choice Analysis: Theory and Application to Travel Demand*, Cambridge, MA and London: MIT Press.

Borgers, A. and H.J.P. Timmermans (1986), 'A model of pedestrian route choice and demand for retail facilities within inner-city shopping areas', *Geographical Analysis*, **18**, 115–28.

Borgers, A., F. Hofman and H.J.P. Timmermans (1997), 'Activity-based modelling: prospects', in Ettema and Timmermans (eds), pp. 339–51.

Bovy, P.H.L. and E. Stern (1990), *Route Choice: Wayfinding in Transport Networks*, Dordrecht: Kluwer.

Brownstone, D. and T.F. Golob (1992), 'The effectiveness of ridesharing incentives. Discrete-choice models of commuting in Southern California', *Regional Science and Urban Economics*, **22**, 5–24.

Brownstone, D. and K. Small (1989), 'Efficient estimation of nested logit models', *Journal of Business and Economic Statistics*, **7**, 67–74.

Burnett, P. and S.M. Hanson (1982), 'The analysis of travel as an example of complex human behavior in spatially-constrained situations: definition and measurement issues', *Transportation Research*, **16A**, 87–102.

Chapin, S.F. Jr (1974), *Human Activity Patterns in the City. Things People Do in Time and in Space*, New York: Wiley.

Charles River Associates (1967), *Disaggregate Travel Demand Model*, Report prepared for the National Cooperative Highway Research Program, Transportation Research Board, Washington, DC: Charles River Associates.

Domencich, T.A. and D. McFadden (1975), *Urban Travel Demand: A Behavioral Analysis*, Amsterdam: North-Holland.

Ettema, D.F. and H.J.P. Timmermans (eds) (1997), *Activity-based Approaches to Travel Analysis*, Oxford: Pergamon.

Fischer, M.M. and P. Nijkamp (1985), 'Developments in explanatory discrete spatial data and choice analysis', *Progress in Human Geography*, **9**, 515–51.

Fischer, M.M. and P. Nijkamp (1987), 'From static towards dynamic discrete choice modelling: a state of the art review', *Regional Science and Urban Economics*, **17**, 3–27.

Fischer, M.M. and P. Nijkamp (1993), 'Design and use of geographic information systems and spatial models', in M.M. Fischer and P. Nijkamp (eds), *Geographic Information Systems, Spatial Modelling, and Policy Evaluation*, Heidelberg: Springer, pp. 1–13.

Gärling, T., J. Säisä, A. Böök and E. Lindberg (1986), 'The spatiotemporal sequencing of everyday activities in the large-scale environment', *Journal of Environmental Psychology*, **6**, 261–80.

Golledge, R.G. and R.J. Stimson (1987), *Analytical Behavioural Geography*, London: Croom Helm.

Golob, T.F. (1985), 'Analyzing activity pattern data using qualitative multivariate statistical methods', in P. Nijkamp, H. Leitner and N. Wrigley (eds), *Measuring the Unmeasurable*, Dordrecht: Nijhoff, pp. 339–56.

Goodwin, P., R. Kitamura and H. Meurs (1990), 'Some principles of dynamic analysis of travel behaviour', in Jones (ed.), pp. 56–72.

Hägerstrand, T. (1970), 'What about people in regional science?', *Papers of the Regional Science Association*, **24**, 7–21.

Hanson, S. and M. Schwab (1986), 'Describing disaggregate flows: individual and household activity patterns', in S. Hanson (ed.), *The Geography of Urban Transportation*, New York and London: Guilford Press, pp. 154–78.

Hausman, J.A. and D.A. Wise (1978), 'A conditional probit model for qualitative choice: discrete decisions recognizing interdependence and heterogeneous preferences', *Econometrica*, **46**, 403–26.

Hensher, D.A., P.O. Barnard, N.C. Smith and F.W. Milthorpe (1989), 'Modelling the dynamics of car ownership and use: a methodological and empirical synthesis', in The International Association of Travel Behaviour (ed.), pp. 141–73.

Horowitz, J. (1979), 'Disaggregate demand models for non-work travel', *Transportation Research Record*, **673**, 56–71.

Horowitz, J.L. (1980), 'A utility maximizing model for the demand for multi-destination non-work travel', *Transportation Research*, **14B**, 369–86.

Horowitz, J.L. (1983), 'Random utility models as practical tools of travel demand analysis: An evaluation', in P.H.L. Bovy (ed.), *Transportation and Stagnation: Challenges for Planning and Research*, Proceedings of the 10th Transportation Planning Research Colloquium, Delft: Colloquium Vervoersplanologisch Speurwerk, pp. 386–404.

Horowitz, J.L. (1986), 'Modeling choices of residential location and mode of travel to work', in S. Hanson (ed.), *The Geography of Urban Transportation*, New York and London: Guilford Press, pp. 207–26.

The International Association of Travel Behaviour (ed.) (1989), *Travel Behaviour Research*, Fifth International Conference on Travel Behaviour, Aldershot: Avebury Gower.

Jones, P.M. (1983), 'A new approach to understanding travel behaviour and its implications for transportation planning', PhD thesis, University of London.

Jones, P. (ed.) (1990), *Developments in Dynamic and Activity-based Approaches to Travel Analysis*, Aldershot: Avebury Gower.

Jones, P.M. (1991), *Some Recent Methodological Developments in our Understanding of Travel Behaviour*, TSU 663, Oxford University: Transport Studies Unit.

Jones, P.M., M.C. Dix, M.I. Clarke and I.G. Heggie (1983), *Understanding Travel Behaviour*, Aldershot: Avebury Gower.

Jones, P., F. Koppelman and J.-P. Orfeuil (1990), 'Activity analysis: state-of-the-art and future directions', in Jones (ed.), pp. 34–55.

Kawakami, S. and T. Isobe (1990) 'Development of a one-day travel-activity scheduling model for workers', in Jones (ed.), pp. 184–205.

Kern, C.R., S.R., Lerman, R.J. Parcells and R.A. Wolfe (1984), *Impact of Transportation Policy on the Spatial Distribution of Retail Activity*, Final report on DOTRC 92024, Washington, DC: US Department of Transportation.

Khattak, A.J. (1991), *Conceptual Issues and Empirical Evidence Regarding the Effect of Information on Travel Behaviour*, TSU 660, Oxford University: Transport Studies Unit.

Kitamura, R. (1988), 'An evaluation of activity-based travel analysis', *Transportation*, **15**, 9–34.

Koppelman, F.S. and M. Hirsch (1989), 'Intercity travel choice behaviour: theory and empirical analysis', in The International Association for Travel Behaviour (ed.), pp. 227–44.

Koppelman, F.S. and E.I. Pas (1985), 'Travel-activity behavior in time and space: methods for representation and analysis', in P. Nijkamp, H. Leitner and N. Wrigley (eds), *Measuring the Unmeasurable*, Dordrecht: Nijhoff, pp. 587–627.

Kroes, E.P. and R.J. Sheldon (1988), 'Stated preference methods. An introduction', *Journal of Transport Economics and Policy*, **22**, 11–25.

Louvière, J.J. and D.A. Hensher (1982), 'Design and analysis of simulated choice or allocation experiments in travel choice modeling', *Transportation Research Record*, **890**, 11–7.

Luce, R.D. (1959), *Individual Choice Behavior: A Theoretical Analysis*, New York: Wiley.

Manski, C.F. (1981), 'Structural models for discrete data: the analysis of discrete choice', in S. Leinhardt (ed.), *Sociological Methodology 1981*, San Francisco: Jossey-Bass, pp. 58–109.

McFadden, D. (1981), 'Econometric models of probabilistic choice', in C.F. Manski and D. McFadden (eds), *Structural Analysis of Discrete Data with Econometric Applications*, Cambridge, MA and London: MIT Press, pp. 198–272.

Meurs, H.J. (1991), 'A panel data analysis of travel demand', PhD thesis, University of Groningen.

Nijkamp, P., S. Reichman and M. Wegener (eds) (1990), *Euromobile: Transport, Communications and Mobility in Europe. A Cross-national Comparative Overview*, Aldershot: Avebury Gower in association with the European Science Foundation.

Recker, W.W. and T.F. Golob (1979), 'A non-compensatory model of transportation behavior based on sequential consideration of attributes', *Transportation Research*, **13B**, 269–80.

Recker, W.W., M.G. McNally and G.S. Root (1983), 'A methodology for activity-based travel analysis: the STARCHILD model', in P.H.L. Bovy (ed.), *Transportation and Stagnation: Challenges for Planning and Research*, Proceedings of the 10th Transportation Planning Research Colloquium, Delft: Colloquium Vervoersplanologisch Speurwerk, pp. 245–63.

Recker, W.W., M.G. McNally and G.S. Root (1986a), 'A model of complex travel behaviour: Part I – theoretical development', *Transportation Research A*, **20A**, 307–18.

Recker, W.W., M.G. McNally and G.S. Root (1986b), 'A model of complex travel behaviour: Part II – an operational model', *Transportation Research A*, **20A**, 319–30.

Sheppard, E. (1986), 'Modeling and predicting aggregate flows', in S. Hanson (ed.), *The Geography of Urban Transportation*, New York and London: Guilford Press, pp. 91–118.

Sobel, K.L. (1980), 'Travel demand forecasting by using the nested multinomial logit model', *Transportation Research Record*, **775**, 48–55.

Thurstone, L. (1927), 'A law of comparative judgement', *Psychological Review*, **34**, 273–86.

Tversky, A. (1972a), 'Elimination-by-aspects: a theory of choice', *Psychological Review*, **79**, 281–99.

Tversky, A. (1972b), 'Choice-by-elimination', *Journal of Mathematical Psychology*, **9**, 341–67.

van der Hoorn, A.I.J.M. (1983), 'Experiments with an activity-based travel model', *Transportation*, **12**, 61–77.

Wardman, M. (1988), 'A comparison of revealed preference and stated preference models of travel behaviour', *Journal of Transport Economics and Policy*, **22**, 71–91.

Williams, H.C.W.L. and J.D. Ortuzar (1979), *Random Utility Theory and the Structure of Travel Choice Models*, Working Paper No. 261, School of Geography, University of Leeds.

Williams, H. and J.D. Ortuzar (1982), 'Travel demand and response analysis – some integrating themes', *Transportation Research*, **16A**, 345–62.

Wilson, A.G. (1969), 'The use of entropy-maximizing models in the theory of trip distribution, mode split and route split', *Journal of Transport Economics and Policy*, **3**, 108–26.

Wilson, A.G. (1970), *Entropy in Urban and Regional Analysis*, London: Pion.

Wilson, A.G., A.F. Hawkins, G.J. Hill and P.J. Wagon (1969), 'Calibrating and testing the SELNEC transport model', *Regional Studies*, **2**, 337–50.

4. External effects of transport

Werner Rothengatter

1 INTRODUCTION

The discussion on the idea of external economies and diseconomies dates back to Alfred Marshall who introduced the term 'external economies' in the first issue of his *Principles of Economics* in 1890. Marshall's concern was to explain that even with the existence of increasing returns to scale (downward-sloping average cost) the paradigm of a perfect market economy would not be destroyed through monopolistic concentrations of the industry – as prophesied by Karl Marx. Marshall argued that the main cause of increasing returns was the 'general development of the industry', which produced 'external economies'. That is, the single firms would not realize the advantage of concentration and keep to the price-taking behaviour of small enterprises.

In the following decades the notion of externalities has experienced a metamorphosis, taking on different meanings, partly aiming at extending the scope of effects, partly intending to narrow the scope, reduce broadness and vagueness and make the concept of externalities more workable for public policy application. Both the origin and the further attempts to widen, to narrow or to clarify the notion of externalities have contributed to an overall fuzziness of the idea (see Papandreou, 1994). Therefore, it is indispensable to develop a clear definition of the concept of external effects in general before coming to the specific situation in the transport sector.

In particular, two contrasting positions have influenced the debate after Marshall. First, his academic successor, Arthur C. Pigou, elaborated on the idea and presented in his *Economics of Welfare* (1924) a comprehensive scientific concept of positive and negative externalities. An externality is characterized here by a divergence between the marginal social product and the marginal private product. Such a divergence occurs if agents are not allocated the costs or benefits that they are responsible for, such that they will neglect these effects in their decision making. The remedy suggested by Pigou is a tax or a subsidy to balance the difference between social and private marginal costs.

Second, Ronald Coase (1960) has presented an alternative view on the nature and the treatment of externalities in his famous article on 'The problem of social cost'. In the first part of his analysis Coase states that externalities occur if property rights are not defined for a resource which is commonly used by different agents. Under restrictive assumptions, he shows that the externality vanishes and equilibrium is restored if the property right is allocated to one of the agents using the resource, regardless of whether he is the 'perpetrator' or the 'victim'. A full allocation of the liability to the 'perpetrator' would not in any case restore optimality.

2 MODELLING THE FUNDAMENTAL CONTROVERSY ON EXTERNALITIES

2.1 A Simple Model of Externalities

Many attempts have been made to translate the notion of and the reasoning about externalities into an abstract modelling context to make the conclusions more precise compared with qualitative discourses. Schweizer (1988) has constructed a simple game-theoretical model that can be used to reproduce the controversial Pigouvian and Coasian positions about externalities by inserting the appropriate assumptions. His model approach will be modified in the following to keep the theoretical treatment as brief as possible.

Suppose there are two agents 1 and 2 with utility functions U and V, and the activity levels x and y, respectively. At these activity levels agent 2 suffers from a damage caused by agent 1 which is defined by $d(x,y)$. Thus, we arrive at the following definitions:

$$U = u(x), \quad V = v(y) - d(x,y) \tag{4.1}$$
$$d(x,0) = d(0,y) = 0; \; d_x(x,y) > 0; \; d_y(x,y) > 0 \text{ (for a damage)}.$$

The subscripts denote the first partial derivatives. As can be seen from (4.1) the damage d results from an interaction between 1 and 2, agent 2 not being able to control the contribution of agent 1, that is, 2 can only manipulate d_y but not d_x. With d_x and $d_y > 0$ or < 0 the externality d would have a reciprocal character as emphasized by Coase. If $d_y = 0$ the magnitude of the externality would depend only on the decisions of agent 1 and the externality would not be reciprocal. This would happen for instance if the externality incurred a fixed cost which is equal for every activity level $y > 0$.

Maximizing the sum of utilities would give the first-order conditions

$$u_x(x^P) - d_x(x^P,y^P) = 0; \quad v_y(y^P) - d_y(x^P,y^P) = 0. \tag{4.2}$$

Index P is used to indicate that the x and y values fulfilling (4.2) give the Pareto-type social equilibrium, supposing also that the second-order condition holds. However, to arrive at position (4.2), the agents would have to form a grand coalition, apply a socially rational calculus and agree on transfer payments to share the surplus achieved compared with the stand-alone situation. The stand-alone situation itself is described by the Nash equilibrium:

$$u_x(x^N) = 0; \quad v_y(y^N) - d_y(x^N, y^N) = 0. \qquad (4.3)$$

Index N stands for the Nash-type equilibrium, which denotes the best position which every agent can achieve by his/her own forces. Under a system without defined liability or compensation agent 1 would maximize his utility u in the variable x, not taking into account the externality d which is transmitted to agent 2. Agent 2 is not in a dominant position such that nothing is left for him but maximizing utility v in the variable y taking into account the additional costs d which are caused by the activity of agent 1. Obviously the Nash equilibrium is individually but not socially optimal.

This stage of the analysis enables us to explain the Coase/Pigou controversy which Coase (1960) started by analysing Pigou's example of a railroad company (agent 1) whose activity causes damage by emitting sparks which destroy the crops of a farmer (agent 2) by fire. Coase interpreted Pigou in a way that making only the railways liable for the damage would restore the Pareto equilibrium. In the terms of the model this would imply that agent 1 would have to bear all external costs d such that the Nash equilibrium would change to

$$u_x(x^L) - d_x(x^L, y^L) = 0; \quad v_y(y^L) = 0. \qquad (4.4)$$

Index L denotes that liability is allocated to agent 1, only. Comparing (4.4) with (4.2) it is obvious that (4.4) is not socially optimal as long as $d_y > 0$. This underlines Coase's argument (Coase, 1960, p. 27):

> The problem which we face in dealing with actions which have harmful effects is not simply one of restraining those responsible for them. What has to be decided is whether the gain from preventing the harm is greater than the loss that would be suffered elsewhere as a result of stopping the action that produces the harm.

If $d_y = 0$, however, (4.2) and (4.4) coincide. We see that the hypothesis of reciprocity (that is, interaction in both directions) is necessary to make Coase's criticism consistent. Then, shifting the responsibility to the initiator of the harm, only, is not socially efficient because the 'victim' contributes to the magnitude of impacts as well.

However, Coase seems to have overinterpreted the Pigou scheme in so far as Pigou does not explicitly allocate the full liability to one party, but rather imposes an 'optimal' tax on the producer in the following way:

$$u_x(x^T) - t = 0; \quad v_y(x^T,y^T) - d_y(x^T,y^T) = 0. \tag{4.5}$$

In this formulation it has been assumed that the tax is proportional to the activity level x.

T denotes the equilibrium achieved after taxation. We can immediately see – comparing (4.5) with (4.2) – that the Pareto equilibrium is restored if

$$t = d_x(x^P,y^P), \tag{4.6}$$

which means that the tax should be equal to the marginal cost of the externality (or marginal benefit in the positive case). After optimal taxation there is still some damage whose cost has to be borne by the 'victim'. The revenues from the taxation go to the public budget and are not used for a full compensation of the 'victim'. This means that reciprocity is also included in the Pigou scheme: in the optimal solution agent 1 pays the tax and agent 2 pays for the remaining damage.

2.2   The Pigouvian Concept

The economic effects of the Pigou scheme are illustrated in Figures 4.1(a) and 4.1(b). In panel (a) the market equilibrium quantity x' represents the amount that is actually produced and consumed and reflects a balance of marginal private costs and benefits (intersection of supply and demand curve). If consumption or production create external costs, however, the marginal social cost (MSC) curve lies above the market supply curve S (= marginal private cost, MPC). The socially efficient solution would be found at the intersection between MSC and the demand curve D. To modify private decision making such that the socially optimal allocation (p^*, x^*) is achieved, a tax of the amount AG should be introduced for the producers. The welfare gain of this measure is approximately represented by the triangle AGE. In this scheme it is assumed that the state will spend the revenue x^*AG in a welfare-maximizing way or reduce other taxes. External benefits create the opposite effect. In Figure 4.1(b) they are represented by a shift from the market demand curve D, which reflects the perceived private benefits to the social demand curve D^*. To create private incentives to produce the quantity x^*, a subsidy has to be offered to the producers. The welfare is increased approximately by the triangle HBF. The subsidies are financed by lump-sum taxation.

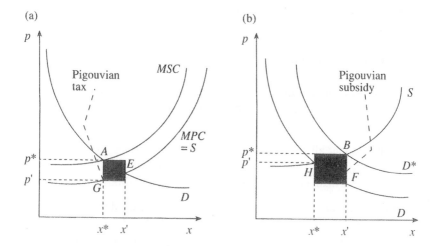

Figure 4.1   Pigouvian taxes and subsidies

The 'correct' taxes and subsidies are not easy to determine, because calculating their magnitude presupposes the derivation of the social equilibrium. Some properties of the Pigouvian taxation/subsidization scheme seem to be important:

- The Pigouvian tax does not allocate the complete externality to the perpetrator but only the 'optimal' amount. This means that in the optimal solution the victim still has to bear the remaining load at production point x^*. Note that no direct compensation is paid because the revenues of the tax go to the public budget.
- If Pigouvian taxes should restore economic equilibrium, then the conditions for a general equilibrium to exist must hold. As these conditions are far from reality, the concept of solving externality problems by pure Pigouvian instruments is also far from being realistic.[1]

2.3   The Coase Concept

The basic terms in the Coasian thinking are 'transaction costs' and 'property rights'. This is reflected in the description of the nature of externalities as well as in the theorem on their internalization.

Nature of externalities

1. Externalities arise if the property rights for a resource jointly used by several agents are not clearly defined.

2. Externalities are reciprocal, that is, the 'perpetrator' and the 'victim' are both contributing to the magnitude of the effect.

Coase theorem and extensions

3. Suppose that transaction costs are negligible and there is an equal distribution of bargaining power of the stakeholders. Then the following theorem holds:

> an efficient allocation of resources will be obtained by allocating the property rights of the jointly used resource to one of the conflicting parties in a clear manner, that is, either to the 'perpetrator' or to the 'victim'.

4. If relevant transaction costs occur it has to be checked whether the gain from removing the externality is greater than the loss for the producer. In a reduction policy scheme the least-cost principle has to be applied.
5. The main reason for the persistence of externalities may be the high transaction costs associated with their removal. If the benefits from removal are lower than the transaction costs occurring, then it is economically rational to live with the externality rather than to remove it.

The clear consequence is that it would be wrong to allocate the liability of an externality completely to the producer. Coase has shown that this would lead to suboptimal results. However, his criticism of the Pigou taxation scheme can only partly be accepted. As the analysis in Section 1 has clarified, Coase would have been right if the effect of a Pigou tax was that the producer would have to bear the full liability. An optimal Pigou tax (equations (4.5) and (4.6)), however, does not generate this result. Rather it optimizes the level of reduction (marginal damage costs equal the marginal prevention costs) and allocates the burdens to both, the producer (has to bear the tax) and the 'victim' (has to bear the remaining harm). By this, the reciprocity property of the externality is implicitly included in the Pigou scheme subject to the condition that all aspects of private decision making of the involved parties are represented by the demand and supply curves.

For practical application, the question remains whether it is possible at all to fulfil the latter condition, remembering that the concept is based on a partial analysis of one market, only. What is apparently not included in Pigou's paradigm is the phenomenon of transaction cost, which Coase introduced in 1937 (Coase, 1937, 1988). The consideration of this important argument leads to the conclusion that a simple one-market paradigm with a calculation of the difference between social and private marginal costs is not sufficient to derive an optimal taxation scheme. The transaction costs have to be taken into account, and, in addition to that, also the impacts on related markets. This leads finally to an overall social cost–benefit analysis of any externality-reducing scheme.

2.4 The Coasian View Extended

According to Pigou, every deviation from social marginal cost pricing appears as a troublemaker in the equilibrium paradise and would have to be treated by a state's intervention. This issue would place the state in the role of an active welfare manager who is permanently controlling the performance of the economic sectors and setting the appropriate taxes. Many doubts have been raised as to the competence of the state with respect to a flexible welfare management. Such doubts seem to have been a stimulus for the Coasian criticism of the Pigou concept. According to the Coasian view there are intrinsic forces in a market economy to cope with externalities, although they are processed outside the market (bargaining option). We shall analyse these forces first, based on static welfare models, which was also the point of departure for the Coase analysis, and second, based on a more dynamic view of social welfare.

Static welfare models
Cooperative bargaining solution   Suppose that the externality is positive and that there are a limited number of agents exchanging such benefits outside the market mechanism. $A = \{1, \dots, a\}$ is the set of partners in the game. Suppose furthermore that the agents have full information on the impact mechanism such that it is possible to establish a characteristic function

$$z: \wp(A) \to \Re \tag{4.7}$$

$\wp$ denoting the power set of A and $\Re$ the set of real numbers. The characteristic function z assigns a utility value (pay-off) to all possible coalitions which can be formed out of A. $z(A)$ is the utility of the grand coalition of all partners. If every partner contributes monotonically, regardless of which partnership he belongs to, to increase the overall utility, then $z(A)$ is the social optimum. In the case of two agents, as described in Section 2, the power-set of coalitions consists of three elements: the stand-alone situations $\{1\}$ and $\{2\}$ and the grand coalition $\{1,2\}$. The characteristic function values of the stand-alone situations are described by (4.3) and that of the grand coalition by (4.2), which is the social optimum. Once a coalition has formed it can be regarded as a club that aims at achieving economic goals commonly. The club can reach a higher utility level than the partners are able to guarantee for themselves. The maximal difference is (4.2) – (4.3). Under a regime of perfect information there is one serious problem left to be solved. This is the allocation of the common utility surplus

(4.2) – (4.3). Cooperative game theory offers a number of intuitive solutions for achieving a fair and efficient allocation (for example: nucleolus or disruption nucleolus concepts, see Schmeidler, 1969), and some axiomatic solutions of which the 'Nash arbiter' or the 'Shapley value' solutions are the most well known.

By applying the Shapley value, for instance, the common utility is allocated in a way – roughly speaking – such that each partner is given his expected marginal contribution to the club. As long as the number of potential partners is low and the common utility high, one can assume that the agents will discover the advantage – or in the case of transaction costs the net advantage – and form coalitions after some time to capitalize the benefit options. In business life this can be realized by mergers, strategic alliances or simply by coordinated behaviour in oligopolistic markets. Consumers can form groups to reduce the cost of travelling by bus or clubs to make sports activities affordable. No specific intervention of the state is necessary to encourage or enforce the agents to go together. The state's role is restricted to supplying the appropriate legal framework.

Non-cooperative bargaining solutions   What Coase seemed to have in mind when he discussed the farmer/rancher and the railway/farmer examples was that the agents do not cooperate directly but discover the impact mechanism and react by offering contracts. For instance, the farmer could offer to pay compensation to a railway company for a reduction in train operation frequency or for using high-quality coal producing less sparking fire. It can be shown that the agents can achieve the socially optimal situation through a multistage bargaining process even if (not too high) transaction costs occur (Schweizer, 1988), which clearly supports the Coase theorem.

However, there are limits for de-central solutions through bargaining:

- dilemma situations (obstacles to contracting);
- high transaction costs;
- high number of involved parties;
- unequal distribution of economic/political power; or
- imperfect information on the impact mechanism,

which lead to situations for which the social optimum can no longer be restored through decentralized individual activity.

Dynamic markets and adaptive efficiency
The above analysis was based on the general assumption of a static neoclassical world. In a dynamic world, driving forces of competition have to be considered:

1. progressive innovative strategies to achieve monopoly power and supernormal profits;
2. consolidation strategies by choosing the right partnerships to make a firm's development sustainable over time; and
3. catch-up strategies to follow the market leader by applying product and process innovation or imitation policies.

In the dynamic context, the notion of Pareto equilibrium is replaced by terms such as 'workable competition' and 'adaptive efficiency' (see Stiglitz, 1990; North, 1990) to indicate that it is much more important for the economic system to adjust most flexibly to a changing environment rather than to achieve a static equilibrium position in a given time period.

It is in the context of these dynamic market phenomena that externalities can partly play an important productive role. In a world of uncertainty, agents try to manage their risks by face-to-face contacts and by constructing networks of individual or institutional relationships. With increasing complexity and risk, the market mechanism changes from the 'invisible hand' of Adam Smith to 'visible and invisible handshakes' (see Rosen, 1985). This means that there are more economic relationships in existence which do not touch the market in the traditional way, that is, through the pricing mechanism. For example, implicit contracting may replace explicit contracts because of high transaction costs of explicit contracting in a dynamically changing environment. Stiglitz (1987) has shown, taking the examples of the labour and the credit markets, that implicit contracts can be an efficient way to insure risks if there is enough trust in the reliability of partners in the network. Contract and spot markets thus can be replaced by implicit '*do ut des*' strategies. Following Rosen (1985, p. 1145) such markets look 'more akin to the marriage market rather than to the bourse'.

While implicit contracts or strategic alliances are examples of voluntary expected externalities, there are a number of involuntary (unexpected) externalities. An outstanding prototype for these externalities is the diffusion of information about innovations. Although innovations can be privatized by patent rights, licences or secret research and development, it is almost impossible to keep them totally private. In the medium term, know-how of firms cannot be hedged such that positive spillovers occur for the imitators.

A further example is trading between two firms, 1 and 2, with one supplier operating under increasing returns. An increase in production of firm 1 will lead to lower unit cost of the supplier and – under competitive conditions – to a reduced price of the input which is also to the benefit of firm 2.

The form and the speed of technical progress in a market economy under uncertainty are crucially dependent on the possibility of creating externalities of this kind. This is because the diffusion process is stimulated such that the interdependence between innovation and imitation becomes more intensive.

So many phenomena which are called externalities in the traditional literature are not at all detrimental to adaptive efficiency of the market system. This holds in particular for the positive external economies of density with which Marshall had started the history of the externality concept. It can hardly be said that effects of this type produce market failure and would call for public corrections. On the contrary they can be regarded as normal market phenomena in the growth cycle of industries.

The insights gained in this section will – all, it may be stressed, within the confines of the single objective of allocative efficiency – have important consequences for the treatment of many effects that are called 'positive externalities' in the literature. In general there are a number of options to internalize these externalities by de-central and market-conforming activities such that state intervention is not necessary.

3   DEFINITION OF EXTERNALITIES

If the concept of externality is intended to be used in practical policy, the scope of the notion has to be defined in a narrow way. Under this premise we suggest defining externalities by the following three properties:

- involuntary interaction among agents who use a resource jointly of which the property rights have not been defined;
- processing of the interaction outside the market, that is without trading or bargaining such that costs occurring or benefits generated are not allocated to the responsible party; and
- relevant market failure which leads to reduced adaptive efficiency through false signalling.

Restricting the externality phenomena to these limits, we are left with effects that are detrimental to long-term efficiency in the absence of any mechanism which could remove the failure by decentralized activity, and this at sufficiently low transaction costs. If the three conditions are fulfilled, then public action becomes inevitable, which can consist in taxation/subsidization, regulation or a change of the legal/institutional framework (thus changing the regime of property rights).

Once this definition is agreed one can bring a clear structure into the fuzzy world of externalities:

1. Pecuniary externalities are excluded. They have to be considered only if they induce technological externalities according to the above description.

Only technological externalities matter, that is, externalities that imply a change of production technology or of the preference settings.

2. Multiplier effects are excluded. The fact that changes in one market lead to repercussions in other markets such that finally agents are affected who have nothing to do with the initial activities on the first market, typically indicates a pecuniary and not a technological externality.

3. Scale effects of production are excluded as long as the production technology does not change, or de-central mechanisms exist for internalization. The economies of density that have been a part of Marshall's reasoning belong to this set as well as the 'unpaid factors' in the sense of Meade (1952), that is, his blossoms/bees example. In these cases, mechanisms exist to internalize the externalities at low transaction costs. If agents do not make use of these mechanisms, they reveal that the relevance of the externality is estimated to be low.

4. Implicit contracting is not a case of externalities. It is simply a way to save transaction costs in a world of uncertainty in which permanent adjustments of explicit contracts could be very costly. The occurrence of implicit contracting cannot, furthermore, be used as an indicator for externalities (referring to the fact that externalities are processed outside the market).

5. Technical progress through dissemination of knowledge is in itself no externality unless the three conditions listed above apply. As long as firms are able to protect inventions by property rights (patents, licences), sufficient mechanisms exist for internalizing the benefits of innovations.

Consequently some of the benefits which are classified as 'external' in the literature by lobby groups disappear from the list of relevant externalities. This results in an asymmetry of the externality concept: a number of positive economies of scale and of scope can be internalized by cooperative or non-cooperative bargaining schemes, assuming that in general agents have a genuine interest in discovering those benefits and in finding ways of capitalizing them. If transaction costs are very high, the number of involved parties is large or knowledge is lacking on the impact mechanism, then there is little chance of solving the externality problem by decentralized actions.

In the case of external costs, however, there are fewer reasons to expect that the conditions for a decentralized solution apply. This is because of the existence of incomplete and asymmetric information, asymmetric distribution of power or high transaction costs for individual action. Furthermore, if there are many affected agents then high transaction costs may make individual bargaining impossible.

As concerns the internalization policy, one has to bear in mind that neither the Pigou nor the Coase approach allocate the full cost of the externality to the producer because of the reciprocity of the externality. Furthermore, the Coase analysis gives the insight that every internalization scheme has to be checked with respect to the transaction costs. In other words, replacing the market failure of externalities by government failure of inefficient taxation or regulation should be avoided.

4   EXTERNAL EFFECTS OF THE TRANSPORT SECTOR

4.1   Types of Externalities

There are four levels on which externalities can occur in the transport sector:

1. infrastructure provision can lead to positive and negative impacts which are not processed through the market;
2. the users inside a transport system can influence one another and thereby cause inefficiency through involuntary interactions;
3. the financial scheme of infrastructure payment may be false such that the wrong parties pay, that is, the taxpayers pay more than the value of the public service while the private users pay less than the cost for the privately used part of the capacity; and
4. the activities on the transport infrastructure can influence third parties outside the transport sector in a way that false signalling reduces the market efficiency.

Levels (2)–(4) are, as may be seen, all connected with the use of infrastructure.

4.2   External Effects of Infrastructure Provision

There are a number of reasons why the state may want to act as a provider of transport infrastructure or at least have this provision take place under its strict control:

1. transport infrastructure is used for public services such as military purposes, basic social communication and other social goals;
2. transport infrastructure may be intended to stimulate growth in remote and underdeveloped regions to catch up and provide a regionally balanced income distribution; and
3. state-based planning of infrastructure provision aims to exploit synergy effects that can be generated by an integrated transport network design.

If such positive spillovers of infrastructure provision are produced and financed by the state, they have to be included in the cost–benefit analysis of the state's infrastructure investment calculus. In the context of the effects of category (2) – effects on the regional distribution of income – a lively debate is going on with regard to the treatment of pecuniary effects in an economic environment of imperfect competition. This discussion was started by Krugman (1991) and followed by Venables and Gasiorek (1998). Briefly, they identify positive spillovers of transport investment policy through improving the competitive situation in remote regions, effected by attracting additional suppliers to the regional markets. Clearly those multiplier effects are pecuniary, as they work through the price mechanism. However, they lead to real changes in the production sector, which means that they have to be considered in the cost–benefit scheme.

If infrastructure is provided by private consortia, an additional problem arises. Apparently there may be benefits from infrastructure provision occurring in market segments, which the providers cannot control and which cannot be capitalized. For example, land prices may rise or firms establishing themselves at motorway junctions may enjoy extra profits which private motorway owners cannot participate in because of limited property rights. In such cases, private infrastructure providers are in the position to negotiate with the state on a public share of the investment cost or on other forms of public participation.

On the other hand, external costs of infrastructure provision can occur, consisting of: (i) pollution of soil and water, sealing of surface; (ii) disturbance of the biosphere, biodiversity and natural habitats; (iii) separation effects on human communication; and (iv) visual intrusion.

External benefits of the infrastructure provision have to be deducted from, while external costs have to be added to, the cost of the bill that has to be paid by the users of the infrastructure. In some countries (for example, France), special regional taxation is imposed on industries that are expected to profit from better accessibility. This can be used as a measure for the minimum economic value of the positive externality.

4.3 External Effects of Infrastructure Use

External benefits of infrastructure provision, which have been introduced in Section 2 above, are initiated by the option of improved accessibility and lower transport prices. The ensuing use of this option by private users is cost induced, that is, inside the market mechanism. Consequently, if the state has included the benefits of new options in the cost–benefit scheme then there is no reason to consider these benefits a second time, that is, there are no external benefits produced by private agents through their traffic activities.

This view contrasts with that expressed in many publications that have been issued or sponsored by motorists' clubs or by the associations of road vehicle manufacturers or of the road haulage industry. They argue that the creation of new consumption patterns and of new kinds of logistic organization ('just-in-time' deliveries) includes external benefits which have to be balanced against other impacts (see Aberle and Engel, 1992; Willeke, 1994; or Baum and Schulz, Chapter 9, Section 7, this volume, for this argumentation). The reason for this different view lies in a wider definition of externalities (for example, as 'effects on third parties', 'effects outside the transport sector' and so on).

External costs of infrastructure use may have a number of different sources, which are shown in Table 4.1.

Table 4.1   Externalities of the use of infrastructure

External costs	External benefits
Traffic congestion, in the sense of additional time and operation costs caused by user interactions	Considered in the option values of infrastructure provision
Uncovered costs of the infrastructure provision (net of the share of the state)	
Environmental impacts related to transport activities, such as noise, air pollution, climate change, separation of communication between neighbourhoods, water and soil pollution as well as disamenities and detrimental effects of operations on the infrastructure	
Traffic accidents that deplete the stock of human resources; the costs are relevant in as much as they are not covered by insurance	

Each of these sources of external costs of infrastructure use will now be considered in more detail (environmental impacts and traffic accidents are treated together).

Congestion costs

Congestion costs are caused by user activities inside the transport sector and consist of additional time and operating costs of the users caused by their interactions. Note that costs of accidents or of environmental pollution are not included in our notion of congestion costs. Defined in this way, congestion costs are 'club internal', as they result from an informational and organizational problem within the transport sector.

As Pigou (1924) argues, people behave according to the perceived average cost of their trips and not according to the marginal social costs which would establish an optimum in terms of the minimum total costs for all users of the system. Therefore, the external congestion cost is the difference between marginal social and average user costs.

The following properties are essential:

* congestion costs are obviously an element of the social costs;
* congestion costs are external with respect to the market and cause inefficiencies; and
* congestion costs are internal with respect to the set ('club') of users.

As congestion costs are externalities, it follows immediately that their reduction increases social welfare. Charging congestion costs according to the marginal cost principle and spending the money for the best public choices would be the best solution in a static world. This is the clear position of standard welfare theory which corresponds with Pigou's taxation principle.

However, there are strong institutional objections against such a simple solution. Congestion cost charging would imply a most flexible pricing scheme and an efficient road management. However, following the observations of institutional economics the state is a very bad manager (see the X-inefficiency argument of Leibenstein, 1978). The organizational structure, the incentive system and the pressure of partial political interest and rent-seeking lobby groups make a large deviation from the efficiency goals most likely. Therefore it is postulated that the state should confine itself to creating the appropriate institutional organizations on the one hand and keep out of the business of short-term operations management on the other. This issue relates to Knight's (1924) proposition that restoring optimality in a market distorted by congestion externalities may be achieved more efficiently by the creation of new market arrangements than by trying to manage the problem through public means, by taxes or public charges.

Infrastructure being congested implies that the properties of non-exclusion and non-rivalry no longer apply. This means that a heavily congested infrastructure is no longer a public good but can be regarded as a club good, with predominantly private characteristics, for which the allocation can be organized according to market rules. A privately organized road network, for instance, would clearly show differentiated user charges, depending on the congestion level and on the willingness to pay, such that the congestion externalities would vanish. In consequence, the transport sector could be planned, managed and financed as a set of self-financing systems, either on a private or a public agency basis.

From the viewpoint of the 'adaptive' welfare concept, the advantage of club organizations is that the dynamic adjustment of the system in the long run is increased because of its higher flexibility and more direct reactions to changes of the market.

There are different opinions on the magnitude of congestion externalities. Quinet (1994) gives an average figure of 2 per cent of GDP, based on a literature survey. This figure is also mentioned by the European Commission (1995b). Prud'homme (1998) has shown that in the literature it is usually the total cost of congestion that is calculated, and not the external cost. Restricting himself to the latter and applying a rigorous approach he shows that the magnitude of this effect, calculated for the Paris region, is only one-tenth of the figure mentioned above. This means that the average figure, including rural areas, would be even lower than 0.2 per cent of GDP.

Uncovered costs of the infrastructure
One of the most heavily debated items of the list of externalities is the uncovered cost of the infrastructure. After a first look at the problem it seems to be clear that uncovered infrastructure cost is an externality because users of the infrastructure shift these costs to the taxpayers, that is to a third party which has not taken part in the decision making on infrastructure provision and thus is affected involuntarily. However, a counterargument is that infrastructure decisions have been taken by the state, which is the representative of the taxpayers. Many of the decisions are not economically based but seek to improve social conditions. Therefore uncovered infrastructure costs could be regarded as a cost burden which the public bears voluntarily.

If it comes to an analysis of market distortions through externalities, the uncovered infrastructure costs indeed play a role because they help to keep prices low on the subsidized infrastructure and thus influence intermodal competition. From the economic point of view, the following rules of calculating infrastructure costs are relevant.

- The state's share has to be deducted, which can be estimated on the basis of the positive externalities of infrastructure provision. The historical role of the state when building up the network also has to be considered in the state's share.
- The cost net of the state's share should be allocated according to rules of fairness and efficiency.
- The total cost includes variable costs and fixed capital costs. For the latter, the future full capital costs (represented by depreciation and interest on capital) are relevant, not just the expenditures.

- The costs for a user category have to be compared with the revenues to calculate the degree of cost recovery. Earmarked taxes and charges have to be treated like market revenues from the infrastructure service.

Under these general assumptions, INFRAS/IWW (1995) have calculated a degree of cost recovery for road transport of about 90 per cent, for rail transport of about 50 per cent and for inland waterways of about 15 per cent in Europe.

5 VALUATION OF EXTERNAL COSTS OF ACCIDENTS AND ENVIRONMENTAL IMPACTS

Two basically different approaches can be identified: the (static) welfare approach; and the (dynamic) risk approach. In this section the different approaches will be further specified and the variants described (see Figure 4.2 for an overview).

5.1 The Welfare Maximization Approach

The traditional approach of neoclassical welfare theory is based on the assumption that information is complete and available to all agents. This means that environmental damages can be predicted with a high degree of certainty. The essential properties of the neoclassical welfare model are:

- material production and environmental (human) resources are regarded as substitutes – a reduction in the latter can be compensated by an increase in the former;
- the societal value system is reflected by market prices – if market prices do not exist for a particular externality, it can be evaluated by market analogy;
- every change of the environmental (human) resources can be expressed in monetary terms.

Mostly the replacement of depleted resources is calculated ('resource approach') or the willingness to pay estimated ('utility approach') in order to evaluate externalities by means of market analogy. The resource (cost) and utility approaches are usually treated as discrete alternatives for the evaluation of accident consequences and environmental impacts. However, using the instruments of dynamic welfare theory, it can be shown that the two approaches coincide when a complete formulation of a dynamic welfare maximization problem under environmental constraints is given (see Kotz et al., 1984).

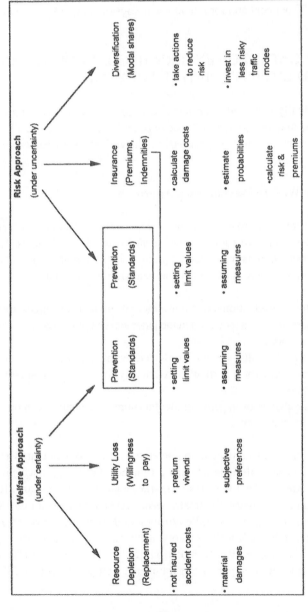

Figure 4.2   Approaches for measuring externalities of transport

Let us assume that society values material consumption C and limited resources S (human and environmental capital) and assesses these by means of a utility function that for simplicity is assumed to be the same for every consumer):

$$u = u\,(C, S),\, u_c > 0,\, u_s > 0. \tag{4.8}$$

This expression differs from the textbook formulation by the inclusion of the available natural resources S. If a prolonged period is considered, each year t of this period will be characterized by a consumption volume C_t with a resource stock S_t. If the annual utility values are integrated by addition into the society's overall assessment and society places a higher value on 'today's' than on 'tomorrow's' unit of utility, we obtain the 'utilitarian' form of the welfare function:

$$W = \int_0^\infty u(C_t, S_t)\exp(-\partial t)dt \tag{4.9}$$

where $\delta > 0$ is the social rate of impatience.

For the production of consumption goods a technology is available which converts labour L, capital K and natural resources R into national product Y:

$$Y_t = F(K_t, L_t, R_t),\, \partial F/\partial v > 0,\, v \in \{K_t, L_t, R_t\}. \tag{4.10}$$

In contrast to the textbook model, the consumption of natural resources appears as an argument of the production function F.

If the stock of natural resources is limited and written S_o, then the current natural resource stock S_t is given by the expression:

$$S_t = S_o - \int_0^t R_\tau d_\tau \tag{4.11}$$

that is, over time, S_t is steadily depleted. By definition

$$R_t = dS_{t/dt}. \tag{4.12}$$

From the welfare-maximizing approach, that is, max (W) under conditions (4.5)–(4.7), and an income disposal equation, it is now possible to derive not only the usual optimum consumption plan but also an optimum plan for resource depletion. The optimality condition that is important for our reasoning (derived from the Hamiltonian of the system) is:

$$\frac{\partial F}{\partial R_t} = \frac{1}{(\partial F / \partial K_t)}\left(\frac{\partial F^0}{\partial R_t} + \frac{\partial U / \partial S_t}{\partial U / \partial C_t}\right). \tag{4.13}$$

The left-hand side denotes the marginal productivity of the natural resource that equals its price in equilibrium. It can be derived from solving the differential equation (4.13) together with the other optimality conditions.

Obviously the price of the natural resource is inversely dependent on the marginal productivity of capital (because of the substitutive relationship between produced capital and non-produced resource). Furthermore the price of the resource is directly dependent on the marginal utility of the natural resource and inversely dependent on the marginal utility of material consumption. Therefore, the (shadow) price of the natural resource increases, *ceteris paribus*, with the preference for the resource. The first important insight of this exercise is that the natural resource has a price although it is not traded on the market. The second insight provided is that in the dynamic equilibrium, damage costs and utility losses coincide because damages have to be evaluated on the basis of opportunity costs, that is, utility losses. The third basic result is that the valuation of external costs varies over time because there is a social rate of discount (see below for further interpretation).

The reason for the resource approach usually generating lower figures compared with the utility approach in empirical estimation lies in the fact that damage calculations are based on present knowledge of future damages, while the utility approach also may include a risk component, dependent on the preferences of people questioned or observed.

Most approaches to measure external effects are *top down*, that is, they calculate the overall costs for each type of external effect for a geographical unit (country) and allocate these costs to the units of transport by breaking the aggregate figures down using key functions. This results in figures of average externality costs, which indicate the magnitude of the problems but cannot be used directly as bases for designing internalization measures. From the viewpoint of neoclassical welfare theory the marginal costs are relevant, which would presuppose that the external cost analysis ends up with a cost function, with the traffic unit as the independent variable, which can be differentiated to result in the marginal cost function. Adding up all marginal cost functions of the different types of externalities would yield the additional social costs that have to be internalized through Pigou taxation.

Taking the club or the transaction cost theories as a starting-point, it would be important to relate every cost element to the best levy point, that is, the level of decision making on which the highest influence of an internalization policy can be achieved. This would lead to a structured or incremental costing concept, which clearly would deviate from the marginal cost approach. In any case, the information stemming from a top-down analysis would not be sufficient.

Recent research therefore has concentrated on developing cost figures by *bottom-up* approaches. These start from the source of disturbance, the traffic unit, and try to construct a consistent impact chain from the source (emission) via the transmission mechanisms (transport of pollutants, concentrations) to the impacts on human beings and nature (health, indicators of local environmental quality). In particular the ExternE project of the EU Commission (1995a) and the follow-up studies (for example: the QUITS project of the EU (QUITS, 1998); Ricci and Friedrich, 1999) go along these lines and provide data for future damages and utility losses by following the impact pathway bottom up.

In the *resource approach*, all cases of loss caused by accidents and environmental impacts are regarded as depletions of resources, which are evaluated by reference either to the costs of replacement or to the lowering of future returns. Human beings, animals and plants are treated here in the same way as material objects, that is, they are conceptually equated with capital goods so that their cost values (purchase or manufacturing costs) or income values (cash values of future returns) can be determined.

For instance, in the case of a fatality, the application of the cost value principle involves calculation of the costs incurred in raising human beings of predetermined age levels, whereas the income value principle requires calculation of all the productive contributions over the expected remaining life of the victim.

Calculations of losses that have occurred or are expected to occur can be performed on a 'net' or 'gross' basis. That is, the consumption of the accident victims can be deducted, with the argument that they no longer take place in the society concerned, or it can be included, arguing that the loss of consumption of the person killed is also a utility loss for society. When evaluating accident prevention, for example, in the cost–benefit analysis of traffic safety precautions, the gross consumption is the relevant measure because society intends to preserve the lives of people, including their consumption.

The resource approach can quickly impinge on ethical problem areas, as is frequently demonstrated by the example of accident deaths. In principle, cost value determinations imply that lost capital goods (here, human beings) can be reproduced, while calculations of income value on the basis of age level and social position can also generate negative results. For this reason, the debate on accident costs has been accompanied by constant efforts to blunt the sensitive points by the use of suitable average concepts and reference quantities. Standardized evaluation techniques for transport investment (see PLANCO, 1990) or externality charging (see Ricci and Friedrich, 1999) employ average quantities of this kind.

The *utility approach* is founded on the individual value estimates of those concerned by the external effects. The theory is based on hypotheses of individual behaviour of the type used in general equilibrium theory. The most important, '*homo oeconomicus*', hypothesis consists of two elements. First, the information premise assumes that all agents are fully aware of the economically relevant data or can completely safeguard themselves in uncertainty by contingent claims. Second, the judgement premise postulates that an individual is capable of consistent evaluation (order of preferences, utility function) in all possible economic circumstances. Individuals' notions of utility are expressed by their demand behaviour, so that this behaviour can also provide the basis for measuring changes in utility.

The decisive element is that individuals respond to changes in their economic situation by a willingness to pay or to sell. This willingness can be measured by stated or revealed preference techniques. In the first case, people are questioned and express the magnitude of their response to an external effect by virtual payments or contingent claims. Revealed preference approaches try to derive the economic valuation of an externality from observed behaviour of affected people.

An approach that is increasingly applied is the 'hedonic pricing' method. In this contingent method, a demand function is constructed which includes – beside other market parameters – the environmental quality as an additional argument of the function. The values of the parameters of the demand function are estimated on the basis of field study results. If the specified demand function also comprises market prices, which is usually the case, then it is possible to calculate the monetary value of the environmental parameter by taking the elasticity of substitution. A field study for estimating the value of noise has been carried out by Pommerehne (1986) for the city of Basle (Switzerland).

One of the most comprehensive surveys for the application of a willingness-to-pay approach has been designed by Schulz (1985), who asked a total of 4500 Berliners what maximum monthly sum they would be prepared to pay for different air qualities. If the result of this survey is extrapolated for the whole of the population of the Federal Republic of Germany, the costs of air pollution (= the utility of improving air quality to 'holiday air quality') are close to 3 per cent of GDP for 1985. The willingness to sell would have to be put at a still higher figure.

For some externalities it might be impossible to give valuations in money terms, based on damage costs or willingness to pay, because the impact path of the mechanisms from the emission source to the damaging impacts on people cannot be constructed (for example, the emission of carbon dioxide (CO_2)). In these cases a *prevention approach* is applied, which basically estimates the cost of avoiding the harm by prevention measures. Prevention measures are related to standard settings, whose magnitude depends on:

- the level of prevention defined by specified limit values; and
- the preventive technology used.

Setting limit values can be based on expert judgements that occasionally are given in the form of benchmarks recommended by particular institutions. In the case of CO_2, reference is usually made to the Intergovernmental Panel on

Climate Change (IPCC). This panel has recommended that emissions of CO_2 be reduced by 50 per cent until the year 2040, based on the 1990 level (for the industrially developed countries even by 80 per cent).

The setting of rules for limit value measurements is crucial to the formulation of possible preventive technologies. For instance, it is important for noise emission limits to define the point at which these are to be measured – for example, the boundary of the land plot or an inside wall of the house or flat of the affected individual.

It is well known that private investors will discount future earnings and costs in an investment calculus and that also society prefers today's consumption to that of tomorrow. When it comes to the evaluation of external diseconomies, one has to assume that there is some sort of *social discount* that has to be applied to make the effects occurring at different periods of time comparable. The basic question is: is the social rate of discount the same as that applied in business finance, is it the same as the rate of discount which is applied in cost–benefit analysis or are there reasons to deviate from such benchmarks?

The model outlined in Section 5 above gives a first answer. The social rate of discount results from the optimal solution of the dynamic programme in the form of the optimal value of the marginal efficiency of capital. This value will be dependent on:

- the parameters of the utility function (intergenerational preference, preference for the natural resources);
- the parameters of the production function (production elasticities of labour, capital and natural resources, rate of technical progress);
- the social rate of impatience ('rate of rapacity') that is applied for discounting the utilities of the single periods of the time horizon.

Kotz et al. (1984) have shown that the resulting social rate of discount is considerably lower than the private rate of discount. There are also reasons for the discount rate for environmental externalities to deviate from the discount rate for internal benefits and costs (time and cost savings). However, it depends on the preferences of future generations whether savings of generalized costs are evaluated lower than reductions of external costs. As these preferences are not known, the use of a uniform discounting rate can be justified. Kotz et al. suggest a rate of 3 per cent, which lies at the lower bound of discount rates internationally applied in cost–benefit analysis.

5.2 The Risk Approach

The economic theory that has formed on the basis of this understanding of natural resources may be called 'economic ecology' (Pearce et al., 1993;

Hampicke, 1992). It is intrinsically based on the assumption that the future is not perfectly predictable but that risk and uncertainty are basic phenomena associated with deteriorating environmental quality. Therefore the set of these approaches is summarized under the notion of the risk approach.

The focus of the risk approach is not the question what the cost of an environmentally harmful activity might be. This cost might be infinitely high if risks for the existence of humankind occur. Therefore the main issue postulated by the risk approach is risk management, according to the precaution principle. Risk can be managed through a strategy mix consisting of diversification, insurance and prevention. These three components will be further elucidated below, followed by an analysis of opportunity costs in relation to the issue of a 'safe minimum standard'.

The *diversification strategy* is of specially close concern to the theory of business finance, as investors are inclined to opt not for bonds or equities carrying the maximum expected yield but for a portfolio embracing a range of risk categories so that their risks are spread. Society may adopt a similar strategy for transport by not exclusively backing one type of vehicle such as the car – notwithstanding the preference of individuals for the car now and in the foreseeable future. Instead it may be catering for the parallel development of alternative (for example, public transport) modes in order to reduce human and environmental risks and provide other options in the event of acute threats to safety or to the environment. This is exemplified by the smog alarms, when people are obliged to use public transport if the concentration levels for defined exhausts exceed critical limits.

The reason why countries provide ample and high-standard loss-making public transport facilities may be explained as an attempt to spread risks. Therefore the deficits of public passenger services may be seen as the price of risk diversification (they are indeed often referred to as 'survival precautions').

In the area of safety and the environment under consideration, *insurance contracts* could be a suitable means of placing future risks into economic categories. For analytical purposes it is for the moment expedient to disregard the existence of insurance companies and to look at insurance contracts as a reciprocal obligation.

Where two individuals are exposed to a risk which may materialize for one or the other of them, the risk can be covered by a reciprocal insurance in which each partner pays a premium measured in such a way that the ratio of the premiums equals that of the respective probabilities of loss. The reciprocal insurance of a pool comprising many insured individuals functions in a similar manner as long as the risks are not mutually correlated (see Markowitz, 1959). However, as soon as the risks borne by individuals are correlated, they can no longer be allocated with actuarial fairness on the principle of the probabilities of loss. The issue then becomes one of social risks, which in an unsafe world are the counterpart to external effects.

Accident and environmental risks bear a heavy social imprint, and private sector willingness to insure these risks is therefore too weak to provide full cover from the premium payments. In these circumstances the state may react by imposing mandatory insurance, and we do indeed find that many countries lay down compulsory third-party insurance. Such insurance covers both material and intangible losses by lump-sum payments (damages, compensation for loss of limbs), although the amounts in Europe are very modest. It is possible, in principle, to extend the insurance premiums to the still uncovered additional social costs, for instance, for the external costs of accidents. Such an extension can be prepared by the usual calculation of a risk premium on the base of risk utility functions and the random income losses caused by accidents (for the mathematical background of calculating such premiums, see Heilmann, 1990).

In the context of the risk approach the *prevention cost* estimation is no longer an auxiliary method which is applied if direct measurements of damage costs or of willingness to pay fail, but it gets a strong theoretical underpinning through the foundation of economic ecology. This theory is based on the central hypothesis that 'safe minimum standards' describe the long-term sustainability of the economic and social systems. Technology and human behaviour have to be developed and organized in such a way that the safe minimum standards for all environmental and safety indicators are guaranteed over time.

Hirshleifer and Riley (1979) have given the risk-theoretical background of this approach by introducing the concept of 'state-related utility'. According to this concept it is quite possible that the individual utility level depends not only on material consumption but also on the nature of objects which cannot simply be described by income equivalents. This would, for instance, be true for an irreplaceable heirloom, the individual's own life or that of his child. In the loss state the utility curve drops to a lower level.

The question whether or not the individual wishes to be insured against such loss depends on the extent to which income and the state-related variable are substitutes, that is, are mutually exchangeable in terms of utility compensation. In the case of the child's life, taking out an insurance policy on the life of the child would, from an economic point of view, be irrational. This is because the family concerned would need less income in the loss state compared with the non-loss state. In a case like this it would be rational to transfer income from the 'state with loss' to the 'state without loss', that is to practise a kind of reverse insurance by doing everything to prevent the occurrence of the loss. Where preferences are distorted ('merit quality') or where social risks occur, it is up to the state to make the optimum provision for loss.

The previous example can be transferred to environmental phenomena of a social dimension, in particular to the risk of global warming. Instead of insuring against risk an active management towards risk reduction would appear the rational response.

We shall now discuss briefly the question of *opportunity costs* (shadow prices) for the situation when the 'safe minimum standard' issue of the risk approach applies. Suppose that material welfare of a time period, C, is dependent on an activity variable x, which, for instance, denotes traffic volume. Assume further that producing the activity variable (traffic) causes environmental impacts and that the 'safe minimum standard' issue of the risk approach applies. Then a general formulation of the welfare problem, written in a static way for simplicity, can be given as follows:

$$\max \{C(x)\}, \text{ s.t. } g(x) \leq R, \tag{4.14}$$

$g(x)$ denoting the externality production function and R the safe minimum standard.

If the constraint is biting then the associated shadow price is positive, otherwise it is zero. A positive shadow price denotes the gain in material welfare C if the constraint is extended by one unit. The ways to achieve the safe minimum standard can consist of prevention measures associated with prevention expenditures and changes of the production volume for the variable x, that is, reduction of traffic activities (see IWW et al., 1998).

6   EMPIRICAL FINDINGS

6.1   Accidents

In 1991, a total of 57 000 fatalities and 1.8 million injuries were reported for the roads of all EUR 17 countries (member countries of the EU plus Norway and Switzerland), and 613 fatalities/1352 injuries in the rail systems. This comparison indicates that the market competition between road and rail is distorted: the railway companies are enforced by the states to fulfil high safety standards while this does not hold for road transport. The magnitude of market distortion can be measured by the external costs that both competitors produce. The external costs of traffic accidents are composed of three elements: the resource consumption; the production losses; and the evaluation of human value.

Resource consumption costs consist of administrative costs, cost of medical treatment and cost of rehabilitation. The production losses include all missing contributions of accident victims to the GDP, or the production potential, respectively (the latter macro-indicator being used to make the approach independent of the employment situation in the economy). If a human value is added then the production loss has to be computed net of the consumption of the victim. The human value, finally, expresses the willingness of society to spend money to reduce a fatal accident. It can be derived from stated preference surveys or from revealed preference analysis of public safety programmes in transport. Usually the human value (in some studies denoted as 'risk value') dominates the other cost elements. Therefore in countries in which human values are a part of the cost calculation, the resulting figure of the cost of a (saved) human life are much higher compared with computations which are based on resource cost and gross production loss.

INFRAS/IWW (1995) suggest a human value of €1.1 million. In the ExternE study mentioned above, the human value used is as high as €4.1 million (see Ricci and Friedrich, 1999). If such high values for human life are used in empirical valuations, then the human value becomes by far the dominating factor in every externality evaluation.

Concerning the shape of the accident cost function for roads, an evaluation of German accident data shows that this function is U-shaped for motorways and concave for all other road types. The aggregate function is strictly concave such that the marginal cost function on the aggregate level is strictly decreasing with the traffic volume.

6.2 Noise

About 80 million EU citizens (that is 20 per cent) are exposed to daytime noise above 65 dBA (decibel A), which can cause serious health impacts. An additional 170 million citizens are exposed to noise levels which cause serious annoyance (defined by the World Health Organization as between 55 and 65 dBA, see EU Commission, 1995a,b). As the data over the past 15 years do not show significant improvement, fighting traffic noise is one of the most important challenges of transport policy. Noise is a local phenomenon such that some type of a bottom-up approach is necessary to start with a quantification.

The first basic element of a noise assessment is the estimation of noise production curves and the way these depend on traffic characteristics. These functions are concavely shaped because of the logarithmic relationship between the dBA level and the traffic volume.

The second component is the valuation of noise by people exposed to different noise levels. The Swedish noise values that are given by Hansson (1997) lead to a strictly increasing function of noise cost, with increasing levels of noise exposure (dBA). Amalgamating the data, the resulting function, based on the (comparatively high) Swedish noise evaluations, is concavely shaped. This means that the marginal cost of noise is decreasing with growing traffic volume.

Table 4.2 *QUITS methodological approach of the externality analysis*

Traffic modes (technologies)	Burdens (emissions)	Dispersion modelling, concentrations	Quantification of impacts	Valuation of impacts (burdens)
Road traffic:	*Air pollutants*	Emission source: linear	*Human health*	*Direct valuation methods*
a) Passengers	CO_2	*Integrated model*	Mortality	Contingent valuation
'car'-mix: petrol	CH_4 (CO_2-equivalent)	0–200 m: ln-function	Morbidity	method (CVM)
with and without cat,	CO (CO_2-equivalent)	from MLuS-model		Market simulation
diesel	SO_2	200–5000 m: empirical	*Environmental*	
b) Goods	NO_X	exp.-function	*Materials*	*Indirect valuation methods*
mix of vans, light and	Particulates ($PM_{10}, …$)	>5000 m: EcoSense	Maintenance of façades	Hedonic price analysis
heavy trucks	Benzol	*Results*	of buildings	(HPA)
Rail traffic:	HC	Concentration changes:	Crops	Wage risk analysis
a) Passengers	Non-methane HC	SO_2, NO_X, PM, nitrates,	Yield losses	(WRA)
conventional	Pb	sulphates, acid deposit.	Forests	Travel cost approach
high-speed	Other micro-pollutants	Emission source: point	Timber losses	Production losses
b) Goods	*Other pollutants*	*Model used*	*Climate*	Avoidance costs
only electric powered	Soil	EcoSense	Global warming	Costs of illness (COI)
trains	Water	*Results*		
Air traffic:	*Accidents*	Concentration changes:	*Non-environmental*	
Passengers, different	Noise	SO_2, NO_X, PM, nitrates,	Infrastructure	
aircraft	*Others*	sulphates, acid deposit.	Subsidies	
	Vibration	Emission source: linear		
	Cutting-off-effects	Rough calculation with		
	Visual intrusion	EcoSense		

Source: Weinreich et al. (1998).

6.3 Exhaust Emissions

In the EU project ExterneE (EU Commission, 1995a) and the follow-up project QUITS (1998) the valuation procedure follows the 'impact pathway' as shown in Table 4.2. In QUITS the emissions per trip from different transport modes on the route between Frankfurt and Milan are modelled and then weighted with average marginal cost values. The external costs caused by air pollutants, then, are estimated as given in Table 4.3.

Table 4.3 External costs for different traffic categories on the Frankfurt to Milan route (€/1000 pkm or tkm)

Traffic category	Air pollutants	Total external costs
Road passenger	15.63	44.26
Rail passenger	1.71	4.87
Air passenger	9.60	21.91
Road freight	15.74	30.62
Rail freight	0.68	2.80

Source: QUITS (1998).

The overview shows that road traffic produces the highest air pollution and total external costs on the Frankfurt to Milan route. Even air traffic is environmentally superior because of significantly lower air pollution costs that are not offset by higher costs of climate change. As accident costs are almost zero for rail and air traffic, the comparison results in large specific cost differentials not only between road and rail, but also between road and air traffic. In the case of freight traffic, rail is environmentally advantageous when air pollution is taken as an indicator. If noise is added, the relative distance is diminishing because the noise disturbance by freight trains is high, even if a so-called railway noise bonus of 5 dBA is applied. The latter is motivated because of the different spectrum of noise frequencies for road and rail traffic which make rail noise less disturbing (see INFRAS/IWW, 1995, for further details).

6.4 Greenhouse Gases

The resource cost estimations of climate change show an extremely high variance. Based on the expected global damages induced by CO_2 concentrations in the atmosphere, Nordhaus (1991) estimates a cost value of roughly US$5 per tonne of CO_2, while Azar's (1996) results show a value of US$510 per tonne of CO_2. Both apply an equity weighting approach, based on estimated damages of global warming, aggregating the damages by countries and time periods and weighting these by the inverse of income. The different results are caused not only by the damage calculations, but also by the weighting procedures (rich countries against poor) and in particular the choice of a discounting rate (see Section 5) are responsible for the huge differences. In the QUITS research quoted above, the authors have tried to reduce the variance and result in a band between US\$66 and US\$170 per tonne CO_2.

In the INFRAS/IWW study, the authors argue that it is not possible yet to give reliable figures on expected damages and their distribution over time and space. Therefore they prefer to apply a prevention approach which starts from the IPCC assumption that the global CO_2 production has to be reduced by 50 per cent until the year 2040, which means that the industrialized countries have to reduce emissions by about 80 per cent. Assuming a particular allocation of the reduction target among the countries, the INFRAS/IWW results give a figure of 50 €/t of CO_2. Inserting this value in the cost calculations for the different traffic modes, they show that road and air traffic are the main polluters. In particular, the specific climate costs of freight transport by air give rise to the question whether the prices have been set right for this sector, remembering that air traffic pays neither fuel taxes nor value added tax on international routes.

6.5 Other Externalities

There are a number of further external cost components which are mentioned and sometimes quantified in the literature. In a study for the German Environmental Agency, IWW et al. (1998) present cost estimations for some types of effects which are usually treated as intangibles:

- risk of cancer from particulate matter and benzenes;
- health risks from ozone;
- risks for flora and fauna;
- noise damage outside of homes; and
- risks for biotopes and biodiversity.

Furthermore, risks from salting roads in winter, oil spills and chemical treatment of rail tracks are also mentioned. Finally, the upstream and downstream effects (production of vehicles, disposal of vehicles) have to be considered if a complete documentation of the total balance of externalities is to be given. Such effects are discussed qualitatively in INFRAS/IWW (1995).

Table 4.4 Relative external costs of transport in EUR 17, 1991

Effect	Road			Rail		Aviation		Ship
	Cars (€/1000pkm)	Buses (€/1000tkm)	Freight (€/1000tkm)	Passengers (€/1000pkm)	Freight (€/1000tkm)	Passengers (€/1000pkm)	Freight (€/1000tkm)	Freight (€/1000tkm)
Accidents	32.3	9.4	22.2	1.9	0.9	–	–	–
Noise	4.5	4.2	12.7	3.1	4.7	3.0	16.5	–
Air pollution	6.6	4.1	13.0	2.0	0.7	5.0	26.3	4.2
Climate	6.6	2.7	10.6	3.0	1.1	9.8	50.5	1.9
Total	50.0	20.4	58.5	10.0	7.4	17.8	93.3	6.1

Source: INFRAS/IWW (1995).

6.6 European Study

INFRAS/IWW (1995) have studied the external costs of transport for the West European countries (EUR 17 = member countries of the EU plus Norway and Switzerland). The basic approach was:

- to restrict the list of external effects to be quantified in the study to accidents, noise, air pollution and climate change;
- to select a country-based state-of-the-art valuation by type of effect;
- to define a simple cluster for reference values by regional types, modes, and vehicle categories;
- to project the reference value to the clusters of the EUR 17 countries; and
- to weight the results by purchasing power parity.

Because of this unified methodology, the resulting figures are comparable and can be added or used for a European synopsis for external costs of transport.

The total external costs of transport in the EUR 17 countries sum up to about €270 billion for the year 1991. This corresponds to 4.6 per cent of GDP on average. The country values vary considerably. The lowest value is shown for Norway (4.0 per cent) while the highest value is computed for Portugal (10.3 per cent). The higher external costs of transport in the less-developed countries such as Portugal or Greece are caused mainly by the high accident rates.

The total external costs of road transport are €250 billion, while those for rail transport are €5 billion. The reason for this discrepancy is twofold: first road traffic has the highest share of the total traffic (roughly 80 per cent), and second, the relative costs of road traffic are much higher compared with rail transport or inland waterway shipping. As about 57 000 fatalities and 1.8 million injuries were reported for the EUR 17 road sector in the year 1991, compared with about 600 fatalities/1400 injuries for the rail sector, the external costs of accidents are dominating the figures in the external costs breakdown. The relative external costs of road passenger traffic are given in Table 4.4.

7 INTERNALIZATION OF EXTERNALITIES OF TRANSPORT

7.1 The Goals of Internalization

The policy goals behind internalization of external effects can be manifold:

1. optimal use of existing capacity;

2. abolishing of subsidies that are not justified by public good characteristics of the transport system;
3. allocation of the costs to the agent who is responsible for their production (polluter should pay);
4. achieving defined long-term environmental/safety quality standards;
5. better balance of regional development;
6. better balance of social development; and
7. developing new markets and new technology with lower consumption of natural resources.

Aspects 1. to 7. are normative issues. The first three reflect the static efficiency view of neoclassics, which corresponds to the theoretical background of the Green Paper (EU Commission, 1995b). Aspects 4. to 6. concern sustainability issues of the environment and for the social balance. Finally, aspect 7. bridges the gap between long-term environmental and economic development in so far as the latter may show a new quality dimension after making the former a matter of permanent market decisions of firms and consumers. Aspects 4. to 7. bring in what one can call the issues of 'adaptive efficiency' which should be added to 1. to 3. to result in a comprehensive long-term view of efficiency and sustainability.

7.2 Instruments of Internalization Policy

Pricing policy is the uniform remedy in the neoclassical approach, following the Pigouvian idea of correcting the markets that are disturbed through externalities by a system of taxes and subsidies to restore the general equilibrium. In more practical applications, market segments of the transport market are defined (by type of region and type of transport infrastructure) and studied using the Marshallian demand/supply model where the social marginal cost and the individually perceived average cost functions represent the supply side. Optimal policy strategies follow from maximizing consumer/producer surpluses subject to budget constraints.

This kind of approach has been tested in the TRENEN project of the EU (TRENEN, 1995). Externalities have been included through a marginal cost approach, which in the case of the environment is based on dose-response relationships to measure social marginal costs. Analysis results in optimal taxation/charging schemes for every defined market segment. This approach can be regarded as a challenge in itself to show that the neoclassical welfare approach can be filled with empirical figures and produces results that can be used as baseline benchmarks for discussing pricing strategies.

Yet, there is some scepticism whether the neoclassical marginal costing approach can be applied in reality. It has already been shown in Section 6 that some externalities (noise, accidents) do not show an upward-sloping marginal cost curve such that marginal costing conflicts with issues of full cost recovery and the polluter pays principle. Furthermore, looking at the list of normative and positive political issues of internalization policy discussed above, it is obvious that it is hardly possible to achieve a set of different goals in a balanced way using only one political instrument. Different objectives call for a set of different instruments, each of which should be simple, transparent and acceptable to the majority of agents.

INFRAS/IWW (1995) have proposed categorizing the instruments that might be appropriate for internalization policy using the typology given in Figure 4.3. Instruments are classified on the basis of increasing intensity of government intervention, or – conversely – of decreasing scope for independent decision making by individuals and firms. The most important message that is given by this figure is that the set of different goals described cannot be achieved efficiently by one uniform instrument. An optimal policy mix implies different instruments directly addressing the various levy points of decision making in transport. The pricing instruments used in this policy mix can consist of several elements, such as fuel taxation, emission certificates, mandatory insurance or multipart tariffs as they are applied in the energy or communication sectors.

8   SUMMARY AND CONCLUSION

First, external effects occur if a resource is used commonly by different agents, of which the property rights are not defined. In a narrow definition, external effects are characterized by three properties: involuntary interaction, processing outside the market and disturbance of adaptive efficiency. According to Pigou all externalities have to be removed by taxes and subsidies. The optimal level can be computed as the difference between the private and the social marginal cost in the equilibrium situation. According to the Coase theorem, externalities can be internalized through allocation of property rights – no matter to which party – and private bargaining. This presupposes that the transaction costs are very low and there are no problems of asymmetrical market power. As these assumptions are usually not given, Coase recommends checking the social benefit situation with and without internalization of externalities. Externalities should be removed only if the net benefits are positive. In the case of the transport sector the externalities which, from the pure point of view of efficiency, call for public interventions are the consumption of non-renewable resources by pollution and the impacts of accidents which are not paid for by private parties, that is, by their insurance.

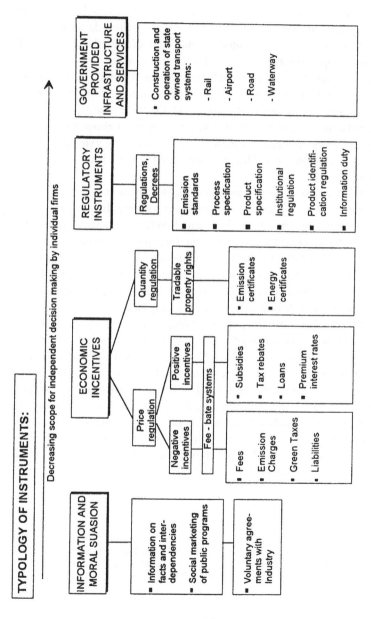

Source: INFRAS/IWW (1995).

Figure 4.3   Typology of policy instruments for internalizing external effects

Second, congestion costs, which are often denoted as one of the most challenging externalities of the transport sector, basically indicate that the organization of transport infrastructure management is wrong. Therefore, instead of trying to find out the correct Pigouvian taxes, an alternative solution could be to manage road capacities according to private management rules. The quantification of external effects can be done on the basis of neoclassical utility theory or by risk analysis. In most valuation approaches, damage costs or contingent valuations are estimated. In the light of uncertainty and risk, prevention and opportunity cost (shadow price) approaches also have a valid theoretical foundation and are relevant for practical application. The calculation of external costs leads to a widespread band of results, depending on the approach chosen. Using moderate values, an EU-wide study comes to the conclusion that the external costs of transport sum up to about 5 per cent of GDP (not including congestion externalities). Internalizing external costs by public policy instruments would lead to a substantial increase in the variable cost of transport.

Third, the fuzziness of social cost calculations is by no means an argument to reject public policy instruments for reducing externalities of transport. However, it shows that basing environmental policy on social costing is not enough. It is not a substitute for a clear public setting of goals to achieve a sustainable development of the transport sector. Unlike rigid regulatory provisions, pricing strategies have the advantage that they are flexible and perceptible and can provide strong incentives for behaviour consistent with the aims pursued. Nevertheless, pricing policy can only be a part of internalization policy for externalities of transport. Founding pricing policy on a uniform concept such as social marginal cost pricing might lead to serious caveats.

Finally, while there may be considerable external benefits of transport infrastructure provision by the state, no external benefits of infrastructure use by private agents could be identified. Most positive externalities of transport mentioned in the literature (for example, development of new consumption patterns or logistic concepts) are either induced by the state's infrastructure provision or they are usual market phenomena processed by the price mechanism. Therefore it is not justified to subtract external benefits of infrastructure use from external costs.

NOTE

1. Important conditions are: convexity of preferences and technology (increasing marginal cost curves), perfect divisibility, perfect foresight, atomistic competition. Furthermore the Pigou analysis is based on a partial one-market analysis. It has to be assumed that other markets are not affected.

REFERENCES

Aberle, G. and M. Engel (1992), 'Theoretische Grundlagen zur Erfassung und Bewertung des volkswirtschaftlichen Nutzens' (Theoretical foundations of measurement and evaluation of social benefit), *Internationales Verkehrswesen*, **44**, 169–75.

Azar, C. (1996), 'Discounting and distributional considerations in the context of global warming', *Ecological Economics*, **19**, 169–84.

Coase, R.H. (1937), 'The nature of the firm', *Economica*, **4**, 386–405.

Coase, R.H. (1960), 'The problem of social cost', *Journal of Law and Economics*, **3**, 1–44.

Coase, R.H. (1988), *The Firm, the Market and the Law*, Chicago: University of Chicago Press.

EU Commission (1995a), *ExternE. Externalities of Energy*, Luxembourg: Office for Official Publications of the European Communities.

EU Commission (1995b), *Towards Fair and Efficient Pricing in Transport*, Green Paper, COM(95)691/FIN, Brussels.

Hampicke, U. (1992), *Ökologische Ökonomie. Individuum und Natur in der Neoklassik. Natur in der Ökonomischen Theorie. Teil 4*, Opladen: Westdeutscher Verlag.

Hansson, L. (1997), 'The internalization of external effects in Swedish transport policy – a comparison between road and rail traffic', Dissertation, Lund: Lund University.

Heilmann, W.-R. (1990), 'Risk management and insurance', *Forensic Engineering*, **2** (1–2), 119–34.

Hirshleifer, J. and J.G. Riley (1979), 'The analytics of uncertainty and information – an expository survey', *Journal of Economic Literature*, **17**, 1375–421.

INFRAS/IWW (1995), *External Effects of Transport*, Study for the Union Internationale des Chemins de Fer, Zürich and Karlsruhe: IWW.

IWW, IFEU (Institut für Energie- und Umweltforschung), Kessel and Partner, PÖU (Planungsgruppe Ökologie und Umwelt) and PTV (Planung, Transport, Verkehr Consult) (1998), *Entwicklung eines Verfahrens für die Bestimmung umweltverträglicher Fernverkehrskonzepte* (Methodology for designing an environmentally sustainable concept for long distance transportation), Study on behalf of the German Environmental Agency, Karlsruhe: IWW.

Knight, F. (1924), 'Some fallacies in the interpretation of social cost', *Quarterly Journal of Economics*, **37**, 582–606.

Kotz, R., P. Müller and W. Rothengatter (1984), *Entwicklung eines Verfahrens für dynamische Investitionsplanung und Ermittlung des bei der Fortschreibung der BVWP anzuwendenden Zinssatzes* (Development of a dynamic investment planning method and determination of the interest rate to be applied to the Federal Road Transport Plan evaluations), Expert report commissioned by the Federal Minister of Transport, Ulm.

Krugman, P. (1991), *Geography and Trade*, Cambridge, MA: MIT Press.

Leibenstein, H. (1978), *General X-Efficiency. Theory and Economic Development*, New York: Oxford University Press.

Markowitz, H.M. (1959), *Portfolio Selection: Efficient Diversification of Investments*, Cowles Foundation for Research in Economics Monograph 16, New Haven, CT: Yale University.

Marshall, A. (1920), *Principles of Economics*, 8th edn, London: Macmillan.

Meade, J. (1952), 'External economies and diseconomies in a competitive situation', *Economic Journal*, **62**, 54–67.

Nordhaus, W.D. (1991), 'To slow or not to slow? The economics of the greenhouse effect', *Economic Journal*, **101**, 920–37.

North, D.C. (1990), *Institutions, Institutional Change and Economic Performance*, Cambridge: Cambridge University Press.

Papandreou, A. (1994), *Externality and Institutions*, Oxford: Clarendon.

Pearce, D., E. Barbier and A. Markandya (1993), *Blueprint. Measuring Sustainable Development*, London: Earthscan.

Pigou, A.C. (1924), *The Economics of Welfare*, London: Macmillan.

PLANCO-Consult GmbH (1990), *Externe Kosten des Verkehrs: Schiene, Straße, Binnenschiffahrt* (External costs of transport: rail, road and inland waterways), Report for the Deutsche Bundesbahn, Essen.

Pommerehne, W. (1986), 'Der monetäre Wert einer Flug- und Straßenlärmreduktion: Eine empirische Analyse auf der Grundlage individueller Präferenzen' (The monetary value of a reduction in aircraft and road noise: an empirical analysis based on individual preferences), in Umweltbundesamt (ed.), *Kosten der Umweltverschmutzung* (The costs of environmental pollution), Berlin: Schmidt, pp. 199–224.

Prud'homme, R. (1998), 'Road Congestion Costs in the Paris Area', Paper prepared for the 8th World Conference on Transport Research, Antwerp.

Quinet, E. (1994), 'The social costs of transport: evaluation and links with internalisation policies', in European Conference of Ministers of Transport, *Internalising the Social Costs of Transport*, Paris: OECD, 1994, pp. 31–75.

QUITS (1998), *External Quality Validation*, Draft of the Final Report, EU Project, Brussels.

Ricci, A. and R. Friedrich (1999), *Interim Report of Infrastructure Pricing Working Group 21 'Environmental Costs of Transport'*, Report to the European Commission, Brussels.

Rosen, S. (1985), 'Implicit contracts: a survey', *Journal of Economic Literature*, **22**, 1144–75.

Schmeidler, D. (1969), 'The nucleolus of a characteristic function game', *SIAM, Journal of Applied Mathematics*, **17**, 1163–70.

Schulz, W. (1985), *Der monetäre Wert besserer Luft* (The money value of better air), Frankfurt: Lang.

Schweizer, U. (1988), 'Externalities and the Coase Theorem: Hypothesis or Result?', *Journal of Institutional and Theoretical Economics*, **144**, 245–66.

Stiglitz, J.E. (1987), 'The causes and consequences of the dependence of quality on price', *Journal of Economic Literature*, **25**, 1–47.

Stiglitz. J.E. (1990), 'On the economic role of the state', in A. Heertje (ed.), *The Economic Role of the State*, Oxford: Blackwell.

TRENEN (1995), *Final Report of the TRENEN Project in the Context of the EC – Joule II Research Program*, EU project, Brussels.

Venables, A.J. and M. Gasiorek (1998), *The Welfare Implications of Transport Improvements in the Presence of Market Failure*, Report prepared for the Standing Advisory Committee on Trunk Road Assessment (SACTRA) Committee, London.

Weinreich, S., K. Rennings, P. Friedrich and A. Ricci (1998), *External Costs of Road, Rail and Air Transport – a Bottom-up Approach*, Working Paper of the Zentrum für Europäische Wirtschaftsforschung (ZEW), Mannheim: ZEW.

Willeke, R. (1994), 'Germany', in European Conference of Ministers of Transport, *Benefits of Different Transport Modes*, Round Table 93, Paris: OECD, pp. 5–37.

5. Imperfect competition in transport markets

Emile Quinet

1 INTRODUCTION

Transport demand and supply having been discussed in the two previous chapters, it is logical to consider next the interface between them, that is, the transport market. The present chapter will attempt to survey the recent literature in this field both for passenger and goods transport.

In Section 2 the characteristics and main structural features of transport markets will be analysed: how many markets exist, how do they interrelate and what are the channels of competition? Section 3 is devoted to the way transport markets operate: the scope of imperfect competition, the importance and effects of instability and unsustainability and the role of public interventions. Section 4 summarizes the findings and provides some general policy-orientated conclusions.

The word 'market' has several meanings. It can be the place where people buy food and other commodities for the home. It can be the business 'marketplace' where goods and services are traded. Or it can be the abstract concept of economists (in the tradition of Walras, 1874), providing the interface between supply of and demand for a particular good where the price and quantities to be bought and sold are determined.

The latter kind of market is known to be no more than a theoretical ideal, and this is perhaps especially true in the field of transport. To begin with, much of the sector's activity lies outside the market and is regulated by government (see Chapter 9). Second, a large part of transport activity is transport for own account and this is the case for car passenger transport, and also for a significant part of road haulage and inland waterway transport. Third, transport markets are far removed from the archetypes of the pure and perfect competition producing stable long-term equilibrium among many buyers and sellers.

2   CHARACTERISTICS OF TRANSPORT MARKETS

That part of the transport industry which is subject to market forces obeys them according to its own inherent characteristics. In traditional economic theory, a market consists of a particular good – for which offers of sale and purchase are made – and a price-setting mechanism that establishes the equilibrium between supply and demand. It also has a spatial scope, as determined by the locations of operators, and a dimension in time: the interface between supply and demand usually occurs at intervals between which both are held in abeyance until the next market session.

This is the 'ideal' case. But there is hardly any instance of a market for a perfectly defined and reproducible good with a price-setting mechanism that immediately establishes the equilibrium between supply and demand. Transport, moreover, has its own characteristics, often omitted in current textbooks, but nevertheless entailing important consequences.

Let us first look at these characteristics which, as will be further elaborated below, result in a profusion of transport markets (Section 2.1). These markets may, however, as will also be set out, be interrelated by similarities in either demand or supply (Sections 2.2 and 2.3). Then, we shall examine the way prices are formed and publicized in transport (Section 2.4). Next, two forms of competition which are characteristic in transport will be considered (Section 2.5). Finally, some concluding remarks will be made with regard to the nature of the transport market (Section 2.6).

2.1   Heterogeneity of Transport and the Profusion of Transport Markets in the Narrow Sense

Transport, as a marketable good, can be defined as 'the carriage of an object of given specifications, for example weight, size, or of a person, from A to B in a given time, under given conditions of safety, reliability and comfort'. It is easy to see that each of these specifications is essential to the definition of transport as a marketable good, since changing any one of them changes the value of transport to the consumer (compare Chapter 2) or its cost to the supplier, which is to say that the market will be different. In the case of home-to-work travel, for example, the time of travel is fundamental to the definition of the good, and also the reliability of that time. Starting-point and destination are other obvious essentials. The offer of transport from Paris to New York is not much use if you want to go to Moscow. In the case of goods, the type of freight carried is crucial. Fresh fruit and vegetables have very different requirements from, say, metal ore. Taken in this sense, there is a wide range of transport markets, each with its own generally limited supply and demand structure and with a set of features drawn from all those which define transport as a marketable good.

How can order be found in this profusion, and how can we identify similarities between those markets? There are a number of different ways of classifying and interrelating aspects of the demand for transport on the one hand and the supply of it on the other.

The assumption that the transport market is just the confrontation of suppliers (the transport operators) and final customers is obviously too simple. In fact there is a series of vertically interrelated markets, the structure of which is shown in Figure 5.1. In this figure the first two rows (infrastructure management and rolling-stock industries) represent providers of inputs for transport. For transport operators, the corresponding markets clearly are input markets. These markets are related to the markets for the final product (the output of transport operators, that is, transport services) in the way shown by the links between the last three rows.

Let us say just a few words about the markets of rolling stocks and the auxiliaries' markets. The market for rolling stocks is highly competitive in the car, truck and shipping industries. It has some interesting and specific features in the aircraft industry, structured as an oligopoly with a dominant firm, Boeing, and a challenger, Airbus Industries, which was lucky to benefit from unoccupied niches in the 1970s, when it was created. The market for railway rolling stock is highly fragmented in Europe, where a double vertical monopoly exists in

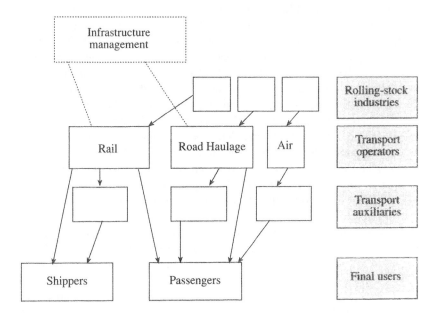

Figure 5.1   Transport production process

several countries, with a strong integration between rolling-stock manufacturers and railway undertakings.

The transport auxiliaries perform several economic functions. Some trade uncertainty, providing a commercial insurance to the transport operators, as are the non-vessel-operator-common-carriers in maritime transport.[1] Others perform technical optimization through matching parcels inside vehicles, or sorting parcels between different vehicles; still others, like travel agencies, provide information to the customers.

Relations between auxiliaries and operators take various forms. In some transport sectors, auxiliaries dominate the operators, as is the case in road goods transport, where many truckers depend on auxiliaries on financial or commercial grounds.[2] In air transport, the reverse is true: air companies must be prevented from abuse towards travel agencies, due especially to the power that is given to them by the Computer Reservation Systems (CRS).

From here, we shall leave these markets and concentrate on the market confronting transport operators and shippers or passengers with each other.

2.2   Interrelating Markets with Regard to Demand

'Quality of service' is one important criterion applying to transport as a good. Clearly, transport services that differ in quality are of a different kind. Quality of service may be quantified by reference to the generalized cost of transport: the transport decisions made by users depend on a linear combination of service quality and monetary cost considerations. Even with identical service quality characteristics, however, different modes of transport are not in general perfect substitutes. The question may be asked, what is the degree of substitution and parallelism between these goods? Some idea about this may be gained from the MATISSE demand model developed by Julien and Morellet (1990) to analyse interregional passenger traffic. The figures in Table 5.1 reveal the direct and cross-price elasticities of demand for each of a number of transport modes.

The transport modes considered are: air, rail exceeding 150 km/h commercial speed, rail under 150 km/h commercial speed, motorway and ordinary highway. Elasticities are calculated with reference to: motor vehicle fuel prices for all road transport; motorway toll charges; rail fares in each of the two categories; and air fares.

The figures in Table 5.1 relate to current supply of transport in France, which is plentiful in all modes, especially as compared, for instance, with rail in North America. The table none the less shows that transport modes are fairly close substitutes. Rail and road are closer over shorter distances and rail and air over longer ones. But where all three modes are available, competition arises and patronage substitution leads to the interlinking, by demand, of the corresponding markets.

Table 5.1   Direct and cross-price elasticities in interregional passenger transport

	Price elasticities for			
	Motor fuel	Rail (< 150 km/h)	Rail (> 150 km/h)	Air
Journey of 100–300 km				
Ordinary highway	−1.2	0.1	0.0	0.0
Motorway	−1.3	0.4	0.0	0.0
Rail (< 150 km/h)	1.4	−1.3	0.0	0.0
Rail (> 150 km/h)	0.0	0.0	0.0	0.0
Air	0.3	0.4	0.0	–
Journey of more than 700 km				
Ordinary highway	−0.4	0.05	–	0.05
Motorway	−0.6	0.1	0.05	0.1
Rail (< 150 km/h)	0.2	−1.0	−1.4	0.4
Rail (> 150 km/h)	0.2	0.05	0.3	0.4
Air	0.1	0.05	0.3	−1.4

Source: Julien and Morellet (1990).

2.3   Interrelating Markets with Regard to Supply

Interrelating markets with reference to demand can never produce a single market for transport operations which have different origins and destinations, such a difference being categorical. If one looks at supply, it is possible to classify together markets where the suppliers are the same, use the same kind of equipment or can move easily from one market to another. Thus it is possible, for example, to speak of a 'more than 100 km' goods transport market, to the extent that long-distance carriers can cover a given territory and change routes rapidly at no extra cost. In these circumstances, it may be noted that a rise in transport demand over a route from A to B would begin by pushing up A to B transport prices and would then attract long-distance carriers from other routes, driving up transport prices on those routes, the end result being a uniform long-distance transport price rise over the whole area in question. The scope and speed of the process would depend on whether the transport equipment can be switched easily from one area to another and on the speed with which information on market conditions can be transmitted from place to place.

The above considerations give some indication of patterns of interrelating markets.

1. In the case of long-distance (greater than 100 km) goods transport, road haulage forms closely interlinked markets, more so than transport by inland waterway – especially in many parts of Europe, where canal systems are inadequately connected.
2. For passenger transport, similar considerations suggest that urban transport in different cities – to the very limited extent that this obeys market forces – will show little interrelationship. Facilities are usually tailored to each individual city, and operating staff are settled in the urban areas where they work.
3. Considering long-distance passenger transport, market interlinking occurs along the same lines as for goods transport. This effect takes specific features for air transport, as will appear from the following.

Nero (1996) models the effects of European airline deregulation through a network as represented in Figure 5.2.

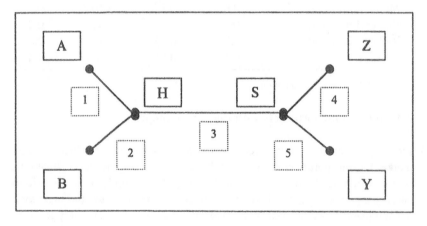

Source:　Nero (1996).

Figure 5.2　Model of intercountry air competition

H and S are capitals of the two countries. HS is, of course, the international relation, AH and BH are the domestic relations in country 1, ZS and YS the domestic relations in country 2. If q_{ij} represents the volume of transport on the link between two adjacent airports and Q_{ij} the volume of transport from an origin i to a destination j, for the case of the network depicted in Figure 5.2 the following relation holds:

$$q_{BH} = Q_{BS} + Q_{BH} + Q_{BA}. \tag{5.1}$$

If the cost function of an airline operating for instance routes AH and BH has the expression:

$$C = C(Q_{AH}, Q_{BH}) = \alpha + c_1(Q_{AH}) + c_2(Q_{BH}) \tag{5.2}$$

where C is the cost function of the firm, α is the fixed common cost of the firm, and $c_i(.,.)$ are the incremental costs of each link $i = 1, 2$, then:

$$C = \alpha + c_1(Q_{AH} + Q_{AB}) + c_2(Q_{BH} + Q_{AB}), (Q_{AS} = 0, Q_{BS} = 0). \tag{5.3}$$

It follows that the marginal cost of product Q_{AB} depends not only on the quantity of product Q_{AB} but also on the quantities of products Q_{AH} and Q_{BH}. It can be seen that the same is true for the products Q_{AH} and Q_{AB} (their marginal costs depend on Q_{BH} and Q_{AB}). This result is known as the cost complementarity, and this complementarity happens even if the costs on each link only depend on the traffic of that link.

In all the above situations, the speed of adjustments and market linking depend on a factor of vital importance to the transport market, namely the way in which prices are formed and published.

2.4 Formation and Publication of Prices

In the 'ideal' market of economic theory, prices are determined at the point of equilibrium between supply and demand. This ideal, however, is seldom achieved. Some reasons which are of particular relevance to the transport sector are as follows.

A first reason, which is found in public passenger transport, is that of prices resulting from a published fare structure on display to the public. This would seem to be an ideal instance of publishing prices, but it is only an illusion in cases where the published fares system is very elaborate. Only a handful of initiates will then be capable of sorting through the maze of information provided. This is the situation wherever yield management, that is, instant adjustment of prices to demand, and market segmentation are the rule, in other words where there are many complex fares and rates which fluctuate frequently in response to changes in the conditions governing demand. Examples are air passenger and rail freight transport.

A second reason, usually encountered in goods transport, is that of secrecy. In this case prices are not known to others than the contracting parties. Rival operators learn of them through leaks, by word of mouth or by deduction. Knowledge of market strains travels quickly, however; it is based less on prices than on such other trade criteria as delivery times or the volume of transport services on offer to shippers.

2.5   Other Channels of Competition

Traditional textbooks allow the market outcome to be defined by one quantity and one price. Things are much more complicated, however, especially in transport, as suppliers make a wide use of price discrimination and compete on many other factors than price. The three kinds of price discrimination usually distinguished in literature (see, for instance, Tirole, 1988) all occur in transport.

For instance, railway operators use first-degree discrimination (that is, perfect discrimination: each customer is charged the maximum price he can pay) towards big shippers: they know the willingness to pay of each of them (usually, it is roughly the cost of the alternative mode of transport, in a pure Bertrand competition manner). Furthermore, they can set a perfectly personalized price for each of them.

Second-degree price discrimination is the situation where customers can be differentiated using some objective parameter, for instance, the age of the customer, or the day of the trip, or the length of the trip. Classically, the best device is then for the supplier to use Ramsey–Boiteux prices; this device is widely used in passenger transport.[3]

Third-degree price discrimination is the situation where there are several types of users, for instance frequent or 'captive' users versus infrequent or 'non-captive' users. The firm cannot distinguish between them by means of any kind of objective criterion, but it can offer several kinds of package, for instance, package and unit tickets. This type of behaviour by the supplier, which leads to reduced fares for large quantities, is also widely used in transport, both that of passengers and that of goods. Third-degree discrimination, when applied to quality and comfort, also provides a clear explanation of the existence of first and second class in rail and in air transport.

Competition is also channelled through other factors, for instance, time of departure or arrival, frequency, size of network or quality of service. Problems of competition through time of departure and size of network have been studied both on a theoretical and an experimental level.

On a theoretical level, Encaoua and Perrot (1992) analyse the equilibrium conditions of a market formed by several companies operating on a network. Their cost functions present economies of scale and of scope (see Chapter 2, Section 2). Demand is fixed for each pair of origins and destinations ('O–D pair') and users choose the company according to price, duration of trip and connecting costs. The competition between operators is a two-stage game: first they set the network on which each of them operates, then they compete in price. The authors show that several equilibria exist, one of them being also a collective optimum.[4]

Knowledge on time competition (that is, the choice of a time schedule for its services by each of the competing firms) began with Farrell and Saloner (1987) and the results have been synthesized by Perrot (1993). The general result of the model is that when two companies having networks of different size compete in time coordination:

1. the company which has the smallest network always gains from time schedule compatibility;
2. the company which has the largest network always gains less from compatibility (it may even lose in some cases); and
3. customers always gain from compatibility.

As for quality of service, we have previously seen that, when users each have a different willingness to pay, the operator can benefit from the situation by offering several (usually two) levels of quality at different prices. In the other situation where the willingness to pay is similar among users, it can easily be seen that the supplier supplies the optimal quality provided that the demand has the expression:

$$q = q(p + a\theta), \tag{5.4}$$

a being a constant and θ being the quality of service level. Profit is then:

$$\Pi = pqC(q,\theta), \tag{5.5}$$

where $C(q,\theta)$ is the cost function of the firm. Collective surplus is:

$$CS = \int_0^q p(u,\theta)du C(q,\theta), \quad (u = \text{individual utility}). \tag{5.6}$$

Π is maximum when:

$$q\frac{\partial p}{\partial q} - \frac{\partial C}{\partial \theta} = 0. \tag{5.7}$$

CS is maximum when:

$$\int_0^q \frac{\partial p}{\partial \theta} du \frac{\partial C}{\partial \theta} = 0. \tag{5.8}$$

Both are equal if $\partial p/\partial\theta$ is constant, which means that:

$$p = f(q + a\theta). \tag{5.9}$$

Regarding competition in terms of timetables and frequency of service on given routes, Quinet (1991) has shown that monopoly situations, and to a lesser extent competition, usually lead to less social welfare than cooperation, and that competition is often unstable.

2.6 The Nature of the Transport Market – in Conclusion

By and large, transport operates in a market system far removed from the ideal market model, whereby a well-defined good has its price fixed by the play of supply and demand. Instead of one single market, there are many. However, these are interlinked on the demand side by the possibility of substitution (for example, between modes), and on the supply side by the fact that inputs can switch from one market to another and that costs of different products are inter-related. The system by which prices are formed and published is far from being as pure and transparent as it would be under ideal market conditions. Furthermore, operators largely use price discrimination and compete on many other fields than price, and especially on departure time and quality of service.

3   HOW THE TRANSPORT MARKET OPERATES

We shall now consider how transport markets operate, a subject of vital importance both to the strategies of private companies and to government economic policy. Let us try to answer the following four questions:

1. Where do transport markets locate in the range between monopoly and competition?
2. Are transport markets stable or unstable?
3. How and why do public authorities intervene?
4. How does competition work?

3.1 Between Monopoly and Competition

Chapter 2 has analysed the cost function of transport firms, and the situation where economies of scale and scope exist. From these results it is possible to compile Table 5.2, which is of course approximate and valid mainly for areas the size of Europe. From the table it is clear that the most frequent situation is oligopoly. A question is then 'what kind of oligopoly?'.

Table 5.2   Transport market structures

	Monopoly	Oligopoly	Competition
Rail	X		
Road goods transport		X	X
Road passenger transport			
Regular services	X		
Chartered services		X	
Inland waterway transport			
Dumb barge convoys		X	
Powered craft			X
Air			
Intracontinental	X		
Intercontinental		X	
Sea			
Liner traffic	X	X	
Tramp traffic			X

Source: Quinet (1990)

The essential decision parameters are prices and not quantities. This point is specially clear for the customer. Then it would be rational to think that competition is of the Bertrand type and so is of a cut-throat nature.[5] This happens in some markets, such as road goods transport, where there is not much product differentiation and no problem of capacity (trucks can move easily). But in many other situations milder forms of competition appear, through product differentiation (for instance, by logistic services in goods transport) and capacity constraints (in air transport). The result is that the competition is more often of the Cournot type.[6] This result is confirmed by econometric analyses (see, for example, Brander and Zhang, 1993), which show that the reaction function of competitors – the way their price reacts to changes in the price of the other firm) exhibits either collusion or Cournot competition characteristics.

In the past a monopoly has been considered, in many situations, as rather innocuous, due to its contestability features. As may be known, a contestable market may be defined as a market where entry and exit are easy, quick and cost free (Baumol et al., 1982). In such a market, a monopolist or an oligopolist cannot profiteer, as a rival could step in, win customers by offering slightly lower prices and then withdraw if the former counterattacked.

The contestability of a market depends on several factors, such as client mobility, price flexibility and absence of entry or exit barriers. Do clients switch easily among suppliers according to the commercial policy of the latter?

Passengers certainly do, but goods forwarders tend to be less mobile, mainly because of the increasingly frequent practices of long-term contracts, and the impact of logistics which tighten the links between forwarders and shippers.

Contestability also depends on the flexibility of prices. If these can be adjusted without difficulty, an established firm can easily hold off the trade offensive of a new competitor and the contestability of the market will be correspondingly reduced. Price flexibility varies according to the mode and type of transport. In the case of maritime conferences – or of 'alliances' – tariffs can be changed only with the agreement of all partners to the conference, which can be a cumbersome and slow process. On the other hand, some air carriers continually change their rates in prompt response to steps taken by their competitors.

The absence of entry and exit barriers is the main feature of a contestable market. Where barriers exist, potential competitors either are completely excluded or are discouraged from entering the market. The chief barrier is non-recoverable outlay, that is, expenditure needed to enter the market but which cannot be recovered on leaving it, a case in point being fixed infrastructure that cannot be re-sold easily. By and large, transport operations involve only a limited amount of non-recoverable outlay. Investment in equipment can mostly be recovered since there are markets for second-hand lorries, aircraft and ships just as for cars. Where the firm entering the market already exists, moreover, or where a firm intends simply to operate a new route, non-recoverable outlay is reduced.

The public authorities may raise artificial barriers of different kinds, mostly to entry: by granting a firm an operating monopoly; and by setting quotas or imposing permit requirements.

On the other hand, the authorities may remove barriers to entry or exit by awarding, for example, vessel-scrapping grants in waterway transport or investment incentive payments in shipbuilding. More subtle barriers may exist on the technical and organizational side, such as requirements relating to logistical services, computerized data transmission systems and airport congestion. Logistical services – storage, packing – were introduced in the mid-1970s when a demand economy supplanted the supply economy. Firms which can provide these services have a competitive edge where the shipper is concerned and therefore have an advantage over rivals. Logistical services are of course closely bound up with the introduction of systems for transmitting and processing data regarding goods forwarded. Computerization, which is the backbone of data transmission and processing, is therefore itself a barrier to entry in that it gives rise to discrimination between firms which have access to computer networks and those which do not.

A similar situation is found in air passenger transport as regards computerized booking systems. Only a small number of competing systems exist, and these are controlled by a few large airlines or by a few groupings of airlines.[7] The systems' value lies in their broad scope, so they form a barrier to entry controlled by the airlines running them.

One final example of a barrier to entry is the natural or organized scarcity of infrastructure such as air terminals. When an airline has its own terminal, competitors may have difficulty in obtaining facilities, thus coming up against a barrier to entry. Reversely, the goods transport market is highly contestable, in so far as freight rates are very close to the costs.

On the whole, it seems that contestability is not so frequent now as it was thought about ten years ago (Borenstein, 1992). The main reasons are that incumbent firms are able to devise prompt answers to the entrant (through, for instance, yield management), that they have developed fidelity practices (for instance, frequent flyer programmes), and that it appears that costs of entry and exit are not zero.

3.2   Market Stability and Sustainability

Market stability, defined as the sustainability of a given level of prices, is a major concern for government and the private sector. The fact that stability is a matter of particular concern in the transport sector may be seen by one of the few series of transport prices for which detailed and reliable statistics are available, namely those of maritime oil freight (Bauchet, 1991) (see Figure 5.3).

Stability may be analysed by examining in turn the supply and demand sides of the transport market. Expressed simply, an industry – let us say a monopoly – is said to be sustainable if a potential competitor cannot take up some or all of the demand by undercutting the prices set by the monopolist. Broadly speaking, sustainability is equivalent to stability, essentially seen as the maintenance of steady prices. Unsustainability is relatively common. We may take the example of a monopoly which produces a single product. As may be seen from Figure 5.4, unsustainability occurs in the rising part of the average cost curve. A monopoly is the most advantageous form of organizing production for the community. But the monopolist's market would be broken by a competitor who served only a part of the market at a price lying between p_0 and p_m.

The same would apply to oligopolies in the falling or rising segments of the average cost curve for the sector. As with a monopoly, unsustainability occurs when capacity is not, or cannot be, geared to the volume of demand. It is obviously very difficult to determine whether these conclusions are corroborated by any particular real life situation, especially as Figure 5.4 relates to an enterprise producing a single product. In practice, enterprises tend to produce more than one product. This makes analysis more difficult; the calculations for

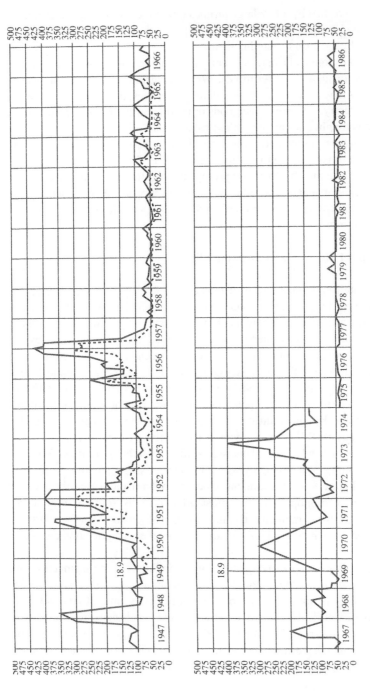

Source: Bauchet (1991).

Figure 5.3   Trends in maritime oil freight (tankers)

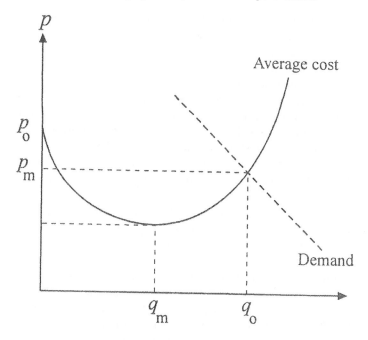

Figure 5.4   Unsustainability

determining a monopoly's sustainability become much more complicated and even harder to verify.

Where there is cross-subsidization, a monopoly is not sustainable. In the transport sector, cross-subsidization has several features:

- cross-subsidization in space, as between profitable trunk rail routes and money-losing branch lines; or, in the case of urban transport fares, the balance struck between the profits made on central city services and the losses incurred by services in outlying areas;
- cross-subsidization in time: the difference between peak-hour and off-peak fares, as evidenced by urban or rail passenger ticket prices, is usually much smaller than the corresponding difference in cost.

Cross-subsidization, as mentioned above, is usually practised by the public authorities, who find it a convenient way of financing the public service obligations they impose on carriers: serving sparsely populated areas, ensuring transport regardless of the level of demand, application of uniform prices in time and space. To offset these constraints, the authorities must in all logic protect the monopoly from the weakness induced by the obligations. Otherwise, and this is where its unsustainability lies, they expose the monopoly to 'creaming off' by smart competitors who will take the most profitable segment of the clientele by offering lower prices.

The above kinds of unsustainability are static, but there are others of a dynamic nature which may be produced by shifts in demand. In the case of a contestable monopoly, a steady rise in demand may lead to instability. At a given moment, the monopoly operates with a certain stock of capital equipment. But, as time goes on, this stock will be inadequate to cope with rising demand. A competitor can then move in with a superior stock of equipment, satisfy the demand at a lower cost and drive out the first monopoly, with a consequent loss of efficiency. The public authorities are obliged therefore to protect the first monopoly.

Technical change may produce the same effect, with demand remaining constant. Changes in technology may render existing equipment obsolete so that the monopoly operating with it is exposed to competition from a new operator using more modern equipment at a lower cost. But effects like these, linked to increased demand or technical progress, are less common in the transport sector than situations in which the average production cost is higher than the minimum average cost. These, as we have seen, are unsustainable situations in which the monopoly can be bested by new arrivals who serve only part of the market (this point can also be approached through game theory and core existence; see Button (1996) for an application to air transport competition).

What are the cases in which the average production cost can be higher than the minimum average cost? In the transport sector, this situation can arise as a result of a number of factors.

1. *Cyclical fluctuations*, notably in periods of crisis: equipment – here meaning vehicles – is geared in size and number to requirements in a 'normal' economic climate. But at a time of crisis, capacity cannot be reduced promptly owing to the long operating life of equipment, ships and aircraft for example, and the surplus capacity entailed can persist for a considerable length of time.
2. *Seasonal fluctuations*: transport flows are subject to wide seasonal variations. The amount of equipment needed is calculated to cope with peak periods, but outside of these periods the surplus capacity has the same effects as those described above.
3. *Empty return runs*: this particular example of imbalances between capacity and demand is very common in road haulage. The road haulier carrying a load from town A to town B will enter the transport market in B to avoid returning empty to A, and will thus increase the total capacity of B's market. Accordingly, B's capacity is clearly determined by chance as a result of a process that is not correlative with the determination of demand.

Where there is a great deal of empty return traffic, there is usually a disparity between transport capacity and transport demand which is attributable to chance and will lead to fluctuations in freight rates, keen competition for contracts in the event of surplus capacity, cartel-type agreements and the like.

4. By and large, as set out under 1. and 2. above, the transport sector suffers from chronic surplus capacity since it is equipped to meet peak traffic needs and is therefore overequipped at other times. Operators do not seek to reduce capacity for seasonal troughs and, in the event of a crisis, are unable to do so because of the long operating life of their equipment. This inflexibility of supply has its counterpart in inflexibility of demand, which is inelastic, at any rate where freight transport is concerned. Quite independently of the theory of sustainability and its applications, here we have conditions whereby equilibrium, though attained at each particular instant, differs considerably from one moment to the next, as may be seen from Figure 5.5.

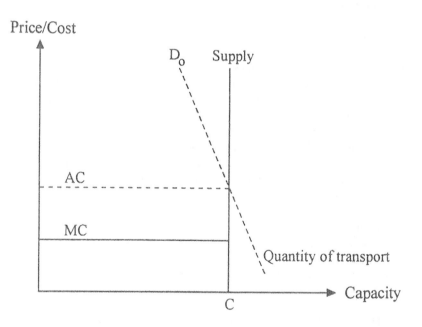

Figure 5.5   Market instability

Demand fluctuates around a mean point D_0 owing to seasonal or cyclical variations. Supply is shown in simplified form by the horizontal segment MC, which corresponds to the marginal cost of transport (when demand is inadequate, carriers cover variable costs and write down some of their fixed costs by selling at or slightly above the marginal cost), and by the vertical with capacity on the x-axis. In a free market, the mean financial equilibrium of enterprises requires that capacity C be determined in such a way that the break-even price – the point where the supply and demand curves intersect – is equal to the average cost AC.

The structure of the graph shows that slight changes in installed capacity (empty return runs, breakdowns and so on) or in demand (seasonal variations, crises) will produce far greater changes in the break-even price and be a source of endemic instability in the market, as evidenced by trends in maritime freight. On the whole, transport markets are by no means stable. On many of them the instability of demand in conjunction with the inflexibility of supply and the frequent occurrence of surplus capacity can lead to sharp price fluctuations. Moreover, where certain activities and types of tariff structure, such as those connected with cross-subsidization, are concerned, the market cannot be sustained, that is, its equilibrium may be upset by an entrant with a 'creaming off' approach.

3.3 Role of Public Intervention

How and why do public authorities intervene? Risks of instability and imperfect competition are, together with public service obligations, reasons for the public authorities to intervene in transport markets.[8] As will be argued much more extensively in Chapter 9 ('Transport policy') this intervention has taken various forms and intensities throughout the years. A decade ago, it was very strong. In every country, private markets were tightly regulated: entry, prices, quantities were submitted to strict regulations, as well as social and technical regulations. Many monopolies were publicly owned, others were controlled and protected by public authorities. Now markets have been almost fully deregulated in all countries. In Europe, full competition has been introduced in air transport. Freight transport by road and by inland waterways has been fully deregulated, and public authorities intervene just for safety and environmental reasons. Public intervention remains important in rail transport and in regular road passenger transport, though the public authorities try in almost every country to decrease their intervention.

3.4 How Does Competition Work?

The experiences of deregulation show that competition is difficult to set up. This result is partly due to economies of scale, scope and network. It is also due to the actions of the incumbent firms, and also in many cases to the failure of public authorities (see also Chapter 9), and to the phenomenon of capture which more or less happens.[9]

Deregulation in air transport (USA) and in road passenger transport (USA, UK) led to some kind of competition in the beginning (new entrants, mergers, bankruptcies), and also to restructuring with the appearance, in air transport, of the hub-and-spoke form. But eventually many new entrants or former operators were eliminated, and a new oligopolistic structure appeared, where firms benefit from some market power: monopolistic position on a hub, control of information to the customer, and control of scarce resources such as slots or terminals. Public authorities have generally had little success in their attempts to eliminate those distortions in the competitive process.

In rail transport, full competition has so far appeared nowhere, and it does not seem that it will appear anywhere. Competition just exists in the form of fringe competition, yardstick competition, or competition for the market. In this last situation many problems appear, related to the length of the franchise (especially when there are specific assets), to the renewal of franchise (a situation where the incumbent has many advantages), and also to the set-up and monitoring of the contract (asymmetry of information, incentives, and so on).

4   CONCLUSION

To sum up, the concept of transport markets would seem to cover a complex set of realities. Much of the transport sector is not subject to regulation by market forces and falls directly or indirectly within the sphere of regulation by the public authorities. There is not one market but a host of small markets, all interrelated either by virtue of the fact that some of them share a common source of supply, which may therefore switch from one market to another within the same category, or by similarities in demand as, for example, when the demand may be catered for by interchangeable services offered by different modes of transport.

These markets are far from perfect. Quite aside from methods of determining prices, there are many external factors and strong evidence of monopolistic or oligopolistic tendencies, due both to the features of the cost functions and to the strategic actions of the firms. Whereas some markets, such as road haulage, are highly contestable, others involving infrastructure are not, because the contestability is often eroded by firms seeking to create customer loyalty or to set up barriers to entry. Competition based on quality (for example, service frequency, number of routes) generates effects that are not easy to analyse and its consequences in terms of social welfare are unclear. There are strong tendencies towards instability. To set up fair and efficient competition is a difficult task. The transport markets operate far from perfectly, thus illustrating the generally accepted fact that regulation by market forces is not a law of nature but something to be striven for each day.

NOTES

1. Those operators do not hold any physical assets. They merely play the role of go-between, renting capacities on vessels and selling them to forwarders or shippers.
2. For instance, an auxiliary induces a driver to establish himself as a (small) road transport operator; the auxiliary gives the driver a loan and provides him with freight transport which the auxiliary has obtained from the shippers with whom he is associated.
3. In Ramsey–Boiteux prices, the mark-up (that is, the ratio: {price less marginal cost}/price) is inversely proportionate to demand elasticities.
4. Nash equilibria, that is, situations where no player regrets his choice, given the other's choice.
5. In Bertrand duopoly the decision variables are prices. The customers will buy from the firm whose price is the lowest. It can be shown that, under commonly admitted assumptions, at the market equilibrium the price is equal to the cost of the less efficient firm.
6. In Cournot duopoly, the decision variables are quantities. The price is fixed by the market mechanism in such a way that at that price the market is cleared and all the quantities supplied are bought by the customers. It can be shown that in Cournot duopoly, firms make a profit which is intermediate between the monopoly profit and the competition profit (which is zero).
7. For instance, in the United States the SABRE system has been developed by American Airlines and the APOLLO system by United Airlines. In Europe, Air France, Iberia and Lufthansa together operate a system called AMADEUS, while Alitalia, British Airways, KLM and Swissair founded the system GALILEO.
8. Examples of public service obligations are: uniform tariffs not linked to costs (universal service); obligation to run unprofitable services; and prohibition of tariff differentiation.
9. The mechanism of capture is that through which the regulator is convinced by the thesis and opinions of the firm he has to regulate, and for which he becomes its advocate.

REFERENCES

Bauchet, P. (1991), *Le Transport International dans l'Economie Mondiale* (International transport in the world economy), Paris: Economica.

Baumol, W.J., J.C. Panzar and R.D. Willig (1982), *Constestable Markets and the Theory of Industry Structure*, New York: Harcourt Brace Jovanovitch.

Borenstein, S. (1992), 'The evolution of US Airline competition', *Journal of Economic Perspectives*, **6**, 45–73.

Brander, J. and A. Zhang (1993), 'Dynamic oligopoly behaviour in the airline industry', *International Journal of Industrial Organization*, **11**, 407–35.

Button, K. (1996), 'Liberalising European aviation: is there an empty core problem?', *Journal of Transport Economics and Policy*, **30**, 275–91.

Encaoua, D. and A. Perrot (1992), *Concurrence et coopération dans le transport aérien en Europe* (Competition and cooperation in European air transport), Report for the EC, Paris: Université de Paris II.

Farrell, J. and G. Saloner (1987), 'Competition, compatibility and standards: the economies of horses, penguins and lemmings', in L. Gabel (ed.), *Product Standardization and Competitive Strategy*, Amsterdam: North-Holland.

Julien, H. and O. Morellet (1990), *MATISSE*, Report 129, Paris: INRETS (Institut National de Recherche sur les Transports et leur Sécurité).

Nero, G. (1996), 'A structural model of intra European Union duopoly airline competition', *Journal of Transport Economics and Policy*, **30**, 137–56.

Perrot, A. (1993), 'Compatibility, networks and competition a review of recent advances', *Transportation Science*, **27**, 62–72.

Quinet, E. (1990), *Analyse Economique des Transports* (Economic analysis of transport), Paris: Presses Universitaires de France.
Quinet, E. (1991), 'Organisational structure of public transport and assessment of schedules', *Transport Planning and Technology*, **16**, 145–53.
Tirole, J. (1988), *The Theory of Industrial Organization*, Cambridge, MA: MIT Press.
Walras, L. (1874), *Eléments d'Economie Politique Pure* (Elements of pure political economy), Paris: Librairie Générale de Droit et de Jurisprudence, reprinted 1976.

PART III

Infrastructure

6. Transport infrastructure: the investment problem

Jan Owen Jansson

1 DEFINITION OF TRANSPORT INFRASTRUCTURE

'Infra' means (in Latin) 'situated below', and transport infrastructure is, accordingly, in the first place roads for cars, buses and trucks, and rails for trains. Natural transport infrastructure is water and air. Inland waterways often require heavy investments in canals and locks, but also sea transport and air transport require manmade supplements – navigational aids, traffic control devices and so on – to make complete fairways and airways.

Freight transport vehicles need special infrastructure as well as elaborate gear for loading and unloading. This is obviously less important in passenger transport. Certain facilities for boarding and alighting are required for different modes of public transport, whereas a private car can take on or let go a passenger almost anywhere at the roadside. Somewhat inadequately, these parts of the transport infrastructure are called 'terminals', as if they were ends of journeys. From the point of view of a traveller or shipper, terminals are places where a change of mode of transport is made.

Idle transport vehicles have to be put somewhere where they are out of the way and/or safe. Again, there is no good collective name for this third part of the transport infrastructure. It is really important for just one type of vehicle, the private car, because cars are idle more than 90 per cent of the day on average. Therefore 'parking facilities' will do as the general term.

It can be argued that 'transport infrastructure' should also include pipelines for oil transport, underground pipes for transport of water and so on, and possibly electric powerlines and telecommunication networks, too. The following discussion is confined to the items mentioned above, not because such a narrow definition is inherently superior, but because the subject of transport economics has traditionally been confined to transport of persons and material goods. An extension of the subject in the way hinted at above is long overdue, but this chapter is not the proper place for such an enlargement.[1]

2   PURPOSE AND PLAN OF THE CHAPTER

This chapter deals with investment in transport infrastructure (TI), both non-urban and urban. The purpose is to discuss the theory and practice of investment appraisal in this field, taking account of the actual TI development in the postwar period in Western Europe. The chapter is organized in the following way: first, the salient features of the product 'TI services' are described (Section 3). Then the postwar development of the main type of transport infrastructure, that is, the road network, is briefly sketched (Section 4). This serves as a background to the main topic of the chapter, which is investment appraisal by cost–benefit analysis (Sections 5–7). Section 5 presents 'classical' cost–benefit analysis of non-urban road investment, and Section 6 deals with the first necessary mod-ification of the classical approach in the case of significant intermodal competition. The recent boom in railway investment is the main event calling for a new look at the topic. Schematic models are outlined both of railway investment and road investment in the long-distance, intercity travel market, where the modal split between road, rail and air is the main issue for the future.

Section 7 discusses the very substantial modifications of the classical model for investment appraisal required when it comes to urban transport systems, and Section 8 concludes the chapter.

The discussion of investment criteria needs a solid basis of facts about the fundamental characteristics of the cost of, and demand for transport infra-structure, which follows immediately below.

3   GENERAL CHARACTERISTICS OF TRANSPORT
INFRASTRUCTURE

3.1   Organizational Disintegration of the Natural Production Function

TI is the fixed capital of transport systems. With the main exception of traditional railway transport companies, transport firms do not own the fixed capital used in the production process, that is the transport infrastructure, but acquire TI services on a 'pay as you go' basis. The reason for this apparent oddity is, of course, that sharing the fixed capital with others is normally more economical than acquiring the required pieces of transport infrastructure for one's own exclusive use.

The organizational disintegration of the essential factors of production typical of transport systems is analytically a little confusing, because the scope of the analysis had better be the 'natural' production function rather than set by the formal limits of the organization concerned, providing TI services.

3.2   TI Service User Costs are Dominant in the Total Transport System Costs

We are here concerned with optimal investment and optimal use of transport infrastructure. It would be unnatural, however, to confine the analysis to just the plants producing 'TI services'. The 'natural' production function is a transport system consisting of transport vehicles, and transport infrastructure – bearers of moving vehicles, terminals for change of mode of transport, and parking facilities for idle vehicles – producing a traffic flow, or throughput of goods so far as freight terminals are concerned. Including the external costs, the corresponding total transport system costs (*TC*) are conveniently divided into three parts:

$$TC = TC_{prod} + TC_{user} + TC_{ext}. \tag{6.1}$$

Transport users both demand the services provided and supply some essential inputs to complete door-to-door transport chains by driving their own vehicles, or walking, waiting, and riding on public transport vehicles. In transport demand analysis the translation of quality of service into user time cost in order to obtain a 'generalized cost' in place of just the monetary price has been standard practice for several decades. So far as investment appraisal for transport infrastructure is concerned, the user inputs in the production of transport services (that is, driver/passenger time, vehicle operating costs including fuel consumption, and transport system internal accident costs) can be handled in the same way as different producer inputs.

The external (to the transport system) costs comprise all possible costs falling on 'third parties', that is, the rest of society. It is not always obvious where the line should be drawn between TI users and external subjects in the case where the transport infrastructures of different transport systems partly overlap.

In terms of total transport system cost share, transport infrastructure comes third in importance. Considerably greater are the user time costs and capital and running costs of the transport vehicles. This means for all kinds of transport infrastructure that in optimization of facility design, maintenance policy and so on, a narrow limitation to the producer costs could be very misleading.

The external costs of third parties are very important in some cases: for example, the environmental damage that would be caused by a new road, railway, or airport is often critical for the possibility of expanding the capacity of the transport system, especially in urban areas.

The cost of the environmental damage is often larger than the sum of the costs of measurable externalities such as air pollution and noise. The residual can be described as loss of 'beauty, comfort and security'. It is caused by the new piece of transport infrastructure itself rather than just the new traffic on it.

The term 'encroachment cost' is used in this and the following chapter to mark the existence and importance of some less measurable costs of transport production.

An illustration from the road transport sector of the total cost structure is given in Figure 6.1. As is seen, for the transport produced on the state-owned road network in Sweden, the total user costs of time, vehicles and traffic accidents are some ten times greater than the total road expenditure, of which repair and maintenance make up the lion's share. Road users also pay taxes on motor vehicles and fuel, which together outstrip total road expenditure by a factor of four.

This cost structure is representative of other transport systems in so far as the user costs are dominant, but stands out by the high proportion of accident costs. In view of the fact that the road transport volume constitutes some 80 per cent of total transport – personal and freight – it is apparent that (the lack of) road safety is of utmost concern.

The substantial excess of tax revenue over expenditure on roads is unheard of for the infrastructure of other modes of transport. The economic justification for the 'overcharging' of road users has to do with the structure of the external costs, and traffic congestion. This is a main topic of Chapter 7. Let it only be said at this stage, that the proven low elasticity of demand is probably a contributory explanation of why the strict earmarking of revenue from taxes on

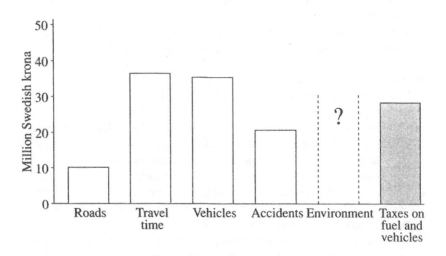

Figure 6.1   Cost components in the total costs of road transport on the Swedish state-owned road network, 1990

motor cars and fuel for road finance has been abandoned in most countries, with the notable exceptions of Japan and the USA.

3.3 The Nature of the Product Makes Production under Constant Returns to Scale Atypical

The top diagram in Figure 6.2 gives the *general* shape of the long-run total cost (LRTC) as a function of the output volume (Q) for *all* kinds of products, goods as well as services, according to elementary production and cost theory (just about as axiomatic as the notion that demand falls when the price rises). Initially increasing returns to scale prevail, which means that the LRTC increases degressively with respect to Q. After that a relatively wide interval follows, where basically constant returns to scale apply, but sooner or later decreasing returns to scale set in, and the LRTC will increase progressively with respect to Q.

Needless to say, the course and relative extent of the three cost–output intervals can vary widely between different types of products. The general feature is that all three intervals exist for all products.

Observations in the third output interval are difficult to make in reality, because a production plant with such a large capacity is a failure: the same output could be produced at a lower cost per unit of output by two plants, each one with half the capacity. Real observations could be expected to be rare also in the first output interval for a similar reason, at least as far as manufacturing

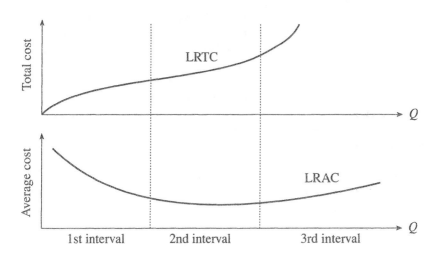

Figure 6.2   General shape of long-run total and average costs defines three cost–output intervals

industry is concerned. Small firms, or rather production at low-capacity plants of storable and transportable goods, could not exist, if it is possible to produce such goods for substantially lower average costs at plants with higher capacity. Engineering cost studies of long-run cost and output relationships, which examine technically possible, not necessarily observable, production solutions, and consider plants of widely differing capacities representing different technologies, regularly arrive at distinctly L-shaped average cost curves.[2] There is ample evidence in the engineering cost literature that small-scale production is often very uneconomic compared to large-scale production.[3]

Mainstream microeconomics is focused on the second cost–output interval, because it is assumed that most industrial production takes place in this interval. When discussing TI services, on the other hand, one should focus on all three intervals, not least on the first interval, because in terms of the number of plants, this is the most frequent one. Why this is so can be explained as follows.

TI services have the common characteristics of most services, that is they are non-storable and non-transportable, and are in addition 'spatially unique' in the sense that transport between C and D is normally not a substitute for transport between A and B.[4] This means that the number of separate, potential markets for TI services is very great indeed, which in turn means that the average market size is very small in terms of the demand base (see also Chapter 5, Section 2, 'Characteristics of transport markets').

The qualification 'potential' is important. Bearing in mind the spatially unique character of transport demand, it can be argued that the most common market form as regards TI services is *apoly*, that is, there is no supply at all. The routes concerned are too thin or, in other words, the average TI cost would be too high for a direct road or railway connection. As far as air transport is concerned, the population of most towns, let alone villages and hamlets, is too small for an airport of its own, which is an expression of the same small-scale diseconomies.

3.4 The Root Cause of Small-scale Diseconomies

Factor indivisibility and the law of large numbers make for pronounced small-scale diseconomics in the production of non-storable services provided at departmentalized facilities. The standard multichannel queuing model can be used for predicting to what extent queuing time depends on the rate of capacity utilization and the number of service stations of the facility. Since this model is mathematically quite involved, it is helpful to derive the steady-state mean queuing time in two steps.

The facility consists of n identical service stations. With random arrivals, let p be the probability that an arrival will find all channels occupied, s is the service time, and Φ is the occupancy rate. The mean queuing time can then be written as

$$q = \frac{s}{n(1-\Phi)}\, p. \tag{6.2}$$

The left-hand factor represents the expected queuing time for those customers who actually meet with a delay, which is inversely proportional to n. The probability that a delay occurs, p, is a function of n and F. As n is increasing, p will continuously decrease, given the occupancy rate. This function is rather complicated, and not spelled out here (see, for example, Saaty, 1961).

From numerical simulations it is clear that the combined effect of these two factors makes the advantages of multichannel service facilities truly remarkable. A reflection of this relationship is given by the series of numbers in Table 6.1. Keeping the quality of service constant by fixing the expected queuing time per arrival at a given level – a fifth of the service time in the numerical example – the required rates of capacity utilization for facilities of successively more service stations are as shown.

Table 6.1   Possible rates of capacity utilization for maintaining a given quality of service (constant expected queuing time) at a departmentalized facility

Number of service stations	Rate of capacity utilization
1	0.20
2	0.43
3	0.57
4	0.65
5	0.70
6	0.73
7	0.76
8	0.78
9	0.80
10	0.82
11	0.83
12	0.84
13	0.85
14	0.86
15	0.87

Queuing models are a standard analytical tool among other things for seaport capacity optimization. How does the long-run cost and output relationship look in practice? Econometric cross-section studies of seaport cost functions to verify the theoretical conjecture of pronounced economies of plant size are difficult, because of the very heterogeneous cargo handled in the different ports to be compared. Since a main source of the economies is expected to be that much higher rates of capacity utilization could be obtained in large than in small ports, a measurable proxy for the scale economies to focus on could be the rate of capacity utilization of the main capital resources such as berths, cranes and storage space, as well as permanently employed labour. Such a study was made of 35 Swedish seaports in the middle of the 1970s (Jansson and Rydén, 1979) and the result was that the elasticity of the rate of capacity utilization with respect to the resource stock concerned (≈ number of service stations) was to be found in a range from 0.5 to 0.9 for different resources. This implies substantial economies of scale.

Long-run airport cost functions are more tractable so far as the dominant passenger business is concerned, because of the homogeneity of the units of output. The airport owner's total cost per passenger for the 24 primary airports in Sweden illustrates the magnitude of the small-scale diseconomies in that sector. The impression given by Figure 6.3 is a little distorted by a systematic cost difference between two categories of airport – partly military and/or municipality-owned versus state-owned airports. By including an appropriate dummy variable in the regression of average airport cost on passenger volume the main message is very clear: airports in the range of 100 000–200 000 passengers per

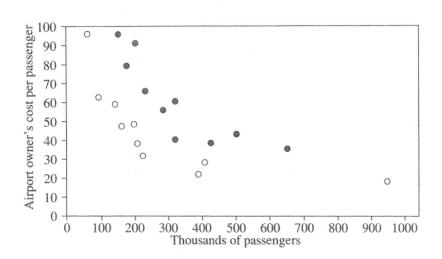

Source: Flygplatsutredningen (1990, p. 55).

Figure 6.3   Airport cost per passenger against passenger volume

year are some five times more costly than airports serving one million passengers. A similar cost picture for British regional airports is given by Doganis and Thompson (1975).

By international standards one million passengers per year is not a large volume. There are three Swedish airports handling traffic volumes exceeding that limit; they did not fit into the diagram of Figure 6.3, especially not Arlanda, the biggest, which handles 15 times more passengers than the biggest airport represented in the diagram. Big airports have a more diversified line of products than small airports. It is more difficult to calculate a single, comparable unit cost; it seems, however, that all three 'outliers' are at the cost level of the two airports with the lowest cost in the diagram.

4 ROAD INVESTMENT IN THE CAR AGE

When it comes to common facilities like roads, the highway engineering manuals indicate very marked diseconomies of small-scale operations, too. From the experience of the build-up of the road network in the postwar period of motorization, it seems that the scale economies are largely exhausted in the traffic volume range where motorway standards are justified. Since topography and the condition of the soil can differ greatly from one region to another, the variability in construction costs is quite significant. The figures in Table 6.2 from the Swedish National Road Administration are rough averages: within each class of road, capital costs that are twice as high per kilometre, or only half the value given, are not rare.

Table 6.2   Road capital and running costs for roads of optimal design (€ per 100 passenger-car-equivalent-km, 1996 price level)

Traffic flow per day	Cross-section (paved width in metres)	Speed limit (km/h)	Mean speed (km/h)	Road costs per traffic unit
400	Two lanes $(5 + 2 \times 0.25)$	70	69	15
1 350	Two lanes $(6 + 2 \times 0.25)$	90	78	6
7 000	Two lanes $(7 + 2 \times 0.5)$	90	83	2
14 500	Two lanes $(7 + 2 \times 3)$	90	87	1.4
27 000	Four lanes	90	90	1.3
40 000	Motorway	110	96	1.3

Sources: Statens Vägverk (1978); Vägverket (1996).

In Small (1992), some empirical results of returns to scale in road building are surveyed. The traffic volume range studied in the included works corresponds to the range of the three highest flow figures of Table 6.1, and beyond, and as the cost figures above indicate, the economies of traffic volume seem to be almost exhausted in that range.

4.1 Road Cost Reduction and Quality Improvement Have Walked Hand in Hand

In addition to the pronounced initial economies of traffic volume in the road costs come the road-user cost savings due to the higher quality of service that goes with successive road upgrading as the traffic volume increases. Time cost savings are partly achieved by road shortening – low-volume roads have to go round natural obstacles in order that building costs per traffic unit do not run away – and partly by road widening and alignment improvements, which allow higher speeds without increasing the accident risks. In fact the accident cost per unit of traffic falls with higher road standards in spite of increasing speed, which is illustrated in Table 6.3 (see below). The only offsetting user-cost effect is that the fuel consumption per vehicle-km rises slightly with speed from a minimum in the 50–70 km/h range.

4.2 Complementarity and (Non-)substitution between Spatially Separate Links of the Road Network

A reflection of the diseconomies of small-scale operations is the markedly hierarchical structure of the road network. When it comes to transport over longer distances, it is desirable to consolidate separate transport flows originating in the same area but from strictly different places and with more or less different final destinations on to a trunk road system, rather than extending the branch and twig feeder roads all the way from origin to destination in accordance with the 'shortest distance' principle. The fact that a motorway for a traffic flow of twenty thousand vehicles per day produces road services at a fifth or less of the cost per vehicle-km of a small road designed for a thin traffic flow is obviously of basic importance for constructing a rational road network, which in principle should connect all houses in the nation to one another.

At the same time as the complementary aspect of individual links of the network is held up, it should be pointed out that individual roads are local nature monopolies in many cases. That a particular motorway produces road services at a fifth of the cost per vehicle-km of a small road between two villages in a different part of the country is of no consequence for the viability of the latter as a transport connection between the two villages. In manufacturing industries, on the other hand, the average costs of all plants and/or firms of a particular industry making easily transportable goods should be more or less on the same level; a high-cost plant or firm could not survive where all plants in the industry serve the same national or global market.

4.3   Unprecedented Road Traffic Growth

The postwar period has seen a complete transformation of the transport infrastructure in Europe as an integral part of major technological change in the transport sector. During the period of motorization, which in Europe occurred in the 1950s and 1960s, the principal cause of road investments was, of course, the steady growth in car traffic, which has largely paralleled the growth in car ownership. Successively shifting demand curves to the right meant that it became profitable to move downwards along the steeply falling LRAC curve in most relations.

In the postwar period, non-urban road investments can to a large extent be characterized as replacements of existing road links, justified as socially profitable upgradings, rather than additions to the road network. Despite the fact that the postwar period has been an unprecedented road-building era, the total length of the main road network in a country like Sweden increased only by about 10 per cent in the first twenty years, and since then has not increased at all.

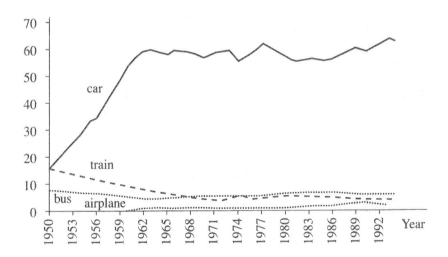

Figure 6.4   *Postwar development of travel volumes by car, train, bus and air relative to the real GNP in Sweden*

As seen in Figure 6.4, car travel volume had already caught up with train travel volume by 1950. During the period of the private car breakthrough, train travel was decreasing in absolute terms, and relative to GNP the drop was almost as dramatic as the booming car travel. The railway passenger travel development has been normalized since then, that is, train travel has developed by and large in proportion to GNP.

5   CLASSICAL COST–BENEFIT ANALYSIS OF NON-URBAN ROAD INVESTMENT

In the context of the concentration of TI investments in the road sector, cost–benefit analysis was introduced and developed as the main method for road investment prioritizing. Later, the use of cost–benefit analysis was extended to other types of TI, such as airports and seaports, and in Sweden to railway investment after the separation of rail track and train operations in 1988.

5.1   The Highway Engineering Approach: Total Social Cost Minimization

Cost–benefit analysis for non-urban road investment was quickly adopted by highway engineers when it was realized that it could be operationalized in a rather 'practical' way, which was not obvious from its theoretical, primary formulation. With the supply and demand paradigm of economics, cost–benefit analysis of transport infrastructure investment boils down to calculating the change in consumer and producer surplus as a result of an upgrading of a particular link in the road network. Since there are literally thousands of links that could be interesting to upgrade, a formidable task for road transport demand modelling looms large. In view of the fact that genuine origin– destination (O–D) road transport data are rare, and difficult to collect (due to the dominance of do-it-yourself transport in the road network, requiring no recorded transaction), a strict adherence to the theoretically ideal social surplus calculation is impossible. Fortunately, there is a reasonable proxy close to hand, which saves the trouble of estimating demand functions for thousands of O–D pairs in order to be able to calculate changes in the consumer surplus. It is enough to calculate changes in the total system costs for a given set of trips. Then no more than five to ten values of different user inputs are involved, which have to be estimated.

The crucial simplification is that road investments do not induce new traffic. The main rationale for this assumption is the clear-cut pattern of car traffic growth: only the number of cars is growing, while the trend in car use (kilometres per car) is constant. Since it is difficult to prove that road building is a significant determinant of the rate of car ownership, it is acceptable to view all new traffic as 'autonomous traffic growth'.

In the hands of highway engineers the road investment appraisal has thus turned from a very difficult task of demand-curve fitting to a relatively simple problem of selecting the investment projects that will minimize the total transport costs in the system. With a set of general values of time, a value of a 'statistical life' and so on, the main additional information required about each investment project is:

1. the existing traffic flows on the roads affected (which can be obtained from traffic counts on the roads); and
2. the change in travel time, accident risk and so on that would be achieved by the proposed road improvement. This the highway engineer can predict, and if, in addition, a traffic growth rate can be derived from a car ownership forecasting model, the total benefits are easily calculated to set against the estimated costs.

With this information the total benefits can finally be calculated to set against the estimated investment costs.

5.2 The Economist's Contribution: 'The Rule of Half'

The aforementioned 'rationale' for ignoring induced, newly generated traffic can be questioned, among other things on the ground that the apparent constancy of the annual kilometres per car is not an inherent characteristic of car use, but the result of a number of balancing forces: on one hand, car use tends to increase with increases in income, and on the other hand, the rise in the price of petrol during the 1970s and first half of the 1980s and the continued car diffusion among women and pensioners have worked to reduce total kilometres driven per car.

However, the realization that car use is generalized-cost-elastic should not ruin the attractive simplicity of classical, highway engineering investment appraisal. For economists it is easy to calculate the benefit of newly generated traffic: the present generalized cost is the minimum value of the benefit, and the previous generalized cost (which the new traffic was unprepared to pay) is the maximum value of the benefit of new traffic. The 'rule of half' is convenient when the empirical evidence of short-run demand elasticities seems robust enough to provide standard values for taking newly generated traffic into account in a rough and ready manner.

It is true that the long-run demand elasticities are more uncertain. The question is whether they are still appreciably different from the short-run ones.

Infrastructure

Looking back at the road network of 1950, which was to a considerable extent unpaved, it is obviously unreasonable to think that the radical improvements obtained by road investment up to now have not induced car traffic. Some of the total traffic growth assumed as exogenous was probably induced traffic. It is a little ironic that now, when large-scale sophisticated travel demand models, which were badly needed in the initial period of motorization, have been developed at last, the old, simplifying assumption that all traffic growth is autonomous is much more reasonable than in the early postwar period.

5.3   Benefit Components in TI Investment Calculations

Looking forward it is interesting to notice that the composition of the total benefit side of road investments seems to undergo a substantial change. In the left-hand column of Table 6.3, the percentages of the main benefit components in the aggregate benefits of all Swedish (non-urban) road investment planned for the 1990s are given. Road-user time savings is the most important component. This used to be a general feature (see the Leitch report – UK Department of Transport, 1978 – for a retrospective view). In the second place comes accident cost reduction. The relative importance of this component and the vehicle operating cost savings differs somewhat between countries, depending on circumstances such as the value put on risk reduction. In the residual, the two biggest items are increased 'comfort' and decreases of 'severance', or 'barrier effects'.

Table 6.3   *Shares (%) of the main benefit components of planned road investments in the state-owned Swedish road network in the ten-year planning periods before and after the turn of the century, respectively*

	1991–2000	1998–2007
Time saving	42	37
Accident reduction	26	42
Vehicle operating cost saving	12	15
All other benefits	20	6
Total	100	100

Sources: Lindberg (1992); SAMPLAN (1995).

Of course, for safer modes of transport, this order of importance of benefit components is different. Time savings of passengers are dominant on the benefit side in cost–benefit analyses for typical railway (track) and airport investments. For seaport investments 'vehicle cost savings', that is, laytime reduction for ships, but also savings due to new possibilities for using bigger ships or ships with special requirements, which could not be accommodated before, are the most important benefits. This is because freight time cost, although appreciable, is still only a fraction of passenger time cost.

An important factor for new investments in TI is changes in values of the benefit components. Such changes have occurred in the 1990s: emission costs have gone up, and so has the value of accident risk reduction relative to time savings. This is clearly reflected in the road investment benefit components in the right-hand column of Table 6.3, where accident reduction has taken the place of time savings in the order of importance.

It is first a little puzzling that accident risk reduction is such a prominent reason for road investments now and in the foreseeable future, bearing in mind that the road traffic accident risk, measured as the number of traffic accidents per motor-vehicle-km, is nowadays some ten times lower than in the 1950s (see Figure 6.5). The achievement of a continuous decline of the traffic accident risk is no longer sufficient as a goal for traffic safety policy. Not even the decline in absolute numbers of road traffic fatalities and serious injuries that has been obtained in Sweden during the 1990s is good enough. Now the official road safety goal is the 'zero vision'.

In striving for the utopia of zero serious traffic accidents, it is helpful to raise dramatically the values of accident risk reduction for road investment cost–benefit analysis. However, it is uncertain whether the absolute number of

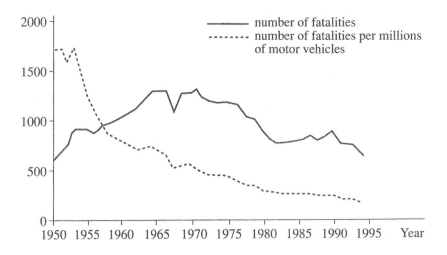

Figure 6.5   Road traffic fatalities in Sweden since 1950 (absolute numbers and relative to the number of motor vehicles)

accidents will continue to go down, if the stagnation in car ownership is halted and car traffic starts to grow again. One thing, which is sure, is that motorway construction will be boosted.

As is exemplified in Table 6.4, the greatest advantage of motorways is the relatively low accident risk associated with them compared with roads of inferior standard.

Table 6.4   Cost of accidents on different types of non-urban road in France

Type of non-urban road	Cost (FFr per car-km)
Two lanes, 6–7 m	0.13
Three lanes, 9 m	0.15
Three lanes, 10.5 m	0.11
Four lanes, 14 m	0.12
2 × 2 lanes, level intersection	0.08
2 × 2 lanes, grade separated intersection	0.04
Motorway	0.03

Source: Direction des Routes (1986).

6   MODIFICATION OF CLASSICAL ROAD INVESTMENT COST–BENEFIT ANALYSIS I: THE CASE OF INTERMODAL COMPETITION

The development of the railway network up to the 1990s has been quite the opposite to the road network development. Discontinuation of twig and branch lines, closure of small stations, and disinvestment in the railway network were the main measures taken by the Swedish railways (SJ) in that period in the continued struggle to make ends meet.

6.1   The Recent Railway Investment Boom – a Revival of Rail Transport?

In the 1980s, the Swedish government decided that something else must be done. Sweden was the first country to separate the rail track planning and operation from the production of train transport services. The main rationale for the creation of the Swedish rail track administration, Banverket, in 1988 was that the 'road transport model' should be adopted by the railways. This meant that rail infrastructure, like the roads, should be managed separately, and be free for all (train operators) who both fulfil strict safety requirements and pay rail track charges based on the marginal costs. Investment in rail track should be based on the same kind of cost–benefit analysis as road investments.

The revenue from the rail track charges has so far covered just a fraction of the total expenditure on rail track investment, repair and maintenance. Banverket has no cost-recovery obligation, and is financed by grants from the central government. In recent years, these grants have been relatively large, because a salient feature of the current transport and environmental policy in Sweden is to bring about a renaissance of electrically driven rail transport. Heavy investments in new rail track making much higher train speeds possible are the main means to that end.

In the interurban travel markets, the main issue for the future is the modal split. With the introduction of high-speed trains, and total railway investments raised to a level comparable with total road investments, the new challenge from rail transport could change the picture in the long-distance travel markets radically.

6.2   Diagrammatic Illustration of the Benefits of a Railway Investment

In the cost–benefit analyses underpinning the new wave of railway investments in Sweden during the 1990s, the second most important benefit component – after time savings – has been the benefits of induced railway transport, that is, traffic transferred from road and air as well as newly generated traffic.

The principal necessary modifications of traditional road investment cost–benefit analysis are illustrated in Figures 6.6 and 6.7.

The example used refers to a long-distance route between two big cities, 'Here' and 'There'. In the initial situation, the total volume of passenger transport is fairly evenly divided between train, car and airline travel. It should be observed first that, since it is just the market for travel between Here and There that is considered, only the total air traffic on the route, being a typical long-distance mode of transport, coincides with the volume of travel illustrated in Figures 6.6 and 6.7. Total rail-passenger-km on the route may be twice as high as the volume of rail travel just between Here and There, and total km on the route would typically be many times higher than the total car-km of the trips going the whole way. It should be noted that this is one of the great advantages of roads, that is, their flexibility in being able to serve everything from very short-distance to very long-distance travel demands. Now consider a railway investment, the effects of which are illustrated in Figure 6.6. The investment, undertaken to accommodate the expected increase in rail transport demand, is assumed to include both an upgrading of the rail track and a concomitant improvement in train speed as well as frequency. It is appropriate to make the traffic benefit calculation in two steps. For the first step, from position (a) to position (b), the generalized costs (GCs) of the modes alternative

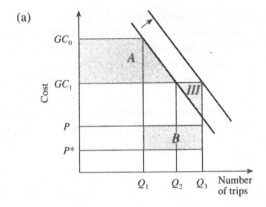

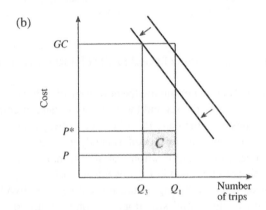

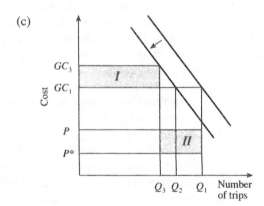

Figure 6.6   Total traffic effects of a railway investment: (a) train; (b) car;
(c) airline

to the improved mode are assumed to stay constant. A second step is required if this assumption does not hold good, which it does not as a rule when a public transport mode is among the alternatives. The left-hand shift in the airline demand curve is likely, sooner or later, to lead to an increase in GC_{air}. The second step in the traffic benefit calculation leads from position (b) to position (c), where the repercussions of that increase are accommodated in a final equilibrium.

- *Step 1*   The consumers' surplus A for the train passengers between Here and There is enhanced by the area B when the train fare P_{train} exceeds the price-relevant marginal cost P^*_{train}. On the markets for car travel and air travel, the respective demand curves shift to the left because of the decrease in GC_{train}. This results in an additional benefit on the former market equal to C, if it can be assumed that the road-user charge for cars, P_{car}, is below the price-relevant marginal cost P^*_{car}. On the air travel market, on the other hand, it is possible that a disbenefit will have already arisen after the first step, provided that the airline's fare P_{air} exceeds the price-relevant marginal P^*_{air}.
- *Step 2*   The decrease in demand for air transport leads to fewer flights, which raises GC_{air}. This in turn gives rise to a right-hand shift of the train demand curve. This does not increase the consumers' surplus of train passengers; on the contrary, train travellers gained from the competing airline are worse off in position (c) compared with position (b) by the triangle area *III* in Figure 6.6. With regard to car travel, the demand shift illustrated represents the sum of the two steps; since it can be assumed that GC_{car} stays constant all the time, a separation of the first and second steps is not necessary. The total benefit for travellers between Here and There of the railway investment considered thus amounts to $A + B + C - I - II - III$.

In the diagram, the benefits of induced rail traffic are, like in the real cost–benefit calculations of big rail track investments, of a comparable order of magnitude as the time cost savings of existing traffic. Of crucial importance for this outcome is the assumption that the price-relevant marginal cost of train transport services is well below the level of train fares. Similarly, the positive addition C to total rail track investment benefits is entirely dependent on the assumption about the relative size of P_{car} and P^*_{car}.

6.3   Diagrammatic Illustration of the Benefits of a Road Investment

When, as shown in Figure 6.7, a road investment is considered in the same relation, it is seen that, against the consumers' surplus A' on the market for car

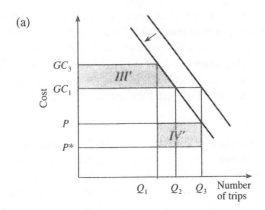

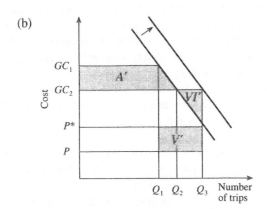

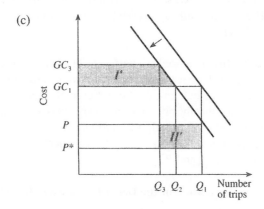

Figure 6.7   Total traffic effects of a road investment: (a) train; (b) car;
(c) airline

travel between Here and There, under the same assumptions as in the previous case, possibly six disbenefit items arise. The total sum of benefits for travellers between Here and There is $A' - I' - II' - III' - IV' - V' - VI'$.

It is now that one should remember that the major part of total road-user benefits would fall on car travellers not going the whole way. To get a complete picture of total benefits for all travellers on the route, similar sets of diagrams should be prepared for all the markets for successively shorter travel distances. The air alternative will be absent, as explained before, and the benefits for car trips will be counterbalanced to a successively smaller extent by disbenefit for train travellers, as the market share of road transport is increasing.

The main point, however, is that when private (individual) transport and public (collective) transport are competing, a road investment creates indirect disbenefit because public transport is a pronounced decreasing-cost activity, that is, due to the 'Mohring effect' (see Chapter 7, Section 8).

A final reflection is that it seems more grand than wise to give priority to the fulfilment of a national or international motorway network as a main strategy for an infrastructure investment programme. Interurban, long-distance transport is the natural niche for both the railways and airlines. Therefore, road investments for short- and middle-distance transport, in particular where the density of demand is too low to support adequate public transport, often show a higher benefit–cost ratio than investing large sums of money in the upgrading of long thoroughfares to motorway standard. But, alas, to an 'empire builder' many smaller road improvements here and there is less appealing than an inter-regional, let alone international, motorway system.

7   MODIFICATION OF CLASSICAL ROAD INVESTMENT COST–BENEFIT ANALYSIS II: INVESTMENT IN URBAN TRANSPORT SYSTEMS

As regards non-urban TI investment, it can be argued that in many cases the indirect traffic effects are of secondary importance compared with the direct benefits as calculated by traditional cost–benefit analysis, restricted to a single mode of transport. This is not true for urban TI investment appraisal. The indirect urban traffic effects are all-important in major travel markets. The situation is further complicated by congestion in the system, that is, by the fact that operations regularly take place at a much higher rate of capacity utilization than in non-urban road networks, which makes cost and output relationships non-linear in the relevant range. Even long-run decreasing returns may set in, that is, the third cost–output interval of Figure 6.2 (above) can be applicable in urban transport systems. It is clearly seen in all examples given above (seaport, airport, non-urban road) that the long-run average cost (LRAC) levels out sooner or later. In Table 6.1 (above) it is clear that the economies of number of service stations are almost exhausted for *n* in the range 10–15. This is a feature which reappears in many other cases. Large-scale diseconomies may set in to balance and eventually offset the initially very prominent plant-size 'economies'.

At the system level, there is at least one important example of decreasing returns in the production of road services. For radial road transport in big cities there is a long-run capacity limit that shows itself in increasing costs of various kinds as more and more of the extremely scarce space is taken up by roads and parking facilities. In mega-cities like Tokyo, New York and London, the car share in the market for central city commuter trips does not exceed 10 per cent. The passenger flow capacity of car traffic per metre of track width is relatively low, which means that elevated expressways have to be constructed if the market share of car traffic on radial routes of urban areas is to be substantially increased, and this is obviously an increasingly costly option, if it is an option at all in view of the environmental damage it would do.

7.1   The Futility of Urban Road Capacity Expansion

One major unsettled issue of urban transport investment policy that should be a focus of transport economics is simply: can urban road capacity expansion really relieve congested cities, or is that a basically futile pursuit?

When the demand for car travel is much more elastic than assumed in Figures 6.6 and 6.7 because of a good public transport alternative, cost–benefit analysis of a road investment is quite tricky – that is, in the absence of efficient road pricing. This problem is addressed here by a sort of cautionary tale, which has its roots in early work by Mishan (1967) and Thomson (1978). Their contributions seem close to fading into oblivion. This would be unfortunate because, although both Mishan's and Thomson's models are exceedingly simple, they make some relevant points, and to quote the methodological justification of the classic 'urban transport parables' by Strotz:

> [D]ue to the immense complexities of the problem a prescientific approach has to be adopted ... telling simple little stories, each of which highlights a particular though ubiquitous problem. From each of these, we wish to draw a moral, a principle that ought not to be overlooked when a more complex situation is to be faced. (Strotz, 1965, p. 1298)

7.2   Mishan's Parable: A 'Corner Equilibrium' Model of the Travel Market

Mishan's parable is an attempt to put the car era in a nutshell as far as urban areas are concerned. A diagrammatic summary of it is shown in Figure 6.8.

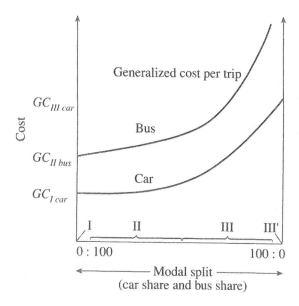

Figure 6.8   Diagrammatic account of Mishan's parable

A given total number of commuters are all travelling by bus to begin with. The generalized cost of bus transport as a function of patronage should be read from right to left. Since it is a decreasing-cost activity in the whole range, the average generalized cost, $GC_{I\,bus}$ is at a minimum when all are travelling by bus, that is, when the story begins. However, anyone who can get hold of a car can improve on this. Therefore, in the transitional phase II the first car travellers are incurring the lower generalized cost $GC_{II\,car}$. However, the more motorists there are, the higher the generalized cost of car travel will be because of congestion. In the intermediate phase III, car trips are already costlier than the bus trips in phase I. Still, car traffic is on the increase because going by bus is at present a worse alternative. This is the heart of the matter: bus travel will always be at a disadvantage from an individual's point of view because the congestion will have the same adverse effect on buses as on cars. In phase III, the ultimate, logical consequence is that the bus services close down, since everybody is travelling by car. The mean generalized cost, $GC_{III\,car}$, is at its highest ever, according to Mishan's basic presumption.

An appropriate qualification is that there is no general law saying that the total generalized cost of everybody travelling by private car has to be higher than the total generalized cost of everybody travelling by bus. That depends on a number of circumstances, in the first place on the existing road capacity relative to total travel demand. Mishan's parable, however, was intended 'to reveal some of the circumstances under which consumers' surplus, when used as an index of the benefits to be derived from private automobile travel, may give perverse results ... leading to over-investment in road construction' (Mishan, 1967, p. 184), rather than to make an empirically based social cost comparison of different modal splits on particular routes. The modal-split equilibrium is continually a corner solution determined by current car availability. This makes Mishan's parable inapplicable to the central city-bound travel market. In this travel market, Thomson's parable, where GC_{car} and GC_{bus} intersect owing to the sharply rising shape of the former in the face of a long-run capacity limit is applicable.

7.3   Thomson's Parable: an 'Interior Equilibrium' Model of the Travel Market

In his seminal study *Great Cities and Their Traffic*, Thomson (1978) argued that an increase in road capacity, when existing capacity is less than the potential demand for it, may well lead to a final equilibrium which is worse both for road users and for public transport passengers.

In the illustrative example of Figure 6.9, an interior equilibrium is assumed. Two capacity levels for car traffic are considered and the question is: what are the costs and benefits of expanding the car transport capacity from level I to level II? The basic proposition is that the modal-split equilibrium occurs where the average GC_{bus} and the average GC_{car} intersect. In towns and cities without urban railways it is unlikely that such an equilibrium could ever occur, unless separate bus lanes or busways existed. By the capacity expansion considered, the equilibrium point will move upwards to the right. The result is that, contrary to the intention, the average generalized cost for all trip makers increases from GC_A to GC_B! This constitutes an equivalent social cost increase, assuming that the fare component of GC_{bus} equals the operator's average cost.

The cost side of the road capacity investment consists of the highly tangible capital costs of the new roads and the less tangible environmental costs. But where are the benefits? The usual case of road investments is that the capital costs are compensated for by savings in road users' running costs. In this case such savings are non-existent or, rather, have turned into additional costs at least in the peak period. Only in off-peak periods is it conceivable that some benefits have been obtained.

The moral of Thomson's cautionary tale is very provocative: no matter how large the pressure of demand for extended radial road capacity is, the right policy is to reduce road capacity and increase public transport capacity (see also Mogridge et al., 1987; Holden 1989; Mogridge, 1990). It is obviously

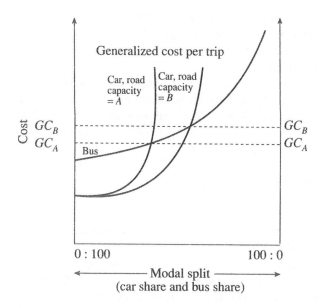

Figure 6.9   Illustrative picture of the effects of radial urban road capacity expansion

very important to examine whether this basic conclusion is true in a less simplistic model.

7.4   Additions for Greater Realism to Thomson's Model

The main limitations of Thomson's parable are its insufficient recognition of:

1. the fact that two rather different categories make up total car traffic, that is, commercial vehicles and private cars with substantially different time values;
2. the fact that car trips and public transport trips along a particular route towards the centre have systematically different origins as well as destinations; and
3. that traffic conditions can be substantially different in peak and off-peak periods. Therefore it is too strong an assumption to postulate that, in equilibrium, the GCs are typically the same for all. This point has been elaborated in a model by Jansson (1987).

The 'addition for greater realism' in this model has modified, but not basically changed, the moral of Thomson's parable: when public transport is the main alternative mode of transport, large investments in road capacity can be very unprofitable and bad for both car travellers and public transport users. The right policy direction is likely to be just the opposite, that is, to expand the capacity of separate-track public transport.

This cautionary tale cannot replace a fully fledged cost–benefit system analysis including a travel demand model based on extensive origin and destination matrices. However, when working with large and complex urban transport models, there is a risk that one could get lost, or 'would not see the wood for the trees', if a basic strategy is lacking.

7.5   What Did We Do Wrong in the Past?

Another fundamental difference between the investment problem in urban versus non-urban transport infrastructure is the close connection between transport and town/city planning.

Most city governments now seem to be well aware of the need to integrate transport planning and general land-use planning in a way that takes the strong interdependence between transport and the location of various activities into account, as well as making them cooperate towards the overall goal of improving the quality of life of the citizens. Looking back, however, a fairly general value judgement by transport experts about the urban transport development during the period of motorization in Western Europe is that too much road and parking capacity was offered to motorists in urban areas, and that in this process cuts were made in the old city structure which were too deep (see, for example, OECD, 1975, 1985 and 1995 for how this insight has developed over the years).

What could have been done instead? Many critics of our reshaped cities find it difficult to give a consistent answer to this question. It is important to pay due attention to the 'historical' question in view of the fact that the developing countries are now at the beginning of motorization. The situation in many of the rapidly growing great cities in the developing world is alarming. Even though car ownership is much less than in the developed countries, cities like Mexico City, Caracas, São Paulo, Rio de Janeiro, Buenos Aires, Teheran, Bangkok, Kuala Lumpur and Manila are literally coming near to being choked by motor traffic. Also in very poor cities like Calcutta, Mumbai (Bombay), Jakarta, Cairo and Lagos, where car ownership is still only a small fraction of that in Western Europe, chronic traffic congestion rules the streets (see World Bank, 1975, 1986). The general advice that they should not make our mistakes is not very helpful, unless we specify more exactly what our mistakes were.

7.6 Which Urban Development Do You Want?

One lesson has been learned at long last: radial road capacity expansion above ground seems to be out of the question in European cities. If this generalization can be ventured, the next question is: what about ring roads through more or less built-up areas and/or parts of a green belt or green wedges?

Since the main rationale of ring roads is to divert central city through-traffic, this strategy might seem acceptable also to environmentalists. Two problems which exist are that the ring roads do a lot of harm by their sheer existence both in built-up and in recreational areas, and that the through-traffic that can be diverted on to them is rarely large enough to justify their huge investment costs, caused to a considerable degree by an expensive design necessary to minimize the visual intrusion and environmental damage or 'encroachment costs'.

If ring roads could be combined with central city road pricing, the latter problem would be much less. Such a rational combination remains to be seen in practice. What is more likely to appear, unfortunately, is toll-financed ring roads, in the worst case with free central city entrance.

To be financially viable, and to show a reasonable traffic benefit–road cost ratio, it is often necessary to add substantial newly generated traffic to the diverted traffic. There is typically an appreciable potential for traffic generation by ring roads. In the absence of such roads, relatively little travel is made between suburbs in different outskirts. After some time of adjustment, such travel can grow very substantially, if the generalized cost is reduced radically.

The big question is thus: should we, in the name of higher car mobility, start to connect distant suburbs of a big city by urban expressways – justified on the political scene by their capability to divert central city through-traffic – which will open up new land where sprawling new developments can find a new outlet? Or should we continue to concentrate new settlements along radial, separate-track public transport lines? Let us make this big issue more concrete with some data from typical large cities in the old and new worlds, respectively.

West of Mississippi, with the outstanding exception of San Francisco, American cities are rather similar in basic layout, and are almost completely car dependent. If the population is about 1.5 million, as in Denver and Phoenix, the figures in Figure 6.10 are typical: the built-up area is about 1500 km² and the population density is consequently 1000 persons per square kilometre. The total length of the roads in the urban area is 15 000 km. People travel some 10 000 km annually per person almost exclusively by car.[5]

Traditional European cities of the same size in terms of population have quite a different layout. The population density in Copenhagen, Munich and Vienna, which represent the data to the left in Figure 6.10, is five times higher than in Denver and Phoenix. Total road-kilometres, on the other hand, are only a fifth.

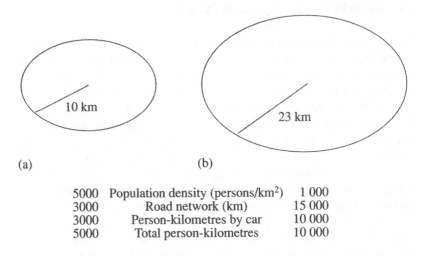

(a)   (b)

5000	Population density (persons/km^2)	1 000
3000	Road network (km)	15 000
3000	Person-kilometres by car	10 000
5000	Total person-kilometres	10 000

Source: Newman and Kenworthy (1989).

Figure 6.10   Salient features of big cities in Europe and the USA, 1980:
(a) European 1.5-million city (Copenhagen, Munich, Vienna);
(b) American 1.5-million city (Denver, Phoenix)

The average mobility in the big European cities is, as seen, about half of that in the wholly car-dependent cities of the American West.

Characteristic of the car cities in the new world is that, apart from a few skyscrapers constituting the central business district, a central city of European type is difficult to identify. Car mobility is almost the same in every direction, wherever you are. A main advantage of this could be that all the jobs in the city are accessible to everybody who has a car at his or her disposal. The conditions for matching supply and demand on the labour market should be very good.

Taking a long view, however, a note of caution is required: the car city tends to grow much faster by area than by population, which tends to make the general mobility somewhat illusory. In the American cities west of Mississippi one travels twice as many kilometres per day as in typical European cities of comparable population. The question is whether Americans reach a greater number of important destinations than Europeans.

It should be added that, although the approximation to zero of the public transport share in the above-mentioned typical cities of the American West is not too far from the truth, New York and a number of other cities in the North-East have well-developed public transport systems. In the aggregate, however, the role of public transport appears minor compared with Europe. According to the *Nationwide Personal Transportation Study 1990* (US Department of

Transportation, 1991), the share of bus and railways in total personal travel is only 2.3 per cent in the USA.

8 CONCLUDING REMARKS

Cost–benefit analysis has proved its potential for investment appraisal as far as rural and interurban transport infrastructure is concerned. There are still problems to be solved concerning values of time, frequency of public transport services, accident costs, noise and visual intrusion (for this the reader may be referred to Chapter 4), but the systematic structure for the relevant information provided and the discipline of thought required by cost–benefit analysis are indispensable for rational decision making. It is then a little hard to concede that in urban transport cost–benefit analysis is insufficient as the basis for strategic choices. Transport system design and city shape are too mutually dependent.

Economic analysis nevertheless has an important role in furthering the understanding of the dynamics of city evolution in general, and, in particular, to settle the issue of whether it makes sense or is nonsense to 'build roads to get rid of traffic'. In particular instances it can be correct to claim that, by building a certain bypass, traffic in the town or village passed by will decrease, but it is too opportunistic to hold up traffic diversion, if not outright total traffic reduction, as the guiding-star for road investment policy, just because 'environment' is the password of the day, and carry on with road building more or less as before. Looking back at the postwar history of cities, there are some clear-cut cases where every major road investment was meant to divert traffic from densely populated built-up areas. The ring roads have been located successively further away from the city centre, and the end result is that there is today as much or typically more traffic in practically every place in the city.

A reinforcing factor in the process was parking policy, which also aimed at getting rid of cars in the street. Town and traffic planners thought that it was necessary to provide low-priced or free off-street parking facilities and/or force developers and property owners to do the same at their premises.

A great challenge for the future is still to demonstrate how the fine slogan 'better towns with less traffic' (OECD, 1975) can be realized. This is a main theme of the next chapter, on the optimal use of transport infrastructure.

NOTES

1. It can be argued that the economic principles for road, railway, seaport and airport investment appraisal have considerable bearings on the problems of investment in pipelines, electric powerlines and telecommunication infrastructure.

2. The decreasing returns to scale in the third output interval, necessary for the commonly assumed U-shape of LRAC, which are caused by organizationl 'diseconomies of size' rather than technical limitations, are more difficult to verify by theoretical engineering calculations.
3. See the classic, empirical studies by Haldi and Whitcomb (1967) and Pratten (1971), as well as reference works such as Sherer and Ross (1990) and Carlton and Perloff (1994).
4. To transport transport (sic!) is just as impossible as transporting, for example, hairdressing services.
5. This figure seems to have gone up by at least 25 per cent from 1980 to 1990 according to the *Nationwide Personal Transportation Study* (NPTS) of 1990 (US Department of Transportation, 1991).

REFERENCES

Carlton, D.W. and J.M. Perloff (1994), *Modern Industrial Organization*, New York: HarperCollins.
Direction des Routes (1986), *Méthodes d'évaluation des investissements routiers en rase campagne* (Methods for the evaluation of road investment in the countryside), Paris.
Doganis, R. and G.F. Thompson (1975), 'The economics of regional airports', *International Journal of Transport Economics*, 2 (2), 167–78.
Flygplatsutredningen (1990), *Flygplats 2000: de svenska flygplatserna i framtiden: betänkande* (Airport 2000: the Swedish airports in the future), Statens offentliga utredningar; 1990: 55, Stockholm: Allmänna.
Haldi, J. and D. Whitcomb (1967), 'Economies of scale in industrial plants', *Journal of Political Economy*, 75 (4), 373–85.
Holden, D. (1989), 'Wardrop's third principle, urban traffic congestion and traffic policy', *Journal of Transport Economics and Policy*, 23, 239–62.
Jansson, J.O. (1987), *Investment Policy in Highways for Central-city-bound Travel*, VTI (Statens Väg- och Transport forskningsinstitut: Swedish National Road and Transport Research Institute) working paper, Linköping.
Jansson, J.O. and I. Rydén (1979), *Swedish Seaports – Economics and Policy*, Stockholm: EFI (Ekonomiska Forskningsinstitutet: Economic Research Institute), Stockholm School of Economics.
Lindberg, G. (1992), 'Mikro- och makroekonomiska ansatser i vägplaneringen' (Micro- and macroeconomic approaches to road planning), in P.O. Hesselborn (ed.), *Infrastruktur och samhällsekonomi*, TFB (Transportforskningsberedningen: Transport Research Board) report 21, Stockholm.
Mishan, E.J. (1967), 'Interpretation of the benefits of private transport', *Journal of Transport Economics and Policy*, 1 (2), 184–9.
Mogridge, M.J.H. (1990), *Travel in Towns: Jam Yesterday, Jam Today, Jam Tomorrow?*, London: Macmillan.
Mogridge, M.J.H., D. Holden, J. Bird and G.C. Terzis (1987), 'The Downs–Thomson paradox and the transportation planning process', *International Journal of Transport Economics*, 14, 284–311.
Newman, P. and J. Kenworthy (1989), *Cities and Automobile Dependence. An International Sourcebook*, Aldershot: Avebury Gower.
Organization for Economic Cooperation and Development (OECD) (1975), *Better Towns with Less Traffic*, Conference Proceedings, 14–16 April, Paris: OECD.

Organization for Economic Cooperation and Development (OECD) (1985), *Co-ordinated Urban Transport Pricing*, Road Transport Research, Paris: OECD.

Organization for Economic Cooperation and Development (OECD) (1995), *Urban Travel and Sustainable Development*, Paris: OECD.

Pratten, C. (1971), *Economies of Scale in Manufacturing Industry*, Cambridge: Cambridge University Press.

Saaty, T.L. (1961), *Elements of Queuing Theory*, New York: McGraw-Hill.

SAMPLAN (1995), *Resultat av inriktningsanalyser – Grundalternativet* (Results of the analysis of alternative investment directions – the base alternative), Stockholm: Swedish National Institute for Communication Analysis (SIKA).

Sherer, F. and D. Ross (1990), *Industrial Market Structure and Economic Performance*, Boston: Houghton-Mifflin.

Small, K. (1992), *Urban Transportation Economics*, Chur: Harwood.

Statens Vägverk (1978), *En studie av vägstandard* (A study of road quality), P003, Stockholm: Swedish National Road Administration.

Strotz, R. (1965), 'Urban transportation parables', in J. Margolis (ed.), *The Public Economy of Urban Communities*, Washington, DC: Resources for the Future.

Thomson, J.M. (1978), *Great Cities and Their Traffic*, Harmondsworth: Penguin.

UK Department of Transport (1978), *Report of the Advisory Committee on Trunk Road Assessment* (Leitch report), London: HMSO.

US Department of Transportation (1991), *Nationwide Personal Transportation Study 1990*, Washington, DC: Federal Highway Administration.

Vägverket (1996), *EVA – Effektberäkning vid väganalyser. version 2.1* (Cost–benefit analysis for roads. Version 2.1), Borlänge: Swedish National Road Administration.

World Bank (1975), *Urban Transport*, Sector Policy Paper, Washington, DC: World Bank.

World Bank (1986), *Urban Transport*, World Bank Policy Study, Washington, DC: World Bank.

7. Transport infrastructure: the problem of optimum use

Jan Owen Jansson

1 INTRODUCTION

While in the previous chapter the problem was how to determine, from the point of allocative efficiency, the optimum size for any piece of transport infrastructure (TI), in this chapter size – or capacity – of infrastructure is a fixed quantity. Again, the problem is how to derive rules for obtaining an optimum. This optimum now relates, however, to the use of transport infrastructure.

Optimum use of existing transport infrastructure means in standard economic analysis that the rate of capacity utilization is such that the marginal utility of further use equals its marginal cost of queuing and/or congestion.

However, there are other costs involved, which do not, in the same way, critically depend on the rate of capacity utilization but on the behaviour of the drivers, the technical characteristics and conditions of the transport vehicles and infrastructure, and the quality of the fuel burnt. Traffic accidents, noise, exhaust emissions, and other externalities of transport production make up the latter cost category. Traditionally these costs have been contained by rules of the road, standards and regulations concerning transport vehicles and fuel, and information and education of the travelling public, including drivers of private cars. The economics of transport regulation (see, for example, Crandall et al., 1986) is an important branch of transport economics besides transport price theory. In view of the fact that the pricing for optimizing the rate of capacity utilization prescribed by transport economists is a relatively rare phenomenon in reality, it could be argued that the economics of transport regulation should have a much more prominent place in that part of transport economics that deals with the use of infrastructure. This chapter is traditional in its focus on price theory. The justification for this is that proper congestion tolls, accident externality charges, and polluter payments could be the solution to the immense traffic and environmental problems of the big cities of the world.

In addition, pricing of TI services is a means of financing the transport infrastructure. The central question, whether charges bringing about the optimum use of transport infrastructure will also pay for the facilities, is a main theme of the following discussion. At the end of this chapter, however, the complementarity of pricing and regulation in the solution of urban traffic problems will be emphasized by an urgent plea for integration of road pricing and 'traffic calming' theory.

The plan of the chapter is as follows. First the concept of the price-relevant marginal cost is defined (Section 2). Then, the characteristics of the relationships between the short-run producer marginal costs, price-relevant user costs and transport volume are discussed (Sections 3 and 4). The possibility of having markets for whole pieces of transport infrastructure – such as parking facilities – is discussed in Section 5.

This leads on to the long-lived issue of short-run versus long-run marginal cost pricing, which is clarified in Section 6. After that comes an analysis of the financial consequences of optimal pricing of TI services (Sections 7 and 8).

Transport system external costs play an important role for central government tax revenue, so some of the intricacies of these costs are tackled next (Section 9). In the concluding Section 10 the analytical results are summarized, and the conflict between the two opposite goals of equity and efficiency in the pricing policy for transport infrastructure services – in turn, non-urban and urban – is considered.

2 THE PRICE-RELEVANT MARGINAL COST

Modern pricing theory for TI services started with a number of studies of congestion costs in the 1960s (Walters, 1961, 1968; Ministry of Transport, 1964). In these studies the marginal cost pricing principle was applied to urban road transport.

From the point of view of welfare theory, pricing with a view to maximizing the sum of producer's and consumer's surplus as well as internalizing all possible negative transport system external costs is 'optimal pricing'. It is generally thought of as 'marginal cost pricing', and in spirit, if not quite formally, that is what the present discussion is all about. However, with a system definition including 'users' in the double role of suppliers of essential inputs (time) as well as consumers of the output (movement) – compare the total cost equation (6.1) in Chapter 6, Section 3.2 – optimal price will strictly be different from the derivative of the total social cost with respect to output, or traffic volume (Q), which is the usual definition of the marginal cost. To avoid confusion, the prefix 'price-relevant' is put in front of 'marginal cost'. It is this marginal cost that should be equal to the price in optimum.

The definition of the price-relevant marginal cost is the following in the case of TI services:

$$MC = \frac{dTC}{dQ} - AC_{user} = MC_{prod} + Q\frac{\partial AC_{user}}{\partial Q} + MC_{ext}. \qquad (7.1)$$

For the discussion of optimal pricing of TI services, it is appropriate in most cases to assume the transport infrastructure to be fixed. So far as the producer costs are concerned the cost and output relationship to be considered is thus that between the costs of wear and tear, traffic control and so on, and the traffic volume. The middle term of (7.1) represents the influence of an additional user on the costs of fellow transport system users.

Mathematically, the product of Q and the derivative of AC_{user} with respect to Q equals the difference between MC_{user} and AC_{user}, and the latter formulation makes, of course, economic sense, too: AC_{user} is perceived as the private marginal cost, when a good number of independent transport consumers make use of the transport facility concerned. It is the difference between the social and private marginal user costs that is price relevant. In the exceptional case, the 'fellow transport system users' belong to the same enterprise as the additional vehicle considered. In that case the middle term vanishes from the MC expression. For example, the charges that a separate rail track owner levies on the national railway enterprise should not contain a congestion cost component, where no other operators of railway services exist, provided, it should be added, that the railway enterprise levies optimal fares on its passengers.

The transport system external marginal costs represented by the third term of the MC expression above include a number of separate items. Of these, intersystem accident costs, together with the emission costs, are the most important in most cases.

3   MARGINAL PRODUCER COST OF TI SERVICES

It is true that MC_{prod} is the least important of the three main price-relevant MC components. Still it is surprising that very little serious work has been done on the theory and measurement of the price-relevant producer costs of transport infrastructure, apart from replicating conventional cost-accounting figures for the average variable costs. In a recent survey (Jansson and Lindberg, 1997), the main conclusion both for road and rail track operating costs – maintenance, repair and restoration costs – is that for a number of reasons the price-relevant marginal cost falls well short of the producer average cost. The reasons are as follows:

1. a good portion of the operating costs is fixed, that is independent of the traffic volume;

2. the short-run marginal cost falls with the traffic volume for activities such as road resurfacing and reconstruction, and rail restoration;

3. some maintenance activities produce public goods, that is, qualities that can be enjoyed by an unlimited number of road users. Clearing the road of snow, road information, and grass cutting on the verges are some examples. Irrespective of whether these costs increase with the traffic volume or not, they are price irrelevant, because the benefits are increasing in parallel with the producer costs. A marginal cost expression like that in equation (7.1), considered in the short- versus long-run marginal cost discussion, where the total benefits (B_t) just offset the total costs (C_t) to make the social marginal cost equal to zero, is applicable also in this case.

4   PRICE-RELEVANT USER COSTS OF TI SERVICES

4.1   User Costs at 'Departmentalized' and 'Common' Facilities

Terminals, such as airports and seaports, are typical departmentalized facilities: a slot or berth is assigned to the users one at a time, among other things for safety reasons, and this is true also for 'blocks' of rail track for trains. The user costs of TI services produced at departmentalized facilities consist in the first place of service time costs, and queuing time costs incurred on occasions of excess demand. The service time cost per customer can often be assumed to be independent of the total traffic relative to the number of service stations (that is, the rate of capacity utilization, or occupancy rate), whereas the expected queuing cost rises sharply with the occupancy rate.

With a common facility like a road, the users' interference with one another takes two related forms – a reduction in speed to avoid collisions when traffic density goes up and (multi-)vehicle accidents that occur in spite of speed moderation. The main user-cost components are in this case the travel time cost, the vehicle operating cost, and the accident cost, which are all of a comparable order of magnitude in road transport. However, one general finding of empirical research in this area is that the accident cost component of the price-relevant user cost is negligible in many cases (Satterthwaite, 1981; Vägverket, 1993; Nilsson, 1996).

On the other hand, as will be seen in Section 9, the price-relevant external accident cost is often quite important.

4.2   Congestion Costs at Common Facilities

The congestion cost component in the price-relevant cost is obtained by: (i) estimating the relationship between speed or travel time and traffic volume, and (ii) determining the appropriate value of time. A large amount of literature exists in these two subject fields.[1] Here, two issues will be considered that usually do not get much attention:

1. the method of calculating optimal congestion tolls for traffic with and without an absolute time restriction respectively, and
2. the question why optimal congestion tolls are close to zero in the larger part of the non-urban road network.

Is it true, as is often claimed when the absence of congestion is pointed out, that there is an oversupply of non-urban road capacity? The answer to this question is that most non-urban road investments are made with a view to raising the quality of road services, and this cannot be done, with existing technology, without also expanding the road capacity. For Sweden, for example, there is ample evidence that interurban and rural roads are practically uncongested (see Swahn, 1992, and Vägverket, 1997).

It is interesting – and surprising – that this also seems to be the case in Britain, where there is a population density ten times that of Sweden, and a similar rate of car ownership. According to Newbery (1994), around the year 1990, only 2 per cent of the total congestion costs in Britain did occur in non-urban road traffic, whereas no less than 73 per cent of total motor-vehicle-km were produced on the road network outside urban areas.

As is well known, the situation is entirely different in big cities. The structure of optimal congestion tolls in major urban areas has some interesting characteristics, which should be taken into account when introducing urban road pricing. First, it can be noted that in central cities commercial traffic is of the same order of magnitude as traffic for private purposes (see, for example, Stangeby, 1997). Due to the much higher costs of drivers' time in commercial traffic than in traffic for private purposes, and the fact that the production period for transport (the period during which the transport activity must take place) in the central city is fixed for many road users, the level of optimal road-user charges will have to be relatively high all day in the central city. The only parts of the road network where matching charges would have to be levied are the main arterials into the central city during the morning and afternoon peaks.

The conventional 'fixed production period' model, just referred to, does not seem fully applicable to non-urban traffic, or to urban car commuting. In the latter case, what happens as the demand for road space goes up is that the peak period becomes wider and wider. Because of this it is not the relationship between travel time and traffic volume per hour that should be the basis for the congestion cost calculation, but the relationship between travel time and the number of car travellers completing their trips in the morning peak, taking into account that the morning peak is not of fixed duration, but will expand into the previously off-peak time. A curve representing the relationship between travel time and the number of car trips in the morning would rise more gently than a curve representing the relationship between travel time and flow per hour (see further Jansson, 1969).

A numerical example will show the great difference in congestion tolls according to which model is used and which composition of the traffic is assumed. In Table 7.1, a standard urban traffic model is used (Underwood, 1961) and optimal congestion tolls have been calculated at different rates of road capacity utilization (after tolling), on one hand for central city traffic during the day and on the other for traffic on roads going into the central city. The former is assumed to comprise private and commercial traffic in a fifty–fifty proportion, the latter to consist of 100 per cent private car commuters.

Table 7.1   *Optimal congestion tolls at different rates of road capacity utilization in two cases*

Rate of capacity utilization	Congestion toll, €/10 car-km	
	Central city traffic during the workday, case (a)	Commuter traffic before/ after the workday, case (b)
0.01	0	0
0.1	0.13	0.03
0.2	0.3	0.07
0.3	0.5	0.11
0.4	0.8	0.16
0.5	1.2	0.23
0.6	1.8	0.3
0.7	2.8	0.4
0.8	4.7	0.6
0.9	9.5	0.9
1	–	2.2
0.9*	–	5.9
0.8*	–	8.8

Note: * Total car-km per hour are less, but the number of cars in the system greater than at maximum capacity.

Remember that this is just a numerical example, based on Swedish time values, and some rather schematic assumptions as to the traffic composition. In reality, pure cases as to the production period fixity or flexibility, such as cases (a) and (b) in Table 7.1, are relatively rare. The point made here is that the conventional way of calculating congestion tolls where a fixed period for the production of transport services is being assumed is applicable mainly in central cities, where commercial traffic dominates. Strictly speaking, in non-urban areas it is inapplicable. This does not matter very much, however, because the optimal congestion toll will come out anyway as rather low, irrespective of which assumption is made concerning the production period.

Urban commuter traffic is a different matter. The highest rates of capacity utilization occur on the roads to/from the central city in the peak hours. It is interesting to see, for a given rate of capacity utilization, that the congestion toll level is many times higher for central city traffic than for the car commuters. For low rates of capacity utilization this is mainly due to the difference in the average values of time. Close to the capacity limit – where the optimal toll is some ten times higher in the central city than on the arterials between the suburbs and the city – the additional effect of the different models for calculating congestion tolls is quite important.

A further fact relevant for urban road-pricing policy is that during peak hours the capacity utilization normally is much higher on the arterials than in the central city road network. This works towards levelling out the structure of optimal congestion tolls over the city. It can be noted, for example, that the tolls should be about the same (€2.2) in both places in the network when the rate of capacity utilization is at its maximum on the arterials into the city, and just two-thirds of the maximum in the central city, or €0.4 0 per 10 car-km when the rate of capacity utilization is 0.70 on the radial arterials, and 0.25 in the central city network. This indicates that the level of congestion toll adequate for the central city traffic during the whole day may also be about right for the commuter traffic during peak hours. Only in off-peak hours on the radial arterials is a substantially different (lower) toll level indicated.

4.3   User Costs of Excess Demand at Departmentalized Facilities: A Queuing Model Illustration

While roads are common facilities, railways are better characterized as 'departmentalized' facilities. When a train uses a certain section of the track – a 'block' – other trains cannot use the same block at the same time. If there is excess demand in the short run, queuing costs are incurred. In the long run, queuing costs should be provided against in the scheduling, but the operator of the railway service cannot, of course, get away with scarce rail track capacity with impunity. The 'scarcity costs' will appear as accelerating user costs in one form or another as the rate of rail capacity utilization is increased.

The main point concerning pricing policy is that, if there is just one train operator in the system, the rail track scarcity costs are internalized in the planning of the timetable. Time-slots are made simultaneously for all train services in the railway network. There is no need for rail track scarcity charges to be levied by the track owner on different trains. It should be the task of the railway enterprise to design a peak-load pricing structure with a view to optimizing the rate of capacity utilization over time, taking into consideration both rail track and rolling-stock capacity limitations.

In a situation where a considerable number of independent railway companies are using the same rail track, a system of rail-track charges is indicated. This can be thought of as a set of 'access charges' for blocks where excess demand would occur in the absence of such charges.

Terminals for change of mode in door-to-door transport chains (seaports, airports and so on) and parking facilities for idle vehicles are naturally divided into separate 'departments', for example, the berths of a seaport. The general-purpose seaport supplies service to ships, cargo and land transport vehicles arriving more or less at random and making different demands on port resources. The short-term demand for port services will therefore vary – one week all resources may be occupied and the ships will be waiting in the roads, the next week there may be no ships in the port at all. What is the correct trade-off between the two objectives of a high level of utilization of port facilities and a low likelihood of delays for ships?

This can be illustrated, using elementary queuing theory, on the basis of the following standard assumptions:

1. customers arrive at random, which means that the distribution of arrivals can be described by the Poisson probability distribution;
2. similarly, the duration of the service time is a random variable, fitting the negative exponential probability distribution; and
3. there is no upper limit to the length of the queue, that is, customers are indefinitely 'patient'.

In the simplest case of a single-channel facility, the expected queuing time in static equilibrium will then be:

$$q = \frac{As^2}{1 - As} = s\frac{\Phi}{1 - \Phi} \qquad (7.2)$$

where q is the expected queuing time per customer (days), A is the expected number of arrivals per day, s is the expected service time per customer (days) and Φ is the occupancy rate $(= As)$.

A characteristic of this model, like many other, more complicated queuing models, is that, given the occupancy rate, the mean queuing time q is proportional to the mean service time s. As can be seen, q moves towards infinity as

Φ approaches unity. The sharp rise in the mean queuing time as the occupancy rate increases is shown in the middle column of Table 7.2, which gives the ratio of q to s for different values of Φ. The price-relevant cost, given in proportion to s in the right-hand column of the table, rises even more sharply, as the occupancy rate goes up.

Table 7.2 *Queuing time in the single-stage single-channel model*

Occupancy rate	Mean queuing time (as a proportion of service time)	Expected additional queuing time (as a proportion of service time) caused by another arrival
0.1	0.11	0.12
0.2	0.25	0.31
0.3	0.43	0.61
0.4	0.67	1.11
0.5	1.00	2.00
0.6	1.50	3.75
0.7	2.33	6.26
0.8	4.00	20.00
0.9	9.00	90.00
1.0	–	–

The root cause of the queuing that occurs is, of course, the variability of A and s. The laytime of similar ships varies because a great many more or less random factors significantly affect the actual value of the service time. Such factors include the weather, and stoppages due to breakdown of handling or other equipment. In addition, the type and size of ships and the type of cargo can vary considerably. What difference does it make, if the variability of s can be reduced?

The Pollaczek–Khintchine formula provides a general answer to the question of how the mean queuing time is affected by the distribution of service time. It states that for any arbitrary distribution of s it is possible to express the steady-state mean queuing time q as a function of the arrival rate A, the mean service time s and the variance, var(s) of the service-time distribution:

$$q = \frac{A\left[s^2 + \text{var}(s)\right]}{2(1 - As)}. \tag{7.3}$$

In the case of a negative exponential distribution of s, the variance is s^2. It is easily checked that expression (7.2) for the mean queuing time is obtained by inserting s^2 for var(s) in (7.3). In the case of constant service time, the variance of s is zero and the general formula gives:

$$q = \frac{s}{2} \frac{\phi}{1-\phi}. \tag{7.4}$$

The elimination of service-time variability will, *ceteris paribus*, reduce the mean queuing time by half.

It is clear from expression (7.3) above that, given the occupancy rate, the mean queuing time is proportional to the sum of the service time and its relative variance (s + var(s)/s). Consequently, to reduce the queuing time it is as important to achieve a reduction in the variability of the service time as it is to achieve a reduction in the mean service time itself. In the case of seaport operations this means that the expected queuing time may be reduced either by increasing the handling speed or by making each call by the ships more homogeneous, for example, by specializing in serving a particular type of ship or cargo.

In practice it can be rather difficult to calculate the applicable queuing cost function (see Jansson and Shneerson, 1982), but it is even more difficult to estimate accurately the matching demand function. Some trial and error is necessary before the right solution can be found, that is before the price is found which equals the price-relevant expected marginal cost.

5 PRICING OF TI SERVICES AND PRICING OF PIECES OF TI

The queuing model above is still a relatively simple case. Much greater difficulty in monetizing the user costs of excess demand arises in cases where these costs assume the shape of frustration of not attaining possession of service at the facility concerned, because queuing would be out of the question – the case of impatient customers at departmentalized facilities.

In this case a reasonable alternative to calculating short-run price-relevant user costs (assuming the capacity to be fixed) can be to take the average producer cost of a marginal department, including capital costs, that is, a proxy for the long-run marginal producer cost, $LRMC_{prod.}$ For common facilities like roads, the indivisibility problem – the fact that road capacity may be increased only with given, discrete units – makes LRMC calculation a tricky business. However, an alternative way of looking at TI services is as very short-term renting of space of a TI facility, where the 'first come, first served' principle is applied. It is then interesting to note that this transaction form is one end-point of a continuum, where the other end-point is to purchase a whole piece of transport infrastructure for one's own exclusive use. The latter option is quite frequently chosen by big users as regards departmentalized facilities (for example, an airport). A middle form is the renting of a piece of transport infrastructure on a long-term basis, for example, a berth with supplementary transit storage facilities in a seaport. Liner shipping companies often choose this transaction form to avoid the risk of queuing time. In the case of what is usually regarded as common facilities, buying or renting a whole piece is more rare, but strictly private roads exist, as well as private sidings complementing the national rail network. From a pricing-theoretical point of view this difference in transaction form is really fundamental: it can change the market form from one extreme of (local) monopoly to the other extreme of almost pure competition.

In the parking market, for example, the whole continuum of transaction forms is well represented. Since parking is an important TI service in its own right, it is worthwhile to look closer at this.

For a car commuter working in the Central Business District (CBD) of a city with a population of more than a million, the parking cost is the dominant component in the daily travel cost, provided that he has to pay the full market price for a parking space. Then the daily parking cost can be anything from US$6 upwards depending on city size, whereas the private car operating cost of the journey itself is normally below US$6. In a city like Stockholm the cost of renting a parking space on a monthly basis is about US$6–10 per day in the CBD. In central Tokyo, for instance, or in lower Manhattan it is many times more. Such prices cannot, with relatively few exceptions, be afforded by private motorists paying out of their own pockets. The car commuting to the CBD is based on employers subsidizing the parking, often because the employees concerned need the car for business trips during the workday.

Looking at the parking market from the demand side, a useful distinction is between 'parking at the base' and 'parking away from the base'. Like its owner, every car has a home, or 'base', where the car is kept when it is not in use. The characteristics of the demand for base parking are that each parking period is fairly long term, and that it occurs frequently, and at the same place. When the car is used for various trips to destinations away from the base – to shops, to visit customers, to run different errands – short-term occasional parking in many different places is needed.

In the base-parking market segment, parkers typically own parking space, or hire it on a long-term basis, and in the other market segment parkers pay per hour of parking space occupation. This is the same market segmentation as in the market for accommodation with owner-user apartments at one end and hotel rooms at the other. The interesting additional fact, however, is that whereas the price of a hotel room per night is many times higher than the rent of a comparable flat, this rational price ratio is often upside down in the parking market, because of artificially cheap on-street parking.

Optimal on-street parking pricing is a fairly complex matter when it comes to the detailed structure of the charges by time period. A basic feature, all the same, is that the average level of charges should not deviate too much from the value of the land used. If the average level of on-street parking charges is much higher, more kerbstone spaces should be provided, and if it is much lower, better use of some of the existing kerbstone parking space could probably be found.

Bearing this in mind, the appropriate relative prices of on- and off-street parking can be considered: normally, on-street parking should be substantially more expensive than off-street because:

1. the former is on a per hour basis, whereby a rather modest average rate of capacity utilization is to be expected, whereas garage space and so on can be leased on a monthly, or more often annual, basis, in which case nearly all spaces could be let; and
2. the cost of the land taken up by the latter can be distributed between several floors when the parking space is in the basement of a block of flats or office building, or in a multi-storey parking garage typical of central cities.

With such a price structure, which in fact is reversed in many cities in the world, a rational division of short- and long-term parking would arise: long-term parkers could simply not afford to park in the streets, where generally only short-term parkers would be found.

6   SHORT- VERSUS LONG-RUN MARGINAL COST PRICING: WHY ALL THE ARGUMENT?

When the marginal cost principle was applied to roads in the 1960s, one important message was that no road investment or capital costs are price relevant. Short-run variable costs must be distinguished from the costs that are fixed in the short run, because it is the short-run marginal cost that is to be estimated and combined with the corresponding demand function to obtain the optimal price.

In retrospect, one can wonder why there was so much argument on the subject of short- versus long-run marginal costs. How could this issue get such a prominent place in the debate, in view of the fact that short-run marginal cost (SRMC) is equal to long-run marginal cost (LRMC) along the expansion path? Were there reasons to believe that systematic under- or overinvestments were made in the road network, which made the two diverge? There is nothing wrong in principle with the LRMC pricing approach. It could even be preferable for practical reasons in some cases, which was exemplified above in the discussion of the parking market. The reason why the debate could go on for so long is simply that the cost calculations presented as an alternative LRMC basis for road-user charges were wrong. The result did not represent a price-relevant LRMC, and therefore appeared to give a much higher optimal price than came out of correct SRMC calculations.

6.1   The Double-counting Fallacy

One common mistake was to add the infrastructure capital costs in the form of a marginal capacity cost, or something like that, to the short-run price-relevant marginal cost. Then the outcome is obviously that the short-run price-relevant cost is considerably exceeded. What is overlooked is that by increasing road capacity, more traffic can be accommodated without inflicting congestion costs on the original traffic. A trade-off is involved: when capacity-expanding investments are justified, an equivalent traffic (time, accident and vehicle-operating) cost is saved, which would occur if the investments were not made. The additional traffic consequently does not cause any congestion costs for the original traffic under these circumstances. Therefore a congestion cost component should not be added to the LRMC calculation.

6.2   Quality Improvements Must Not Be Overlooked in the Calculation of the Price-relevant LRMC

The type of departmentalized facilities found in the base-parking market is a relatively simple case for calculating a long-run marginal cost. There are more complicated cases. If a long-run costing approach is chosen, one must not forget to check whether a user-cost component or an external cost component appear in the long-run version of marginal cost. In road transport, in particular, a long-lived misunderstanding of what the price-relevant LRMC cost consists of boils down to forgetting that investments in the non-urban road network, where serious congestion is generally absent, are made primarily to raise the quality of road services (in other respects than eliminating traffic congestion). Let us consider this fact in the light of the empirical approach to LRMC estimation known as 'development cost' calculations. By time-series analysis of the total costs of the whole interurban road network and the steadily growing total road traffic, it is thought that the indivisibility problem of LRMC calculations could be avoided: what appears as a marked indivisibility on an individual road link being improved is smoothed out in the context of the whole road network. The error of the development cost school of thought is, however, that one decisive term of the price-relevant long-run cost expression is overlooked. Only under the unrealistic assumption that the road investments are purely capacity expanding, without any joint quality-raising effect such as road shortening, or improved alignment, would it be reasonable to take the ratio of the annual capital costs of new investments to the additional traffic on the roads as a proxy for the price-relevant LRMC. Since, on the contrary, non-urban road investments are almost wholly justified by cost savings for the existing traffic (including the autonomous traffic growth), a large error is made by ignoring the negative user-cost term in the LRMC expression. The correct proxy for the price-relevant LRMC of the interurban road services has the following form:

$$LRMC_{proxy} = \frac{C_t - B_t}{\Delta Q_t},$$
(7.5)

where:

C_t = capital cost of new investments year t,
B_t = benefits for existing traffic year t in the form of user cost savings thanks to the new investments, and
ΔQ_t = addition to the traffic on the roads in year t.

As is well known, the traditional practice of the national road administration for calculating the benefits of prospective investment projects is to disregard newly generated traffic; only cost savings to existing traffic and the forecasted autonomous traffic growth are included on the benefit side. Provided that the selected projects have a positive net benefit/cost ratio, it follows that B_t is equal to, or greater than C_t, which means that the price-relevant cost is zero or even negative.

There are, of course, in-between cases. In particular, in more populous countries than, for example, Sweden, it is presumably less rare that road investments (outside urban areas) are made, partly because capacity is truly scarce. Then it is likely that the benefits to existing traffic, B_t, given the rate of capacity utilization, fall well short of the capital costs, C_t, and there is a positive value of the LRMC proxy, which is consistent with a positive congestion toll in this case.

The lessons from the long discussions of optimal charges for non-urban road services are generally relevant for all transport infrastructure, including railways. The interurban railway investment boom that we have seen in recent times is to a large extent justified by train-user benefits in the form of straighter lines, and above all higher speed. Applying formula (7.5) for the LRMC proxy would most likely result in rather low marginal costs. We see much less of urban (overground) rail investments in spite of the fact that there are strong demand pressures from commuters in many large cities. The big obstacles are land scarcity and encroachment costs. Again this problem is similar for urban roads and railways.

6.3 The Importance of Unaccounted-for Encroachment Costs for the Relationship between Short- and Long-run Marginal Costs

The equality of SRMC and LRMC presupposes that investments are optimal (defined by the goal of social surplus maximization). The problem in practical cost–benefit analysis is that all relevant costs are not easily monetized. The unaccounted-for costs may still have a strong influence on the relationship between SRMC and LRMC, in particular the encroachment costs of new infra-structure. These costs are very difficult to monetize and include in cost–benefit analysis of transport infrastructure investments, but can nevertheless play an important role in the decision-making process. Many planned roads, railways and airports will never be built, or the building-start is greatly postponed, because of lengthy efforts to persuade politicians and residents in the area of threatening encroachment to accept the projects in their original design.

Financing difficulties are another common reason for lagging infrastructure investments. This is strengthened if, as often happens, the original projects are substantially modified to lessen the encroachment costs, which leads to additional building cost. This means that SRMC and the calculable LRMC can be substantially different. As it is always right to base the costing for price making on the short-run cost (letting sunk capital costs be bygones) it is good to bear in mind that SRMC is *higher* than LRMC under the circumstances described above. The discarding of long-run marginal cost as a basis for calculating the price-relevant road transport cost will consequently not bias the result downwards, as is often claimed by LRMC proponents.

A conceivable alternative might be to charge a price smoothing out the rise and fall in SRMC that follow from growing congestion over time and eventual congestion relief as a result of capacity-expanding investments, on the ground that some users of transport infrastructure take current prices as the basis for long-run locational decisions which lock them into particular patterns of transport. This may be sensible in some cases. It is still SRMC pricing, because the price level resulting from such an averaging would coincide with LRMC only in the case where investments are truly optimal.

7   WILL OPTIMAL CHARGES FOR TRANSPORT INFRA-STRUCTURE SERVICES PAY FOR THE FACILITIES?

To answer this question it is essential to ascertain long-run cost structure. The normal procedure in pricing theory when the question of the financial result of optimal pricing is taken up is to explore whether or not economies of scale apply. When both short- and long-run efficiency conditions are fulfilled, a well-known implication is that the ratio of optimal price to average total cost equals the inverse of the scale elasticity of the production function concerned. Economies of scale imply a financial deficit and diseconomies of scale a surplus as a result of optimal pricing.

When it comes to TI services, there is an additional condition that tends to make the financial result of optimal pricing much more sensitive to deviations from constant returns to scale. This will be explained in what follows.

7.1   Congestion Tolls as a Contribution to the Capital Costs of the Facility

Suppose that a particular TI facility is run by a private firm operating in a competitive environment. In addition to the requirement to cover the total costs of operations (that is, including the capital cost of the facility), it is assumed that the firm has to pay compensation to people living nearby incurring certain damage costs (for example, noise disturbance) caused by the operations at the TI facility. Below, the three main components of the price-relevant cost as defined in equation (7.1) above of the TI services concerned are compared to the full cost price charged by the imaginary private operator.

$$PC = SRMC_{prod} + Q \frac{dAC_{user}}{dQ} = MC_{ext},$$

Full cost price $= AVC + AFC + AC_{ext},$

where:

AVC = average variable cost,
AFC = average fixed cost, and
AC_{ext} = average external cost.

Although the 'cost responsibility' is normally defined for the totality, it is illuminating to make the comparison item for item.

It was concluded in Section 3 above that MC_{prod} in most cases (for different modes of transport) falls short of the accounting cost concept, AVC, that is, the producer average variable cost.

The average fixed cost, AFC, has no direct counterpart in the price-relevant producer costs, but should be set against the price-relevant user-cost component. The revenue from congestion tolls or the equivalent type of charge for regulating the capacity utilization is the first-hand source for facility capital cost recovery. This is a well-established view of the matter.

It is less clear which attitude is most sensible to the possibility that a difference between AC_{ext} and MC_{ext} can exist. This will be discussed further in the next section. Even if transport vehicles eventually become silent, clean and safe, the basic reason for charging for their use of the various kinds of infrastructure will remain where and when various pieces of this infrastructure are scarce resources. So the basic question is whether optimal congestion tolls or queuing charges would pay for the facility concerned.

The form of the organization of the transport activity has an interesting role to play in this connection. A number of cases can be distinguished. The first case below is imaginary, but instructive as a starting-point.

7.2 Imaginary Fully Integrated Road Transport System (Case a)

Imagine a road transport concern where the road owner is also the seller of transport services (the unit of output is a standard truckload-km). It can be assumed either that the road owner also owns all the trucks or that he acts as a forwarding agent and just hires truck inputs on behalf of shippers. The objective is profit maximization, and our seller of truck transport is assumed to be a price taker on a competitive transport market.

Average variable cost of truck operations rises gradually as the capacity limit of the road network is approached. Since the road owner controls all truck movements, he calculates the short-run marginal cost by taking the derivative of the total transport system cost function with respect to total output, which is the basis for determining optimal output (where price equals marginal cost).

Just as in the case of rail track services used by a monopoly train operator, mentioned in Section 4, there is no allocative need for a separate road track charge. The congestion costs are internal to the transport firm. The difference between the marginal cost (that is, the price) and the average cost of truck transport constitutes the 'contribution margin', that is, the financial contribution towards covering the road capital costs. In microeconomics textbooks this is often called 'quasi-rent'.

It is assumed that operations take place at the 'expansion path': for each actual level of output the least-cost solution, including the road costs, is found. It is then helpful to introduce the scale elasticity, E, of the road transport production function: $E = 1$ means that constant returns to scale apply, $E < 1$ means decreasing returns to scale, and $E > 1$ increasing returns to scale.

If marginal cost pricing is applied, the following holds:

$$\frac{1}{E} = \frac{\text{marginal cost}}{\text{average road transport cost} + \text{average road cost}}. \qquad (7.6)$$

This means that the financial result of the whole firm, measured by the ratio of total revenue to total costs, is equal to the inverse of the scale elasticity, E.

This is, of course, elementary and very well known. The question focused on here is how the contribution margin is related to the road capital costs under different conditions to the returns to scale. The main point should be intuitively clear: the contribution margin is a residual by nature; in the first place the short-run variable factors of production are fully remunerated – in this case the road transport costs. The contribution to the road capital costs, which are fixed in the short run, will be what is left of total revenue after that remuneration is paid out.

The ratio of the contribution margin per unit of output to the road capital cost is written:

$$\frac{\text{contribution margin}}{\text{average road cost}} = \frac{\text{marginal cost} - \text{average road transport cost}}{\text{average road transport cost}}. \qquad (7.7)$$

When constant returns to scale apply, the difference between the marginal cost and the average road transport cost equals the average road cost, and the contribution margin will be just sufficient to cover the latter. However, this harmonious state of affairs is atypical, and, as we shall see, if the road capital cost is just a fraction of the transport cost, which is true in reality, the contribution margin relative to the average road cost is very sensitive to deviations of E from unity.

7.3   One Road Owner Serving Many Independent Truck Transport Operators (Case b)

With the organization of road transport production mostly existing in actual practice, the road owner has no direct coordinating power over road vehicle traffic but has to rely on incentives such as congestion charges. In the present case the road users and the road authority make separate financial accounts. The financial result of the road authority corresponds to the accounting ratio of the contribution margin to the road capital cost in the previous case. The fact that this ratio can take on values in a much wider range than follows from 'normal' deviations from unity of E is a matter of some concern.

The cost picture is exactly the same as before except for the following changes in designation:

average cost $\Rightarrow AC_{prod}$
average road transport cost $\Rightarrow AC_{user}$
contribution margin per traffic unit $\Rightarrow$ congestion toll.

Expression (7.7) for the ratio of the contribution margin to the road capital cost is renamed 'the ratio of the congestion toll to the road capital cost', and it can be written as follows (see further Jansson, 1984):

$$\frac{PC}{AC_{prod}} = \frac{1}{E} + \frac{AC_{user}}{AC_{prod}}\left(\frac{1}{E} - 1\right). \tag{7.8}$$

7.4 Bad News about the Financial Result of Optimal Congestion Tolls

The first practical observation is that the ratio AC_{user}/AC_{prod} normally takes on relatively high values. In the total costs of a transport system – be it road, air or sea transport – the transport infrastructure costs are a relatively minor part. In personal transport, in particular, AC_{user} is typically many times greater than AC_{prod}, because the time and effort of persons are dominant items. This gives the above formula a markedly high-geared character: as soon as E is different from unity, the last term becomes operative, and when AC_{user}/AC_{prod} has a high value, the financial result, PC/AC_{prod} will deviate widely from the value of $1/E$.

In Table 7.3 this is illustrated by some examples where the scale elasticity is varied around unity, and where the ratio of the user cost to the producer cost of transport infrastructure services increases from 0 to 5. It is interesting to note, for example, that in interurban and rural road transport the AC_{user}/AC_{prod} ratio is at least 5. The scale elasticity is not constant with respect to traffic volume. It seems to be gradually falling towards unity. In the range of 400–20 000 vehicles per day it is about 1.2, on average, according to highway engineering cost studies (see Jansson, 1994, for the above figures). This is consistent with practically zero congestion tolls, as can be seen in Table 7.3 (right-hand column, bottom line).

By pointing out the jointness of road capacity and quality, Walters (1968) argued that roads approximate public goods in a wide initial range of traffic volumes. A simpler and more general explanation is apparently to hand, which also explains the dramatic change in optimal charges from zero to a level of twice the road capital costs or more (see Table 7.3, left-hand column). It does

Table 7.3   Marginal accident cost components on Swedish interurban roads

Ex ante and *ex post* cost components	€/10 car-km	%
Cost of death and injury based on willingness to pay for safety of the person exposed to risk, *ar*	0.46	65
Direct material accident cost for the victim's household, *a'r*	0.03	4
Indirect material accident cost for the victim's household (lost consumption), *a"r*	0.02	3
Costs of death and injury based on willingness to pay for safety of relatives and friends of the person exposed to risk, *br*	0.17	24
Accident cost for the rest of the society, *cr*	0.08	11
Total marginal cost $(a + b + c)r$	0.71	100

not contradict Walters's original idea, but labour (time)-saving capital investment is not special to road transport. In many industries the larger plants often have a marked labour-saving potential. The special feature of road transport is that the capital services are disintegrated from the labour and charged for separately.

The problem is that zero charges for public goods for which excludability is technically possible are not easily acceptable for reasons other than allocative efficiency. At the other end of the scale it is probable that road pricing for central-city-bound traffic that brings in revenue that covers radial road investment costs many times over is consistent with the efficiency conditions. However, now that the technique for charging urban traffic exists, the lasting difficulties of getting acceptance for urban road pricing bear witness to the opposition to the idea that the motorists of a particular city should pay two or three times more than is spent on the roads of the city. What should be done with the surplus revenue from congestion tolls on top of the fuel tax (which should cover external costs of fossil fuel burning) is a main, knotty issue in the urban road-pricing debate.

A similar impasse exists as far as the congestion problems of big city airports (and airways) are concerned: efficient congestion tolls would most probably cover the costs of those airports many times over, but no one seems to have the determination and/or voter support to introduce them.

In previous literature exploring the relationship between short- and long-run costs of road transport (notably Mohring and Harwitz, 1962; Mohring 1976; Small et al., 1989), the point that has been emphasized is that optimal congestion tolls exactly cover the total road investment costs in the case of constant returns to scale. This was presented as good news, and it is no doubt a soothing possibility for the conflict averse, but it is representative neither of rural and interurban roads, nor of urban roads.

8   IMPLICATIONS FOR RAIL-TRACK CHARGES, AIRPORT AND SEAPORT PRICING

Other modes of transport should also be considered in this connection. A few comments on the infrastructure for trains, airplanes and ships are made below.

8.1   Fully Integrated Railway Transport System (Case c)

The national railways have been the only example of the fully integrated form of organization of case (a), above. This is gradually changing: Sweden (long ago), Britain, and most other European countries are creating separate rail-track administrations/companies with a view to making competition in the operation of railway services possible. In a traditional vertically integrated railway company for freight transport, the ratio of the contribution margin, in the fares, to the rail-track cost by and large obeys the same formula (7.8) as was derived above. The interpretation of E and AVC, however, is different when a scheduled passenger transport undertaking is the track user. The 'Mohring effect', that is, the fact that additional passengers lead to positive external effects on the original passengers via a rise in the frequency of service, makes a substantial difference compared to the previous case (a), where full-load transport for hire makes up the system output.

8.2   One Rail-track Owner Serving One Independent Train Operator (Case d)

In the present Swedish case where only one main-line train operator (SJ) exists, the social surplus maximizing track owner (Banverket) should not charge any congestion tolls, provided that SJ also has the objective of social surplus maximization. The congestion costs are already internalized in SJ's accounts. A track congestion toll would mean that SJ pays for congestion twice, both in a direct monetary form, and in the form of delays, which SJ should be entirely aware of. This would result in too little congestion in the railway network, as it were, that is, in too low a rate of track capacity utilization.

From the point of view of Banverket, the financial situation looks rather odd. No matter whether constant, decreasing or increasing returns to scale prevail in the railway transport system, SJ should make no contribution to the track costs of Banverket; only traffic-dependent rail-track wear and tear should make up the rail-track charges. In a variant of the present case (d), where SJ is a pure producer-surplus maximizer, a rather complicated situation would arise if the overall objective is still social (= consumer and producer) surplus maximization for the whole railway transport sector. This second-best problem is facing the Swedish government. One solution might be to adjust the rail-track charges to offset the tendency to monopoly pricing on the part of SJ. This would not be easy, among other things because the rail-track charges are already relatively low compared to the train fare. Further subsidization of Banverket is problematic. Another idea is to make competitive tendering for each particular railway line, or competition on the rail, prevent monopoly pricing.

8.3   One Transport Infrastructure Owner Serving a Few Independent Transport Service Producers (Case e)

An implicit point of the Swedish separation of track and trains was that, eventually, train service competition should be possible. The road and rail transport systems would then be organizationally more or less on an equal footing. Congestion charges on trains could be justified provided that there is a fairly large number of independent train operators, which are rivals for rail track capacity. However, if this situation were to come true, the operators would probably argue that they can coordinate timetables and so on by negotiation without the stimulus of rail-track congestion charges.

That hypothetical situation resembles the present state of affairs of congested airports, where peak-load pricing is long overdue. Airlines would naturally view peak surcharges as just another unwanted cost increase. It may well be true that the allocation of slots between airlines can be managed without resort to the price mechanism. The main economic problem, however, is that airlines individually and/or collectively manifestly fail to establish the peak/off-peak differentials in their fare structure which would be forced upon them by airport congestion tolls.

In seaports a similar case can be made for congestion or queuing surcharges on cargo and ships, although the situation of excess demand in the 1960s and 1970s with long queues of ships has turned to excess supply of port services. Generally speaking, cost consciousness is not very prominent, either in port pricing or in the elaborate rate-making of liner shipping. The ancient principle of 'charging what the traffic can bear' is still very dominant (see Jansson and Shneerson, 1982, 1987).

9   TRANSPORT SYSTEM EXTERNAL COSTS

The main reason for the current, new interest in 'fair and efficient pricing in transport' (European Commission, 1995) is the reportedly large external costs of primarily road transport, which are incurred by 'third parties' (that is, nature), and human beings not taking a direct part either as producer or user of the transport system concerned. The target is 'internalization of the externalities', which is a separate issue from the question that has just been discussed – whether optimal charges will pay for the different TI facilities. Externality charges on account of the air pollution caused by exhaust emissions, noise disturbance and accident spillovers are not meant to finance TI construction and operation.

The basic theory and empirical problems posed by the transport system external costs are also rather different from what has been previously discussed in dealing with the two other components of the price-relevant marginal cost, MC_{prod} and $Q(dAC_{user}/dQ)$.

A main point here is that the short-run cost and output relationship does not take the 'standard' rising shape in all cases as the capacity limit is approached. In fact three typical cases for the shape of the short-run marginal external costs can be distinguished: (a) constant cost, (b) decreasing cost, and (c) increasing cost, as depicted in Figure 7.1. Components of the external accident cost are represented in all three typical cases. The marginal cost of traffic noise belongs to the decreasing-cost variety, whereas most components in the exhaust emissions have a similar increasing relationship with traffic volume as the fuel consumption itself.

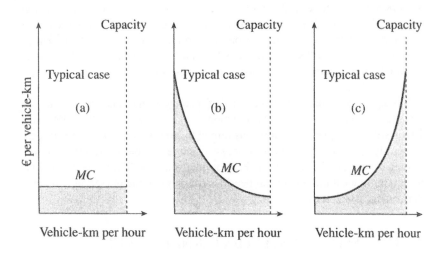

Figure 7.1   Three typical cases for the relationship between short-run external costs and traffic volume

The three mentioned traffic externalities (which are not the only ones) are discussed below, of which the accident externalities get the fullest treatment because of their complexity and potential importance for road-pricing policy.

9.1 Accident Externality Charges

Looking at the rather complex details of optimal accident externality charges, it seems that accidents occurring where different transport systems are physically overlapping or crossing each other give rise to the highest externality charges. Basically, the reason is that it is known beforehand that if a train and a car collide, or a car hits a cyclist, the lighter vehicle takes most of the damage, whereas it is not known *ex ante* which of all the cars will be most seriously damaged in the expected multi-car accidents.

Let the number of intersystem accidents be denoted as X, the number of intrasystem accidents as A, car traffic volume as Q and the risk of injury for a car traveller as r. In a non-urban road network, r, which equals A/Q, seems by and large independent of the traffic volume. That is, the number of accidents A and the traffic volume Q are proportional, given the type of road. When the risk is constant, the risk elasticity with respect to car traffic volume (E_{rQ}) is zero. This means that the price-relevant user cost does not contain any accident cost. In the absence of vulnerable road users in the main part of the non-urban road network, the price-relevant accident cost consists only of the external costs that are imposed on society at large (typical case a).

In urban areas, with many intersections, the risk elasticity is above zero. A value around 0.2 is derived from the accident prediction model of the computer program EVA used for investment appraisal by the Swedish National Road Administration (Vägverket, 1993). The risk elasticity with respect to motor traffic volume related to unprotected road users (E_{RQ}) seems to be around 0.5 (Brüde and Larsson, 1993).

Let M be the volume of travel by bicycle and on foot. Then, as the number of motor vehicles increases, while M is kept constant, the accident risk $R = X/M$ will increase for vulnerable, or 'unprotected' road users in proportion to the square root of the car traffic volume, while the risk for cars hitting unprotected road users, $r' = X/Q$, is decreasing in proportion to the inverse of the square root of the car traffic volume.[2]

Besides the estimation of the risk functions, the monetizing of the accident costs is a crucial part of the price-relevant cost calculation. Total *ex post* accident costs are literally incalculable. They consist of profound grief and sufferings in the cases of death and disability, and different material losses in all the cases. After an accident has happened, only the latter costs can be assessed in monetary terms. In Figure 7.2, the material costs of a fatal accident are given by $a' + a''$. The value a' stands for the direct and the value a'' for the indirect material costs of the victim's household. The latter mainly consist of lost production that would have been consumed by the victim's dependants.

Material costs, taken as the sum of direct and indirect material costs, are just a fraction of 'the value of a statistical life', a. This item is an *ex ante* cost. It is obtained by asking for the total willingness to pay for increased safety (for a full overview of different methods for the valuation of accidents/safety, see Chapter 4, Section 4). For the development of a theory of accident externality charges we should define three components of the *ex ante* accident cost:

$f(r) =$ willingness to pay for complete safety on the part of the household to which a certain person exposed to the risk r belongs; $f(r) \approx ar$ for low values of r;

$g(r) =$ willingness to pay for complete safety on the part of relatives and friends of the above person; $g(r) \approx br$ for low values of r;

$h(r) =$ willingness to pay for complete safety on the part of the rest of society; $h(r) \approx cr$ for low values of r;

where b and c are the values of a statistical life to relatives and friends and the rest of society, respectively.

The assumed general shape of $f(r)$ is presented in Figure 7.2. The discussion is facilitated, if the reasonable assumption is made that this function is approximately linear for very small risks, coinciding with a ray (ar) from the origin, which obviously takes a value of a at a risk level of unity. The very point of the depicted shape of the function $f(r)$ is, however, that for substantial risk levels, the curve bends upwards at an accelerating rate, and will never reach the range close to $r = 1$.

The great difference between *ex ante* and *ex post* valuation of serious casualties should be obvious. Let it be assumed that r stands for fatality risk, and that a representative household is prepared to pay $f(r)$ ($\approx ar$ for low risks) for complete safety for a particular household member. If l/r households have a similar willingness to pay for safety, it can be concluded that one life will be saved for a total payment of $f(r)/r \approx a$, the so-called 'value of a statistical life'. However, no normal household would be willing to sacrifice a member for a sum of money equal to a. Life is invaluable.

The function $g(r)$ is presumably (but not necessarily) less steeply rising than $f(r)$, and the function $h(r)$ could be approximated by cr in the whole range, and represent the material cost which follows from assuming that the rest of society looks at victims of traffic accident in the same way as hard-hearted slave-owners. The corresponding functions for the willingness to pay for safety at different risk levels for the vulnerable road users are written $f(R)$, $g(R)$, and $h(R)$. We ignore the possible willingness to pay on the part of motorists for avoiding the risk of their vehicles hitting vulnerable road users, $r' = X/Q$.

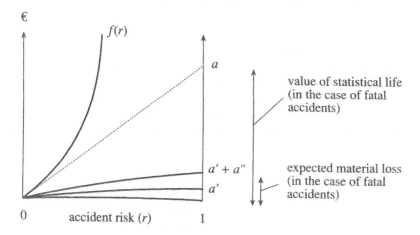

Figure 7.2   Household willingness to pay for complete safety, f(r) for a particular household member/motorist and expected material loss of the household, (a' + a")r, at different risk levels

Assuming that accidents of a given severity, for example, fatalities, are valued the same for motorists, cyclists and pedestrians, the annual total expected accident costs can be approximated in the following way:

$$TC = TC_A + TC_X = (a + b + c)(rQ + RM) \qquad (7.9)$$

where TC = annual total expected accident costs, TC_A = annual total expected intrasystem accident costs, and TC_X = annual total expected intersystem accident costs.

From function (7.9), the price-relevant accident costs or 'accident externality charges' are easily derived. Informally it can be put like this: if your entry by car into a road network increases the accident risk for the existing road users, the expected external accident cost that should be charged to you is $(a + b + c)rE_{rQ}$ and/or $(a + b + c)r'E_{RQ}$. Irrespective of whether your entry increases the risk for others, there is the external cost $(b + c)r$, which, it could be argued, should also be included in the accident externality charge; b represents the immaterial external cost, and c the material external cost. That only cr is a generally accepted item of such charges is a sign of the materialism characterizing current transport policy; road users should be responsible for the material costs that their risk taking incurs on the rest of the society, but not for the immaterial costs. In the present case the latter costs are likely to be of a different (higher) order of magnitude than the former. In Tables 7.4 and 7.5 the total accident externality charge is given, both including and excluding the item *br*.

Ignoring the cost of accidents with only material damages, the marginal accident cost for interurban car traffic on an average Swedish road broken down by cost components is presented in Table 7.4.[3] It can be seen that the immaterial components of the total marginal accident cost are dominant; they make up four-fifths of the total. An accident externality charge excluding *br* should be about €0.08/10 car-km. Including *br*, the charge increases to €0.25/10 car-km. The accident externality charge is thus between 11 and 35 per cent of the total marginal accident cost of non-urban road traffic.

Table 7.4   *Illustrative example based on the accident prediction model of the Swedish National Road Administration of optimal accident externality charges on cars in a representative central city area (€ per 10 car-km)*

Traffic flow	A-accidents			X-accidents	Total accident externality charge	
	br	*cr*	$(a+b+c)r\,E_{RQ}$	$(a+b+c)r\,E_{RQ}$	Including *br*	Excluding *br*
500	0.19	0.07	0.16	1.60	2.04	1.85
5 000	0.23	0.08	0.19	0.53	1.02	0.79
10 000	0.25	0.09	0.21	0.37	0.92	0.67
25 000	0.29	0.10	0.24	0.24	0.87	0.58
40 000	0.32	0.11	0.26	0.19	0.88	0.56

Source: Jansson and Lindberg (1998).

In urban areas, the level of the accident externality charge would be of a different order of magnitude. The cost structure is more complex than on interurban roads. As the traffic volume increases, the somewhat less important component, that is the price-relevant cost of A-accidents, will gradually increase, while the more important price-relevant cost of X-accidents will decrease sharply. On balance, the relationship between the total price-relevant cost and car traffic volume is L-shaped in the relevant range, as seen in Table 7.5. From the summations in the right-hand column it is clear that the treatment of *br* as regards A-accidents is, relatively speaking, less crucial for the final result.

It can be concluded that the total accident externality charge may be many times higher in a central city area than on interurban roads.

Table 7.5 *Financial result for the owner of transport infrastructure of optimal pricing, PC/AC$_{prod}$ for different values of the scale elasticity E and the ratio of the user cost to the producer cost*

AC_{user}/AC_{prod}	Scale elasticity E				
	0.8	0.9	1	1.1	1.2
0	1.25	1.11	1	0.91	0.83
1	1.50	1.22	1	0.83	0.66
2	1.75	1.33	1	0.72	0.49
3	2.00	1.44	1	0.64	0.32
4	2.25	1.55	1	0.55	0.15
5	2.50	1.66	1	0.46	0.00

Source: Jansson and Lindberg (1998).

9.2   Noise and Barrier Effects of Car Traffic

First considering noise, the price-relevant noise disturbance cost also seems to belong to the decreasing-cost typical case. On one hand, the physical level of traffic noise (decibels) increases in a markedly degressive way with the traffic volume. On the other hand, when it comes to the disturbance *cost*, the willingness to pay to reduce noise increases progressively with the noise level. Which effect is the strongest? One authoritative source states that 'a halving of the traffic will reduce the noise level by 3 dBA, but a reduction of 8–10 dBA is required in order that the noise level will be perceived as halved' (SOU, 1989, 43, p. 66). Further evidence on these two relationships is badly needed.

Next considering barrier effects, it is clear that in a street system without cars, pedestrians can cross the street everywhere. As soon as cars are allowed, the pedestrian behaviour has to be disciplined: pedestrians have to cross streets only at marked crossings, and when pedestrian lights are green. The complete feeling of security for the unprotected road users also disappears with the first car entering the streets. Insecurity grows with the number of cars using the streets, but the marginal additions to total insecurity will probably become smaller and smaller.

9.3   Exhaust Emission Costs

The main point here is that regulation in the form of standards concerning fuel, engines and exhaust fume cleaning devices seems to lead the way, since the ultimate goal is anyway to get rid of harmful emissions. For petrol-driven cars it seems to be possible to solve the exhaust fume emission problem – apart from CO_2 – by catalytic cleaning of exhaust fumes. The catalytic converters seem effective enough to make the price-relevant cost of NO_x, CO, HC, VOC and SO_2 emissions almost trivial.

Given the unit costs of these emissions presented in the literature (see, for example, Small and Kazimi, 1995, and Eyre et al., 1997; for a thorough discussion see Chapter 4 of this book), it is clearly cost-effective to make catalysers compulsory. During the period of transition to a car fleet where all cars have catalysers, the petrol tax component in question should be based on the emissions of present 'cat-cars'. This is because it seems very unreasonable to make catalysers compulsory on all new cars, and yet tax the petrol used by new (and old) cars as if there were no catalytic cleaning. An ownership tax differentiation between cat- and non-cat-cars would be fair, as well as encouraging a quicker introduction of catalytic converters to the whole car fleet.

Comparable cleaning devices for aircraft, diesel-burning ships and lorries are currently too expensive to introduce, given the relevant relative prices. Concerted EU action could most likely solve the problem in a fairly short time by economic incentives (for example, substantially raising the diesel tax) to develop proper cleaning devices and/or much cleaner fuels and engines. Moreover, if an electronic kilometre charging system is applied to HGVs and buses, differentiated kilometre charges could to a large extent replace the diesel tax as pollution payment. The diesel tax would be too blunt a means of control, when improved engines and exhaust fume cleaning devices are introduced on the heavy vehicles.

Adopting such a policy, Europe would soon get rid of most of the NO_x and SO_2 emissions from the transport sector without serious harm to trade and industry. Carbon dioxide – CO_2 – however, is an entirely different matter. It cannot be cleaned away. In Europe as in developed countries elsewhere in the world, the aim is to start to actually reduce the total CO_2 emission rather than letting it continue to rise. The cost-efficient way of attaining this aim would be to introduce a common CO_2 tax in all sectors of the economy sufficient to induce different kinds of substitution and mobility restraint.

Such a tax exists in many countries. A key issue both for climate policy and transport policy is the value of the CO_2 tax. A proper damage cost approach to calculating the expected costs of threatening global warming is, unfortunately, very difficult. The range of values suggested by different attempts at damage cost estimation is very wide indeed (see Chapter 4). In the concluding section below, the strategic choices facing policy makers in this connection are put into the perspective obtained by the analysis of this chapter of the price-relevant marginal cost for the use of transport infrastructure.

10 CONCLUSIONS

10.1 Marginal Cost and Present-day Taxes

One result of the survey of the short-run price-relevant cost components for road services is that, so far as non-urban car traffic is concerned, the total price-relevant marginal cost is well below the prevailing average level of the total tax imposed on petrol. In Sweden, as in a number of other European countries, the price of petrol at the filling station is about €1 per litre (1999 prices), of which €0.8 is tax, whereas the price-relevant cost on uncongested non-urban roads expressed per litre of petrol is no more than €0.2. In Table 7.6, the total petrol price is divided into five components to make this relation clearer.

Table 7.6   Composition of the total petrol price for non-urban car traffic, Sweden

	Price (€/litre)
Petrol price before tax	0.2
Price-relevant marginal cost (apart from CO_2 emissions)	0.2
Value-added tax (25% of the above two items)	0.1
CO_2 tax	0.1
Excess tax	0.4
Total petrol price	1.0

The total petrol tax excluding the CO_2 tax exceeds by far the price-relevant cost of non-urban car traffic. This relation is to some extent disguised, among other things by giving suggestive names (such as 'energy tax') to different tax components, and by calculating the value-added tax after all other taxes have trebled the petrol price. Politicians, and, in particular, the minister of finance, seem to be unaware of this awkward fact, or at least they do not show that they are aware of it. As in many other countries, the petrol tax is a very important source of revenue for the central government. A petrol tax reduction down to the level of the price-relevant marginal cost would be very difficult for financial reasons.

For urban, and, in particular, big city road networks the picture looks quite different. The price-relevant marginal cost varies substantially over time and space. It can be argued, however, that, on average, the 'excess tax' component in Table 7.6 is changed to a tax shortfall, that is, the total petrol price is too low to cover the price-relevant marginal cost of congestion, accidents, noise, and emissions of NO_x, HC, CO and VOC. It should be apparent that road-pricing differentiation between urban and non-urban areas is an issue of foremost importance. Raising the petrol tax to bring the price of urban road use in line with the price-relevant cost is obviously not the right way to go. The urban net benefits of such a policy could easily be offset by non-urban disbenefits. Separate urban road pricing is the right way. If that way is chosen, the remaining question concerning non-urban car traffic is: what should be done about the present excess tax on petrol in this sector?

The CO_2 tax is the crucial factor in this connection. Although, in the example of Sweden, the present level of the CO_2 tax is high by international standards, it is still far too low for achieving the objective of substantial CO_2 emission reduction. A quadrupling of the present CO_2 tax is probably necessary for keeping within the desired emission limits. This would wipe out the 'excess tax' item in Table 7.6, but nothing else so far as non-urban car traffic is concerned; the only thing that would be achieved is that the petrol taxes change names. The real effects of such an ambitious climate policy would arise in other sectors than non-urban car travel. First, in urban traffic, road pricing would have to be introduced to match the price-relevant costs of congestion, accidents, and other externalities, since the petrol tax is mainly used to curb CO_2 emissions. Second, a multiplication of the CO_2 tax would be a great challenge for other sectors of the economy, where fossil fuels are used in large quantities.

A quadrupling of the present Swedish CO_2 tax corresponds to a tax of €0.2 per kg of CO_2. This would be a very demanding target for pricing and taxation policy for other modes of transport, as well as some parts of industry, which is realistic only if all EU member states do the same thing. In that case the transport sector would be the least problem. If, for example, air travellers had to pay €0.2 per kg CO_2, total demand for air transport would be noticeably affected, but if all airlines were treated in the same way, no serious allocative problem would be created.

10.2   The Urban Problem

When it comes to urban TI services, and in particular, big city road services, the goal conflict has the opposite character to that of non-urban road transport illustrated in Table 7.6, above. Optimal road pricing would typically give revenue covering road capacity costs many times over. The same is true for big city airports located not too far out, and seaports (which, however, in most cases are relocated to external sites to avoid the increasing costs of central city location).

However, to judge from the considerable difficulties in carrying the forty-year-old idea of urban road pricing through the political decision-making process, the efficiency and equity goal conflict is just as severe in the case of an expected large financial surplus as in the more familiar case of a deficit resulting from optimal pricing. In addition, in the present case there is the fear that many commercial activities, which make the central city 'flourish', would move out, if road motor vehicle transport was made more expensive by road pricing – just as central city seaports have moved to seashores out of the city, as we have already mentioned. External supermarkets completely designed for motorized customers, replacing department stores in the central city and/or traditional food markets, and suburban high-street retailing are a well-known, hotly debated issue.

There are three different approaches to solving the efficiency and equity goal conflict in urban road transport worth mentioning: (1) returning the financial surplus to the paying motorists; (2) tradable ration coupons; and (3) administrative restraints on urban motor vehicle traffic. Each of these approaches will be considered in turn.

1. *Returning the financial surplus to the paying motorists*   In an exceptional case this could be done completely by selectively (geographically) lowering car ownership taxes by a corresponding amount. The snag is that the existing level of car taxes is too low to admit full compensation, and a negative car ownership tax seems anomalous. In addition, the necessary geographical selectivity (in order that the compensation should not be too diluted) will create administrative border problems regarding car registration. A partial return of the road-pricing surplus to the paying motorists seems to be the most practicable and reasonable option. This will be the result if the surplus is used for lowering the local income tax level, or local rates, which would be in line with a 'green' tax shift.

2. *Tradable ration coupons*   If it is considered very important that existing motorists as a collective are not 'taxed' more than at present, tradable ration vouchers, or permits to travel by car in certain places at certain times could be issued and distributed (free) among town and city motorists. The resulting income redistribution then takes place within the motorist collective, from those who want to drive relatively more to those who are willing to sell some or all of their allotted share of coupons. The big, perhaps insurmountable, problem with such a system is to find a reasonable criterion for who should get ration coupons in the first place. Should some have more coupons than others? If all citizens get a ration card, a large redistribution of income between car owners and carless people would follow. And if only car owners get a ration card, an unwanted incentive to become a car owner is created. It goes without saying that if the local government sells the permits rather than gives them away, no solution to the equity problem has been found.

3. *Administrative restraints on urban motor vehicle traffic*   Instead of rationing scarce road space by the willingness to pay for it, innovative forms of traffic regulation can be introduced. In the best case it may achieve approximately the same allocation of road space as a proper price system, without a wholesale transfer of money from urban motorists to the local government. In the worst case it can result in a big loss of social surplus.

10.3   Towards Integration of Urban Road-pricing and Traffic-calming Theories

In the road-pricing literature, the unprotected road users – cyclists and pedestrians – play a secondary role. This is right and proper so far as the interurban road network and the main urban arteries are concerned. Those roads are meant for medium- and long-distance travel by fast motor vehicles, and to the extent that the slow, short-distance traffic by foot and two-wheeled vehicles take the same routes, separate lanes should be provided alongside the roadway. An 'industrial economics' view of the 'output' of motor vehicles in the road system is appropriate, by which the pricing objective is to ensure that an optimal rate of capacity utilization of the transport production plants is obtained in terms of traffic flow and travel time.

In the streets of the central city, or in residential areas in the suburbs, things can look quite different, at least in the cities of the old world. Short-distance trips dominate (through-traffic should use bypasses). A substantial proportion of the trips could be made by foot or bicycle, if it is safe and if pedestrians and cyclists are not too hampered by traffic lights and other restrictions. Speed limits for cars are applied in the interest of unprotected road users in the first place. 'Traffic calming' is nowadays equally as prominent as traditional traffic management by which the travel time of car trips should be minimized. The extreme of car-free streets is no longer exceptional but an increasingly prominent feature of the central city.

The theory of road pricing should similarly differentiate between roads for motorized traffic and central city streets (and residential areas). This will be achieved automatically by paying proper attention to the component in the pricing-relevant cost constituted by the accident externality charges (see Figure 7.3).

The relationship between the optimal accident externality charges on motor vehicles and the volume/capacity ratio takes the very opposite shape to that between the optimal congestion toll and the volume/capacity ratio (compare Tables 7.1 and 7.5). The optimal congestion toll is zero in a relatively wide range, and begins to rise when traffic density is such that the speed limit is difficult to reach. It will accelerate as the volume/capacity ratio approaches unity. This may cause some unexpected problems in finding the true optimum. If car traffic demand is fairly elastic, the demand curve may well intersect the curve of total price-relevant cost from below the first time (intersection point B), and a second time from above (intersection point C). Point B corresponds to a minimum of the net benefit and point C to a maximum. However, a third point of interest is the starting-point A, where, clearly, the net benefit is zero. Although point C corresponds to a maximum, it may still represent a negative net benefit, in which case the corner solution A is to be preferred. Complete

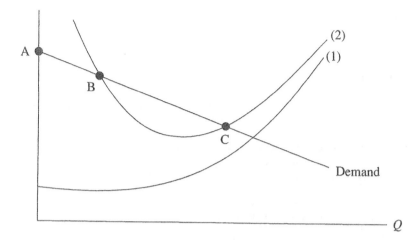

Figure 7.3   Accident externality charges on top of congestion tolls and polluter payments

freedom from motor vehicle traffic may turn out to be the true optimum in many cases.

This possibility complicates the already complicated and controversial issue of urban road pricing, but it may be seen as an important reminder that it is not just in certain residential areas that freedom from car traffic is very natural. 'Pedestrianization' is a measure as worthy of attention as road pricing in the city centre.

When the possibility of prohibiting car traffic in certain areas is up for discussion, many road-pricing enthusiasts argue that it is most unlikely that a corner solution could be optimal anywhere, since threshold costs (costs that manifest themselves as soon as a quantity > 0 is being produced) are absent. This is plainly wrong. The truth is instead that when accident risks as well as noise and barrier effects are considered, the price-relevant cost can initially be very high, which under certain circumstances speaks for complete freedom from car traffic.

NOTES

1. An excellent book covering both topics is Small (1992). A recent value of time survey can be found in Wardman (1997).
2. As stated in the text, the elasticity of R with respect to Q according to Brüde and Larsson (1993) is 0.5. This means that the number of accidents involving unprotected road users (X) is proportional to $Q^{0.5}$, which, of course, can also be written as the square root of Q.

3. The fatality risk for motor vehicle-only accidents (r) is 7.7, and the corresponding risks for severe and light injuries, corrected for underreporting, are 113 and 474, respectively, per 10^9 vehicle-km.

REFERENCES

Brüde, U. and J. Larsson (1993), 'Models for predicting accidents at junctions where pedestrians and cyclists are involved. How well do they fit?', *Accident Analysis and Prevention*, **25**, 499–509.

Crandall, R.W., H.K. Gruenspecht, Th.E. Keeler and L.B. Lave (1986), *Regulating the Automobile*, Washington, DC: Brookings Institution.

European Commission (1995), *Towards Fair and Efficient Pricing in Transport. Policy Options for Internalising the External Costs of Transport in the European Union*, Green Paper, COM(95)691/FIN, Brussels.

Eyre, N.J., E. Ozdemiroglu, D.W. Pearce and P. Steele (1997), 'Fuel and location effects on the damage costs of transport emissions', *Journal of Transport Economics and Policy*, **31** (1), 5–24.

Jansson, J.O. (1969), 'Optimal congestion tolls for car commuters. A note on current theory', *Journal of Transport Economics and Policy*, **3** (3), 300–305.

Jansson, J.O. (1984), *Transport System Optimization and Pricing*, New York: Wiley.

Jansson, J.O. (1994), 'Accident externality charges', *Journal of Transport Economics and Policy*, **28** (1), 31–43.

Jansson, J.O. and G. Lindberg (1997), *Transport Pricing Principles in Detail*, European Commission, DG VII Project No: ST-96-SC.172, Brussels.

Jansson, J.O. and G. Lindberg (1998), *Accident Externality Charges – With Emphasis on Urban Transport Problems*, Proceedings of 1st Asia Pacific Conference on Transportation and the Environment, 13–15 May, Singapore: Center for Transportation Research, National University of Singapore.

Jansson, J.O. and D. Shneerson (1982), *Port Economics*, Cambridge, MA: MIT Press.

Jansson, J.O. and D. Shneerson (1987), *Liner Shipping Economics*, London: Chapman & Hall.

Ministry of Transport (1964), *Road Pricing: The Economic and Technical Possibilities* (Smeed Report), London: HMSO.

Mohring, H. (1976), *Transportation Economics*, Cambridge, MA: Ballinger.

Mohring, H. and M. Harwitz (1962), *Highway Benefits: An Analytical Framework*, Evanston, IL: Transportation Center at the Northwestern University.

Newbery, D. (1994), 'Pricing and congestion', in R. Layard and S. Glaister (eds), *Cost–Benefit Analysis*, Cambridge: Cambridge University Press, pp. 396–417.

Nilsson, G. (1996), *Trafiksäkerhetssituationens variationer i tiden* (Road safety variations over time), VTI Rapport 15, Linköping: Swedish Road and Transport Research Institute.

Satterthwaite, S.P. (1981), *A Survey of Research into Relationship between Traffic Accidents and Traffic Volumes*, Transport and Road Research Laboratory Supplementary Report 692, Crowthorne.

Small, K. (1992), *Urban Transportation Economics*, Chur: Harwood.

Small, K. and C. Kazimi (1995), 'On the costs of air pollution from motor vehicles', *Journal of Transport Economics and Policy*, **29** (1), 7–31.

Small, K., C. Winston and C.A. Evans (1989), *Road Work*, Washington, DC: Brookings Institution.

Stangeby, I. (1997), *Persontransport i arbeid* (Business travel), Transportøkonomisk Institutt rapport 375/1997, Oslo: Norwegian Institute of Transport Economics.

Statens offentliga utredningar (SOU) (1989), *Storstadstrafik 3 – Bilavgifter* (Report on road pricing by the Committee of Inquiry into big city traffic problems), Stockholm: Allmänna Förlaget, 43.

Swahn, H. (1992), *Framtida transporter i Sverige. Tekniska underlagsbilagor* (Future transport in Sweden. Technical appendices), VTI notat T117:3–6, Linköping: VTI (Swedish National Road and Transport Research Institute).

Underwood, R. (1961), 'Speed, volume, and density relationships', in Bureau of Highway Traffic, *Quality and Theory of Traffic Flow*, New Haven, CT: Yale University Press.

Vägverket (1993), *EVA-Effectberäkning vid väganalyser* (Cost–benefit analysis for roads), Borlänge: Swedish National Road Administration.

Vägverket (1997), *Nationell plan för vägtransportsystemet* (National plan for the road transport system), Borlänge: Swedish National Road Administration.

Walters, A.A. (1961), 'The theory and measurement of marginal private and social costs of highway congestion', *Econometrica*, October, 676–99.

Walters, A.A. (1968), *The Economics of Road User Charges*, World Bank staff occasional papers no. 5, Washington, DC: International Bank for Reconstruction and Development.

Wardman, M. (1997), *A Review of Evidence on the Value of Travel Time in Great Britain*, Working paper 495, Leeds: Leeds University, Institute of Transport Economics.

8. Transport infrastructure and regional development

Piet Rietveld and Peter Nijkamp

1 INTRODUCTION

In several parts of the world (Europe, North America, ASEAN) various clearly visible processes of economic integration take place, implying a transformation of regions into a network economy with an open access to, but also with a strong competition between major areas in this network. As a result of this competitive process, some regions will become losers and others winners. Thus, the regional development issue seems to become a factor of critical importance. This is also witnessed by the new national and supranational plans (such as the STAR programme of the EU) to invest in sophisticated infrastructure in backward regions in order to ensure relatively equal competitive advantages for all regions. In many countries, transport infrastructure is regarded as a critical success factor for competitive performance and internationalization of regional economies. The awareness has grown that missing links – and even more so, missing networks as a whole – mean a significant reduction in the potential productivity of a region or nation.

It is increasingly recognized that regional development is not only the result of a proper combination of private production factors such as labour and capital, but also of infrastructure in general and transport infrastructure in particular. Improving infrastructure will then lead to a higher productivity of private production factors. Conversely, a neglect of infrastructure will lead to a lower productivity of the other production factors.

The desired balance between private capital and infrastructure in regional development has been the subject of much theoretical and ideological debate. Hirschman (1958) has already pointed out, however, that it is illusory to think that a structural balanced development is possible. Given the lumpiness of transport infrastructure projects, one will often have relatively long periods of excess supply or demand.

Governments have different options with respect to transport infrastructure decisions. First, they may invest in infrastructure as a response to serious bottlenecks taking place due to an expansion of the private sector. This leads to a *passive* strategy: transport infrastructure is following private investment. Another option is that governments use transport infrastructure as an engine for national or regional development. This implies an *active* strategy, where transport infrastructure is leading and inducing private investments. The latter strategy has a risky element, because the response of the private sector to infrastructure improvement may be unpredictable and even disappointing. In many countries one can easily find examples of infrastructure projects which failed because of an insufficient response from the private sector.

It is important to note, at this stage, that in general the concept of infrastructure is used in a rather loose way in the literature. Most definitions, however, include one or both of the following elements. First, infrastructure is mostly a capital good for which users do not pay a full market price: infrastructure is perceived as a source of external economies (compare Youngson, 1967; Lakshmanan, 1989). Second, provision of infrastructure to an area will mean a relatively high cost for the first user and a small marginal cost for an extra user. This implies essentially that infrastructure is regarded not as a set of things, but as a set of attributes (Youngson, 1967).

In the past decades there has been an ongoing debate on the economic impacts of the supply of infrastructure. A major issue here is whether infrastructure – as a set of connected public goods – should be a main responsibility of public authorities or whether it can be left to the private sector (see Chapter 9, Section 4; see also Nijkamp and Rienstra, 1996). Issues such as fiscal federalism also play a role in this context. It is often argued that a meaningful distinction of possible governmental tasks can be made into: regulatory systems, management and operation, and ownership of infrastructure (see Lindfield, 1998). The long-range impacts of infrastructure provision may depend on the type of institutional arrangement chosen (see also Crihfield and McGuire, 1997; Cain, 1997; World Bank, 1994).

The impact of infrastructure on the economy consists of various elements (see Table 8.1). Temporary effects will occur in the construction sector (directly) and indirectly in all other sectors via intermediate deliveries. An additional, negative effect, which is often overlooked, concerns crowding-out (especially for large-scale investments): infrastructure must be financed, for example, by means of government bonds, which may lead to higher interest rates and lower investments elsewhere in the economy.

Among the permanent effects is the influence on the quantities of production factors needed for operations and for maintenance. In the present chapter attention will mainly be focused on still another type of permanent effect: the 'programme' (induction or spin-off) effects. Programme effects refer to long-term indirect changes in income, employment or investment in the private

Table 8.1   Effects of transport infrastructure investments

Type of effect	Demand side	Supply side
Temporary	Construction effects; Crowding-out	–
Permanent (structural)	Cost of operations and of maintenance	Effect on productivity and location of new activities

sector, that is, effects which are induced by the new opportunities offered by the improvement or extension of infrastructure.

The distinction between temporary and permanent effects of infrastructure is important. The permanent effects by definition are often difficult to trace, that is, because they materialize only in the long run. They are, therefore, difficult to disentangle from other factors impacting on regional development.

The dynamics of the impacts is often complex. Since preparation and implementation of infrastructure projects take much time (in some countries, 15 years is no exception), there is ample time for other actors in the economy to anticipate the completion of infrastructure. For example, private sector developers may construct industrial sites or large office buildings before the transport infrastructure has been completed. On the other hand, because of locational or organizational inertia it may often take a long time before the actors in the economy have fully adjusted to changes in infrastructure. Relocations of firms are usually not induced by changes in transport infrastructure, but by lack of space for those firms that want to expand. Only after the decision to relocate has been made does infrastructure start to play an important role.

Another example concerns the organization of distribution patterns. Improvement of infrastructure may make changes in distribution patterns worthwhile – for example, a reduction in the number of distribution centres. But firms are usually not fast in realizing such changes. As a consequence the programme effects of infrastructure investments materialize in a gradual way.

The dynamic pattern of infrastructure impacts has not received much attention in research thus far, but it is clear that it depends, among other things, on the speed of overall economic growth. In a dynamic economy one may expect a faster pattern of adjustment. The purpose of the present chapter is to review studies which assess the permanent impacts of transport infrastructure investments on the spatial economy. Environmental effects will not be discussed: these are reviewed by Rothengatter (Chapter 4 in this book).

This chapter has links with several other chapters in this volume, especially with those on transport policy (Baum and Schulz, Chapter 9), transport infrastructure investment (Jansson, Chapter 6), and transport in developing economies (Gwilliam, Chapter 13).

The further organization of the chapter is as follows. Some theoretical notions on infrastructure and regional development are discussed in Section 2. Section 3 is devoted to studies which focus on the impact of transport infrastructure on productivity in regions. In Section 4, studies are reviewed which focus on the role of transport infrastructure as a location factor, that is, influencing the location of private investment or employment. In Section 5, an integrated analysis of productivity and relocation effects of transport infrastructure on regional development is given. Section 6 offers concluding remarks.

2   TRANSPORT INFRASTRUCTURE AND REGIONAL DEVELOPMENT: THEORY

Improvement of transport infrastructure influences both production and household consumption. It leads to a reduction in transport costs and/or travel times. This may give rise to substantial redistribution effects among economic groups and also among regions. In order to analyse the differential effects of

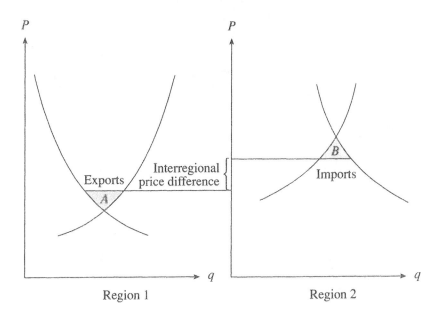

Figure 8.1   Supply and demand in two regions

improvements of transport infrastructure on regional development, we shall discuss the relationship between transport and interregional trade.

The standard model of interregional trade is illustrated in Figure 8.1. Export takes place from region 1 to 2 when transport cost is less than the difference in equilibrium price for a certain good in both regions (that is $(p_2 - p_1)$ in Figure 8.1). Compared with the situation without trade, an additional surplus is created consisting of areas A (accruing to producers in region 1) and B (accruing to consumers in region 2). Thus, both regions benefit from trade according to the model. Improvement of infrastructure leads to a decrease in transport costs and hence to an increase in transport volumes. The equilibrium price in region 1 will increase, and the price in region 2 will decrease. Thus, in region 2, consumers benefit from the improvement of infrastructure, whereas producers are negatively affected. In region 1 it is the other way around. In employment terms, region 1 benefits, but region 2 is hurt by the improvement of transport infrastructure.

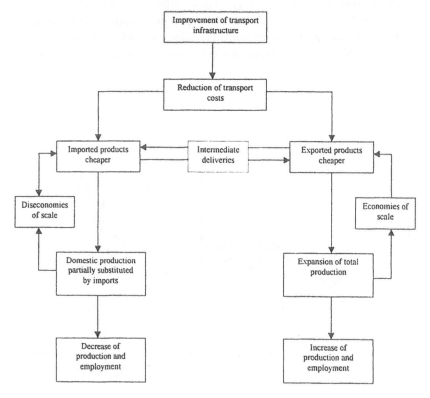

Figure 8.2   Effects of improvement in transport infrastructure

The two models sketched above are partial equilibrium models. They deal with the market for only one good. General equilibrium models are better for analysing the effects of changes in infrastructure, but they are of course more complex (see, for instance, Takayama and Labys, 1986; Takayama and Judge, 1971; Tinbergen, 1957; van den Bergh et al., 1996).

Figure 8.2 (which has been taken in adjusted form from Pluym and Roosma, 1984) presents some of the main effects when more than one sector is considered. In this case, the net effects are difficult to predict. Intermediate deliveries play a complicating role. In addition, there may be compensating forces in the regions in which employment was negatively affected by increased competition. Prices of the products concerned will decrease, so that consumers can spend more on other products, part of which will be produced in the same region.

Processes in the long term (relocation of capital and persons) caused by changes in transport infrastructure are even more difficult to predict. Thus, operational models have to be developed to trace the effects of changes in (transport) infrastructure on regional development. This will be the subject of the next sections.

3 TRANSPORT INFRASTRUCTURE AND REGIONAL PRODUCTIVITY

3.1 Introduction

In addition to production factors such as labour and private capital, transport infrastructure plays a role as an input in production processes. An improvement of transport infrastructure services implies that a regional economy can make use of its private production factors in a more productive way. Better transport infrastructure means that lower capital and labour needs to be able to reach the same production level.

There are essentially two ways of analysing the productivity gains induced by transport infrastructure improvements. The first one takes place at the firm level by measuring carefully the reductions in (transport) costs which can be achieved by infrastructure improvements. The second one occurs at the aggregate regional level by investigating the contribution of the production factor infrastructure to regional production, taking into account the contribution of other production factors. This entails the use of regional production functions.

3.2 Analysis at the Firm Level

Micro analysis can be helpful in tracing behavioural determinants and responses of individual firms as a result of new infrastructure. An interesting example can be found in Forkenbrock and Foster (1990) who describe the results of various studies concerning the impact of infrastructure on regional development all using quasi-experimental control group analysis and macroeconomic indicators (for example, population, employment, income per capita and so on). It is remarkable that the results of these studies appear to differ from one another: some authors find a positive relationship and others a negative or inconclusive one. Thus controlled micro experimentation does not necessarily guarantee satisfactory outcomes. Other results on cost shares can be found in Diamond and Spence (1989) and Anderson (1983). We shall present two examples of a micro approach, taken from Dutch research in this field.

A study by NEA (1990a) addresses the economic costs of inadequate infrastructure in the province of Noord Brabant on the regional economy. The study focuses on the congested S20 road connection between Nijmegen and Eindhoven. Firms in the region were reported to suffer from excessive transport costs. A careful series of interviews with firms in the region led to the conclusion that firms with a regional orientation experience an increase in total transport costs of about 1.6 per cent due to the congested conditions, including both capital and labour costs. For firms with an international orientation this figure is 0.7 per cent. For most non-transport firms the transport costs do not exceed 30 per cent of total costs.

It appears that the impact of the delays on productivity of firms is low, except for transport firms themselves. The overall effect of inadequate transport infrastructure on regional productivity will therefore be low in this case. Of course, the impact on the profit rate of individual firms will be higher, even much higher in certain individual cases. An interesting result of the study is that the actual time losses for firms are much smaller than the time losses as perceived by the firms themselves. This is also an important point for the impact of infrastructure on location decisions of firms. Perceptions deserve more attention in studies of firm behaviour than they usually receive.

A second case study was carried out by NEA (1990b) in the province of Zuid-Holland. In contrast to the former study, the latter is an *ex post* study: it deals with a realized infrastructure improvement.

In the 1980s an industrial area near The Hague, the provincial capital and seat of the government of the Netherlands, received a much better connection with the national highway system. The time gains for cars or trucks operated by firms in this particular area varied from 2 to 10 per cent. For firms located outside the industrial area the average time gains were of course much smaller. It appeared from the interviews that firms made little systematic effort to make use of the time gains. A rescheduling of trips did not take place, for example, so that part of the time gains was absorbed by an increase of slack in firms. The overall reduction in transport costs and the related productivity increase due to the transport infrastructure improvement were relatively small in this case study.

It may be said that a disadvantage of micro case studies of the above type is that they focus only on productivity improvements for firms directly affected by infrastructure improvements. Indirect effects on other firms are usually not taken into account. Another disadvantage of these studies is that only one type of infrastructure is considered. Therefore, it is interesting to combine the case-study approach with modelling approaches, using aggregate production functions, where such elements can be taken into account. This will be the subject of the next section.

3.3 Production Function Approach

A general formulation of a production function for sector i in region r, with various types of infrastructure, is:

$$Q_{ir} = f_{ir}(L_{ir}, K_{ir}; IA_r, \dots, IN_r) \tag{8.1}$$

where:

Q_{ir} = value added in sector i, region r,
     = L_{ir} employment in sector i, region r,
     = K_{ir} private capital in sector i, region r,
     = $IA_r, \dots, IN_r$ infrastructure of various types in region r.

Among the types of infrastructure distinguished are: transport, communication, energy supply, water supply, education, health services, and so on.

As far as transport infrastructure is concerned, it is not easy to take into account its network properties in the production function approach. One possible approach is to distinguish various types of transport infrastructure according to their spatial range: intraregional, interregional, and possibly international.

For transport infrastructure, a related problem is that its impact may transcend the boundaries of regions. A certain region may not have its own airport but still benefit from an airport nearby. This problem may be solved by using the concept of accessibility of certain types of infrastructure (terminals, like ports and airports) in the production function.

Most of the work on the contribution of infrastructure to productivity has been carried out at the national level. For example, Aschauer (1989) found for US time-series data an output elasticity of infrastructure of no less than 0.40 (that is, one extra unit infrastructure leads to an increase in productivity of 40 per cent). However, in more recent research much lower coefficients are often found (see, for example, Munnell, 1993).

Regional studies on the contribution of transport infrastructure to productivity have been less numerous. A sample of such models is given in Table 8.2. In most of the models a simplified version of the above production function approach is used. The most complete ones are those developed by Mera (1973) and Fukuchi (1978) for Japan, Snickars and Granholm (1981) for Sweden, and Pinnoi (1994) for the USA.

Table 8.2   *Regional production functions with infrastructure as a production factor*

Author	Country	Number of sectors	Number of types of infrastructure	Presence of: Labour	Presence of: Private capital	Form of production function
Biehl (1986)	EU	1	1	yes	no	Cobb–Douglas
Blum (1982)	Germany	3	8	yes	no	Cobb–Douglas
Andersson et al. (1989)	Sweden	1	7	yes	yes	Cobb–Douglas (with modification)
Snickars and Granholm (1981)	Sweden	21	5	yes	yes	Leontief
Nijkamp (1986)	Netherlands	1	3	yes	no	Cobb–Douglas
Fukuchi (1978)	Japan	3	3	yes	yes	Cobb–Douglas
Kawashima (1978)	Japan	8	1	yes	no	Linear
Mera (1973)	Japan	3	4	yes	yes	Cobb–Douglas
Costa et al. (1987)	USA	3	1	yes	yes	Translog
Deno (1988)	USA	1	3	yes	yes	Translog
Holtz-Eakin (1994)	USA	1	1	yes	yes	Cobb–Douglas
Pinnoi (1994)	USA	3	3	yes	yes	Cobb–Douglas
Seitz (1995)	Germany	1	1	yes	yes	Translog
Prud'homme (1996)	France	1	1	yes	yes	Cobb–Douglas

Sectoral detail is of importance in these studies. This is shown by Fukuchi (1978) and by Blum (1982), who found that the productivity increase due to infrastructure may be quite different among different economic sectors. This is also confirmed by Biehl (1986), who found that an index of the sectoral composition of regional economies explains much more of the variance in regional per capita income than infrastructure does.

The most detailed treatments of infrastructure are by Blum (1982) and by Andersson et al. (1989). As far as transport infrastructure is concerned, Blum distinguished (in a regional study of the Federal Republic of Germany) four types of infrastructure: long-distance road infrastructure, all other roads, railways and ports. For both types of roads and for ports, significant results were obtained. For railways, Blum found zero and even negative effects.

Andersson et al. distinguished the following aspects of transport infrastructure for the Swedish regions: main roads, railways, airport capacity, travel time to major metropolitan area and interregional travel time. For 1970, they found that the impact of railways on regional production was stronger than that of main roads. In 1980, this situation had reversed. Airport capacity on its own does not have an influence on regional production, according to the estimates. However, if taken in conjunction with research and development, it is shown to have a positive effect.

As appears from Table 8.2, the form of the production function chosen is in most cases a Cobb–Douglas function. This implies a considerable degree of substitutability among production factors, for example, between private and public capital. By investing in private infrastructure regions can extend their production capacity, even when infrastructure is fixed at a low level. An interesting modification of the Cobb–Douglas function is used by Andersson et al. in order to allow for zones with increasing and zones with decreasing returns to scale. An entirely different approach is followed by Snickars and Granholm (1981). The Leontief structure they use implies that infrastructure imposes a limit on the extension of employment and private capital in a region.

4 INFRASTRUCTURE AND THE LOCATION OF ECONOMIC ACTIVITY

4.1 Introduction

Provision of infrastructure in a certain region leads to an increase in productivity of private production factors such as labour and capital (see Section 3). This may in turn lead to expansion and relocation of these production factors in this region. This effect is the subject of the present section.

The response of labour and capital to changes in regional infrastructure could be studied by means of the production functions discussed in Section 3. These production functions may then be used to derive demand functions for labour or capital with relative prices and infrastructure endowment as explanatory variables. In most empirical studies, this approach is not followed, however.[1] Rather, the levels of employment and capital are studied in the context of a rather loose location theory in which relative prices and infrastructure play a role next to a series of other location factors. Among these factors are urbanization economies, sectoral structure, quality of labour, accessibility of markets, and particular regional policies.

Four approaches can be observed in analysing the influence of infrastructure on the location of employment and private capital:

* the role of transport infrastructure is modelled via its influence on accessibility;

- the role of transport infrastructure is modelled via its influence on marginal transport costs, which are computed by means of a linear programming transport model;
- investments in infrastructure are directly linked to private investments in regional economic models; and
- the role of transport infrastructure is analysed by means of surveys among entrepreneurs on the importance of infrastructure relative to other location factors.

4.2 Infrastructure and Accessibility

Improvement of transport infrastructure leads to a reduction of travel time or cost and hence to an improvement of accessibility of markets or inputs. This may in turn lead to a relocation of labour and capital. Accessibility of a certain variable Z in regions can be defined as:

$$ACC_r(Z) = \sum_{r'} Z_{r'} f(c_{r'r}) \qquad (8.2)$$

where $c_{r'r}$ is an index of travel costs between regions r' and r, and $f(c_{r'r})$ is a distance decay function (for reviews on the accessibility concept, refer to Song, 1996, Handy and Niemeier, 1997 and Bruinsma and Rietveld, 1998). The variable Z may refer to employment, production, inputs and so on.

Botham (1983) uses the following relationship between regional employment and accessibility:

$$\Delta E_r = a_1 ED_r + a_2 W_r + a_3 LAPE_r + a_4 ACC_r(Z) \qquad (8.3)$$

where *ED*, *W* and *LAPE* denote employment density, wage rate, and an index of labour availability. For Z, several variables mentioned above have been tried. Finally, ΔE is the differential shift in employment, as defined by shift-share analysis.

The above equation has been estimated for 28 regions in the UK for the years 1961–66, the period just before the construction of the UK national highway system. The equation was used for simulating the impact of the highway system as it developed on the distribution of regional employment.

The reduction in transport costs induced by the highway system leads to an increase in accessibility of the regions. The effects on employment shifts have been computed by means of the equation. The general conclusion reads that the impact of the highway system on the regional distribution of employment is rather small. A similar conclusion is reached by Dodgson (1974), who used the same approach for the effects of the M62 in the UK, and Bruinsma et al. (1997), who studied the topic for the Netherlands. However, a similar study carried out by Kau (1976) in the USA gave rise to the conclusion that some regions experienced substantial positive impacts from an extension of the highway system.

Another application of the accessibility concept is given by Evers et al. (1987) in an *ex ante* study on high-speed rail connections in central and northern Europe. The study is more refined than the ones by Botham and Kau, in that some attention is paid to the problem of multiple modes of transport: focus on only one mode of transport may give a distorted view on accessibility as a location factor. It can be shown that the approach adopted by Evers et al. is (under certain conditions) consistent with a utility-based theory of the location of the firm (compare Rietveld, 1990). The result of the study was that employment relocation induced by the high-speed rail connection would be quite modest. A similar result was obtained by Sasaki et al. (1997) in a study on high-speed rail in Japan.

Illeris and Jakobson (1991) used the accessibility concept to study the effects of a fixed link across the Great Belt in Denmark. Their conclusion is that the competitive position of the regions concerned will not change much by the fixed link so that relocation will remain of limited importance.

In other studies, accessibility is also included but in a much simpler way, that is, by using travel time from a region to the economic core region in a country. This approach is a feasible option for countries dominated by a single centre (see, for example, Folmer and Nijkamp, 1987; Florax and Folmer, 1988).

Still another approach to accessibility is followed by Mills and Carlino (1989). They measure accessibility by means of the density of the interstate highway network and find that it has a clearly positive impact on employment growth in US counties.

In the studies cited in this section, a positive relationship is found between accessibility and total employment. As discussed in Section 2, this result is by no means guaranteed by theory. In terms of Figure 8.2 it means that the balance between the sectors benefiting from a reduction in transport costs and the sectors hurt by a reduction is positive for the regions. At the level of specific sectors, one might still have negative effects on employment, but this is not reflected by the models discussed here, because a sectoral subdivision is not used.

4.3 Infrastructure and Marginal Transport Costs

The accessibility concept used in the previous section is closely linked to the gravity model.[2] It allows for cross-hauling, and it yields spatial interaction matrices with a small number of zero interactions.[3] An alternative approach to transport modelling is the linear programming (LP) model, which does not allow for cross-hauling and which entails many zeros in the spatial interaction matrix (see Nijkamp and Reggiani, 1992). The model deals with the minimization of total transport costs among a set of regions under constraints concerning total supply and demand. The dual variables of total supply and demand per region represent the marginal costs of receiving inputs and shipping outputs. As indicated by Stevens (1961), the dual variables can be interpreted as location rents.

Harris (1973, 1980) has developed a model on industry location in which the dual variables play a central role. Investments in infrastructure leading to changes in transport costs give rise to changes in the dual variables. The dual variables in turn are determinants of industrial location. In this model, other factors influencing industrial location are: the cost of labour, the value of land, prior investments and agglomeration variables. The model has been developed for the USA. It allows for a high degree of spatial detail (approximately 3000 counties), and also the sectoral detail is substantial (up to 100 sectors). An interesting application of the model is discussed in Harris (1980). According to the model, investments in road and rail infrastructure in a rural county in the USA gave rise to substantial and positive direct effects on employment during the first two years. The structural spin-off effects of the infrastructure are negative, however, according to the model. After the fourth year, a negative, though modest, effect takes place on regional employment. This is an illustration of the lower part of Figure 8.2: regions may be negatively affected by an improvement of transport infrastructure.

4.4   Direct Links between Investments in Infrastructure and the Location of Private Investments

The effects of government investments on the regional or national economy and especially on private investments can be studied by means of standard regional or macroeconomic models. Several types of effects have to be taken into account (see also Table 8.1). *Multiplier effects* of public investments have a positive influence on private investments. On the contrary, *crowding-out effects* may occur which have a negative influence on private investments. Crowding-out occurs because financing infrastructure investments leads to higher interest rates for projects that are financed by means of government bonds. This implies a disincentive for private investors. Another type of effect consists of *spin-off effects*. These effects, on which the present chapter is focused, are usually not taken into account in these models, however (compare Houweling, 1987).

A possible approach to detect spin-off effects of infrastructure investments is the use of causality analysis. For example, in the approach of Pierce and Haugh (1977), statistical tests are developed for correlations between time series with different lag intervals. Using this approach, den Hartog et al. (1986) found for the Netherlands that there is indeed a causal relationship between public and private investments, taking place within an interval of three or four years. For the reverse relationship (that is, public investments are caused by private investments), no statistical confirmation could be found.

This result is important in the context of Hirschman's (1958) notion of 'unbalanced growth'. 'Unbalanced growth' means that private and public investments do not follow parallel paths. Periods with a strong emphasis on public investments alternate with periods with a strong emphasis on private investments. The result from the Netherlands suggests that public investments are the leading variable in this process.

A disadvantage of the approach above is that it is not possible to separate indirect, crowding-out and spin-off effects. Since the lag interval is rather short (three or four years), it is not clear whether the causal relationship refers to short-run (indirect or crowding-out) effects or long-run spin-offs. In order to overcome this difficulty, one may introduce different spatial levels in the analysis. An important part of the short-term effects of an infrastructure project will take place outside the region in which the project takes place. Long-run spin-off effects are likely to be concentrated in the project region, however. Therefore, den Hartog et al. (1986) also carried out an analysis at the provincial level. In each region, private investment IP as a share of the gross domestic product Q is explained by government investment IG as a share of the gross domestic product:

$$\Delta\left(\frac{IP}{Q}\right)_{r,t} = \sum_{i=0}^{k} \alpha_i \Delta\left(\frac{IG}{Q}\right)_{N,t-1} + \sum_{i=0}^{k} \beta_i \left[\Delta\left(\frac{IG}{Q}\right)_{r,t-i} - \Delta\left(\frac{IG}{Q}\right)_{N,t-i}\right]. \quad (8.4)$$

The subscripts t and r refer to time and region. The national level is represented by N. Thus in the above equation, for each region private investments are explained by government investments at both the national and regional level with certain lags (see also Nijkamp and Blaas, 1992).

Spin-off effects can be detected by means of the β_i coefficients in a cumulative way ($\Sigma_{i=0}\beta_i$). Empirical results show that spin-off effects are indeed significant for an interval of 0 to 5 years. However, den Hartog et al. (1986) indicate that this positive result depends strongly on one particular province (Zeeland), which happened to attract high levels of government investment during the period considered. If this province is left out, spin-off effects are no longer statistically significant. Thus, with the given approach, only when infrastructure investments are large is it possible to show that significant spin-offs take place in the regions.

4.5 Entrepreneurial Statements about the Importance of Infrastructure as a Location Factor

As a complement to the above modelling approaches one may also make use of direct interviews among entrepreneurs in order to study the relative importance of infrastructure. See, for example, Armstrong and Taylor (1993) and Healy and Baker (1995) for results at the European level. An example of this approach is given by Bruinsma (1990), who studied the impact of infrastructure improvements in three Dutch regions. About 15 per cent of the entrepreneurs state that improved or new infrastructure has played a very important role in the development of employment in the firm. One should not exaggerate the importance of infrastructure, however, since market developments and the availability of space for expansion played a more important role according to the entrepreneurs.

A special category concerns firms which relocated recently: in about 35 per cent of these cases, infrastructure is mentioned as an important or very important location factor. In each of the regions concerned there has been a major improvement of an existing highway or the construction of a new one. The average share of firms which reported that these activities had a positive impact on the firm's employment varied among the regions from 14 to 26 per cent. In one of the regions the data available allow one to make an estimate of the (minimum) number of jobs created by a new highway per amount of investment. The outcome is that an investment of about US$325 000 in highways leads to the creation of one permanent job. As a contrast one may use the amount of investment which is needed to generate one man-year of work in the construction sector and related sectors: taking into account the multiplier chain, a US$50 000 investment in highways generates work for one person during one year. The difference between the two figures is of course that the first impact has a permanent character whereas the second impact takes place only in the short run.

An obvious disadvantage of the approach described here is that there is no guarantee that actual behaviour of the entrepreneur has been in agreement with his statements. Another disadvantage is that such an interview-based analysis does not take into account indirect effects on other entrepreneurs, possibly located in entirely different regions (see also Vleugel et al., 1991). This raises the issue of generative versus distributive effects which will be discussed in the next section since it is of particular importance for our discussion.

4.6 Distributive versus Generative Growth

Improvement of infrastructure may lead to both distributive and generative effects. Distributive effects relate to a redistribution of economic activity among regions, the national total remaining constant. On the other hand, generative effects occur when the national total (or more generally the total in a system of regions) changes. A difficulty is that the balance between distributive and generative effects depends on the demarcation of the system of regions. For example, improvement of a national airport in a country may – apart from an interregional redistribution in the country – induce larger flows of air traffic in the country concerned. This might be interpreted as a generative growth effect, but it may also be the consequence of a redistribution of air traffic at a higher international level. In the latter case, the share of other countries would show a decline.

Thus, generative growth effects may simply be an illusion caused by a delimitation of a study area which is too narrowly defined. This does not mean to say, of course, that all generative growth effects are illusory. But one will often observe the tendency that generative growth effects will be smaller, the larger the system of regions studied.

We conclude that a considerable variety exists in terms of the analytical approaches *vis-à-vis* the impact of infrastructure on locational behaviour of firms. The attractive feature of the first two approaches discussed in this section is that they take into account the network character of transport networks. A consequence is that spatial spillover effects of infrastructure are taken into account. The third approach does not consider such spillover effects. It is strong in another respect, however: it addresses the temporal aspects of the consequences of infrastructure. The last approach is clearly different from the others in that it is carried out at the level of individual firms rather than at an aggregate level; in addition, the responses have the character of stated rather than revealed preferences. Clearly, the approaches outlined here are all partial. In the next section we consider possibilities for an integrated approach.

5   AN INTEGRATED ANALYSIS OF PRODUCTIVITY AND RELOCATION EFFECTS OF INFRASTRUCTURE

In the preceding sections we discussed the productivity and relocation effects of transport infrastructure separately. Of course, it would be preferable to use models where the two effects are treated in an integrated way. We shall discuss some interregional models which are suitable for this purpose. Figure 8.3 gives a schematic example of a model of this type (derived from Amano and Fujita, 1970).

For an appropriate analysis of the element of transport costs in the model one needs a detailed treatment of transport networks, route choice and modal choice. This leads to a degree of spatial detail which is difficult to meet in other

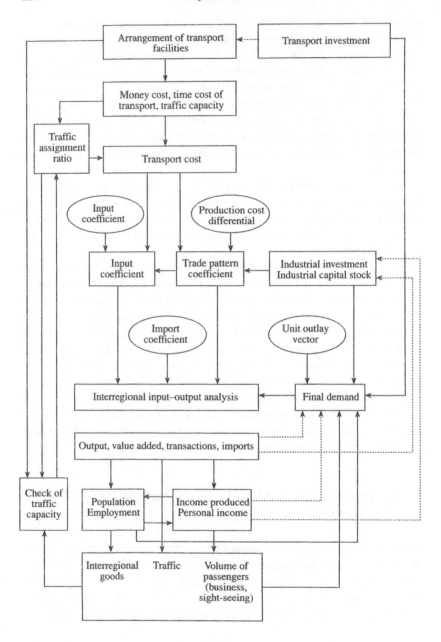

Note: A dotted line indicates a time lag of one year.

Figure 8.3   System chart of the Amano–Fujita interregional model

parts of the model. Los (1980) proposed solving this problem by linking models with different degrees of detail, that is, by using a transport model with a high sectoral and spatial detail. This approach has not become very common, however. Most operational models in this field give a rather crude treatment of networks, route choice and modal choice. In this chapter we shall focus on the relationship between transport costs and trade flows.

Amano and Fujita (1970) put forth the following formulation for a Japanese interregional model:

$$t_{irs} = \frac{K_{ir} \exp\left[-\beta_i\left(p_{iv} + v_{ivs}\right)\right]}{\sum_q K_{iq} \exp\left[-\beta_i\left(p_{iq} + v_{iqs}\right)\right]} \tag{8.5}$$

where the subscripts q, r and s refer to regions, and i refers to sectors. K_{ir} and p_{ir} denote capacity and price level in sector i of region r. Furthermore, v_{ir} is transport cost per unit of i between r and s, and t_{irs} is the share of regions r in the deliveries to region s for goods produced in sector i. As indicated by Bröcker (1984), this formulation can be based on theories of stochastic choice.

A simple illustration of this equation on the sensitivity of interregional trade flows for changes in transport costs is given in Figure 8.4. In a system consisting of regions A, B and C, infrastructure between A and B is improved, leading to a decrease in transport costs between A and B for all goods in both directions. The effect on the trade share of region C (the region not directly involved) is unambiguously negative according to this equation. For the regions directly involved, the effect on trade shares is not clear, however. The loss on the home market has to be traded off against an increased penetration on the market of the other regions. One thing is clear, namely, that the sum of trade shares for A and B will increase as a consequence of the improvement of infrastructure. The conclusion reads that although it is not obvious which of the regions directly involved in the improvement of transport (infrastructure) will be the winner, the regions not involved will certainly be losers.

According to the formulation above, improvements of infrastructure lead to a zero-sum game: $t_{irs} = 1$ for all i and s. However, as can be understood from Figure 8.1, it is not only trade shares which change but also total trade volumes. Improvement of infrastructure not only redistributes existing trade flows but may also generate larger trade volumes. Taking into account this generation effect and other indirect effects, it is no longer obvious that a zero-sum result will arise. In the Amano–Fujita model, generation effects occur among others because the reduction in transport costs leads to an increase in value added which leads in turn to an increase in labour supply and investments.

Liew and Liew (1985) propose another modelling procedure. Their point of departure is a Cobb–Douglas production function with capital, labour and inter-

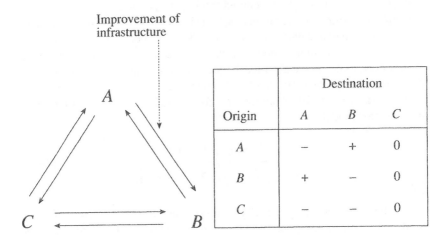

Figure 8.4   Response of trade flows to transport costs, cost reduction in a three-region framework

mediate purchases for each sector and each region. Liew and Liew assume that consumers fully absorb the advantage of a decrease in transport costs: the equilibrium purchase price in region s is the sum of the equilibrium price of the good in region r plus the cost of shipping it from region r to s. Another assumption is that in equilibrium, transport costs are a constant fraction of the equilibrium price. Using a profit-maximizing approach, Liew and Liew derive a linear logarithmic system of price frontiers. Changes in transport costs give rise to changes in equilibrium prices in the various regions. These in turn give rise to substitution effects in the production process. Thus, it is not only inter-regional trade shares which change as a consequence of changes in transport costs, but all input–output coefficients may change as a result of it. In this respect, the model of Liew and Liew is more general than the model of Amano and Fujita where input–output coefficients are assumed to be constant. Other examples of integrated approaches can be found in Sasaki et al. (1995, 1997), Elbers (1992) and van den Bergh et al. (1996).

6   CONCLUDING REMARKS

A wide variety of approaches towards analysing infrastructure can be observed. For another review of studies we refer to Vickerman (1991). The findings in this chapter can be summarized as follows.

It should first be noted that transport infrastructure is a generic term which would deserve much more detailed qualification in order to render itself appropriate for focused policy analysis. It is a pity, for example, that much of the empirical 'infrastructure contribution to productivity' literature does not contain distinctions in terms of infrastructure types. Another basic and often neglected transport policy question concerns the relationship between transport infrastructure and land-use patterns: are large-scale geographical concentrations of public and/or private activities (for example, offices, warehouses, facilities) a response to existing transport infrastructure, or have transport developments merely helped to accommodate what would have occurred anyway? Thus, the assessment of economic impact of infrastructure requires a clear specification of causality mechanisms. Infrastructure is also subject to decreasing marginal productivities. When a region is already well provided with infrastructure, adding infrastructure of the same type is of little value. The provision of an extensive network of highways makes more and more industries footloose. As a result, the importance of road infrastructure as a location factor decreases (compare Wilson et al., 1982). It is in developing countries with low infrastructure qualities that one expects the highest impacts of infrastructure investments on regional development.

As a corollary to the above, it is important to assess the potential effects of new types of infrastructure versus existing types (for example, telecommunication versus roads). Infrastructure types clearly have their life cycles. Life cycles must not be used in a simplistic way, however. For example, after a long period of decline in Europe, rail traffic is regaining momentum by the introduction of high-speed trains.

Consider an improvement of a link in a transport network. The programme effects tend to be largest in the regions connected by the link concerned (and other regions for which the link is important). The effect is not necessarily positive for all of these regions. Some of them may be negatively influenced, for example, by the loss of markets due to increasing competition. The effect on the other regions, for which the improved link is not important, is much smaller, but it tends to be negative (compare Section 5).

Improvement of infrastructure is not a sufficient condition for regional development. Many other intermediary factors play a role. The interplay between infrastructure and other relevant factors is often only formulated in a superficial way in the studies surveyed. Especially for studies on specific infrastructure improvements, it is advisable that model-based studies be complemented with micro studies based on interviews with actual and potential users of infrastructure. Improvement of infrastructure gives rise to both distributive and generative effects (Section 4). Distributive effects tend to be small when in all regions improvements of infrastructure take place at the same speed.

Generative effects of infrastructure can easily be overestimated when the spatial delimitation of the area of study is too narrow. Part of the effects may simply result from an unobserved redistribution at a higher spatial level (Section 4).

Improvement of transport infrastructure leads to a decrease in transport cost. This advantage may be absorbed by entrepreneurs or land owners in the form of profit or rents; it may also be absorbed by employees (via wages). Another possibility is that the advantage is passed over to consumers in the form of lower prices. This distribution issue receives little systematic attention in the models surveyed, which is regrettable since the regional incidence of infrastructure improvements depends on it strongly.

Infrastructure is a multidimensional phenomenon. The importance of synergetic effects between various types of infrastructure has been recognized at the theoretical level. In the present generation of operational multiregional economic models, however, the occurrence of such synergetic effects is usually neglected. Models on infrastructure tend to focus on its use for firms. The use for households must not be neglected, however. Infrastructure is an important location factor for households when relocating. In the long run, this will also have implications for the location behaviour of firms.

Most of the models have been formulated as tools for impact studies: a change in infrastructure is supposed to lead to a change in the private sector. Infrastructure is an exogenous variable in the models. This is not necessarily an adequate way of modelling infrastructure. As indicated in Section 1, infrastructure may not only lead the private sector, it may also follow. It is challenging to broaden the scope of models by introducing the possibility of this two-sided relationship.

Dynamic aspects of infrastructure impacts are important. First, demand- and supply-side effects are quite different in terms of their permanence (see Table 8.1). But also for the latter group of effects it may take a long time before the benefits of infrastructure investments are fully exploited. This holds true for both the effects on productivity and on the location of economic activity.

NOTES

1. It is not so easy to understand why this opportunity for an integrated analysis of productivity and location has not been exploited more intensively. A possible explanation is that the data needed for the estimation of regional production functions are often not readily available.
2. The background of this link is the fact that accessibility can be defined as the sum of opportunities for interaction with certain points in space (see, for example, Bruinsma and Rietveld, 1998).
3. That is, matrices with flows between all relevant origins and destinations of trips.

REFERENCES

Amano, K. and M. Fujita (1970), 'A long run economic effect analysis of alternative transportation facility plans – regional and national', *Journal of Regional Science*, **10**, 297–323.

Anderson, D.L. (1983), 'Your company's logistic management: an asset or a liability?', *Transportation Review*, **17**, 111–25.

Andersson, A.E., C. Anderstig and B. Harsman (1989), *Knowledge and Communications Infrastructure and Regional Economic Change*, Umeå: University of Umeå.

Armstrong, H. and J. Taylor (1993), *Regional Economics and Policy*, Oxford: Allen.

Aschauer, D.A. (1989), 'Is public expenditure productive?', *Journal of Monetary Economics*, **23**, 177–200.

Biehl, D. (1986), *The Contribution of Infrastructure to Regional Development*, Brussels: European Community, Regional Policy Division.

Blum, U. (1982), 'Effects of transportation investments on regional growth', *Papers of the Regional Science Association*, **58**, 151–68.

Botham, R. (1983), 'The road programme and regional development: the problem of the counterfactual', in K.J. Button and D. Gillingwater (eds), *Transport, location and spatial policy*, Aldershot: Gower, pp. 23–56.

Bröcker, J. (1984), 'How do international trade barriers affect interregional trade?', in A.E. Andersson, W. Isard and T. Puu (eds), *Regional and Industrial Development Theories, Models and Empirical Evidence*, Amsterdam: North-Holland, pp. 219–38.

Bruinsma, F. (1990), *Infrastructuur en werkgelegenheid* (Infrastructure and employment), The Hague: Organisatie voor Strategisch Arbeidsmarktonderzoek (OSA).

Bruinsma, F. and P. Rietveld (1998), 'The accessibility of European cities', *Environment and Planning A*, **30**, 499–521.

Bruinsma, F., S. Rienstra and P. Rietveld (1997), 'Economic impacts of the construction of a transport corridor: a multi-level and multi-approach case study for the construction of the A1 highway in the Netherlands', *Regional Studies*, **31**, 391–402.

Cain, L.P. (1997), 'Historical perspective on infrastructure and US economic development', *Regional Science and Urban Economics*, **27**, 117–38.

Costa, J. da, R.W. Ellson and R.C. Martin (1987), 'Public capital, regional output and development: some empirical evidence', *Journal of Regional Science*, **27**, 419–37.

Crihfield, J.B. and T.J. McGuire (1997), 'Infrastructure, economic development, and public policy', *Regional Science and Urban Economics*, **27**, 113–17.

den Hartog, H., K.A. Heineken, B. Minne, R.J.J. Roemers and H.J. Roodenburg (1986), *Investeren in Nederland* (Investing in the Netherlands), Onderzoeksmemorandum 17, The Hague: Centraal Planbureau.

Deno, K.T. (1988), 'The effect of public capital on US manufacturing activity', *Southern Economic Journal*, **55**, 400–11.

Diamond, D. and N. Spence (1989), *Infrastructure and Industrial Costs in British Industry*, London: HMSO.

Dodgson, J.S. (1974), 'Motorway investment, industrial transport costs and subregional growth, a case study of the M62', *Regional Studies*, **8**, 75–80.

Elbers, C. (1992), *Spatial Disaggregation in General Equilibrium Models*, Amsterdam: VU University Press.

Evers, G.H.M., P.H. van der Meer, J. Oosterhaven and J.B. Polak (1987), 'Regional impacts of new transport infrastructure: a multisectoral potentials approach', *Transportation*, **14**, 113–26.

Florax, R. and H. Folmer (1988), *Regional Economic Effects of Universities*, Enschede: Twente University.

Folmer, H. and P. Nijkamp (1987), 'Investment premiums: expensive but hardly effective', *Kyklos*, **40**, 43–72.

Forkenbrock, D.J. and N.S.J. Foster (1990), 'Economic benefits of a corridor highway investment', *Transportation Research A*, **24**, 303–12.

Fukuchi, T. (1978), 'Analyse Economico-politique d'un Développement Régional Harmonisé' (Economic-political analysis of harmonized regional development), *Collections de l'INSEE*, **61**, 227–53.

Handy, S.L. and D.A. Niemeier (1997), 'Measuring accessibility; an exploration of issues and alternatives', *Environment and Planning A*, **29**, 1175–94.

Harris, C.C. (1973), *The Urban Economies 1985*, Lexington, MA: Heath.

Harris, C.C. (1980), 'New developments and extensions of the multiregional multi-industry forecasting model', *Journal of Regional Science*, **20**, 159–71.

Healey and Baker (1995), *European Real Estate Monitor*, London: Healey and Baker.

Hirschman, A.O. (1958), *The Strategy of Economic Development*, New Haven: Yale University Press.

Holtz-Eakin, D. (1994), 'Public-sector capital and the productivity puzzle', *Review of Economics and Statistics*, **76**, 12–21.

Houweling, A. (1987), *Bereken zelf de macro-economische effecten van een investeringsprogramma* (Calculate the microeconomic effects of an investment programme yourself), Onderzoeksmemorandum 33, The Hague: Centraal Planbureau.

Illeris, S. and L. Jakobsen (1991), 'The effects of the Fixed Link across the Great Belt', in Vickerman (ed.), pp. 75–85.

Kau, J.B. (1976), 'The interaction of transportation and land use', in P.F. Wendt (ed.), *Forecasting Transportation Impacts upon Land Use*, Leiden: Nijhoff, pp. 112–34.

Kawashima, T. (1978), 'Regional impact simulation model BALAMO', in H. Straszak and B. Wagle (eds), *Models for Regional Planning and Policy Making*, Proceedings of the Joint IBM/IIASA (International Institute for Applied Systems Analysis) Conference, Vienna, pp. 183–201.

Lakshmanan, T.R. (1989), 'Infrastructure and economic transformation', in A.E. Andersson, D. Batten, B. Johansson, P. Nijkamp (eds), *Advances in Spatial Theory and Dynamics*, Amsterdam: North-Holland, pp. 241–61.

Liew, C.K. and C.J. Liew (1985), 'Measuring the development impact of a transportation system: a simplified approach', *Journal of Regional Science*, **25**, 241–57.

Lindfield, M. (1998), *Institutions, Incentives and Risk*, Brisbane: Australian Housing and Urban Research Institute.

Los, M. (1980), *A Transportation Oriented Multiregional Economic Model for Canada*, Publication 178, Centre de Recherche sur les Transports, Montréal: Université de Montréal.

Mera, K. (1973), 'Regional production functions and social overhead capital', *Regional and Urban Economics*, **3**, 157–86.

Mills, E.S. and G. Carlino (1989), 'Dynamics of county growth', in A.E. Andersson, D. Batten, B. Johansson and P. Nijkamp (eds), *Advances in Spatial Theory and Dynamics*, Amsterdam: North-Holland, pp. 195–205.

Munnell, A.H. (1993), 'An assessment of trends in and economic impacts of infrastructure investment', in OECD, *Infrastructure policies for the 1990's*, Paris: OECD, pp. 21–54.

NEA (1990a), *Congestie en het functioneren van bedrijven, een case-study rondom de S20 in Noord Brabant* (Congestion and the functioning of firms, a case study around the S20-road in the Province of North Brabant), Rijswijk: NEA.

NEA (1990b), *Plaspoelpolder bedrijfsonderzoek* (Investigation of firms in the Plaspoelpolder), Rijswijk: NEA.

Nijkamp, P. (1986), 'Infrastructure and regional development; a multidimensional policy analysis', *Empirical Economics*, **11**, 1–21.

Nijkamp, P. and E. Blaas (1992), *Impact Assessment and Decision Support in Transportation Planning*, Boston: Kluwer.

Nijkamp, P. and A. Reggiani (1992), *Interaction, Evolution and Chaos in Space*, Berlin: Springer.

Nijkamp, P. and S. Rienstra (1996), 'Privatisering van transport infrastructuur' (Privatization of transport infrastructure), *Economisch en Sociaal Tijdschrift*, **50**, 65–86.

Pierce, D.A. and L.D. Haugh (1977), 'Causality in temporal systems, characterizations and a survey', *Journal of Economics*, **5**, 265–93.

Pinnoi, N. (1994), 'Public infrastructure and private production', *Journal of Economic Behaviour and Organization*, **23**, 127–48.

Pluym, W.K. and S.Y. Roosma (1984), *Economische Betekenis van Transportinfrastructuur* (Economic significance of transport infrastructure), Groningen: Federatie van Noordelijke Economische Instituten.

Prud'homme, R. (1996), 'Assessing the role of infrastructure in France by means of regionally estimated production functions', in D.F. Batten and C. Karlsson (eds), *Infrastructure and the Complexity of Economic Development*, Berlin: Springer, pp. 37–48.

Rietveld, P. (1990), 'Employment effects of changes in transport infrastructure: methodological aspects of the gravity model', *Papers of the Regional Science Association*, **66**, 19–30.

Sasaki, K., S. Kumihisa and M. Sugiyama (1995), 'Evaluation of road capacity and its spatial allocation', *Annals of Regional Science*, **29**, 143–54.

Sasaki, K., T. Ohoski and A. Ando (1997), 'High speed rail transit impact on regional systems: does the Shinkansen contribute to dispersion?', *Annals of Regional Science*, **31**, 77–98.

Seitz, H. (1995), 'Public infrastructure, employment and private capital formation', in *Investment, Productivity and Employment*, Paris: OECD, pp. 123–50.

Snickars, F. and A. Granholm (1981), *A Multiregional Planning and Forecasting Model with Regard to the Public Sector*, Laxenburg: IIASA (International Institute for Applied Systems Analysis).

Song, S. (1996), 'Some test of alternative accessibility measures', *Land Economics*, **72**, 474–82.

Stevens, B. (1961), 'Linear programming and location rent', *Journal of Regional Science*, **3**, 15–26.

Takayama, T. and G.C. Judge (1971), *Spatial and Temporal Price and Equilibrium Models*, Amsterdam: North-Holland.

Takayama, T. and W.C. Labys (1986), 'Spatial equilibrium analysis', in P. Nijkamp (ed.), *Regional Economics* (Vol. I of P. Nijkamp and E.S. Mills (eds), *Handbook of Regional and Urban Economics*), Amsterdam: North-Holland, pp. 171–98.

Tinbergen, J. (1957), 'The appraisal of road construction', *Review of Economics and Statistics*, **39**, 241–48.

van den Bergh, J., P. Nijkamp and P. Rietveld (eds) (1996), *Recent Advances in Spatial Equilibrium Modelling*, Berlin: Springer.

Vickerman, R.W. (1991), *Infrastructure and Regional Development*, Pion: London.

Vleugel, J., P. Nijkamp and P. Rietveld (1991), 'Network infrastructure and regional development', in M. de Smidt, A. Granberg and E. Wever (eds), *Regional Development Strategies and Territorial Production Complexes, a Dutch–USSR Perspective*, Amsterdam: Koninklijk Nederlands Aardrijkskundig Genootschap, pp. 189–208.

Wilson F.R., A.M. Stevens and T.R. Holyoke (1982), 'Impact of transportation on regional development', *Transportation*, **10**, 13–16.

World Bank (1994), *Infrastructure for Development*, Washington, DC: World Bank.

Youngson, A.J. (1967), *Overhead Capital*, Edinburgh: Edinburgh University Press.

PART IV

Policy

9. Transport policy

Herbert Baum and Wolfgang H. Schulz

1 PUBLIC AUTHORITIES – THEIR FUTURE ROLE IN THE TRANSPORT SECTOR

At the beginning of the 1990s, after half a century of national regulations and interventions on the markets of freight and passenger transport, the transport sector in Europe was mainly liberalized. The impetus came from the transnational markets in the European Union and was justified by the freedom to provide services in the Single European Market. By the end of the 1990s, this process of liberalization was nearly completed. With this transition of the transport sector from regulated to competitive markets, the national authorities lost most of their power to intervene. Transport firms are now free to take decisions according to their own economic interests. They are subject only – like any other type of firm – to monitoring by the competition authorities. However, from this it does not follow that governments can no longer influence market processes. Now as ever, governments have certain functions as regards market processes and competition activities. Yet, the quality of the interventions has changed. Old types of regulation have been abolished, but governments have shifted their activities to other aspects of the framework for the functioning of transport markets (Hensher, 1994). Partly, in order to retain a certain influence on these markets, simpler possibilities were looked for and found, and new tasks were added.

The fact is that in the transport market no complete state abstinence has been achieved. This is because the transport sector has continued to be seen not only as an economic issue, but also as an action field for other policy issues. Therefore, transport authorities have had to adopt objectives of environmental protection, employment, international competitiveness, social and regional reconciliation and so on (Dempsey, 1989). This complex formation of decisions is the reason why state intervention is still effective in the transport sector despite the valid freedom of markets. Therefore, a market system has evolved that is restricted by political frameworks and by competing organizational objectives. The political task is to guarantee that allocation will be reached by competition, as well as to enforce the various other requirements of transport policy. The following questions are inherent in such a concept.

1. To what extent can privatization and deregulation of the complementary markets for transport infrastructure secure the market process in the markets for transport services?
2. Can competition policy guarantee an efficient competition on the transport markets (transport services and infrastructure)?
3. Which tasks does transport policy have to fulfil for the harmonization of competitive conditions with respect to intermodal and international aspects?
4. To what extent are political requirements legitimized? How can these requirements be implemented? How can conflicts between the allocation by markets and the allocation by administration be avoided?

The above questions will be discussed below.

2   THE SCOPE FOR MARKETS IN THE TRANSPORT SECTOR – THEORETICAL CONSIDERATIONS

For a long time the transport sector was treated as exceptional from the point of view of competition. Political interventionism prevailed. Administrative interventions were used to correct the operation of markets. The empirical analysis of regulatory policy shows that the objectives of the intervention regime were not achieved. It appeared that regulation had led to excessive prices, deviations from cost-optimal modal split and to bottlenecks in capacities. Thus, cost–benefit analyses for the USA pointed to losses of between four and ten billion US dollars per year because of regulation (Friedlaender, 1975; Braeutigam and Noll, 1984). Impact analyses for Europe point out the weakness of regulation, with the following results (Baum, 1991; Bernadet, 1991):

1. In freight transport, tariff parity between the different modes prevented transport rates from developing in different directions. By this 'over-coordination' relative rates could not develop according to the respective quality and cost characteristics of the different modes. The consequence was that certain modes operated in market segments from which, normally, they would have withdrawn. Other modes have not been as active in certain markets as they could have been, given their advantages. The intermodal division of labour became inefficient.

Because of the limited competition on regulated markets, prices for transport services were too high. This put a strain on costs, both for the economy as a whole and for individual users of transport.

2. The restrictions on competition weaken innovation efforts of transport firms and lead to underused rationalization potentials and to a slow-down of productivity improvements. The sharp increase in own-account road transport is an indication of the weakness of competition in the transport industry.

3. Market regulation was one of the reasons for the concentration in freight transport that has taken place since the 1970s. Market entry for new suppliers has been restricted and business take-overs together with the corresponding concessions have been possible only for the larger transport firms.

4. Market regulation has not been able to achieve the objective that was considered essential in a number of countries: protection of the railways. The result of the competition-neutralizing tariff coordination was that the railways have lost traffic to the roads. Public service obligations have forced the railways to retain unprofitable transport.

5. The result of the lack of competition has been increasing subsidies, especially for the railways but also for urban public transport operators that were protected in their monopoly. This has swallowed up public financing resources which would have been more profitably used for extensions and improvements of the service capacity. The regulation of transport markets must be held partly responsible for the capacity bottlenecks which up to now exist in the transport system.

In view of these apparent misallocations caused by regulation policy for the transport sector, there was a call for liberalized markets and for competition. Thus, above all, various efficiency objectives could be achieved, such as an optimal division of labour between transport modes, high-quality standards in transport supply, productivity and cost minimizing, bottleneck-free transport infrastructure, promotion of innovations and technological progress, profitability of transport operating firms and provision for infrastructure and external costs (Deregulierungskommission, 1991).

For a long time it had been felt that for the transport sector an allocation by means of markets and competition would be inefficient. It has now been shown convincingly that this thesis does not hold (Fokkema and Nijkamp, 1994).

Certainly there are 'special features' of production in the transport sector, such as relatively high fixed costs, minimum sizes and indivisibilities of investment. Nevertheless, these characteristics are nothing extraordinary compared with industrial production and the rest of the service sector. They do give rise to certain adjustment problems for firms, but it is still possible to resolve these problems under market conditions.

Because of the relatively low elasticity of demand, a vital entrepreneurial action parameter would be unable to fulfil its function. In fact, the phenomenon of inelastic demand applies only to overall demand for transport ('total elasticity'). The reason for this is that transport demand is determined by the overall production activity of the economy ('derived demand') and there are limited substitution possibilities for transport services. Of decisive importance for the effectiveness of competition, however, are the 'partial elasticities' for the various competitive relationships. Empirical market analyses have shown (Baum et al., 1990) that the cross-price elasticities are far from zero and hence there is partial scope for competition between the different modes. In addition, relatively high values were determined for 'quality elasticities', so that there is a workable non-price competition on transport markets.

Even the 'natural monopoly' of the railways is no argument against competition. Economies of scale with L-shaped cost functions exist for network monopolies. However, the network argument will beome weaker in the case of a separation of operations and infrastructure. Hence, the market entry for third parties is made possible.

Competition in transport will function if the markets are contestable. If contestability exists, the competition process – independent of market structure – by itself ensures that optimal results are achieved (Schwegmann, 1998). Contestable markets exist where the following conditions are fulfilled:

1. established firms and potential entrants must have access to similar technologies; economies of scale or economies of scope do not exist;
2. market exits must be possible without causing any costs, that is, there must be no sunk costs (for example, liquidation losses on capital goods);
3. there must be no significant information or transaction costs; and
4. there must be a reaction-free period on the part of the established firms; that is, old suppliers react to the more favourable supply of newcomers only after a certain delay.

The analysis of contestability for the different transport markets shows a differentiated picture (Baumol et al., 1982; Bailey, 1981).

Serious economies of scale do not exist in the markets for road freight transport and inland navigation. In general, the markets for transport vehicles are opened for all interested parties. Additionally, there are no sunk costs. Transport vehicles have fixed costs; because of their spatial mobility, they can be sold at any time. Economies of scale exist, however, in the forwarding industry (for example, infrastructure for stocks, handling and communication; Harmatuck, 1991).

By the separation of infrastructure and operation in the railway sector and free market entrance for third parties, competition in transport operating is made possible. However, barriers of contestability still exist in the network sector of railways because of high sunk costs. This situation is similar for the infrastructure of other transport modes (road transport, inland navigation and air transport). Thus, those operating markets are contestable, while in the infrastructure sector limits of contestability exist because of economies of scale and sunk costs.

External effects can cause market failures. In particular, road and air transport produce external costs to a considerable extent. These externalities are not charged to the responsible parties, so that the demand is excessive. We can try to reduce external costs of transport by formulating regulations that will restrict supply by emission-intensive modes (notably road and air transport). This is a variant of a prohibitive solution, which is generally inadequate. Furthermore, there will be no real incentives to reduce emissions. A more appropriate solution that could be applied within the market economy framework would be the internalization of the external costs (see Chapter 4, Section 7).

In addition to deregulation, a second step in the implementation of the market economy is the creation of a private ownership system. The fact is that major transport suppliers (for example, railways, public urban transport and airline companies) have been until now either completely or to a large extent state owned. Furthermore, transport infrastructure is owned mainly by the state. In the case of public ownership, it is also possible that the coordination of markets can be achieved on a non-regulated and decentralized basis. Nevertheless, it is doubtful whether the market performance still fulfils the principles of market allocation.

Optimal behaviour by firms is possible only if the market decisions are sanctioned by loss of property. As long as the state is the owner of all or a substantial share of the capital, there is certainly such a *de jure*, but not *de facto*, responsibility.

Responsibility and performance of firms are closely linked. State ownership opens the way for many claims and intervention possibilities for politicians. Responsibilities are thus not clear-cut: in many cases inefficiency is the result of broadly spread property rights. The upshot is that the competitiveness of public transport firms suffers and the market share that would be desirable from the standpoint of the overall economy is not achieved. Therefore, the task of the transport policy is to create the preconditions, through a change in the ownership system, for entrepreneurial action and, through transferring the risks of responsibility, virtually to force success, but it must guarantee the fulfilment of the public obligation functions.

While the deregulated competition of transport operating markets has proved itself to be functional, the competitive constitution of the transport infrastructure is disputed in economic theory and on the political scene. The supply of infrastructure proves to be not contestable because of sunk costs and economies of scale. Transport infrastructure (for example, road and rail networks, and airports) often has the character of local or regional monopolies with some competitive elements at their spatial edges. There are pragmatic attempts to implement more competition for the provision of infrastructure (for example, for rail transport with competitive rail networks, and for motorways with the provision of alternative routes). However, it is so far unclear whether adequate market solutions can be found.

A conflict exists for infrastructure markets between competitive solutions and the public interest. Transport infrastructure creates external benefits, among other things, development effects, increases in the productivity of the transport sector and decreases in accident costs. Private owners of infrastructure will hardly consider these effects for their investment decisions. Therefore, other means must be found, which will protect the public interest against private profit maximization (for example, through contracting or public supervision of bidding processes).

3   DEREGULATION AND COMPETITION OF TRANSPORT OPERATING MARKETS

3.1   The State of Deregulation

With the freedom to provide services in the European market, the central step for the transport operating markets was their integration into a free market constitution. The deregulation extended both to transnational and to domestic markets.

In 1993, market entry contingents for freight transport were abolished at the European level. The system of obligatory forked tariffs was replaced by free prices. Competition in the railway sector was realized by allowing third parties access to the rail network, the basis for this being EC directive 91/440 (Council of the European Union, 1991). Some of the member states followed the directive and made the usage of the rail network against payment of track prices possible. Other countries (for example, France) have not yet done so. Again, some countries practise dumping with the track prices to stimulate the demand for their own rail network.

For urban transport, a more liberalized market environment has also been realized (Council Regulation No. 1893/91). The elements are as follows (DIW, 1998).

1. A sufficient supply of urban transport should be guaranteed by agreements between local institutions and transport operators. Public obligations

concerning the supply of transport services remain exceptions to the general rule.

2. For urban transport companies with public service obligations, it should be realized that this kind of solution produces the lowest costs for the community.
3. All urban transport companies that work under public service obligations can lay a claim on deficit spending by the public authorities.

The transformation of the Council Regulation into national law is realized differently in different European countries. Sometimes free market access is established (for example, in the UK), in other cases access regulations still exist (for example, in Germany).

One future aim of the European Commission is the further opening of the urban transport market with an internationalization of competition (European Commission, 1995). This could lead to a general obligation for public tenders for services in public transport.

Since 1944, with the Treaty of Chicago, the international air transport sector has been dominated by a system of bilateral agreements between single countries. Most of them were based on price-setting rules (IATA as a price-setting organization) and capacity regulations. The starting-point of airline industry deregulation was the US Airline Deregulation Act in 1978 (Kark, 1989). In international air transport the USA has concluded a range of new agreements with other countries and organizations. These agreements were focused on the bilateral expanding of landing rights and the liberalization of prices and capacity. In the early 1990s, this agreement was enlarged by a range of bilateral 'open-sky agreements' (which allow the airlines to introduce connections to every destination in the agreement member states) between the USA and single European countries. For the near future, the European Commission has proposed establishing a general open-sky agreement between the EU and the USA.

Air transport in Europe was also dominated by bilateral agreements. Deregulation started in the middle of the 1980s. The first step was the realization of free market access, the second was the deregulation of capacity and prices, and the last was the removal of cabotage restrictions since 1 April 1997 among the EU member states (for a more extensive treatment of deregulation of air transport in the European Union, see Chapter 10, Section 3).

The UK was the first member state to deregulate its air transport market in 1989. In the 1990s, other European countries began to deregulate by the opening of market access for other airlines. This process has been strengthened in recent years by the privatization of national carriers.

The privatization of the transport industry also has deregulation effects. For example: public-owned rail companies were transferred into private legal forms (for example, British Rail and Deutsche Bahn (DB) – the German railway company). In air traffic, a number of carriers were completely denationalized (for example, Lufthansa and British Airways).[1] Likewise, airports were denationalized (for example, the British Airports Authority). As a result of privatization, the transport firms are freed from the various requirements of the governments or their direct intervention in the business processes. Thus the firms can concentrate on their commercial interests.

Within the EU, market regulations are largely abolished. Market regulations still exist with the CEE (Central and Eastern European) countries as well as within these countries (Baum et al., 1996; see also Chapter 12, 'Transport in economies in transition', of this book).

3.2 Performance of Deregulated Markets

Deregulation and privatization were far-reaching steps for the transport industry and the overall economy. Above all, the long-continuing abstinence of transport operating firms from free market rules made the experiment of deregulation appear to be very risky. Therefore, it is necessary to assess the deregulation effects for the first years.

These effects can be shown most clearly by some examples for the freight transport markets (BAG, 1995; BMV, 1994; Bayliss and Coleman, 1995).

1. First, there was an impressive reduction in freight transport prices. For example, in Germany since deregulation in 1994 the prices have decreased about 25 per cent on average. Second, the prices for transport services are more differentiated. Wide ranges of different price–quality relations for transport services are observable.
2. To prevent price competition, transport firms invest in quality. The satisfying of certain quality standards by transport firms is one aspect of mode choice. Therefore, in all freight transport modes affected, there is a tendency to maintain quality standards or to install new ones. For example, in German road freight transport, despite the high certification cost for maintaining quality standards (approximately €15 000 per truck), 25 per cent of transport operating firms have covered these standards since deregulation.
3. Transport firms are forced to introduce new services according to demand requirements. Consequently, transport markets become more heterogeneous in character. Also, new services consisting of electronic capacity information systems are created by freight transport brokers.
4. Transport firms are forced to introduce modern telematics technology. Examples are EDI (electronic data interchange) technology for a better organization and coordination of transport activities, real-time information systems for the shippers and computer integrated rail routing systems.

Telematics reduces the cost of transport and improves the quality of transport services.

5. High competition may lead to lower profits, and this could lead to a reduction in investments. Alternatively, competition can result in a higher quality of services, which means that additional investments are necessary.

6. The size of transport firms has changed. Especially in road transport and in inland navigation, there is a process of concentration in the forwarding sector and a de-concentration process among transport firms. Existing economies of scale are now used more effectively. This means that the internal efficiency of transport firms is improved. On the other hand, this process leads forwarders to abuse their market power when dealing with the suppliers of transport services.

7. Deregulation gives an incentive to reorganize the internal structure of transport firms in order to create higher productivity. Analyses in the United States found strong evidence for this thesis. For example, management productivity in US road freight transport (turnover per capita in the management team) has increased by approximately 20 per cent in the ten years after deregulation (Corsi et al., 1992). Furthermore, there was an increasing productivity of rolling stock of between 4 and 13 per cent (Boyer, 1981, 1987). On the basis of a cost function these data indicate a substantial reduction of real cost per mile from US$1.25 to US$0.83 (a productivity gain of about one-third in six years) and a nearly stable real freight revenue per mile of US$0.90 and of US$0.84, respectively (McMullen, 1997).

8. Deregulation influences the 'turnover rate' of firms. On the one hand, there is an expansion in market entries. For example, in German road freight transport, between 1990 and 1994 the number of firms increased by about 34 per cent and the number of concessions by about 47 per cent. On the other hand, there is an increasing rate of market exits. For example, in German road freight transport between 1990 and 1994 the annual ratio of bankruptcies to the total number of firms increased from 0.4 to 1 per cent. This is an expression of the increased selection among transport firms in a more competitive environment.

3.3 Industrial Economics and the Transport Industry

The previous analysis of effects of deregulation of the transport industry considers only some selected results. It thus gives the argumentative indications for the functioning of the market allocation and for the workability of competition. A rational and foresighted policy presupposes, however, a theoretically founded knowledge of market structure, conduct, performance and their interactions (Scherer and Ross, 1990; Schmalensee and Willig, 1990; Tirole, 1988). Such a theoretical concept for the industry is given by the theory of industrial organization (industrial economics).[2]

The application of industrial economics to the transport industry is still in its infancy. Because important findings can be obtained, the transport industry is included in the research area of industrial economics. These findings enable a deeper understanding of market processes, which can highlight the need for political action and measures.

A first 'research bubble' of industrial economic research for the transport industry started with impact analyses for the US Motor Carrier Act of 1980 and the US Staggers Act of 1980, which both revised the economic controls over motor carriers and railroads.

Corsi et al. (1992) describe the impact of deregulation on the less-than-truckload (LTL) industry concerning the size of management teams, the rate of stock ownership of LTL carriers, management turnover and performance. Boyer (1987) analyses the effects of deregulation on transport performance (ton-miles per truck, average load, productivity of trucks). Harmatuck (1991) quantified the changes in economies of scale and scope in the motor carrier industry since deregulation. McMullen (1997) deals with market structure, entries of firms, cost functions and revenues in the motor carrier industry.

Research topics that might be useful for decisions of economic policy are tests of market structure, performance and conduct (Bain, 1956, 1968; Stigler, 1968). Using these tests, it is possible to quantify the impact of competition on prices, profits, scale of investments, use of modern technology and supply of new transport services.

The organization of the transport industry is another research area of industrial economics. In the framework of this approach, it would be useful to investigate the impacts of privatization on entrepreneurial objectives, internal organization, costs and productivity of motor carriers and provision of transport infrastructure. Likewise, competition has an impact on the internal organization and the productivity of the management and the employees (X-efficiency).

From the foregoing it may have become clear that making use of the theory of industrial economics may significantly increase insight into the impact of deregulation on transport markets.

4   MARKETS AND COMPETITION FOR TRANSPORT INFRASTRUCTURE

4.1   Options for Property Rights: Public Ownership versus Privatization

The provision of transport services and that of transport infrastructure have a close technical and economic interrelation. An efficient transport infrastructure improves the market success of the transport mode in question. Conversely, market success will also be affected by an insufficient transport infrastructure.

Until now, transport infrastructure has been mainly publicly owned. The state thereby can influence the competitive success of the transport modes through the organization of the infrastructure provision. Obviously, the government has an instrument for the regulation of transport markets through its supply of transport infrastructure. Hence, specific preferences or discriminations of transport modes are possible. The crucial task is to provide infrastructure without creating any distortions for the competitive process in the transport operating markets.

A competitive neutral infrastructure supply can be obtained by two approaches: (i) governmental supply of infrastructure could be made to correspond as far as possible to market forces, which come from the supply side of transport services; and (ii) transport infrastructure could be privatized, which enables an infrastructure provision orientated on rules of profit maximization. In recent years, privatization of the infrastructure has become more important in Europe. Above all, privatization of roads and of rail networks, of terminals for combined transport and of airports stand in the foreground. In addition, in the context of the trans-European networks (TENs), the private financing of the extension of the infrastructure will be strengthened (European Commission, 1994).

4.2 Approaches for Privatizing Infrastructure

The following two different conceptual approaches for privatizing infrastructure facilities may be distinguished.

1. The weakest approach is a formal privatization. In this case only the legal character of the infrastructure provider changes. An advantage is that requirements concerning public bodies that apply to employment may be dropped. Thus a higher flexibility of internal organization processes is reached. On the other hand, it is unlikely that market behaviour will not change significantly. The private legal form will not automatically lead to competitive behaviour.
2. Stronger approaches are 'partial privatization' and 'organizational privatization'. In the case of *partial privatization*, the formerly public infrastructure providers will be responsible only for the existing infrastructure. Planning, building, financing and operating of new infrastructure, for instance a new, high-speed railway line, will be transferred to the private sector. If the government is specially interested in the private financing of the infrastructure, the setting up of a leasing company is the most appropriate way. Leasing is a form of pre-financing of infrastructure by private investors. The infrastructure is available to the government by the payment of the leasing rates.

Organizational privatization means that the government will take the responsibility only for the provision of infrastructural facilities. All other functions that are connected with the infrastructure supply, such as financing, building and operating, in principle are transferred to the private sector. Organizational privatization can take place in different ways. In this context, two concepts for a licensing procedure have been suggested (Roland Berger & Partner, 1995).

- *Licensing concepts with a relatively strong governmental position*: planning and financing responsibilities for the infrastructure remain at the state level. The provision and the operating of the infrastructure will be left to the private sector.
- *Licensing concepts with a relatively weak governmental position*: the government hands over the supply of the infrastructure to a private provider. The company with the lowest prices receives the contract. The government specifies only what minimum standards the private operator must fulfil.

The advantage of both licensing concepts is that the competitive bidding ensures efficiency in the provision of infrastructure. However, those concepts also have some disadvantages. In particular, the fact that the licence is limited in time can be the reason for inefficiency in the investment behaviour of the winning private provider. The provider is confronted with the risk that he will lose the next bidding. In that situation, he will be forced to sell all assets to the new successful competitor. This means that he is normally in a bad bargaining position. Therefore, he tries to anticipate this risk by reducing his investments.

Another crucial point is whether the privatization of infrastructure is accompanied by the introduction of competition. The licence concepts deal only with establishing a competitive process for the provision of infrastructure.

4.3   Privatization – Its Benefits and Risks

Privatization of transport infrastructure is a fundamental modification of transport policy. Therefore, changing the ownership of transport infrastructure must be founded on a benefit–risk analysis.

The following advantages of the privatization of the infrastructure may be expected:

1. increased efficiency and cost reductions for the construction and operating of the transport infrastructure;

2. mobilization of additional, private capital;
3. faster realization of high-growth projects, which also means that infrastructure capacity matches the demand for infrastructure much better; and
4. realization of innovations (for example, integration of infrastructure and telematics).

The advantages of privatization are gained only if workable competition prevails on the market for transport infrastructure. However, it must be seen that for the infrastructure the conditions for free markets and workable competition are in fact fulfilled insufficiently.

The central argument for privatization is that it makes possible the expansion of infrastructure capacity. However, the state will maintain an important role. It will retain responsibility for the legal and administrative frameworks for investment possibilities (among other things public property for land, permission for projects and conditions for regional policy). Therefore, in many cases, the hoped-for push for private investments will not be made. Infrastructure capacity will remain a publicly restricted supply. Better supply, cost decreases and innovations will begin only if market competition prevails in the infrastructure. The question may be asked, however, whether such competition will take place. Private suppliers will insist on regional network monopolies, and they will not accept competitive routes in their spatial neighbourhood. The property rights of the infrastructure could be made marketable by tendering and by auctions. Contracts will have to run for long periods (for example, twenty years). Adjustments of the prices or corrections of the supply during this long contract phase will – by definition – not be according to competitive yardsticks. Therefore this kind of *ex ante* competition among the suppliers of infrastructure is only an imperfect substitute for actual competition on the current market.

The foregoing presupposes that governments are unwilling to give up completely their interest in the provision of infrastructure. In so far as this is true, this type of behaviour will rest on the view that transport infrastructure creates benefits accruing to others than the (private) provider, such as increases in productivity, optimized spatial division of labour, economic integration and provision of various mobility options. It may, therefore, be appropriate to look for solutions that combine the advantages of private markets with governmental responsibilities.

Based on club theory, a cooperative organization of regional transport infrastructure networks is sometimes recommended (Ewers and Rodi, 1995; Newbery, 1988). This concept means that infrastructure users are members in a club sharing a common infrastructure. This membership status enables the club to control the management process efficiently. Nevertheless, the club model has a number of deficits, specially concerning its workability.[3] In view of the competition deficits in the infrastructure sector, intermediate solutions between privatization and government ownership are appropriate (for instance, operator concepts, public–private partnerships and management firms).

Public–private partnerships seem to be a possibility for integrating the incentives of competition (for example, lower costs, greater flexibility in capital investment, higher qualification of employees; European Commission, 1993). However, the governmental agencies will retain the final responsibility for the provision of infrastructure, although the actual provision could be contracted out to the private sector. Establishing public–private partnerships also involves certain risks and new requirements for the governmental agencies.

First, the governmental agencies have the 'make-or-buy' decision problem. They have to investigate whether it is more efficient to contract the service to the private sector or to provide it in-house. Therefore, the public agencies need an assessment tool. If the service is contracted to a private company, they must also establish a cost-control mechanism.

Second, there exists the risk that the governmental agencies are unprotected from price manipulations by the private sector. Therefore, a surveillance system is needed.

Third, private firms could disregard social requirements (for example, environmental protection, working conditions). The government has to anticipate this behaviour and develop instruments and/or incentives which guarantee that private firms will honour the social aspects.

Finally, public–private partnerships lead to new costs. These transaction costs have to be included in the decision process if public–private partnerships are established.

4.4   Separation of Rail Infrastructure from Railway Operations

In view of the unfavourable economic situation of the European railway companies it is found desirable to proceed to their privatization (Dixit, 1997; Nash and Preston, 1992). Privatization should allow the railway companies to have a commercially orientated management and should reduce the political influence on management decisions (ECMT, 1993).

The central problem of railway reform is related to the ownership of rail infrastructure and its operation. At the core of the privatization that had taken place earlier in the USA and Japan was a total shift from public to private decision making, including that concerning rail infrastructure (in Japan, the national rail network was split up into a number of regional networks which were privatized). In Europe (that is, in Sweden, the UK and Germany) another solution has been found. This concept entails the complete separation of rail infrastructure and its operation (Vickers and Yarrow, 1988). The rail operating section is privatized while rail infrastructure remains in public ownership or is formally privatized but with a state majority of capital ownership. In view of the interest of private investors, the privatization of the rail operating section should not be a serious problem.

A separation of the network and its operation has a number of advantages as compared with a complete privatization:

1. It is likely that the restructuring effect of railways would be greater. The deficit is largely a result of the rail infrastructure. Therefore, a privatization in one vertically integrated company would shift the profitability problem towards the private investor. This could reduce the chance of a successful privatization substantially.
2. The problem of profitability in one vertically integrated rail company would lead to a situation of condensing the former network to a profitable size. From a social, as opposed to a commercial, point of view (minimum supply of transport for all members of the society), the workability of the overall transport system could be damaged by a rail network reduction.
3. Concerning the realization of intramodal competition in the rail operating market, it is necessary to guarantee free access to the rail infrastructure for the different operators. A vertically integrated rail company has an incentive to discriminate against other rail operators on the question of infrastructure access in order to realize a joint profit maximum. The creation of competition in the rail sector would be harmed.

The organization of the ownership of the rail infrastructure is controversial. In the case of pure public ownership and network operation the incentives for innovations are low. For completely privatized rail infrastructure companies there are doubts regarding their profitability, which means that the best case would be a cost-covering situation. Therefore, private investors would have little interest in taking over the capital share of such an infrastructure company. The disadvantages of the pure private or the pure public solution could be overcome by a formal privatization of the infrastructure company but with a remaining capital majority in public ownership. This may then gradually be diminished in favour of private investors, after the successful reorganization of the company.

5 HARMONIZATION OF MARKET CONDITIONS IN EUROPE

An important aspect regarding the future workability of competition in the transport sector is the harmonization of market conditions in Europe. 'Harmonization' implies that comparable conditions must be established among the different modes and between the different operators within a given mode of transport. Large differences in market conditions lead to a distortion in competition. Efficiency-based comparative advantages, such as a superior production/cost structure or system advantages, would in that case be eliminated. Experience from the past shows that it is nearly impossible to achieve fully harmonized market conditions in Europe. The reason is that there is a large heterogeneity of interests still existing in the different European countries. Therefore, the general strategy of harmonization on a European scale was to fix minimum standards. Despite the practical success of these agreements, the creation of a common European transport market has renewed the problem of different market conditions. This will be reinforced by the inclusion of the CEE countries in the European Union (see also Chapter 12, Section 5).

5.1 Standards for Market Entry

Qualitative regulations regarding minimum required standards for the market entry of newcomers are important instruments to guarantee a positive performance of deregulated transport markets. These minimum standards include the legal evidence of the personal qualification, the personal reputation and the financial capability of the newcomers. On the other hand, such standards can be used to hinder market entry. In the EU there is the political aim to expand these minimum standards, especially the required financial strength of the newcomers. It is worth emphasizing that this practice favours the market insiders and discriminates against potential competitors.

5.2 Social and Technical Regulations

Differences in social and technical regulations in the various countries favour those operators that work under a relatively low degree of regulation. For example, in road freight transport, different social and technical regulations still exist – such as regarding the size and weight of trucks (between 28 and 50 tonnes maximum permitted truck weight), the required safety equipment and safety controls, and standards regarding work and leisure time of drivers (Bayliss and Coleman, 1995).

The harmonization of technical and social conditions has to be one of the future European transport policy fields in order to complete the common market obligations.

5.3 Fiscal Conditions

Differences in fiscal conditions in the different European countries are the main reason for competition distortions in the transport sector. There are national differences in the fuel, vehicle and company taxes and in contributions to social security systems. These elements have a direct cost character.

The main result of this argument is that the harmonization of fiscal conditions should have priority in order to create comparable competition conditions. On the other hand, past efforts regarding tax harmonization in Europe have demonstrated that there is no simple solution to this problem. Differences in fiscal conditions are caused by different national structures of public financing. This means that before pure fiscal harmonization can be achieved there has to be a process of harmonization of the structures of public financing in Europe.

5.4   Access to Infrastructure

The free access to infrastructure networks is a basic condition for intramodal competition. For all operators the access conditions must be valid in the same way. Discrimination of certain operators distorts the competition process. Especially in rail transport, the scarce infrastructure capacity must be allocated according to market rules. This means that access should be related to the willingness to pay for tracks by the operators. This principle can be guaranteed only if there is a strict economic division between infrastructure provider and transport operator. With Guideline 440/91, the European Commission has created the basis for free access to railway infrastructure. The lack of harmonization because of different national interpretations of Guideline 440/91, for example between Germany and France, creates competition distortions and harms the efficiency of the rail sector within the intramodal competition.

5.5   Infrastructure Cost

Differences in the infrastructure costs of different modes have an important impact on intermodal competition. An efficiency problem arises if these cost differences are not caused by the different nature of the transport systems but by different degrees of covering infrastructure costs for the individual modes or by different financing systems.

The magnitude of infrastructure costs of the individual modes is a matter of controversy (European Commission, 1998). An infrastructure cost financing system, which is neutral to the intermodal competition, could be achieved by introducing overall accounting principles, which should be valid for all modes. These could be the basis for a direct infrastructure pricing system related to the marginal social cost covering principle, for example, by road or track pricing.

Another problem is the different national systems of infrastructure payment that lead to price differences of infrastructure usage in the European countries. This is evident in the rail sector. For example, in the Netherlands there still is a system of free rail infrastructure usage while in Germany the track usage is based on a full cost covering principle. For the use of the 'Freightways' in rail transport, a tracking price of €4–4.5 per train-km has been proposed in Germany, €2.4–2.8 per train-km in Italy, €4.28 per train-km in Switzerland and €1 per train-km in the Netherlands. In a future free market environment it might be more convenient to operate freight passenger transport via low track price countries and to avoid transport through high track price countries. To improve the efficiency of the rail system as a whole, the pricing systems in Europe should be harmonized.

5.6 Different Eastern and Western European Market Environments

There are still large differences in the transport market environments between EU and CEE countries. These are based partly on different national regulations and different social conditions. For example, there are differences in the cost of social security systems and taxation between the CEE and the EU countries of 1:10. Concerning the process of integrating CEE countries into the EU, the non-harmonized market environments are a major problem for future transport policy (see further Chapter 12, in particular Section 5).

6 COMPETITION POLICY FOR TRANSPORT MARKETS

Intra- and intermodal competition on transport markets must be safeguarded against undesirable developments (Blanco and Van Houtte, 1996; Baum, 1991), but this task is incumbent upon the national anti-trust authorities (for national transport) and the European Commission (for transnational transports). Under the former regulation regime, the regulation authorities, as a rule coming under the Ministers of Transport, have performed market interventions for prevailing negative developments of competition. Since the deregulation process, the requirements on market surveillance have changed.

The sole criterion for anti-trust policy is that it should guarantee a high degree of competition, that is, by the prevention of restrictions to competition through agreements or market power. Competition control requires abstinence from regulation; it leaves no possibilities for *dirigiste* manipulation. Restrictions to competition for the purpose of achieving political goals (for example, protection of the rail sector, improvements of traffic conditions on road, environmental protection and road safety) should not be allowed. Inadmissible re-regulations by transport policy must be prevented through the anti-trust courts.

6.1 Cartelization

Cartel agreements have an ambivalent character. On the one hand, cartels can be a source that limits competition and reduces the efficiency of transport markets. On the other hand, they can reduce the cost of transport by rationalization effects and stimulation of innovations (O'Brian and Tulliss, 1989). Taking these arguments into consideration, the anti-trust authorities are facing a trade-off.

In the transport sector, cooperations and joint ventures among private transport companies stimulate cartelization. First, this problem is evident in the airline industry and partly also in freight transport operation and telematics provision. On the European level, in the last few years, the European Commission has investigated several agreements following Article 81 EEC, for example:

1. The agreement between large German charter airlines in 1993 was prohibited. The aim of the cartel was to create a mark-up on travel prices for aircraft fuel consumption.
2. The cooperation between ATG Automobillogistik, Menke Holding and Sillok & Colling for the transport of new cars in Germany was forbidden. These agreements would have created dominant market positions for the three companies involved in this segment.
3. Price agreements within maritime conferences concerning hinterland transport of containers were prohibited. This was because conference members used (abused) their market power in order to charge hinterland operators unreasonably high prices.

6.2 Merging and Concentration

In response to the market liberalization with a higher degree of competition, merging activities are increasing in the transport sector. A higher concentration strengthens the possibility of undesired strategic behaviour on the part of transport companies, for example, by abusing market power or market entry deterrence. The anti-trust legislation on national and European levels (Article 82 EEC, together with Council Regulation No. 4064/89) allows the anti-trust authorities to control mergers. The problem is that mergers do not automatically lead to a limitation of competition. Rather, in some cases mergers enable market entry and lead to cost reduction by reaching the minimum required firm size (Scherer and Ross, 1990). In contrast to the first argument, this would stimulate the competition process. Taking this point into consideration, a disapproval of mergers is appropriate only if the competition is actually limited. The estimation of future market processes, however, gives no clear results. Therefore, a prohibition of mergers, which strictly follows the rule of anti-trust law, is not always convincing. Despite the negative implication of mergers on competition, the positive effects of mergers on industry's competitiveness and on technical progress must be considered. Mergers have to be subject to control under the principle of the 'rule of reason'.

In the early 1990s, several merging activities have been controlled:

1. In the airline industry, a number of take-overs have taken place – for example, Air France took over the Belgian national carrier Sabena; British Airways took over the French domestic airline TAT; and the German national carrier Lufthansa took over the German carrier Aero Lloyd.
2. In the freight transport sector some mergers have taken place. For example, those in Germany between VTG Tanklager und Transportmittel GmbH and BP Transport and Logistik GmbH, and between Vereinigte Tanklager und Transportmitttel GmbH and Lenkering Montan Transport AG.
3. In 1993, a number of airlines, namely Lufthansa, Air France, Cathay Pacific and Japan Airlines, decided to cooperate regarding the common development and use of a computer-based logistics information system.
4. In the maritime transport sector, an agreement concerning regular ferry services for ro-ro (roll-on roll-off) and container cargo between ports in Finland and Belgium/the Netherlands was concluded.

6.3   Dominant Market Positions

A risk of market concentration is that transport companies will abuse their market power by setting excessive prices. In reality this has happened in some cases:

1. There was a case against the German national airline, Lufthansa, regarding the abuse of market power by setting excessive prices for German domestic flights. The case was stopped because Lufthansa revealed economically valid reasons for its pricing behaviour. This example demonstrates the difficulties of testing the abuse of market power in reality.
2. In 1994, German railways, DB, were fined €11 million for abusing their market power. DB had set 42 per cent higher prices in the container hinterland transport for the western seaports of Rotterdam and Antwerp than for the northern seaports of Hamburg and Bremerhaven for the same service.

A major aspect of anti-trust policy will be concerned with the obstruction techniques practised against competitors by large transport companies in order to reduce the degree of competition. This involves reciprocal business between transport companies and shippers – for example, by price discrimination within transport chains, strategic alliances between certain modes and cooperation of transport firms (for example, load pool) – with market exclusion effects regarding third parties. In this context, obstruction practices mean strategically setting prices below the average costs of transport (for example, predatory pricing or limit pricing). For the anti-trust authorities, blocking strategies of this type are in some cases difficult to pinpoint as restrictions on competition.

The competition laws in the majority of European countries make it possible to restrain this type of abuse of market power. The anti-trust authorities will have to demonstrate through appropriate case studies for the transport sector that the legal provisions are adequate and permit the effective maintenance of competition.

6.4 Competition Policy for Infrastructure Facilities

Transport infrastructure itself is a condition for the overall competition between industries among large geographic areas. The degree of intermodal competition is also crucially linked with the transport infrastructure. Traditionally, competition policy for infrastructure has to move in the direction of increasing equal competitive opportunity among the transport modes, minimizing the inequitable distortions of government intervention and enabling each mode to realize its inherent advantages. The competition policy for the infrastructure has to master special situations.

Infrastructure costs are largely sunk costs and infrastructure provision exhibits natural monopoly characteristics. These circumstances will impede the free functioning of competition. In order to obviate this difficulty it is possible to establish competition 'for the market' (competition between potential suppliers for entering the market) rather than competition 'in the market' (the usual form of competition). The tendency in the EU is to establish competition for the infrastructure market by privatization. The competition policy should accompany the privatization process from the beginning. The tasks of the competitive surveillance for the privatization process concern the protection from monopolistic contractors who can manipulate prices; and the preservation of incentives for further investments for the owner of a network.

A new action field for competition policy arises because of the separation of infrastructure ownership from the operation of services within the infrastructure. Therefore, the general task of the competition policy is to enable competition in infrastructure networks (especially for rail networks, airports and seaports; as to rail networks see Section 4.4 above).

Overall competition can be increased if competitive transport operators can share the networks. Therefore, competition policy has the following continuous issues: the preservation of the attractiveness of the joint use of the network; and the possibility for competitive access to the network.

The choice of adequate instruments of competition policy for tackling possible conflicts between infrastructure providers and operators depends on the characteristics of the infrastructure facilities. As examples, infrastructure for rail, for air and for sea transport will be discussed briefly.

The nature of railways requires central timetabling, signalling and planning, and coordination of all movements. These requirements could hinder competitive access. Furthermore, there could be a tendency for the 'established' railway companies to restrict access to the network for new rail operators (for example, by discriminatory track pricing policy, rules for access to stations and to terminal handling facilities). In addition, there is also a potential for discriminatory behaviour among rail operators (for example, excessive purchases of tracks to hinder track access of competitors). Therefore, competition policy must enable competitive access for third parties, but also avoid any negative effects on the service levels and security standards. The most likely market entrance barrier for new rail operators could be the track pricing policy of the rail network provider (Aberle et al., 1995). Therefore, competition policy has to establish models of incentive regulations for infrastructure providers with exclusive rights (for instance, the price cap regulation).

The essential competitive issue for airport infrastructure is the access on equal terms to the airport slots at specific times. Experience with airport deregulation in the USA shows that the large carriers controlled their 'home' airports (Bailey, 1985; Button, 1990; Morrison and Winston, 1986). It is likely that this problem will also occur in Europe. Here, competition policy could solve this access problem by establishing a competitive bidding for slots.

Competition policy for European ports has to master the problem that there is no uniform structure of ports within Europe (ESPO, 1996). Nevertheless, effective competition needs a clarification of the roles of private and public parties in port operations. A crucial point for competition is the bargaining situation between the port authority and the operators. Therefore, a competitive framework for the port authorities has to be established, which should guarantee that all operators are treated on an equal basis.

Many ports, even when run by the public sector, act in the role of landlords, leasing out their land, and in some cases their facilities and equipment, to operators who provide services such as stevedoring and warehousing. In particular, the leasing contracts could contain clauses or agreements that restrict market access for new operators (for example, the leasing contracts required to build new facilities).

7   POLITICAL INTERVENTIONS IN LIBERALIZED TRANSPORT MARKETS

7.1   Reasons for Interventions

Despite deregulation, the state still affects market results, directly or indirectly. This still relatively high degree of intervention results from the following factors.

1. Matters of mobility have a high political value. They are important strategic points in political electioneering programmes because voters have strong personal involvement in mobility questions.
2. Additionally, mobility is strongly demanded by the population. On the other hand, traffic causes large external diseconomies (pollution, noise and accidents). This conflict constellation is one reason for the political management of traffic development.
3. The market system for transport is still in a transition phase from regulation to free competition. In particular, the period of transition requires political surveillance and accommodation to prevent unexpected turmoil.
4. The substitution of a regulatory system by competition affects public interests. Therefore, government may want to guarantee certain standards of service on private markets by 'public orders against payment' (for example, in urban transport). Private demand will have to be supplemented by public demand.
5. Transport technology (for example, new transport systems, the combining of vehicles and telematics systems) is extremely important for the development of the industrial sectors. Generally, new technologies are unprofitable at first. Therefore, the government must adopt a 'door-opener' function.
6. The liberalization of transport operating markets may well cause conflicts with the capacity of transport infrastructure. It is not possible to fulfil all infrastructure needs.

Governmental interventions will not be undertaken by market regulation. This is because, by definition, this instrument is not available for liberalized markets. More particularly, instruments such as infrastructure investment (in facilities, interfaces and assets), subsidies, taxes, fees and organizational measures will be used. It is with these kinds of intervention that market results will be corrected. Thus, conflicts between political requirements and the performance of markets by means of competition can occur.

Finally, the following questions must be clarified: what legitimation exists for governments to intervene, what allocation principle has to take priority, and what limits exist for market corrections?

7.2 Reducing the Growth of Transport

In view of the increasing transport intensity of the globalized national economies, which is also responsible for the negative effects coming from pollution and accidents, the governments intend to lower transport demand. The idea is an 'uncoupling' between the growth of the economy and the growth of transport. There are various levels of uncoupling approaches (Baum and Heibach, 1997):

1. savings of vehicle-kilometres can be made by higher degrees of efficiency in transport operating (for example, fleet management, cooperation and higher degrees of capacity usage in transport operating);
2. substitution of traffic by telecommunication (for example tele-working, virtual processes and electronic commerce); and
3. reduction of traffic-creating structures in trade and industry (for example, new production technologies, weight reduction and miniaturization of products, use of regenerating raw materials, dematerialization of production processes (reduced physical use of factors of production), standardization of product components, modular sourcing, regionalization of procurement and rationalization of plants locations).

The uncoupling approach is sometimes criticized on the grounds that it is a structural intervention, going against the market. Firms would realize traffic-saving potentials more or less spontaneously if these savings were profitable. However, market imperfections are actually recognizable in industrial sectors. In part, the excessive transport demand is the result of governmental interventions (for example, EU agricultural subsidies, structure preservations for outdated industries and regulations for land use). Uncoupling potentials cannot be achieved because of imperfect industry markets (due to, for example, concentration, barriers to entry, sunk costs, economies of scale and of scope, and network economies). These imperfections weaken the pressure for rationalization processes. New technical knowledge produces external benefits. Therefore, governmental support is necessary for research and development.

These market weaknesses may be overcome by measures for supporting a strategy of uncoupling. Nevertheless, it has to be ensured that uncoupling will not become a control instrument for industries. Therefore, market-orientated filters have to be established so that the various possibilities for uncoupling can be checked with regard to their market conformity.

7.3 Internalization of External Costs

In order to harmonize the competition chances between the transport modes, it is necessary to internalize external costs (for example costs of emissions, of noise and of accidents). Such an internalization strategy will lead to the actual costs of each transport mode. For freight transport, it is most likely that this will lead to road transport losing market shares in favour of rail and inland navigation. For passenger transport there will be increasing market shares for rail and urban public transport.

For the European Union, as set out in more detail elsewhere in this book (Chapter 10, Section 3, under 'Road transport'), steps have been taken that are intended to lead to a common method for the internalization of external costs (European Commission, 1998). Nevertheless, beneath the political process to internalize external costs, the discussion of externalities of transport is not yet ended. In particular, for the competition process the question is whether external benefits exist. If they exist, the next question is how they have to be considered in the overall internalization process.

Recent studies have found that transport produces not only external costs, but also external benefits (Baum and Behnke, 1997). Examples of external benefits of transport activities are increases of productivity caused by an intensified division of labour, market extensions and market exploitations, increased technical and economic knowledge by spatial division of labour, exploitation of new resources and materials, accelerations of structural change and increased competitiveness in international trade. How these benefits have to be considered for determining the optimum overall mobility of the economy is controversial. The crucial question is whether the external costs can be balanced against external benefits such as those mentioned.

Some argue that transport activities do create economic benefits, but that these benefits are internalized by the price system (Hansson and Markham, 1992; INFRAS/IWW, 1995; Rothengatter, Chapter 4, Section 4, in this book). They would, therefore, be irrelevant for transport policy. On the other hand, analyses of market interdependencies in modern economics reveal that part of the benefits is not only passed on by markets, but also by other kinds of real transfer mechanisms. In the latter case, these benefits definitely have to be considered as externalities (Laffont, 1987; Greenwald and Stiglitz, 1988; Schulz, 1996).

Technological external benefits, which are not passed on by the market mechanism, arise in the following situations.

- When a firm opens an export market, the foreign market is also opened for other domestic industries. The opening of the export market is only possible if the exports are transported. Therefore, part of the benefits that arise from the opening of the export market is due to transport.
- Because of the spatial mobility of workers, it is possible for a firm to hire employees with higher qualifications. Their higher productivity also increases the efficiency of other enterprises.
- Economies of scale can be made only if the spatial extension of markets is enabled by transport performances. External benefits occur if the market size reaches a certain dimension so that for the manufacturers of other goods new manufacturing technologies become profitable.

- The agglomeration of economic activities creates technological externalities. Agglomerations are only possible because of the markets developed by transport; otherwise, production sites would have to be distributed spatially according to the demand.
- Wealth and growth depend essentially on the availability of technological knowledge. The origin and destination of innovations are determined by, among others, the transport and communication options of an economy. Innovations create technical knowledge, which can be used by others without paying the innovator.

These examples show that external benefits of transport do exist. The 'new growth theory' developed in the USA concludes that such positive externalities, which are provided virtually free of charge for the economic system, are the actual motor of growth and wealth of society (Habakkuk, 1962; Lucas, 1988; Romer, 1990). Since such positive effects in many cases can occur only when transport services are possible, at least part of the external benefits has to be assigned to transport.

7.4   Capacity Allocation

The efficiency of the transport system is considerably affected by limitations on infrastructure capacity. This imbalance between transport demand and infrastructure capacity is caused mainly by the circumstance that infrastructure capacity cannot be adjusted so easily. This is why there is a strong call for publicly controlled allocation of infrastructure capacity.

Bottlenecks in infrastructure capacity of one transport mode could be corrected by transferring the excess to another transport mode or by reducing the demand upon the transport system through changing land use at the origins and destinations of travel. In the case of a general overloading of capacity, the short-term approach is to shift transport to other transport modes. The long-term approach is the extension of capacity.

A further approach is to create incentives for transport operators for a better usage of the capacity of transport means. Transport operating and infrastructure capacity are closely interrelated. Bottlenecks in infrastructure capacity can also be a result of the insufficient degrees of capacity usage in transport operating.

For the case of overcapacity, a wide range of policy measures exist that can assist transport operators in scrapping various means of transport. In inland waterway transport, for example, the scrappage action in Germany took about 4000 vessels out of the market between 1969 and 1990. The 'old for new' regulation of the EU, which was introduced in 1990, provided that in the case of investment in new waterway vessels either old ones had to be scrapped or a penalty equivalent to the scrappage allowance had to be paid. This type of capacity adjustment is sometimes rejected as market-distorting intervention.

Introducing such a system of capacity allocation can, however, be justified as follows. If the capacity is not exhausted, resources are wasted. Thereby the costs of the empty capacities represent the overall economic loss.

Basic economic theory suggests that improvements in transport infrastructure that reduce vehicle operating costs and time costs will induce transport growth. This should not lead to the conclusion that capacity extensions should be viewed as negative. However, insufficient capacity of the transport system results in an overall decrease in system efficiency, because transport demand shifts away from transport modes that maximize system efficiency (in particular for urban transport, see further Chapter 6, Section 7). Hence, the main issues for optimizing the overall transport system are short term to realize an optimal usage of the existing infrastructure capacity and long term to provide adequate infrastructure capacity. Additionally, the price system as an element of a capacity allocation approach has to be enlarged by an information system about infrastructure. This information system should include maintenance management monitoring of the conditions of transport facilities and assets, identifying the deterioration of the facilities and assets and providing the optimal investment strategies that bring the condition of those facilities to a predetermined level of condition.

7.5 Public Interests

A substantial argument for public market interventions is the wish to guarantee certain provision standards for the population and economy. In private markets, the realization of profits on the part of the suppliers is paramount. Because of this, it cannot be ensured that public requirements will be met. This problem results from the fact that both transport infrastructure and transport performances create external benefits, which are not transferred to markets. Therefore, the transport sector has the characteristics of a public good. This leads to free-rider positions on the demand side. In the end, the effective demand is too low, so that the supply is too small with regard to the provision standards judged desirable by the public authorities. This may lead these authorities to supplement private demand with a demand of their own (this demand may relate to infrastructure services – the size and quality of the network – as well as to transport services).

The degree of public market demand depends on a political decision process, which is normally based on the principle of merit allocation. That is, the public authorities practise an 'ordering function' for the supply by private firms it judges of public merit.

This ordering principle will become increasingly important for the transport sector because of the ongoing privatization process. This applies both to rail and to road infrastructure, because of the public interest in the network design and in the operating frequency.

The ordering of private supply can be organized as public tender. Nevertheless, it is necessary to develop a more detailed conceptual frame for this kind of public demand. Procedures to ensure that the bargaining results will be similar to pure market solutions must be found. Both distortions by supply power and abuse of demand power have to be avoided by the government. Public tenders can create competition. For the selection of the suppliers, however, a pure cost comparison is not enough. In the course of the tender 'yardstick competition' between the private firms must take place. Yardstick competition means comparing the performance of the suppliers (performance criteria could be, for example, quality of service and sustainability of supply). Thereby it is possible to force the private suppliers to improve their performance.

7.6   Opening the Markets for New Services

Governments may run a complementary supply strategy for the markets by supporting the market entry of new transport modes, infrastructure facilities and technologies. Examples of such governmental market engagements are the Transrapid (a high-speed railway) in Germany (however, the plans for a line between Hamburg and Berlin were cancelled in March 2000 because of the high cost), large infrastructure projects (for example, bridges, tunnels) or telematics applications to transport systems by providing the infrastructure and/or traffic data. In these cases the government tends to act not directly but indirectly, by holding capital shares of operating companies or by assigning public orders.

These kinds of governmental supplies have to be seen critically under the terms of competition. They initialize the introduction of new services in the market. Normally (that is, under purely private conditions of supply), these services would not have been offered. In addition, they lead to 'suction' effects with the existing offers, thus restricting the competitive position of the private firms. Therefore, for instance, the Transrapid would have withdrawn demand from DB, the national German railway. Infrastructure projects such as tunnels could, for instance, weaken the market position of ferry services. Thus, governmental supply does not fit into the competitive conception of transport markets.

From the point of view of transport policy, it may be thought useful to support new services such as telematics, because they may help to relieve and improve the traffic situation. Furthermore, infrastructure projects may lead to cost savings for users. The more quickly these new services are brought to the market, the larger are the welfare gains.

Additionally, industrial policy also provides arguments for governmental action. Governmental interventions may be considered useful if the effective demand is too low to realize economies of scale or if the market risks are too high for private investors. With the 'door-opener' function of the government, markets can be opened up, and with that the industrial development of the economy is supported.

However, the experiences with numerous projects enforced by industrial policy remind us to be cautious of such governmental engagements. In many cases, especially with new technologies, the hopes for market successes have not been fulfilled. Private firms will normally implement industrial innovations that are likely to lead to real success. Therefore, the scope for governments to introduce new services into a transport setting is likely to be narrow. Governmental engagements will, therefore, have only a subsidiary character.

7.7 Re-regulation

The transition to markets and competition in the transport sector was generally rated a success. The expected distortions occurred only within relatively narrow margins. Meanwhile, the deregulation process in the EU has been more or less realized. Thereby, the liberalized market condition became irreversible. Nevertheless, strong efforts are always required to support frameworks for competition with adjusting elements. This is to prevent the market constitution from undesirable developments.

Intervention in the market may also be required in order to achieve certain modal shifts, particularly from road to rail. Many conceptual ideas exist for such interventions. For example, serious interventions are proposed for the promotion of combined transport (for example, a general prohibition for trucks to make use of motorways, a joining of bilateral agreements between countries with the use of combined transport, and special depreciation rates for vehicles that are used in combined transport).

It is difficult to determine to what extent serious market distortions exist. Empirical studies provide no reference points for this. Governments' answer to undesired developments cannot be to correct the market results, but to organize the basic conditions for the market processes.

The effects of deregulation on accidents and on emissions have been ambivalent. A negative result might be that single firms could use their equipment for longer periods and more excessively in order to reduce the costs. There could be an incentive to less safe behaviour such as the breaching of safety norms (for example, speed limits, driving-time regulations). On the other hand, qualitative improvements in response to deregulation reduce the number of accidents relative to vehicle-kilometres.

In all, a return to a regulatory regime would be essentially inappropriate. Apart from the overall economic disadvantages, it cannot be ensured that profits, which the operating firms can realize because of the (administrative) restraint of competition, will be invested in measures to increase road safety. However, the task of transport policy must be to create such conditions that improvements of road safety simultaneously become profitability factors. The instruments for this approach are, among other things, financial incentives of insurance, advancement of safety standards, stricter technical suitability of new entrants and qualification standards for employers and employees.

Environmental pollution will increase due to the market strength of road freight transport, so it will be necessary to tighten up the emission standards for road haulage to offset this development.

Because competition is increasing and distortions of the market system will occur, there is a demand for a market monitoring system and an administrative crisis mechanism for freight transport. In the European Union, discussions have been held about whether, during fundamental and continuous market distortions, with a strong disproportion between supply and demand, the member state can request stabilization measures (for example, minimum prices, quotas for market entry, financial incentives for market exit) from the European Commission. The justification for a crisis mechanism will depend on the type of crisis.

First, if, due to deregulation, a durable excess supply arises in the transport sector (structural crisis), preservation measures by market regulations would make no sense. In this case, definite capacity adjustments and market exits would have to take place.

Second, in the case of temporary fluctuations of demand, due to the business cycle, transport capacity could be maintained by crisis management. This is because the excess capacity would most likely be needed again during a future boom. On the other hand, during temporary fluctuations, an appropriate adjustment flexibility would have to be demanded from the transport industry. Thus, the justification that is given for a crisis management is not convincing.

In the third place, market distortions could arise in the transitional phase from a regulatory regime to a market constitution. In this case, the government could give temporary financial aid. The transport firms could then use this aid for modernization and adjustments. Such distortions, on the other hand, could be seen as warranting a return to a regulatory market regime. This would endanger a successful transition to a free market economy.

8   RESULTS

Transport markets in the EU countries have been transformed into a competitive economy after long years of regulations and governmental interventions. This development is well advanced for freight transport; competition deficits still exist for passenger transport in urban and regional public transport. Air transport is also largely liberalized. It is a matter of controversy to what extent transport infrastructure should be handed over to market economy allocation. In fact, serious competition barriers exist. Thus, local or regional infrastructure monopolies can be found. In view of this constellation, there are many arguments for keeping infrastructure ownership in public hands, but to find organizational forms for its exploitation on a private economy basis. Therefore, private–public partnerships are a possible organizational solution. The public authorities have the task of providing the infrastructure, but in such a way that the market allocation for transport services is not disturbed by infrastructure interventions.

The transition process of the transport sector from administrative regulations to the rules of a market economy entails frictions, adjustment problems and distortions. The empirical analysis of the market processes, however, shows that no serious misallocation has occurred. The positive effects of competition predominate, with price reductions, cost savings, supply dynamics, quality upgrades and technological progress.

However, it appears that the efficiency of competition is threatened. Thus, the protection of the competitive processes is a crucial political task, which should be taken over by the competition authorities. Focal points in this are the process of concentration, contractual and actual restrictions of competition, the raising of obstacles to competitors, and abuse of dominant positions. New tasks are ensuring the free access to transport infrastructure as well as the implementation of competition on the markets for telematics applications. Only through greater experience can the success of competition policy be guaranteed.

An intensive market monitoring should sharpen an awareness of potentially inappropriate developments. Likewise, the empirical analysis of the competition processes with methods of industrial economics enables the identification and evaluation of such developments. All this can be used for the practical work of the competition authorities.

Competition surveillance is mostly limited to serious offences against fair competition. Therefore, we should examine to what extent such offences (below the level, so to speak, at which the public authorities would intervene – for example, in the case of unfair competition against small transport operators) can be stopped by voluntary agreements (for example, through a code of conduct).

On competitive markets, transport policy above all has the task of harmonizing the conditions of competition. This applies both to competition between the various transport modes and to the international market processes. The main emphasis would be on standards for market entry, social and technical conditions, fiscal measures and infrastructure costs. On the European level, progress has been made. However, the process started will have to be continued and, first and foremost, be extended to transport relations with the CEE states.

Despite the economic freedom of the private sector on the transport markets, it cannot be assumed that governments will completely withdraw from the organization of market processes. Governments will, on the contrary, continue to influence the market processes, for reasons of general public interest, regional aspects, external costs, limitations of infrastructure expansion and, finally, because of the importance of transport for industrial development and technology evolution. To this end, however, governments cannot fall back on regulatory measures, but will use instruments such as infrastructure investments, subsidies, taxes, fees and organizational measures.

Such allocative activities will change market performance. This future distribution of roles between market and state, with strong conflict fields, will be a central problem in transport policy. In the end, this question will have to be decided politically. The decision taken will depend on the question whether the implementation of the political requirements will be organized in such a way that the workability of the market is impaired as little as possible.

NOTES

1. In the Netherlands, the government has kept a 'golden share' (at the time of writing 23 per cent) in the national carrier KLM. This is because it then has a stronger position in negotiations of traffic rights.
2. Industrial economics is a modern quantitative approach within general economic theory and combines the latest theories with empirical evidence about the organization of firms and industries. The objective is to provide diagnoses and prognoses of the market and competition processes. Therefore, empirical observations are undertaken and statistical methods are used, which go beyond the traditional descriptive approaches. In contrast to formal economic theory, which derives its conclusions from certain axioms, empirical evidence stands at the threshold of the study of the structure of firms and markets and their interactions. Theoretical conclusions are based on empirical studies of markets.
3. One crucial question is who becomes a member. First, restrictions for joining a club could occur. Then the risk exists that a club will not reach its optimal size. Second, there is a tendency that the rich will subsidize the poor to join the club, so that the rich will have a high relative status in the club. Third, it is likely that members of a club differ in their valuation of time. In this case, there are distortions of the decision process in a club, because several efficient strategies exist for the extension of infrastructure. This is similar to the liability problem for capital losses.

REFERENCES

Aberle, G., A. Brenner and A. Hedderich (1995), 'Trassenmärkte und Netzzugang' (Track markets and network access), *Giessener Studien zur Transportwirtschaft und Kommunikation*, Band 8, Hamburg.

Bailey, E.E. (1981), 'Contestability and the design of regulatory and antitrust policy', *American Economic Review, Papers and Proceedings*, **71**, 178–83.

Bailey, E.E. (1985), 'Airline deregulation in the United States: the benefits provided and the lessons learned', *International Journal of Transport Economics*, **12**, 119–44.

Bain, J.S. (1956), *Barriers to New Competition*, Cambridge, MA: Harvard University Press.

Bain, J.S. (1968), *Industrial Organization*, 2nd edn, New York: Wiley.

Baum, H. (1991), 'The role of government in a deregulated transport market (access competition, safety)', in European Conference of Ministers of Transport, *The Role of the State in a Deregulated Transport Market*, Round Table 83, Paris: OECD, pp. 5–43.

Baum, H. and N.C. Behnke (1997), *Der volkswirtschaftliche Nutzen des Straßenverkehrs* (Economic benefits of road transport), Schriftenreihe des Verbandes der Automobilindustrie (VDA), No. 82, Frankfurt am Main.

Baum, H. and M. Heibach (1997), *Entkopplung von Wirtschaftswachstum und Verkehrsentwicklung* (Decomposition between growth and transport development), Cologne: Deutsches Verkehrsforum.

Baum, H., M. Gierse and C. Maßmann (1990), 'Aufbereitung von Preiselastizitäten der Nachfrage im Güterverkehr für Modal Split-Prognosen', mimeo (Empirical preparation of price-elasticities of freight transport demand for modal-split forecasts), Essen.

Baum, H., M. Cremer, K. Esser, H. Krumme, S. Pesch and C. Tettinger (1996), *Effects of Regulatory Measures on the Needs for Transport Infrastructure*, Commissioned by Federal Ministry of Transport of Germany and Commission of EC, Cologne.

Baumol, W.J., J.C. Panzar and R.D. Willig (1982), *Contestable Markets and the Theory of Industry Structure*, New York: Harcourt Brace Jovanovich.

Bayliss, B.T. and R.J. Coleman (1995), *Bericht des Untersuchungsauschusses über den Straßenverkehr im europäischen Binnenmarkt* (Report of the investigation committee on road transport in the European 'domestic' market), Brussels.

Bernadet, M. (1991), 'France', in European Conference of Ministers of Transport, *Deregulation of Freight Transport*, Round Table 84, Paris: OECD, pp. 5–39.

Blanco, L.O. and B. Van Houtte (1996), *EC Competition Law in the Transport Sector*, Oxford: Clarendon.

Boyer, K.D. (1981), 'Equalizing discrimination and cartel pricing in transport rate regulation', *Journal of Political Economy*, **89**, 270–89.

Boyer, K.D. (1987), 'The costs of price regulation: lessons from railroad deregulation', *RAND Journal of Economics*, **18**, 408–19.

Braeutigam, R.R. and R.G. Noll (1984), 'The regulation of surface freight transportation: the welfare effects revisited', *Review of Economics and Statistics*, **66**, 80–87.

Bundesamt für Güterverkehr (BAG) (1995), *Marktbeobachtung im Güterverkehr, Jahresbericht 1994* (Market monitoring for freight transport, Annual Report 1994), Cologne.

Bundesminister für Verkehr (BMV) (1994), *Auswirkungen des Tarifaufhebungsgesetzes auf die wirtschaftliche Lage des deutschen Transportgewerbes* (Effects of the Tariff Abolition Act on the economic situation of the German transport industry), Bonn–Bad Godesberg.

Button, K.J. (1990), *Airline Deregulation: International Experiences*, New York: Beekman.

Corsi, T.M., C.M. Grimm and J. Feitler (1992), 'The impact of deregulation on LTL motor carriers: size, structure, and organization', *Transportation Journal*, **32**, 24–31.

Council of the European Union (1989), *Regulation (EEC) No. 4064/89 of 21 December 1989 on the Control of Concentration between Undertakings*, Brussels.

Council of the European Union (1991), *Directive (EEC) No. 440/91 of 29 July 1991 on the Development of the Community's Railways*, OJL237/1991/08/24, Brussels, p. 25.

Dempsey, P.S. (1989), *The Social and Economic Consequence of Deregulation – The Transport Industry in Transition*, Westport: Quorum.

Deregulierungskommission (1991), *Marktöffnung und Wettbewerb, Berichte 1990 und 1991* (Market opening and competition, Reports 1990 and 1991), Stuttgart.

Deutsches Institut für Wirtschaftsforschung (DIW) (1998), *Wettbewerb im öffentlichen Personennahverkehr unausweichlich* (Competition in public transport inevitable), Wochenberichte des DIW, (65), No. 19/98, pp. 311–19.

Dixit, A. (1997), 'Power of incentives in private versus public organizations', *American Economic Review, Papers and Proceedings*, **87**, 378–82.

European Sea Ports Organization (ESPO) (1996), *Report of an Enquiry into the Current Situation in the Major Community Seaports*, London: ESPO.

European Commission (1993), *The Future Development of the Common Transport Policy. A Global Approach to the Construction of a Community Framework for Sustainable Mobility*, White Paper, Brussels.

European Commission (1994), *The Trans-European Network*, Luxemburg.

European Commission (1995), *The Citizens' Network. Fulfilling the Potential of Public Passenger Transport in Europe*, Green Paper, COM(95)601/FIN, Brussels.

European Commission (1998), *Fair Payment for Infrastructure Use: A Phased Approach to a Common Transport Infrastructure Charging Framework in the EU*, White Paper, COM (98)466/FIN, Brussels.

European Conference of Ministers of Transport (ECMT) (1993), *Privatisation of Railways*, Round Table 90, Paris: OECD.

Ewers, H.J. and H. Rodi (1995), *Privatisierung der Bundesautobahnen* (Privatization of the federal motorways), Göttingen: Vandenhoeck & Ruprecht.

Fokkema, T. and P. Nijkamp (1994), 'The changing role of governments: the end of planning history?', *International Journal of Transport Economics*, **21**, 127–45.

Friedlaender, A.F. (1975), *The Dilemma of Freight Transport Regulation*, Washington, DC: Brookings Institution.

Greenwald, B.C. and J.E. Stiglitz (1988), 'Externalities in economics with imperfect information and incomplete markets', *Quarterly Journal of Economics*, **103**, 228–64.

Habakkuk, H.J. (1962), *American and British Technology in the Nineteenth Century*, Cambridge: Cambridge University Press.

Hansson, L. and J. Markham (1992), *Internalisation of External Effects in Transportation*, Stockholm/Paris: Union Internationale des Chemins de Fer.

Harmatuck, D.J. (1991), 'Economies of scale and scope in the motor carrier industry', *Journal of Transport Economics and Policy*, **25**, 135–51.

Hensher, D.A. (1994), 'Transport planning, market and government: challenge for the future', *International Journal of Transport Economics*, **21**, 147–59.

INFRAS/IWW (1995), *Externe Effekte des Verkehrs* (External effects of transport), Zürich-Karlsruhe.

Kark, A. (1989), *Die Liberalisierung der europäischen Zivilluftfahrt und das Wettbewerbsrecht der Europäischen Gemeinschaft* (Liberalization of European civil aviation and the competition law of the EU), Frankfurt am Main: Lang.

Laffont, J.L. (1987), 'Externalities', in J. Eatwell, M. Milgate and P. Newman (eds), *The New Palgrave: A Dictionary of Economics*, Vol. 2, London: Macmillan, pp. 263–5.

Lucas, R.E. (1988), 'On the mechanics of economic development', *Journal of Monetary Economics*, **22**, 3–42.

McMullen, B.St. (1997), *The Impact of Deregulation on Technical Efficiency: The U.S. Motor Carrier Industry*, Report No. TNW 97–10, Oregon State University, Corvallis.

Morrison, S.A. and C. Winston (1986), *The Economic Effects of Airline Deregulation*, Washington, DC: Brookings Institution.

Nash, C.A., and J.M. Preston (1992), *Barriers to Entry in the Railway Industry*, University of Leeds, Institute for Transport Studies, Working Paper 354, Leeds.

Newbery, D.M. (1988), 'Road damage externalities and road user charges', *Econometrica*, **56**, 295–319.

O'Brian, P. and M. Tullis (1989), 'Strategic alliances: the shifting boundaries between collaboration and competition', *Multinational Business*, No. 4, pp. 10–17.

Roland Berger & Partner (1995), *Untersuchung zur Privatisierung von Bundesautobahnen – Zusammenfassender Abschlußbericht* (Report on the privatization of federal motorways – summarized final report), München/Bonn.

Romer, P.M. (1990), 'Endogenous technological change', *Journal of Political Economy*, **98**, 71–102.

Scherer, F.M. and D. Ross (1990), *Industrial Market Structure and Economic Performance*, 3rd edn, Boston: Houghton-Mifflin.

Schmalensee, R. and R.D. Willig (eds) (1990), *Handbook of Industrial Organization*, Amsterdam etc.: Elsevier.

Schulz, W.H. (1996), 'Measuring and understanding external effects of transport', Presentation for the international symposium '*Les neuvièmes entretiens du Centre Jacques Cartier*', Montréal.

Schwegmann, V. (1998), *Preisstrategien im europäischen Linienluftverkehr* (Price strategies for scheduled air traffic), Cologne: Eul.

Stigler, G.J. (1968), *The Organization of Industry*, Homewood, IL/Nobleton: Irwin/Irwin-Dorsey.

Tirole, J. (1988), *The Theory of Industrial Organization*, Cambridge, MA: MIT Press.

Vickers, J. and G. Yarrow (1988), *Privatization: an Economic Analysis*, Cambridge, MA: MIT Press.

10. Transport policy in the European Union

Kenneth J. Button

1 INTRODUCTION

The previous chapter considered transport policy in a general context, although the European Union (EU) was referred to. In the present chapter, which can be seen as a continuation of the previous one, the transport policy of the EU is the central topic. The EU being the most advanced case of an economic union in the world, an analysis of its transport policy may also shed light on the transport policy of an economic union in more general terms.

Transport policy has always held a central place in the development of the EU. One practical reason for this is that transport accounts for about 7 per cent of the EU's GDP and about 17 per cent of its budget. But there are reasons that are more fundamental. The underlying idea of an economic union is to foster trade and allow regions to exploit their comparative advantages. An integral element for achieving this is the creation of an internal market for transport services. Without transport, trade would not occur. Transport acts as the lubricant to trade.

Even with transport, suboptimally high transport costs or insufficient transport provision can impede trade, while manipulation of transport markets can be used to distort patterns of trade. This has long been recognized and the concept of the Common Transport Policy of the EU, only one of two such major common policies, was set out in the Treaty of Rome (which in 1958 laid the foundation for the then European Economic Community).[1]

The development of EU transport policy has its history rooted in the creation of the European Coal and Steel Community (ECSC) under the Treaty of Paris in 1951 (Meade et al., 1962).[2] The founding fathers of the EU were concerned that distortions in the transport market should not interfere with the economic development of Western Europe. More recently, as the economic union has moved closer to a political union, the role of transport as an integrating force has been seen as more important. The EU consists of a large number of countries with different languages, histories, cultures and political systems; many are geographically distant from the core of economic and political activity. Transport is seen as one of the unifying influences that permit national and regional differences to be overcome.

The objective here is not to offer a history of EU transport legislation (see McGowan, 1998, for such an account) but rather it is to highlight some of the key economic considerations that go into reviewing EU transport policy. While there are important trade issues to consider, the creation of a common market poses a number of problems that transcend the basic economics of trade. For example, transport is a major sector in its own right and EU countries have interests in fostering their own transport industries as well as indirectly using transport policy as an instrument to stimulate their exports of other goods and services. Transport provision can also influence the costs of production within a country and act to stimulate development of particular sectors or regions. Reconciling this with the wider needs of an economic union inevitably poses problems.

These problems are made more complex because of the need in many sectors to integrate EU transport into the larger international transport network and to ensure that external EU trade and travel are not excessively impeded by policies adopted for internal transport (Button, 1992a, 1993a). Added to this are issues on the environmental costs associated with transport that have immediate social and economic consequences but can also have trade implications if the full costs of production are avoided because adverse transport externalities are not fully included in production costs.

2   THE ECONOMIC ISSUES

The demand for transport is derived from the desire to cross distance. In the context of the European Union, the issue is one of reducing suboptimal impedance to the movement of goods and people. Basic neoclassical economic trade theory provides the basis for free trade but the full benefits of free trade cannot be reaped if suboptimally high generalized transport costs exist (Button, 1994).[3]

There are also other issues than those stemming from conventional trade considerations. Of particular recent relevance have been issues concerning the need to develop common approaches to economic regulation and matters pertaining to environmental matters.

2.1   Transport and Trade

Two hundred years ago, David Ricardo emphasized the importance of comparative advantage in the creation of trade. One difficulty any nation may have in exploiting its comparative advantage may be inherently high external costs of transport. If costs are naturally high because, for instance, potential markets are distant from production locations or if the terrain is difficult, this will shape the types of goods traded and stimulate local production and consumption. If the benefits of investing to overcome these natural barriers (a reduction in generalized transport cost) exceed the gains from trade then they are not justified. Many barriers are institutional with such things as transport prices being manipulated essentially to set up protective barriers for local production. There may also be institutional regulations regulating the quality and level of supply of transport that have a similar effect to directly manipulating transport costs.

In Chapter 8 (Section 2) it was shown how an improvement in the availability of transport – in this case an improvement in transport infrastructure resulting in a decrease in transport costs – leads to an increase in transport volume between two regions. The purpose of this analysis was essentially distributional and aimed at showing that an improvement in the availability of transport may affect two different regions in different ways: one region may benefit while the other region may be hurt.

The present chapter deals with transport in an economic union. To this end it is of importance to see what role transport – or an improvement in the availability of transport – plays in creating gains for the nations forming such a union. Part of the analysis required for this runs parallel to that already given in Chapter 8. For the sake of clarity, however, the complete derivation of the effect on trade because of an increase in the availability of transport – that is, without referring to the earlier analysis in Chapter 8 – is set out below.

Figure 10.1 offers a simple diagrammatic presentation illustrating the role of transport in trade. The world here consists of just two countries, A and B, with both producing and consuming a single commodity. The demand and supply curves for country A are seen on the left of the vertical axis and those for B to the right. As drawn, B is a higher-cost producer with a higher demand for the commodity than A. With no transport, the price level in B would be higher than in A (that is $P_b > P_a$). The introduction of free, ubiquitous international transport would stimulate potential purchasers in B to seek the lower-priced commodity in country A. With free transport the total demand for the commodity in B would be w', of which w would be met by domestic production and ww' by imports from country A. If transport became available but was not offered freely then fewer imports would be demanded since the effective price confronting consumers in country B is P_a plus transport costs. Also, with higher transport costs the amount of domestic production in B will rise to satisfy demand and further reduce the demand for imports from A (imports being the difference between domestic consumption and domestic production). The demand for imports at different effective prices for B's consumers can be developed from this. In Figure 10.1, I_b is simply the distance ww' taken back to the horizontal, that is, imports in B if the commodity is available at effective price P_a. Since imports would be zero at price P_b, this may be taken as the other extreme of the import demand curve. The line P_bI_b reflects demand for imports when effect prices are between the extremes.

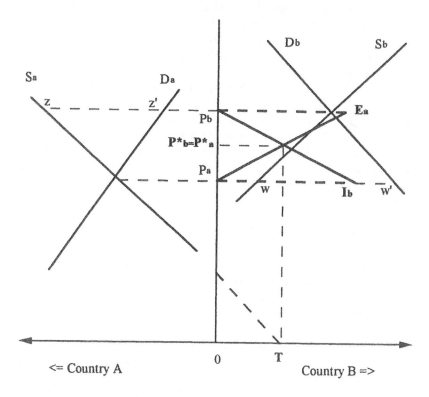

Figure 10.1   Transport and trade

What is going on in country A while B adjusts its demand and production patterns in the face of potential trade? If there was, suddenly, ubiquitous transport and country B, as well as domestic consumers, could purchase at price P_a then the pre-trade production in A would be inadequate to meet the new export demand of ww' from B. The result would be a rise in the price of the commodity. If the price rose to the pre-trade price in B, namely P_b, then production in A would be z' for domestic consumption and zz' for export. The level of the commodity available for export will be the difference between A's supply and demand curve at each price level. Tracing out these points generates A's export supply curve. In the diagram this is transposed to country B's quadrant as $P_a E_a$ (that is, $P_b E_a = zz'$). By doing this, it is possible to bring the export supply and import demand curves together and illustrate the optimal level of trade that will take place (T). Here, with no transport costs, there is a common international price for the commodity where $P_b^* = P_a^*$.

The gains from trade, in terms of consumer and producer surplus generation, are represented by the triangle bounded by the vertical axis and the import demand and expert supply curves. If there is no transport there is no social surplus. If trade is less than T then the social surplus is correspondingly reduced and a price differential will exist between the countries equal to the transport costs involved.

Of course this is a gross simplification. Increasing the number of countries and goods involved adds complexity as does the possibility that trade may take place in imperfect markets. Nevertheless, if transport costs are for some reason artificially high this limits the gains that can be enjoyed from trade. Equally, if they are too low and trade exceeds T then resources are being wasted that can more productively be used elsewhere. Most certainly at the time the EU came into existence there were multiple distortions in both domestic and international transport markets within the EU.

2.2   Regulation and Ownership

There has been a tradition in many EU countries to use transport provision as a tool for regional development and as an input into wider industrial policies. This may be seen from a longer-term classical economics perspective of enhancing the factor endowments of poorer regions (Biehl, 1986) or it may be from a shorter-term Keynesian position of using infrastructure investments as an aggregate demand stimulant. Other member states, however, have been less committed to this approach and have treated transport rather more in isolation with the objective of optimizing its efficiency in a more narrow, sectoral sense. The former approach is associated with the 'Continental Philosophy' of regulation and the latter with the 'Anglo-Saxon School'.

While this dichotomy in approach can be exaggerated, and no country fits exactly into either extreme, it has resulted in difficulties in developing a common economic framework for policy development. The differences were most pronounced in the earlier years of the EU when countries such as France and Germany dominated policy debates. The addition of more market-orientated countries such as the UK and Denmark has shifted the balance somewhat.

Adoption of these different approaches to regulation also has clear trade implications. They directly influence the costs of transport and, thus, indirectly, the costs of the goods and services that are traded. They also have a spatial impact in that they affect the relative costs of production associated with different regions within a country that trade with particular, often geographically adjacent, regions in another country. Efficient trade, therefore, requires some degree of coordination in the way transport is regulated. More recently, concern about the efficiency losses associated with excessive state intervention has led to a reduction worldwide in the ways regulatory regimes are used and a general cutback in their use. Even where the traditional emphasis of regulation has been narrowly on transport, the longstanding focus on containing monopoly power and fostering economies of scale has switched to that of limiting X-inefficiency and stimulating dynamic efficiency. This has meant reductions in state ownership and subsidies and a move to innovative forms of direct regulation such as price capping (setting a limit to prices). These trends can be witnessed at both the individual national level and the EU level.

2.3 Environmental Issues

In Chapter 4 it has been argued that transport is intrusive on the environment (see also Button and Rothengatter, 1997). In that chapter it has also been stated that many of the negative external environmental costs of transport, for example, noise, visual intrusion and atmospheric pollutants such as lead and particulates, have a purely local effect, while others, such as nitrogen oxide (NO_x) and water pollution have wider regional implications or, as with carbon dioxide (CO_2), global impacts. If these costs are not fully internalized then transport is underpriced and transport intensive industries enjoy an artificial comparative advantage. There are also direct economic issues concerning the dispersion of external costs of such things as transport-generated NO_x across other member states.

Economically there is no incentive for any single EU country to initiate internalization strategies beyond those with immediate national implications. Figure 10.2 offers a simple analysis. The country involved has its own marginal costs of abatement and marginal benefits of abatement curves that stimulate abatement of transport-related pollution externalities by Q^*. There are additional external costs due, for instance, to pollution of waterways draining into the watercourses of adjacent EU member countries and transport-induced atmospheric pollution spreading across political borders. Taking these into account would mean the country abating to the point QH in the diagram. There is no incentive, however, for unilateral action on the part of the individual country to pursue such actions and in recent years the EU has put particular attention to developing Union-wide policies to cater for spillover transport environmental effects. One such example of this is EU efforts to develop a strategy to ensure 'sustainable mobility' (European Commission, 1992a) and to foster 'green transport' policies (European Commission, 1992b; 1995b).

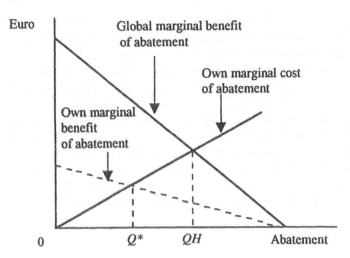

Figure 10.2   Difference between national and EU interests

2.4   Complexity of Transport Policy

While developing an economic framework to ensure that transport provision is consistent with maximizing the benefits of trade between two countries is difficult, the problems involved in this are compounded in an institution such as the EU.

The objective function for transport policy within the EU is a complex one not least because in many areas a consensus of members is needed for EU-wide actions. The situation is made all the more difficult to achieve because of external forces; the EU transport network is an integral part of a multimodal global network. Some idea of the difficulties of attaining anything like a viable economic approach to transport issues can be seen if recent EU transport policy is considered.

Figure 10.3 offers a very simple picture of how EU policy has evolved in this field.

The market was very heavily regulated until the mid-1980s (see below, Section 3) but now almost free market conditions pertain. Demonstration effects from the experiences of the USA in deregulation from 1978 were an important external factor that influenced opinion (Button et al., 1998) but this was also combined with the force of new economic ideas involving such notions as contestable markets, regulatory capture – whereby those intended to be regulated manipulate regulations to their advantage – and dynamic efficiency (see also Chapter 9).

Moving down one level, the market conditions in aviation in the mid-1980s, with many state-owned carriers being unable to compete in an increasingly

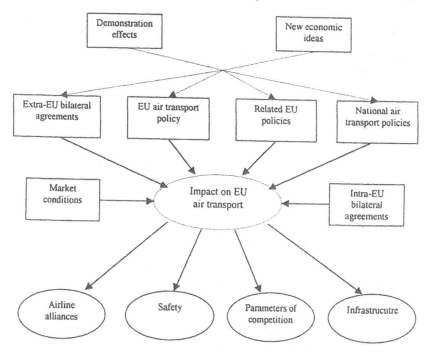

Figure 10.3 Simplified flow chart of factors influencing EU air transport

commercial and expanding market, resulted in some members privatizing airlines and airports unilaterally.

This had both a further demonstration effect and a direct impact on the competitive situation within the Union. A number of EU countries went further and liberalized bilateral air transport agreements with other like-minded members. A similar trend emerged externally with some EU members signing, especially, liberal 'Open Skies' agreements with the USA. The EU air transport policy reforms were part of this process but only, albeit a major, part.

These and other institutional developments have brought about a new market situation that involves innovative industrial structures such as airline alliances, new infrastructure requirements, implications for air transport safety and new competition policy challenges.

2.5 Questions of Transition

Accepting that there were at the outset numerous institutional impediments to optimizing transport provision within the EU, there are many alternative ways in which transition to a more efficient market for transport services could have been achieved. Theoretically, at one extreme is the 'Big Bang' school of thought which favours rapid and radical change while at the other is gradualism involving phased series of incremental regulatory reforms. The time paths of the costs and benefits of reform associated with the two philosophies are stylized in Figure 10.4.

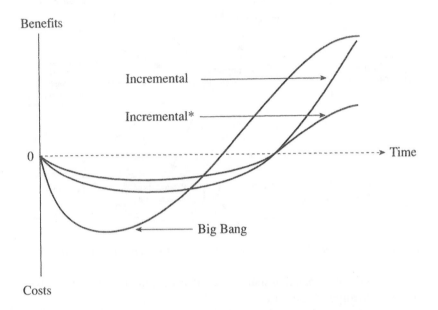

Figure 10.4   Time paths of incremental and Big Bang policy effects

Even if the two approaches result in the same long-term effect, there are important short-term differences. At its simplest, this diagram highlights the importance of the social discount factor in selecting the desirable strategy. Advocates of incrementalism implicitly have a lower discount rate. Essentially, the shock treatment approach has high initial costs of disruption to an industry and possibly consumers but a rapid move to a higher level of total economic welfare. In contrast, incrementalism has fewer initial adverse implications but the benefits of change take longer to materialize. Also the stylization hides important practical considerations. Reforms are seldom as straightforward as the diagram implies and, for instance, the EU liberalization of air transport services (see below, Section 4) has represented a number of separate, often independent, liberalizing initiatives, not a series of pre-planned and advertised incremental changes.

Further, as drawn, the diagram implies that ultimately there is a convergence in the paths of the alternative strategies but there is no reason to anticipate this happening. The incremental path could converge on a lower asymptotic benefit level than the Big Bang curve (for example, path Incremental*). An important factor can be the timing and intensity of external shocks on the market path to equilibrium. Policies and their implementation are also the subject of a diversity of forces and an inevitable degree of regulatory capture occurs. In particular, those most affected by a policy change often have the best access to information and thus the ability to capture the regulatory decision-making processes.

Despite the potential problems, the EU Common Transport Policy has followed an incremental path with periodic, and often seemingly disjointed, phases of activity followed by periods of inertia. The pace changed in the early 1980s as it became appreciated that the creation of the Single European Market in 1992 would require a more liberal transport market if the full potential benefits of freer trade were to be reaped (Button, 1992b).

3   EARLY THINKING ON POLICY

The EU Common Transport Policy, although established as a firm objective in the Treaty of Rome, has evolved rather than emerging from some master blueprint. This was despite attempts in the 1960s to pursue a somewhat more structured path to a common approach to transport (European Commission, 1961).

The early phases in the development of the Common Transport Policy were characterized by a focus on harmonization as a precursor to liberalization (Button, 1979; Gwilliam, 1980). Essentially the argument revolved around the notion that a level playing field was a necessary prerequisite to allowing freer rein to market forces. The domination at the time of countries such as Germany and France, with their proclivity towards interventionist policies in part explains this. Nevertheless the diversity of technical regulations and economic controls that pertained at the time inevitably meant that some initial harmonization was desirable (Munby, 1962).

Table 10.1 offers a very brief outline of the perception of EU transport policy needs in the 1960s together with a summary of some of the early initiatives. The aim here is not to discuss any of this in detail but to pass a few observations regarding some economic considerations.

The forked tariff regime for trucking was aimed at meeting the dual problems of possible monopoly exploitation in some circumstances and of possible inadequate capacity due to excess competition (now commonly referred to as the 'empty core' problem) in others. A 23 per cent differential between the maximum and minimum rate was stipulated and statutory charges established

Table 10.1   Summary of the policy of the 'Six'

Perceived nature of the transport sector

- A high degree of public intervention in the provision of infrastructure
- Low supply and demand elasticities leading to market instability
- Large traditional public service obligation
- Complex relationships between transport and other sectoral objectives

Objectives of policy

- Elimination of obstacles which transport may put in the way of establishment of the Common Market
- Integration of transport at the Community level
- General organization of the transport system within the Community

Basic principles

- Equality of treatment of transport modes and transport enterprises
- Financial responsibility of transport enterprises
- Freedom of action of transport operators. Free choices by users of transport mode and enterprise
- Coordination of infrastructure investment by public authorities

Actions

- Coordination of investment
  Consultation procedure (1996)
- Liberalization of transport services
  Initiation of Community Quota System (1968)
  Greater freedom for unscheduled passenger transport services (1996)
- Organization of the transport market
  Removal of national discrimination in tariffs (1962)
  Experiment with forked tariff (1968)
- Harmonization of competitive conditions
  Agreement on vehicle weights (1963; guidelines, 1972)
  Agreement on driving hours (1969)
  Normalization of transport accounts (1969)

---

on this basis. Practically, there were problems in setting the cost-based rates but beside that, questions must be raised about a policy that is aimed at tackling monopoly and excess competition simultaneously. Capacity limits on the number of international freight movements across borders, which were marginally reduced by the introduction of a limited number of Community Quota Licences (authorizing the free movement of vehicles on the whole of the Community road network), could have led to some quasi-monopoly problems but excessive competition was unlikely given the other institutional constraints in place at the time (Button, 1984).

The initial efforts at infrastructure policy coordination combined with a whole series of harmonization measures, both technical and in terms of accounting practices, can be seen as an effort to get competition on an even basis and to ensure that investments of EU-wide importance were carried out efficiently.

The enlargement of the Union from the original six to nine members in 1973 led to something of a renewed interest in transport policy. The new members, the UK, Ireland and Denmark, tended to be more market-orientated in terms of how transport policy was seen. Also, there is inevitable horse-trading across policy areas and with the enlargement came the opportunity to review a whole range of policy areas. It also followed a period of rapid growth in trade within the Union with a shift towards greater trade in manufactures. As a result, infrastructure capacity issues were coming to the fore and the case for more flexible regulation of road freight transport was being strongly argued (Button, 1990).

As with the previous phase, however, the outcome was hardly dramatic. Some new sectors became important in the debates, most notably maritime transport, and wider objectives such as environmental protection and energy (see Table 10.2).

Again just highlighting some of the points of economic interest, the series of actions can be seen as a further move to liberalization. Making the quota licence system permanent and increasing the number of licences meant that international road freight capacity was expanded. The option of using reference tariffs rather than forked tariffs was a reflection of the inherent problems with the latter. A major element of the measures initiated involved transport infrastructure, both in terms of improving decision making regarding its provision and in terms of the way that charges should be levied for its use.

The subsequent enlargements of the Union as, first Greece, then Spain and Portugal joined, had little impact on the Common Transport Policy. It essentially remained piecemeal. The only major change of importance prior to major developments in the early 1990s was the gradual integration of air transport as an element of policy. Until the early 1980s it had generally been thought to be outside of the jurisdiction of the Commission but following a number of legal decisions by the European Court of Justice (for example, the *Nouvelles Frontières* case regarding the application of competition rules) this changed.[4]

Table 10.2   Summary of the policy of the 'Nine'

Emphasis on

- Links between transport and regional, social, fiscal, industrial, environmental and energy affairs
- Intervention with transport within a Community-level framework
- The joint movement forward on consistency of regulations and liberalization
- The increasing importance attached to coordination of infrastructure
  investment

Policy

- Infrastructure coordination (Importance in the Action Programme,
  1974–76)
      New consultation procedure with a Transport Infrastructure Committee
      (1978)
      Oort's study of infrastructure pricing (1975) (Contained in the 'Green
      Paper' of 1979)
      Creation of an Infrastructure Fund
      Extend interest in the infrastructure of non-members (for example,
      Austria and Yugoslavia) where it affects links between members
- Liberalization
      Reference tariff system (1978)
      Permanent quota system (1976)
      Common method for determining bilateral quotas (1980)

A similar pattern emerged regarding a common maritime policy with moves
to bring the industry in line with Union competition policy.

4   THE NATURE OF CURRENT POLICY

The current shape of EU transport policy owes much to the creation of the
Single European Market in 1992 and to subsequent moves towards greater
political integration. Broadly, the former stimulated a concerted effort to remove
institutional barriers to the free trade in transport services while, combined with
efforts at further political integration, it has led to major new initiatives to
provide an integrated European transport infrastructure – for example the trans-
European networks (TENs) (European Commission, 1989). These strategic,
ultimately multimodal networks are aimed at facilitating higher levels of social
and political integration at the national and regional levels as well as having

purely economic objectives. Accompanying more integrated infrastructure planning, there is now also a greater coordination of investment financing through EU institutions (European Commission, 1994).

The main developments can briefly be summarized by mode, but as mentioned earlier the aim is not to offer a full history but rather focus on some of the important economic dimensions. The modal coverage also reflects the degree of economic reform rather than the absolute importance of any individual mode. Air transport is given particular attention as a sort of case study of how economic policy making regarding transport has evolved.

4.1 Railways

Rail transport is an important freight mode in much of continental Europe and provides important passenger services along several major corridors. At the local level, it serves as a key mode for commuter traffic in larger cities. Much of the important economic reform of European railways was undertaken in the early phase of integration, with important early actions on such things as the removal of discriminatory freight rates coming about under the auspices of the ECSC. The later phase has been concerned less with issues of economic regulation and with operations and more with widening access to networks and with technological developments, especially regarding the development of a high-speed rail network (European Commission, 1986).

The earlier phase had initially sought to remove deliberate distortions to the market favouring national carriers but from the late 1960s and 1970s had shifted to the rationalization of the subsidized networks through more effective and transparent cost accountancy (for example, Regulation 1192/69). The former objectives have met with some success while the impact of the latter has proved rather patchy and the exact incidence of subsidies still often remained uncertain. The Union has also instigated measures that allow the trains of one member to use the track of another with charges based upon economic costs (European Commission, 1995d; Council of the European Union, 1995a, b).

The aim of EU Directive 91/440 (Council of the European Union, 1991) is to develop truly European networks but at the time of writing the open access rules explicitly do not apply to the new high-speed rail lines such as the French and Belgian Lignes à Grande Vitesse and the German Neubaustrecken networks. The implementation of the open access strategy has been slow with limited impact (European Commission, 1998b).

The EU has traditionally found it difficult to devise practical and economically sound common pricing principles to apply to transport infrastructure despite the proposals of the Oort Report as early as 1976 (Oort and Maaskant, 1976).

With regard to railways, the gist of the overall proposals is for short-run marginal costs – which are to include environmental and congestion costs as well as wear of the infrastructure – to be recovered with the inclusion of long-run elements only in narrowly defined circumstances and in relation only to passenger services (European Commission, 1998b). This clearly has implications, especially on the freight side, if genuine full-cost base competition is to be permitted with other modes.

Rail transport has also received considerable support from the Commission as an integral part of making greater use of integrated, multimodal transport systems. Such systems would largely rely upon rail (including piggyback systems and kangaroo trains) or waterborne modes for trunk haulage with road transport used as the feeder mode. This is seen as environmentally desirable and as contributing to containing rising levels of road traffic congestion in Europe (European Commission, 1992a, 1996b).

The success of some of the French TGV services, and especially that between Paris and Lyon where full cost recovery has been attained, has led to a significant interest in this mode. In 1990, the European Commission set up a high-level working group to help push forward a common approach to high-speed railway development. A master plan for 2010 was produced. The Union's efforts to harmonize the development of high-speed rail have not, though, been entirely successful and there are significant technical differences, for example, between the French and German systems – indeed, both countries actively market their technologies as superior (Viegas and Blum, 1993).

4.2   Road Transport

Road transport is the dominant mode of both freight and passenger transport in the EU. The initial efforts to develop a common policy regarding road transport, as we have seen, proved problematic. Technical matters were more easily solved than those of creating a common economic framework of supply although even here issues concerning such things as maximum weight limits for trucks have tended to be fudged over. Economic controls lingered on as countries with less efficient road haulage industries sought to shelter them from the more competitive fleets of countries such as the UK and the Netherlands. There were also more legitimate efficiency concerns over the EU wider social costs of road transport both regarding environmental matters and narrower infrastructure utilization questions.

The Single Market initiative, also later influenced by the potential of new trade with the post-Communist states of Eastern and Central Europe (see further Chapter 12; see also Button, 1993b), has resulted in significant reforms to economic regulation in recent years. From the industrial perspective, road freight transport offers the flexibility that is required by modern, just-in-time production management but from the social perspective can be environmentally intrusive and, in the absence of appropriate infrastructure pricing, can contribute to excessive congestion costs.

Earlier measures had helped expand the supply of international permits in Europe, the EU quota complementing bilateral arrangements, and reference tariffs had introduced a basis for more efficient rate determination. The 1990s have been concerned with building on this rather fragile foundation. In particular, as part of the 1992 Single Market initiative, a phased liberalization was initiated that both gradually removed restrictions on trucking movements across national boundaries and phased in cabotage that had hitherto not been permitted by member states.

The longstanding bilateral arrangements for international licensing led to high levels of economic inefficiency. This was not only because the system imposed an absolute constraint on the number of movements, but also because cabotage was not permitted and combinations of bilateral licences permitting trucks to make complex international movements were difficult to obtain – trucks had to travel long distances without cargo. The system also added to delays at borders as documents were checked. The EU quota system offering multilateral licences had grown very slowly. Besides leading to the gradual phasing out of bilateral controls and the phasing in of cabotage rights, the 1992 initiative also led to considerable reductions in cross-border documentation.

Passenger road transport policy has largely been left to individual member states although in the late 1990s the Commission began to advocate the development of a 'citizens' network' (European Commission, 1995a) and more rational road charging policies (notably systems of congestion pricing – European Commission, 1995b – and infrastructure charges – European Commission, 1998a). Perhaps the greatest progress has been made regarding regulations on such things as the adoption of catalytic converters in efforts to limit the environmental intrusion of motor vehicles. It has taken time to develop a common policy regarding public transport despite efforts in the 1970s to facilitate cross-border coach and bus operations.

4.3   Inland Waterway Transport

Inland waterways had already been an issue in the early days of the Union. This is mainly because it is a primary concern of two founding member countries, the Netherlands and Germany, that in 1992 accounted for 73.1 per cent of EU traffic, with France and Belgium also having some interest.

Progress has tended to be slow in formulating a policy, in part because of historical agreements covering the Rhine navigation (for example, the Mannheim Convention) but mainly because the economic concern has been one of overcapacity.[5] In 1998, this was estimated at between 20 and 40 per cent at the prevailing freight rates. Retraction of supply is almost always inevitably difficult to manage.

As in other areas of transport, the EU began by seeking technical standard-ization (Council of the European Union, 1982). Principles for social harmonization were set out by the Commission in 1975 and 1979 (European Commission, 1975, 1979b). In 1990, under Council Regulation (EEC) 1101/89, the Union initiated the adoption of a system of subsidies designed to stimulate scrappage of vessels. Subsequent measures, such as Commission Regulations (EC) 2812/94 and 742/98, permitted new vessels into the inland fleet only on a replacement basis. This was coupled with an initiative in 1995 to coordinate investment in inland waterway infrastructure (the Trans-European Waterway Network) designed to encourage, for environmental reasons, the greater use of waterborne transport. Guarantees for a minimum income for bargemen that existed in the Netherlands, Belgium and France (through the rota system) have also been taken back in stages and had to be removed entirely in 2000.

4.4 Maritime Transport

Efforts to develop a common policy on maritime transport are relatively recent, dating from the late 1970s. They represent one of the broadenings out of EU transport policy (Brooks and Button, 1992). Since 35 per cent of the interna-tional, non-intra Union trade of member states involves maritime transport (some 90 per cent of the Union's aggregate imports and outputs) it may seem surprising that it took so long for this mode to come within the Common Transport Policy. The reason for this is that the Treaty of Rome required unanimous decisions regarding the extent to which sea transport was to be included in EU policy although it was unclear whether this applied to EU policy as a whole or purely the Common Transport Policy. Inertia was largely, initially at least, a function of a lack of clarity in the Commission's remit.

Initially the membership of countries such as the UK and Greece, with established shipping traditions, brought maritime issues to the table and then the Single European Act of 1986 acted as a catalyst for initiating a maritime policy (Erdmenger and Stasinopoulos, 1988). A series of measures was introduced aimed at bringing shipping within the Union's competition policy framework. The 'First Package' in 1985 sought to improve the competitive structure of the European shipping industry and its ability to combat unfair competition from third countries (see European Commission, 1985). It gave the Commission the power to react to predatory behaviour by third-party ship-owners which when initially applied (for example, the Hyundai case, Council of the European Union, 1989) exerted a demonstration effect, especially on Eastern bloc shipowners. The measures also set out an interpretation of competition policy that allowed block exemptions for shipping cartels (shipping conferences) albeit with safeguards to ensure the exemption was not exploited.[6] An extension of these rules to cover consortia and other forms of market sharing was initiated in 1992 (Council of the European Union, 1992a) and further continues as the nature of maritime alliances have become more complex (European Commission, 1995c).

In 1986 a 'Second Package' – the Positive Measures Package – was initiated by the European Commission with four main regulations aimed at addressing the decline in the competitiveness of the EU's fleets as well as covering such matters as safety and pollution. Greater coordination of fleets was seen as a cornerstone of policy and as part of this a common registry (EUROS – European Commission 1991a, b) was proposed.

It has not, however, proved a success, and fleet sizes have continued to decline (European Commission, 1995e) bringing forth new ideas for capacity reduction from the European Commission (1996c, d). Also, as part of the general effort to liberalize the European market and enhance the efficiency of the industry, agreement on cabotage was reached but with exceptions in some markets, for example, the Greek Islands.

Ports have also attracted the attention of the EU recently. They are major transport interchange points and in 1994 handled about 24 per cent of the world's TEUs.[7] Technology advances have led to important changes in the ways in which ports operate and there has been a significant concentration in activities as shipping companies have moved towards hub-and-spoke operations. The main EU ports have capacity utilization levels of well over 80 per cent and some are at or near their design capacity. Whether this is a function of a genuine capacity deficiency or reflects inappropriate port pricing charges that do not contain congestion cost elements is debatable. The European Commission (1997) has recently produced new proposals for coordinating investment in port facilities.

4.5 Air Transport Policy

The European bilateral system of air transport agreements covering scheduled air services was traditionally tightly regulated. Typical features of bilateral agreements involving EU members meant that:

- often only one airline from each country was allowed to fly on a particular route and the capacity offered by each bilateral partner was also restricted;
- revenues were pooled;
- fares were approved by the regulatory bodies of the bilateral partners; and
- the designated airlines were substantially state owned and enjoyed state aids.

The changing climate began in 1979 when the European Communities Commission put forward general ideas for regulatory reform in its first Memorandum on civil aviation, with more specific ideas following in 1984 with *Civil Aviation Memorandum No. 2* (European Commission, 1979a, 1984).

The practical push for reform came from the European Court of Justice's verdict in the *Nouvelles Frontières* case concerning the cutting of airfares that encouraged the Commission in the view that its powers to attack fare-fixing activities were greater than implementing regulation suggested. The Council decided that the best way to regain control was to agree to introduce deregulation but of a kind, and at a pace, of its own choosing. Hence the 1987 'First Package'. Table 10.3 sets out details of the Packages. The basic philosophy was that deregulation would take place in stages with workable competition being the objective.

A regulation was adopted that enabled the Commission to apply the antitrust rules directly to airline operations (Council of the European Union, 1987a). Only interstate operations were covered; the intrastate services and services to third countries were not at this stage affected by this measure. Certain technical agreements were also left untouched. The Council also adopted a directive designed to provide airlines with greater pricing freedom. While airlines could collude, the hope was that they would increasingly act individually. The authorities of the states approved airfare applications. Also the new arrangements did not constitute free competition – an element of regulation still remained in place. While conditions were laid down that reduced the national authorities' room for manoeuvre in rejecting airfares, they could still do so. However, if there was disagreement on a fare the disagreeing party lost the right of veto under arbitration.

The 1987 package also made a start on liberalizing access to the market. To this end the Council of Ministers adopted a decision in December 1987 (Council of the European Union, 1987a). This provided for a deviation from the traditional air services agreement 50/50 split. The capacity shares related to total traffic between the two countries. Member states were required to allow competition to change the shares up to 55/45 in the period to 30 September 1989 and thereafter to allow it to change to 60/40. Normally they could only take action if capacity shares threatened to move beyond such limits. Fifth freedom traffic was not included in these ratios but came on top. There was also a provision in which serious financial damage to an air carrier could constitute grounds for the Commission to modify the shift to the 60/40 limit.

The decision also required member states to accept multiple designation on a country pair basis by another member. A member state was not obliged to accept the designation of more than one air carrier on a route by the other state (that is, city pair basis) unless certain conditions were satisfied. These conditions

Table 10.3 EU air transport packages

	1st Package From 1 January 1988 International scheduled passenger transport	2nd Package From 1 November 1990 International scheduled passenger transport	3rd Package From 1 January 1993 International scheduled passenger transport
Relevant legislation	Regulation 3975/87 on the application of the competition rules to air transport Regulation 3976/87 on the application of the Treaty to certain categories of agreements and concerted practices Council Directive 87/601/EEC on air fares Council Decision 87/602/EEC on capacity sharing and market access	Council Regulation 2342/90 on air fares Council Regulation 2343/90 on market access Council Regulation 2344/90 on the application of the Treaty to certain categories of agreements and concerted practices	Council Regulation 2407/92 on licensing of air carriers Council Regulation 2408/92 on market access Council Regulation 2409/92 on fares and rates
Fares	% of Fares approved *Fare Type* — *ref. Fare* — *by States* Discount — 66–90 — Automatically Deep discount — 45–65 — Automatically All other — — Double approval	% of Fares approved *Fare Type* — *ref. Fare* — *by States* Fully flexible — 106 — Unless double disapproval Normal economy — 95–105 — Automatically Discount — 80–94 — Automatically Deep discount — 30–79 — Automatically All others — — Double approval	Provisions made for the States and/or the Commission to intervene against: Excessive basic fares (in relation to long-term fully allocated costs) Sustained downward development of fares
Designation	Multiple designation by a State allowed if: 250 000 pass (1st year after integration) 200 000 pass or 1200 rt flights (2nd year) 180 000 pass or 1000 rt flights (3rd year)	Multiple designation by a State allowed if: 140 000 pass or 800 rt flights (from January 1991) 100 000 pass or 600 rt flights (from January 1992)	No longer applicable
Capacity	Capacity shares between states 45/55% (from January 1988) 40/60% (from October 1989)	Capacity shares of a State of up to 60% Capacity can be increased by 7.5% points per year	Unrestricted
Route access	3rd/4th freedom region to hub routes permitted. 5th freedom traffic allowed up to 30% of capacity Additional 5th rights for Irish and Portuguese Combination of points allowed Some exemptions	3rd/4th freedom between all airports 5th freedom traffic allowed up to 50% of capacity Public service obligations and certain protection for new regional routes A 3rd/4th-freedom service can be matched by an airline from the other State Scope for traffic distribution rules and restrictions related to congestion and environmental protection	Full access to international and domestic routes within the EU (exemptions for Greek islands and Azores) Cabotage unrestricted from April 1997. Restricted cabotage allowed for up to 50% of capacity until then. Reformed public service obligations and some protection for new thin regional routes More scope for traffic distribution rules and restrictions related to congestion and environmental protection
Competition rules	Ground exemption regarding: Some capacity coordination Tariff consultation Slot allocation Common computer reservation systems Ground handling of aircraft, freight, passenger and in-flight catering Some sharing of pool revenues	Ground exemption regarding: Some capacity coordination Tariff consultation Slot allocation Common computer reservation systems Ground handling of aircraft, freight, passenger and in-flight catering	Ground exemption regarding: Some capacity coordination Tariff consultation Slot allocation Common computer reservation systems Joint operation of new thin routes
Licensing of air carriers	Not provided for in 1st and 2nd Packages		Uniform conditions across EU; notion of Union ownership and control; and small carriers subject to looser regulatory requirements

become progressively less restrictive over time. The decision also made a limited attempt to open up the market to fifth freedom competition.

In 1989, the Council of Transport Ministers returned to the issue of air transport deregulation. The 'Second Package' involved more deregulation. From the beginning of 1993, a system of double disapproval was accepted. Only if both civil aviation authorities refused to sanction a fare application could an airline be precluded from offering it to its passengers. From the same date the old system of setting limits to the division of traffic between the bilateral partners was totally to disappear in a phased manner.

Member states also endorsed the vital principle, advanced by the Commission, that governments should not discriminate against airlines provided they meet safety standards and address the problem of ownership rules. An airline has typically had to be substantially owned by a European state before it could fly from that country but the Council abolished this rule over a two-year period.

Air cargo services were liberalized so that a carrier operating from its home state to another member country can take cargo into a third member state or fly from one member state to another and then to its home state. Cabotage, or operations between two free-standing states, was not liberalized.

The final reform – the 'Third Package' – came in 1992 and took effect from the following year. This initiated a phased move that, by 1997, resulted in a regulatory framework for the EU similar to US domestic aviation (Button and Swann, 1992). See again Table 10.3.

The measures removed significant barriers to entry by setting common rules governing safety and financial requirements for new airlines. Since January 1993, EU airlines have been able to fly between member states without restriction and within member states (other than their own), subject to some controls on fares and capacity. National restrictions on ticket prices were removed with safeguards only if fares fall too low or rise too high.

Consecutive cabotage was introduced allowing a carrier to add a 'domestic leg' on a flight starting out of its home base to a destination in another member state if the number of passengers on the second leg did not exceed 50 per cent of the total in the main flight. Starting in 1997, full cabotage has been permitted, and fares are generally unregulated. Additionally, foreign ownership among Union carriers is permitted, and these carriers have, for EU internal purposes, become European airlines. This change does not apply to extra-Union agreements where national bilateral arrangements still dominate the market. One result has been a considerable increase in cross-shareholdings and a rapidly expanding number of alliances among airlines within the Union.

Early analysis of reforms by the UK Civil Aviation Authority (1993) and the European Commission indicated that the reforms of the 1990s produced, in terms of multiple airlines serving various market areas, greater competition on both EU domestic routes and on international routes within the EU. The changes varied but countries such as Greece and Portugal increased the number of competitive international services considerably. Many routes, however, either because multiple services are simply not technically sustainable or institutional impediments still limited market entry and remained monopolies in 1994.

More recently, the European Commission (1996a), in examining the impact of the Third Package, reported important consumer benefits. It found that the number of routes flown within the EU rose from 490 to 520 between 1993 and 1995, that 30 per cent of Union routes are now served by two operators and 6 per cent by three operators or more, that eighty new airlines have been created while only sixty have disappeared, that fares have fallen on routes where there are at least three operators and that overall, when allowance is made for charter operations, 90–95 per cent of passenger on intra-Union routes are travelling at reduced fares. A caveat here is that there have been quite significant variations in the patterns of fares charged across routes.

There has been little change in fares on routes that remain monopolies or duopolies. The number of fifth freedom routes doubled to 30 between 1993 and 1996 although this type of operation remains a relatively small feature of the market and seventh freedoms have been little used.[8]

Indeed, much of the new competition has been on domestic routes where routes operated by two or more carriers rose from 65 in January 1963 to 114 in January 1996 with the largest expansions in France, Spain and Germany. The charter market has also continued to grow and in some countries accounts for more than 80 per cent of traffic.

5 CONCLUSION

Developing a common transport policy for a set of economically related but essentially independent states poses a particular set of questions. At one level there is the issue of whether the EU area represents anything like a natural economic market for transport services while at the other there are the problems of overcoming national priorities and legacies. Nevertheless, for an economic union to be fully effective and for trade between members to be conducted efficiently there is the need for at least a reasonable degree of coordination of transport policies.

The underlying economic needs of a common market were recognized at the outset; the problem has been one of moving from a set of fairly well-established broad economic concepts to a tractable policy position. Consensus needs make this difficult in conditions where from a short-term economic perspective there are pressures in each Member State towards protecting the status quo and, in the longer term, to ensure that distribution gains from freer trade benefit individual members. Further, while there may be general agreement about the need for a common transport policy, and setting aside who gains most from it, there are genuine ideological differences on how to attain particular objectives. Finally, there are economic considerations when deciding how the transition to the new position is to be carried through.

The EU has taken its time to tackle the transport needs of a genuine common market. What has emerged, however, while open to a variety of technical criticisms, is something approaching a free market for transport services within the Union – a market that approximates long-established economic ideas of workable competition and from whose experiences perhaps other parts of the world may learn.

NOTES

1. The other common policy being agricultural policy.
2. The Marshall Plan, designed to help restructure European economies after the Second World War, also had elements of a common transport policy and resulted in the establishment of the European Conference of Ministers of Transport (1953).
3. 'Generalized cost': see Chapter 2, note 1.
4. Judgement on discounting practices of a French budget travel company and other recent case law on the applicability of Community Competition Rules to Air Transport and the enforcement mechanism in this sector, joined cases 209 to 213/84, April 1986.
5. In the Mannheim Convention (Revised Convention for the Navigation of the Rhine, signed at Mannheim on 17 October 1868, as amended by the Strasbourg Convention of 20 November 1963) complete freedom of navigation on the Rhine and its tributaries is laid down.
6. 'Block exemption': the allowance of certain practices without the need for their consideration on a case-by-case basis.
7. TEU: trailer equivalent unit; a measurement of cubic capacity used in container transport.
8. Seventh freedom: the right of a carrier to operate stand-alone services entirely outside the territory of its home state to carry traffic between two foreign states.

REFERENCES

Biehl, D. (1986), *The Contribution of Infrastructure to Regional Development*, Brussels: Regional Policy Division, European Communities.

Brooks, M.R. and K.J. Button (1992), 'Shipping within the framework of a Single European Market', *Transport Reviews*, **12**, 237–52.

Button, K.J. (1979), 'Recent developments in EEC transport policy', *Three Banks Review*, **123**, 52–73.

Button, K.J. (1984), *Road Haulage Licensing and EC Transport Policy*, Aldershot: Gower.

Button, K.J. (1990), 'Infrastructure plans for Europe', in J. Gillund and G. Tornqvist (eds), *European Networks*, Umeå: CERUM, pp. 95–118.

Button, K.J. (1992a), 'The future of European transport', in R. Thord (ed.), *The Future of Transportation and Communication*, Borlänge: Swedish National Road Administration, pp. 43–78.

Button, K.J. (1992b), 'The liberalisation of transport services', in D. Swann (ed.), *1992 and Beyond*, London: Routledge, pp. 146–61.

Button, K.J. (1993a), 'Freight transport', in D. Banister and J. Berechman (eds), *Transportation in a Unified Europe: Policies and Challenges*, Amsterdam: Elsevier, pp. 143–70.

Button, K.J. (1993b), 'East–West European transport: an overview', in D. Banister and J. Berechman (eds), *Transportation in a Unified Europe: Policies and Challenges*, Amsterdam: Elsevier, pp. 291–313.

Button, K.J. (1994), 'Transport investment and sustainable development in Europe', in H. Voogd (ed.), *Issues in Environmental Planning*, London: Pion, pp. 114–30.

Button, K.J., K. Haynes and K. Stough (1998), *Flying into the Future: Air Transport Policy in the European Union*, Cheltenham: Edward Elgar.

Button, K.J. and W. Rothengatter (1997), 'Motor transport greenhouse gases and economic instruments', *International Journal of Environment and Pollution*, **7**, 327–42.

Button, K.J. and D. Swann (1992), 'Transatlantic lessons in aviation deregulation: EEC and US experiences', *Antitrust Bulletin*, **37**, 207–55.

Civil Aviation Authority (1993), *Airline Competition in the Single European Market*, CAP 623, London: Civil Aviation Authority.

Council of the European Union (1982), *Directive (EEC) 82/714 Laying Down Technical Requirements for Inland Waterway Transport*, Brussels.

Council of the European Union (1987a), *Regulation (EEC) No. 3975/87 of 14 December 1987 Laying Down the Procedure for the Application of the Rules of Competition to Undertakings in the Air Transport Sector*, OJL374/1987/12/31, Brussels, p. 1.

Council of the European Union (1987b), *Regulation (EEC) No. 3976/87 of 14 December 1987 on the Application of Article 85(3) of the Treaty to Certain Categories of Agreements and Concerted Practices in the Air Transport Sector*, OJL374/1987/12/31, Brussels, p. 9.

Council of the European Union (1987c), *Directive (EEC) 601/87 on Air Fares*, OJL374/1987/12/31, Brussels, p. 12.

Council of the European Union (1987d), *Decision (EEC) No. 602/87 of 14 December 1987 on the Sharing of Passenger Capacity between Air Carriers on Scheduled Air Services between Member States and on Access for Air Carriers to Scheduled Air-service Routes between Member States*, OJL374/1987/12/31, Brussels, p. 19.

Council of the European Union (1989), *Regulation (EEC) No. 15/89 of 4 January 1989 Introducing a Redressive Duty on Containerised Cargo to be Transported in Liner Service between the Community and Australia by Hyundai Merchant Marine Company Ltd of Seoul, Republic of Korea*, OJL4/1989/01/06, Brussels, p. 1.

Council of the European Union (1990a), *Regulation (EEC) No. 2342/90 of 24 July 1990 on Fares for Scheduled Air Services*, OJL217/1990/08/11, Brussels, p. 1.

Council of the European Union (1990b), *Regulation (EEC) No. 2343/90 of 24 July 1990 on Access for Air Carriers to Scheduled Intra-Community Air Service Routes and on the Sharing of Passenger Capacity between Air Carriers on Scheduled Air Services between Member States*, OJL217/1990/08/11, Brussels, p. 8.

Council of the European Union (1990c), *Regulation (EEC) No. 2344/90 of 24 July 1990 Amending Regulation (EEC) No. 3976/87 on the Application of Article 85 (3) of the Treaty to Certain Categories of Agreements and Concerted Practices in the Air Transport Sector*, OJL217/1990/08/11, Brussels, p. 15.

Council of the European Union (1991), *Directive 91/440/EEC of 29 July 1991 on the development of the Community's Railways*, OJL237/1991/08/24, Brussels, p. 25.

Council of the European Union (1992a), *Regulation (EEC) No. 479/92 of 25 February 1992 on the Application of Article 85 (3) of the Treaty to Certain Categories of Agreements, Decisions and Concerted Practices between Liner Shipping Companies (Consortia)*, OJL55/1992/02/29, Brussels, p. 3.

Council of the European Union (1992b), *Regulation (EEC) No. 2407/92 of 23 July 1992 on Licensing of Air Carriers*, OJL240/1992/08/24, Brussels, p. 1.

Council of the European Union (1992c), *Regulation (EEC) No. 2408/92 of 23 July 1992 on Access for Community Air Carriers to Intra-Community Air Routes*, OJL240/1992/08/24, Brussels, p. 8.

Council of the European Union (1992d), *Regulation (EEC) No. 2409/92 of 23 July 1992 on Fares and Rates for Air Services*, OJL240/1992/08/24, Brussels, p. 15.

Council of the European Union (1995a), *Council Directive 95/18/EC of 19 June 1995 on the Licensing of Railway Undertakings*, OJL143/1995/06/27, Brussels, p. 70.

Council of the European Union (1995b), *Council Directive 95/19/EC of 19 June 1995 on the Allocation of Railway Infrastructure Capacity and the Charging of Infrastructure Fees*, OJL143/1995/06/27, Brussels, p. 75.

Erdmenger, J. and D. Stasinopoulos (1988), 'The shipping policy of the European Community', *Journal of Transport Economics and Policy*, **22**, 355–60.

European Commission (1961), *Memorandum on the General Lines of A Common Transport Policy*, Brussels.

European Commission (1975), *Social Harmonisation – Inland Waterways*, COM(75)465/ FIN, Brussels.

European Commission (1979a), *Memorandum on the Contribution of the European Communities to the Development of Air Transport Services*, COM(79)311/FIN, Bulletin of the European Communities, Supplement 5/79, Brussels.

European Commission (1979b) *Social Harmonisation – Inland Waterways*, COM(79)363/FIN, Brussels.

European Commission (1984), *Civil Aviation Memorandum No. 2. Progress towards the Development of a Community Air Transport Policy*, COM(84)72/FIN, Brussels.

European Commission (1985), *Progress towards a Common Transport Policy. Maritime Transport*, COM(85)90/FIN, Brussels.

European Commission (1986), *Report Towards a High-speed Rail Network*, COM(86)341/FIN, Brussels.

European Commission (1989), *Council Resolution on Trans-European Networks*, COM(89)643/FIN, Brussels.

European Commission (1991a), *Amended Proposals for Council Regulations – Establishing a Community Ship Register and Providing for the Flying of the Flag by Sea-going Vessels – on a Common Definition of a Community Shipowner – Applying the Principle of Freedom to Provide Services to Maritime Transport with Member States*, COM(90)54FIN, 22 February 1991, Brussels.

European Commission (1991b), *Amended Proposal for a Council Regulation (EEC) Establishing a Community Ship Register and Providing for the Flying of the Flag by Sea-going Vessels (Presented by the Commission pursuant to Article 149(3) of the EEC Treaty)*, COM(91)54/I/FIN, Brussels.

European Commission (1992a), *The Future Development of the Common Transport Policy: A Global Approach to the Construction of a Community Framework for Sustainable Mobility*, Brussels.

European Commission (1992b), *Green Paper on the Impact of Transport on the Environment: A Community Strategy for Sustainable Development*, COM(92)46/FIN, Brussels.

European Commission (1994), *Proposal for a Council Regulation (EC) Laying Down General Rules for the Granting of Community Financial Aid in the Field of Trans-European Networks*, COM(94)62/FIN, Brussels.

European Commission (1995a), *The Citizens' Network. Fulfilling the Potential of Public Passenger Transport in Europe*, Green Paper, COM(95)601/FIN, Brussels.

European Commission (1995b), *Towards Fair and Efficient Pricing in Transport. Policy Options for Internalizing the External Costs of Transport in the European Union*, Green Paper, COM(95)691/FIN, Brussels.

European Commission (1995c), *Regulation (EC) No. 870/95 of 20 April 1995 on the Application of Article 85 (3) of the Treaty to Certain Categories of Agreements, Decisions and Concerted Practices between Liner Shipping Companies (Consortia) Pursuant to Council Regulation (EEC) No. 479/92*, OJL89/1995/04/21, Brussels, p. 7.

European Commission (1995d), *Communication from the Commission on the Development of the Community's Railways. Application of Directive 91/440/EEC. Future Measures to Develop the Railways*, COM(95)337/I/FIN, Brussels.

European Commission (1995e), *Communication from the Commission to the European Parliament, the Council, the Economic and Social Committee and the Committee of the Regions; the Developments of Short Sea Shipping in Europe: Prospects and Challenges*, COM(95)317/FIN, Brussels.

European Commission (1996a), *Impact of the Third Package of Air Transport Liberalisation Measures*, COM(96)514/FIN, Brussels.

European Commission (1996b), *A Strategy for Revitalising the Community's Railways*, White paper, COM(96)421/FIN, Brussels.

European Commission (1996c), *Communication to the Council, the European Parliament, the Economic and Social Committee and the Committee of the Regions. Towards a New Maritime Strategy*, COM(96)81/FIN, Brussels.

European Commission (1996d), *Communication to the Council, the European Parliament, the Economic and Social Committee and the Committee of the Regions. Shaping Europe's Maritime Future. A Contribution to the Competitiveness of Maritime Industries*, COM(96)84/FIN, Brussels.

European Commission (1997), *Green Paper on Sea-ports and Maritime Infrastructure*, COM(97)678/FIN, Brussels.

European Commission (1998a), *Fair Payment for Infrastructure Use: A Phased Approach to a Common Transport Infrastructure Charging Framework in the EU*, White Paper, COM(98)466/FIN, Brussels.

European Commission (1998b), *Communication to the Council and the European Parliament on the Implementation and Impact of Directive 91/440/EEC on the Development of the Community Railways and on Access Rights for Rail Freight*, COM(98)202/FIN, Brussels.

Gwilliam, K.M. (1980), 'Realism and the common transport policy of the EEC', in J.B. Polak and J.B. van der Kamp (eds), *Changes in the Field of Transport Studies*, The Hague: Nijhoff, pp. 38–59.

McGowan, F. (1998), 'EU transport policy', in A.M. El-Agraa (ed.), *The European Union, History, Institutions, Economics and Policies*, London: Prentice Hall, pp. 247–65.

Meade, J.E., H.H. Liesnr and S.J. Wells (1962), *Case Studies in European Economic Union – The Mechanics of Integration*, London: Oxford University Press.

Munby, D.L. (1962), 'Fallacies of the Community's transport policy', *Journal of Transport Economics and Policy*, **1**, 67–98.

Oort, C.J. and R.H. Maaskant (1976), *Study of Possible Solutions for Allocating the Deficit Which May Occur in a System of Charging for the Use of Infrastructure Aiming at Budgetary Equilibrium*, Brussels: EEC.

Viegas, J.M. and U. Blum (1993), 'High Speed Railways in Europe', in D. Banister and J. Berechman (eds), *Transport in a Unified Europe: Policies and Challenges*, Amsterdam: Elsevier, pp. 75–89.

PART V

Some special cases

11. Urban transport

Martin J.H. Mogridge

1 INTRODUCTION

In earlier chapters of this book (in particular Chapter 6, Section 5) it has already been established that urban transport problems are of a different order to those of interurban or rural transport. Essentially, this arises because there is no possible way in which an urban area, once it is beyond a certain size and concentration of activities, can cater for all potential movements by car. This was first set out by Smeed (1961). The argument can be simplified to state that, for a typical European city, beyond about a quarter of a million people the urban area requires a bus network, beyond a million a light rail network and beyond four million a heavy rail network. The numbers depend on the configuration of the urban area – a linear corridor can support higher levels of public transport, for example Oslo between the mountains and the sea. For western US cities at much lower population densities the values of population required are much higher for a given type of public transport (see Chapter 6, Figure 6.10). Thus problems of modal split become increasingly important the bigger the city.

Because the transport problems become increasingly complex the bigger the city, we use analytical models. For a general treatment of such models the reader may be referred to Chapter 3. In that chapter (Section 3) a number of drawbacks of the traditional four-stage transport planning process were pointed out, which process determines a static equilibrium solution. In particular, the trip generation model is often deficient in its inability to estimate 'hidden' or latent demand when transport costs are changed. Moreover, the interaction between the transport system and land-use patterns is not captured in this type of model. These two deficiencies are especially important in the urban context. Attempts to ameliorate these problems by activity analysis (see Chapter 3, Section 4) and by the development of explicitly dynamic modelling techniques have as yet had little impact on the general use of the static equilibrium model. This is essentially because the data demands of these techniques are much larger.

Jansson, in discussing optimal pricing (Chapter 7), argued that the congestion costs imposed by traffic on other traffic and the external costs imposed by traffic on other people were very significant in urban areas, for all modes. Optimal pricing for road services, where there are diseconomies of scale, implies a financial surplus; on the other hand for public transport, on its own track, where there are economies of scale, it implies a financial deficit.

It is still anathema to many people that congested roads should be charged at a rate which provides a financial surplus. As a result of not charging the optimal price, roads are too cheap, the demand is too high, and road investment has been expanded beyond the optimum level, particularly in urban areas. It is greater anathema to many people that urban public transport should be run at a financial deficit. As a result of not charging the optimum price, public transport is too expensive, the demand is too low, and public transport services are cut back.

Some argue that deficit financing, or subsidization, leads to inefficiencies of operation, higher labour costs and so on. This was a major concern of the Conservative government in the 1980s in the UK, and much effort was expended on trying to prove the point (for example, Glaister, 1982; Bly and Oldfield, 1986a). Thus the privatization of the UK bus operating companies began in 1985 with the aim of eliminating bus subsidies. The privatization of the UK railways began rather later, in 1996, with a similar aim. In the UK as well as in a number of other European countries (for example, Germany, the Netherlands, Sweden), the government set up a separate company for managing the rail network on the one hand and one or more train operating companies on the other in order to separate rail-track and infrastructure costs from operating costs. Road and rail track costs are now separate from operating costs. As argued in Chapter 7 (Section 8), the optimal solution is for the train operating companies to pay the wear-and-tear costs of using the railway but all other costs of the track and infrastructure should be borne by the state, just as for roads.

Also in Chapter 7 (Section 3), the important point was made that, in assessing price, the rent for the space consumed is crucial. In urban areas, it is often the case that the prices charged for road space, parking space, public transport terminal space and so on bear no relation to the price charged for the equivalent space used as homes, offices, factories and so on.

In Chapter 6 it was argued that urban transport investment, whether in roads, public transport, traffic management or parking regulation, is an integral part of the superior aim of creating good living and working conditions for people in built-up areas. If roads and public transport were both providing services, then investing in roads could, in certain circumstances, be counterproductive, such that the net benefits became negative (the Downs–Thomson paradox; see, for example, Mogridge, 1990; also in this book, Chapter 6, Section 7.3, 'Thomson's parable'). This was particularly crucial in the assessment of investment in congested conditions such as central cities and other town centres within an urban area.

These two problems – optimal pricing for and investment in urban transport – have been recognized within the profession for a long time now, but the political willingness to charge optimum prices and to invest in the most efficient facilities – both with the necessary modifications in so far as goals other than maximum efficiency are concerned – is still lacking, because the problems are not sufficiently understood by the politicians or the general public. Some discussion of the history of transport models over the last few decades based on the example of London will demonstrate the way that understanding has gradually developed (Mogridge, 1990, 1997a).[1]

To this end the following stages will be distinguished: single-mode models (Section 2), the first multimode models (Section 3, the developments in the 1970s, the 1980s and the 1990s (Sections 4, 5 and 6), future developments (Section 7) and conclusion (Section 8).

2   SINGLE-MODE MODELS

The early work in London in the 1960s was essentially of single-mode studies. The pioneering work on road pricing in central London by the Smeed Committee (Ministry of Transport, 1964), drawing on the work of Buchanan (1952) and Walters (1954), established the economic case for road pricing but did not tackle the interaction with public transport, although the appendix by Thomson showed that benefits accrue only when the revenue collected is used.

Thomson (1967) developed these ideas, relying on elasticities of demand at different journey lengths for different kinds of journeys, to estimate the effects of two different proposals for traffic restraint in central London. He calculated that the marginal cost was about three times the average cost for the central London road network. His calculations are somewhat spurious since they rely on traffic flows and speeds measured at different times of day when the public transport alternative is slightly different.

The 1962 London Traffic Survey (London County Council, 1964; GLC, 1966) was initially conceived as a road traffic survey; only later was it decided to include public transport.[2] The first modelling of the road network on computer was thus of car and freight movements only. Furthermore, no account was taken of the effects of congestion, and no attempt was made to relate the amount of travel to the capacity of the road system available.

With the formation of the Greater London Council in 1965, covering the majority of the contiguous built-up area, it was soon realized that the public transport networks had to be incorporated into the modelling of transport demand.

3　THE FIRST MULTIMODE MODELS

It was not, however, until 1968 that a modal split model was incorporated into the computer network models (Freeman Fox, Wilbur Smith & Associates, 1968), but this was still extremely simple. Both the rail and bus times were constant for a given trip, irrespective of flow, just like the road network in the unconstrained situation.

This model was used to test three road and two public transport plans, varying from a 'do-minimum' road plan to extensive motorways capable of taking all the demand in 1981, and from extensive improvements to public transport services, especially bus, to a rail plan which connected several of the main-line services across the centre (cross-rail). Many more plans had in fact been defined, but limitations of cost and time prevented further plans from being tested.

The most significant change to the road model was the incorporation of a 'constrained demand' model. By this model, car demand was reduced in destination areas by forcing some car-owning households to behave like non-car-owning households, in order to reduce car demand to a level which left the total road system carrying the maximum traffic within its capacity.

As a result of the procedures, the public transport demand varied only in so far as some trips were transferred from the restraint procedure (about 40 per cent of restrained trips were diverted and about 60 per cent suppressed). In particular, the extensive rail investments only diverted trips from other public transport modes, including from other destinations, rather than attracting any from cars. This appeared to demonstrate that public transport investments were not good value for money.

In effect, the procedures demonstrated the degeneration of traffic, that is that if roads were not provided, then traffic 'demand' disappeared. These points were elaborated in Mogridge's (1977) submission to the Leitch Committee (UK Department of Transport, 1978) in which it was argued that traffic forecasting had to be set in a proper economic framework of supply and demand.

The resulting forecasts of traffic 'demand' formed the basis of the justification for the Greater London Development Plan road proposals (GLC, 1969), an extensive set of motorways, with very little change proposed for the public transport systems. The model procedures became the District Test Model (DTM) for the analyses performed during the Inquiry into the Development Plan (1969–71).

The results were, however, extensively criticized in Thomson (1969). In particular, he argued that the switch of public transport users to car as car ownership increased would cause the public transport operators to reduce services or raise fares, or both, in order to keep within their financial constraints. This would reduce the attractiveness of public transport, and not, as assumed in the modelling, maintain the same level of attractiveness.

He argued, moreover, that the motorway proposals would substantially worsen the general living and working conditions in London. In particular, he argued that the forecasts of population, incomes and thus car ownership and car trips were too high.

As a result of the 'Homes Before Roads' campaign initiated by the London Amenity and Transport Association, based on Thomson's book, the next London election in 1973 was won by the Labour administration which effectively scrapped the motorway proposals.[3]

A second stream of modelling in the 1960s contained calculations of the effect of transferring people from cars to buses of different types in central London on journey speeds (Smeed and Wardrop, 1964; Webster, 1968; Lyons, 1969; Webster and Oldfield, 1972). Despite some unrealistic assumptions on average trip length, waiting times and access times, and parking times, these papers showed quite conclusively that buses could provide quicker journeys, door-to-door, than cars if only cars could be restrained, where demand for travel was as high as in the centres of large cities like London.

The reason is simple. For cars the speed/flow curve shows that there is a rapidly falling speed of cars as their number increases on a given network. This is shown in Figure 11.1 by the region marked A. The maximum flow at equilibrium is marked B. This is unstable because a slight transient addition to flow will cause the curve to drop into the region C where the speed is much lower for a given flow than in the region A. Speeds and flows are both much lower in networks than on single roads because of the delays at junctions.

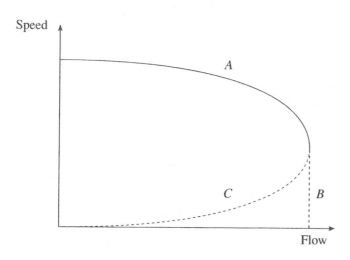

Figure 11.1 Speed/flow curve

Also as the number of cars increases, drivers have increasing difficulty in finding parking space near to the origin and destination, leading to longer parking times. For buses, on the other hand, as the number of passengers increases, so the number of services will increase, and the waiting and access times will fall. If buses are given adequate priority in road space and through junctions, these effects can be enhanced. They can also be enhanced if the appropriate size of buses is used for the demand.[4] Webster and Oldfield (1972) were in fact the first to note that, using an assumption that car access times on a journey were 10 minutes, average car journey direct speeds could be as low as 8 km/hr in central London, that is the same as public transport direct journey speeds and thus at the Downs–Thomson equilibrium speed (Chapter 6, Figure 6.9, using time, not generalized cost).

The crucial point about this work was that it demonstrated that, in central cities, car users could be provided with a quicker journey if only people could be restrained from using cars and thus impeding the buses.

4   THE 1970s: THE ANALYSIS OF ROAD PRICING

The second London Transportation Survey in 1971–72 differed from the 1962 survey in a number of respects.[5] This made the second survey incompatible with the previous, 1962, survey, and thus backcasting for validation impossible, with continuing implications for time-series comparisons up to the present day.

Before the 1971 survey results were available, however, the *London Rail Study* (GLC, 1974a) had reviewed the arrangements for passenger rail travel in London and the commuter region.[6] A number of different population and employment forecasts were used, but the improvements to rail services did not affect trip generation rates, merely the redistribution and modal split. Investment in the rail network was thus not recommended as 'demand' was not sufficient to justify the expense. Nevertheless, a cross-rail route was safeguarded. This outcome is in contrast to Paris, where a 'cross-rail', the Regional Express Railway through the centre of Paris, had been given the go-ahead in the 1965 Structure Plan, on the grounds of improving accessibility, and was well on the way to completion by 1974. Automatic fare collection and a zonal fares system were also backed in the *London Rail Study*, though these had to wait for a new administration (the Labour administration of 1981) before implementation.

Likewise a second stream of work was being developed before the 1971 survey results were available. This was the Circumferential and Radial Investigation of Strategic Transport Alternatives in London (CRISTAL) model (Tanner et al., 1973; Holroyd and Tanner, 1974; and especially Lynam, 1974), in order to assess the effects of road pricing.[7] This was essentially an idealized ring and radial simplified network model, with both road and rail networks, and with buses on the roads (see further Tanner et al., 1973). The model's main drawback from an economic viewpoint was the lack of a proper specification of 'demand' in the trip generation stage.

These results were used in the next study, the Supplementary Licensing Study (GLC, 1974b), which recommended a cordon-entry road charging system for central London, and clearly showed that such a strategy was beneficial (despite the drawbacks in demand specification noted above). The proposal was rejected by the then (Labour) administration in 1975, on the main grounds that poor people, who had to use their cars in the centre, would suffer from the imposition of a charge. This was despite the fact that it could be clearly shown from the analysis that the proportion of cars driven by poor people in and through the centre was a small proportion of the total number of cars in the centre, and that poor people in general would benefit from the better bus services that could be run, and thus, as a group, would be better off. This argument was accepted by the Singapore authorities, who introduced road pricing as an in-bound, morning peak-hour, cordon-entry system in 1976, using pay-and-display licences, with a simultaneous increase in bus services. In London, the Study was referred back with an instruction to examine a system of allocating permits to drivers according to a priority list of 'essential' users with the aim of reducing central area traffic by one-third.

The main model for the second attempt at a road pricing strategy was the Strategic Transport Evaluation Model (STEM) suite of programmes, a detailed multimodal network model developed from the District Test Model (DTM). The main problem with the STEM suite was that it gave the wrong response in modal split between bus and rail for a fare change on one of them. This was resolved by using the London Transport SCENARIO model to assess demand on each mode (Fairhurst and Smith, 1976). The SCENARIO model is essentially a market-share model, with London being divided up into market areas, one of which is the central area.[8]

As for the CRISTAL model, referred to above, there was difficulty in assessing modal change. This was countered by the deliberate introduction of a captive/non-captive element (that is, travellers being able to choose an alternative mode or not) into the process of estimation to damp down the switch of passengers.[9]

Before the production of the STEM analysis of road pricing, the SCENARIO model had in fact been used to evaluate a series of options for the Greater London Council's longer-term transport expenditure – rather inappropriately, since the elasticities were short not long term (and thus probably a factor of two at least too low).[10] It was pioneering in the sense that it set out very clearly a set of policy options based on two extreme positions – called a public transport emphasis and a roads emphasis – and based on four different levels of spending over a 15-year period, namely £2.5, £3.0, £3.5 and £4.0 billion – or €3.7, €4.4,

€5.2 and €5.9 billion (in 1975 prices). Only the latter had different levels of road and rail emphasis.[11]

It was noted that if the Council implemented its target of a one-third reduction in central London traffic, together with additional restraint in inner London and the main strategic centres, by a road pricing policy, the revenue raised could be used to support the Council's transport programme.

It was the first demand analysis in London that used the fact that the public transport cost curves are downward sloping. The most important criterion for selecting public transport policies was that for a given level of financial support for the public transport operator, the passenger-distance it carried had to be a maximum. This is a suboptimal policy criterion, since it does not include the time resources of the passenger, that is, the time spent walking and waiting. There was, however, no optimum criterion for the roads, since there was no measure available of the amount of traffic that would use a given capacity of the road system. It was, therefore, impossible to estimate the value of the expenditure on roads. Since the Council favoured a low fares policy, various options of this kind were also evaluated, within the financial constraints.

Bus marginal costs were estimated at just over half average costs, whereas for rail the value was nearer 0.07, demonstrating that for buses, extra passengers means that extra capacity has to be provided whereas rail can relatively easily carry more passengers if operating well below capacity. These results may be compared to those of Train (1977) in San Francisco.

The improvement of service levels rather than the reduction of fares was also found to be more beneficial, though the preference for the latter by a Labour administration because of its concern for poorer passengers meant that bus projects were favoured over rail. Rail capital projects were found to give a much higher value of passenger-km per unit of expenditure, but owing to the government's restriction on capital spending, and the Council's predilection for revenue support, few rail projects could be funded. Although, therefore, the resulting analysis was suboptimal in efficiency terms, it was the first major exercise of its kind in London and confirmed that quite different demand levels could be achieved with different transport policies.

The STEM analysis of road pricing (Bayliss, 1979; Prestwood Smith, 1979; *Traffic Engineering and Control*, 1979), as well as answering the concerns of the previous administration about the effects on poor people, had shown that people with high values of time would benefit from the faster road speeds when central traffic was reduced by a third. The report had also found that a permit system for 'essential' traffic was impractical. It suggested that a cell-cordon system was more efficient at controlling traffic levels, since many car trips were entirely within the central area and thus would not be affected by a circumferential cordon around the centre. It had also begun to evaluate the effect on the environment of changes in traffic levels. Due to a number of political changes the findings of the report were never put into practice.[12] The ideas developed were, however, applied experimentally in Hong Kong using electronic tolling (Dawson, 1983, 1986; Harrison et al., 1986) but not followed through there after suggestions that the movement of cars and thus people across the charging points could be tracked by the central computer necessary to implement the pricing controls. Road pricing was, however, introduced in Bergen, Norway, in 1986, followed by Oslo in 1990, Trondheim in 1991 and Kristiansand in 1992, using electronic toll gates and including pre-paid passes, though the revenue collected was predominantly to be used for road investments and only marginally for public transport and environmental improvements (typically 20 per cent of the revenue).

5   THE 1980s: MAXIMIZING NET SOCIAL BENEFIT

The STEM model was improved in a number of ways (Blase, 1980) and renamed the GLTS (Greater London Transportation Study) model.[13] The use of marginal costs had not yet, however, been incorporated so that the equilibrium was still a user optimum, not a system optimum.

The GLTS model was used extensively to examine a new set of public transport proposals for London (GLC, 1985). This new plan was notable for proposing a reorganization of rail services, including services which ran on both the London Transport and British Rail networks, hitherto largely separate. It also endorsed the reopening of a North–South cross-rail (the Snow Hill connection, subsequently operational in 1988 as the Thameslink line). It was also suggested that light rail (trams) could replace buses on heavily trafficked roads, given adequate priority.[14]

In the next step, a new model for London, the London Area Model (or LAM) was developed, which incorporated the developing ideas about public transport, and in particular the relationship between fares, service levels and subsidy, that is, the financial constraint (Bly and Oldfield, 1986a). The aim was to reproduce the response to change, that is, the elasticities with respect to fares and service levels (Bly and Oldfield, 1986b; see also Paulley and Oldfield, 1989; the Strategic Transport Model – or STM, Oldfield, 1993). The model was a coarse spatial model; in contrast, the 'trip' types were relatively detailed.[15]

The model was essentially a standard transport model, with a power form in the distribution and modal split functions. Only work trips were doubly constrained; all other trip purposes were singly constrained.[16] Various policies were examined, including policies of halving public transport fares, and charging road users for entry to the central area. Both these policies showed net benefits – which may be the actual reason why the publication was delayed by the government, which was then opposed to such policies.

Nevertheless, the London Planning Advisory Committee (LPAC) decided in 1988 that the model was useful to them in determining their advice to the Secretary of State for the Environment, and commissioned consultants (MVA) to evaluate various scenarios using LAM. They produced the TASTE model (Transportation Strategic Advice: Scenario Testing Exercise). Various of the input assumptions were changed, which was allowed for in the LAM design.[17]

The forecasting date for the study was 2001, using a 1986 base. Four basic scenarios were tested, ranging from a base scenario with currently advocated policies and commitments, one based on public transport infrastructure improvements with a net increase in capital cost of £1.3 billion (€1.9 billion), one based on road infrastructure improvements with a net increase in capital cost of £1.5 billion (€2.2 billion), and one based on road pricing in the central area with no net increase in capital investment. Additional variants of these basic scenarios were also tested to attempt to clarify which policy combinations produced better results, including applying the road-pricing revenues of the fourth scenario to improving rail services and keeping public transport fares constant in real terms, except for a central surcharge.

It must be remembered that the LAM has no mechanism for changing trip rates if trip costs change. Nevertheless, the greatest net social benefit was achieved by a road-pricing scenario together with applying the revenues to improving public transport as just noted above (MVA et al., 1988), even though this probably underestimated the benefits because of the shortcomings in the model. This is the first demonstration in London that such a policy is the best using economic criteria. The consultants noted that the benefit/cost ratios of the different scenarios and their variants suggested that even higher net social benefits could be achieved with a better set of policies, especially if buses were to be given higher priority on the roads with less car traffic. The lower-income households would also gain greater net benefits if bus fares were supported at lower levels. Business would also gain substantially from the faster traffic speeds for users with high values of time and for freight.

A later continuation (MVA and CPB, 1989) explored the sensitivity of the conclusions to some of the input assumptions. It was successfully demonstrated that road pricing, plus using the revenues to increase service levels of public transport rather than reduce fares, could produce even higher levels of net social benefit than the levels suggested earlier, and favoured a cell-cordon system, covering both central and inner London, at different charging rates. Also it was confirmed that a network of tramways on the main radial corridors into central London would bring major benefits to users and to the environment. Furthermore, a number of rail investment options to reduce journey times across central London were suggested.

In 1988 also, the government together with the operators, London Transport (London Underground) and British Rail (Network South-East), began a new study of the central London rail commuting problem, the *Central London Rail Study* (1989). This was stimulated by the fact that commuting numbers had risen dramatically in the 1980s (by a quarter) with the increase in employment because of London's growing importance as a financial and communications centre for Europe. This had led to substantial overcrowding on certain lines.

The model used was the London Traffic Study (LTS) model, a detailed network model (the GLTS model renamed), including a new 'overcrowding' penalty on the rail network where appropriate to reflect the additional 'costs' to commuters with increasing flows. The tests were, however, of a set of rail investment options designed to relieve overcrowding, not to be the best options for transport policy.[18] Interestingly, although a number of schemes gave a benefit/cost ratio greater than unity (and some lower than unity), the government refused to allow any of them to proceed. This was on the basis that none of them gave an adequate financial return on the investment, even when an addition was made for non-user benefits in the relief of road congestion in the centre. In fact, the only scheme to proceed had an assessed benefit (in a further study with different assumptions about employment) just greater than its cost, but it had the promise of a financial contribution from the developer – this is the Jubilee Line Extension (via Canary Wharf and the Millennium Dome in North Greenwich) completed in 1999.

The LTS model was also used by the government to compare a maximum road investment option with a maximum rail investment option for the forecast year of 2001 (MVA, 1989). The roads option was based on the recommendations of the consultants in various local area transport assessment studies, and thus not necessarily the best road schemes that could be devised for London as a whole, whereas the latter was defined before the *Central London Rail Study* and included the operators' preferred schemes, including two cross-rail lines. As one might expect, there are only limited effects on road traffic for both options, since the network is substantially congested and only limited changes are being made, even with these substantial investments. The rail investment does, however, cause substantial shifts between bus and rail flows. Correspondingly, the LTS model was also used to compare the maximum road investment option with the LPAC strategic advice scheme for the same forecast year, with essentially the same input assumptions about population and so on (MVA, 1990). The road scheme in fact includes, besides a set of roads closely comparable to that of the government's maximum roads option, a set of relatively minor rail improvements. The LPAC strategic advice scheme is based on a road-pricing option, with six cell-cordons in central London and two further cordons in inner London at about 5 and 8 km from the centre. It has only one cross-rail in its major rail improvements, but bus fares are held constant in real terms while rail fares are rising by 30 per cent by 2001. There are a number of other minor differences between the government options and the LPAC options. The results show that the maximum road option had costs greater than its benefits, whereas the strategic advice option has a large positive net value. In particular, it showed large increases in accessibility. Thus by the end of the 1980s it was quite clear that, although the roads in London are congested, the solution is not to build more roads, which only worsens the situation, but to charge for their use and to use the money so raised to support public transport. While this conclusion was not achieved using marginal costs, which would allow an optimum to be found, the sensitivity testing that had been carried out was sufficient to ensure the conclusion was robust enough to ensure its validity.

6   THE 1990s: MODELLING THE EFFECT OF TRANSPORT CHANGES ON LAND USE

The 1990s have been notable for the extension of modelling work into the effect of transport changes on land use. One of the main concerns with those who are opposed to road pricing is that increasing the price of travel in the central city area would cause the total area to expand even more rapidly into the countryside. This is the opposite of the argument of Clark (1958) that it was precisely the reduction of travel costs that had caused cities to explode over the countryside.

The UK government in 1988 commissioned consultants MEP to begin an examination of this problem, based on work initiated by Echeniqué et al. (1969).

Before describing the model developed by MEP, a brief description is given of the main model used in the next road-pricing study, commissioned by the government in 1991 as a 'congestion charging' study.[19] The study was reported in MVA (1995) and in a series of six monthly papers in *Traffic Engineering and Control*, beginning with Richards et al. (1996). This model (named APRIL – Assessment of Pricing Restraint in London) is similar in concept to the STM, but at a somewhat finer scale, based on an initial assessment of the most likely charging areas. One noteworthy feature is that there are seven time periods, the two 3-hour peaks, 1-hour shoulders on each side of each peak and a 4-hour inter-peak period, with travellers being able to switch between time periods according to a specified procedure, that is to miminize the effect of any charge on them. This feature is essentially different from any in the STM.[20]

The study investigated the effects of low, medium and high charging levels at each of three cordons, around central London and two in inner London (at about 6 km and 10 km radius) as well as a series of other options including cell-cordon charging and all-day licences. Again the conclusion was that road pricing could give very large net benefits, especially if combined with strategies of reallocation of road space to buses and traffic calming, with rail and bus frequency increases, or with substantial rail infrastructure improvements (up to £20 billion or €29.6 billion). These were not optimum strategies, however, merely arbitrary levels of change. There was no attempt to find a social optimum.

It was noted that substantial rail infrastructure investment could require a large continuing subsidy, as the road-pricing revenues would not be sufficient to cover the costs; there might also be difficulty in raising the finance to build the infrastructure. No cost–benefit calculations were done for the complementary strategies, but it was noted that appropriate policies could ensure that the benefits more than offset the user disbenefits. The then Conservative UK government decided to consult further before taking decisions about implementation.

The model developed by MEP was devised for dealing with the problem of land-use/transport interaction (the London and South-east Region or LASER model) and is an attempt to add to the standard four-stage transport model (see Chapter 3, Section 2) a method of allocating trip origins and destinations to make their location sensitive to travel costs.[21] It is a coarse spatial scale model. The model has a pre-specified distribution of land use, or strictly of floor space or the stock of buildings, divided into business, retail and residential. This is allocated among a number of users, with basic industry being pre-allocated, using an input–output framework. A rent level determines the quantity of space consumed by each type of activity in each zone. The cost of transport between each zone determines where each of the inputs and outputs is located with respect to basic industry, the driving force. Most of the calibration of the relationships was done on 1981 data, since later data were not available.

The unique features of the LASER model are that it links rents of business floor space to the level of demand, and it has constraints on the standard of living of households which reduce consumption of other goods and services when rents rise. The key feature of the model is that population and employment in the region are fixed; changes in travel costs will therefore shift the allocation of homes and workplaces within the region.

The result of this can be seen most clearly in a road-pricing scenario. Higher costs of car travel, which, through decreasing congestion, increase car speeds, allow richer people to buy speed at the cost of money; they thus move inwards towards the centre. Poorer people, however, with a lower value of time, move outwards from the centre, repelled more by the resulting increase in rents in the centre and inner London than by the increase in car costs. Employment changes depend on whether the employer gains from the higher speeds of movement and from the spending of the higher-income households, offset by those who lose by the higher rents, the loss of lower-income employees and lower-spending households. While the values obtained in the model may be questionable, the direction of movement of population and employment is more likely to be valid.

The model can also be run in an incremental manner every five years into the future, predicting changes in the allocation of jobs and homes in the region. It is, however, at a very preliminary stage, since many of the relationships in the model are badly defined through lack of the appropriate data, both cross-section and time-series. It is, none the less, an interesting start to attempting to answer the questions relating to the change in land uses consequent on changes in transport costs.

In parallel to this road-pricing study, the Union Railways, charged with building the high-speed rail link between London and the Channel Tunnel, were using another land-use/transport model to assess the implications of the new link on land-use changes. This was the Leeds Integrated Land-use Transportation (LILT) model (Mackett, 1983). This is an incremental model, working from a known base year in five-year steps. Workers are divided into four types, according to whether or not they have retained their residential or employment location. They are allocated to zones using spatial interaction models with appropriate constraints to ensure that those who are not moving are correctly located and that new construction and demolition controls are met. It is disaggregated by car ownership and mode of travel. Work trips are allocated to the peak period. Shopping and other purpose trips are allocated to the off-peak period. Car ownership is modified by the generalized cost of travel.

Thus the model is effectively a distribution/modal split model which reallocates people according to accessibility.[22] Essentially, the two models – LASER and LILT – do not give the same results when transport policies are changed; they do not even agree on the direction of change in some cases. This means that far more work is needed on the basic mechanisms of the interaction between land use and transport before we can be happy that our models are constructed with the appropriate linkages.[23]

The above results were obtained before the results of the next London Area Transportation Survey (LATS), carried out in 1991–92, the fourth successive decennial survey (with another name change), became available.[24]

A new series of surveys was also started in 1993 to measure direct (or straight-line) journey speeds door to door by different modes over the same random journeys in central, inner and outer London, and between these areas, on a rolling triennial basis (UK Department of Transport, 1994). Strictly speaking, the surveys are a systematic sampling of the random journeys in the LATS, on both the chosen mode and on all other possible modes. This is beginning to substantiate the ideas of Thomson – already discussed in Chapter 6 (Section 7.3) – and of Downs (1962) that in congested conditions there is an equilibrium in generalized costs between alternative modes (or in its simplified form in time alone). In particular, this has demonstrated just how slow car is in central London when the door-to-door journey is considered – that is, taking into account all the access times in parking and walking – and that indeed car journey times are comparable to the best public transport alternative. In other parts of London, car is generally the fastest mode.

Mogridge (1997a) went on, using the new data on journey speeds, to demonstrate a revised set of calculations of the optimum direct journey speed that could be obtained from improving central area buses, thus updating the calculations of Webster and Oldfield (1972). While this speed was still low, it gave a substantial improvement on current journey speeds.

A somewhat similar one-off journey speed survey has been reported in a series of US cities, defining congested corridors to the central area, and measuring random door-to-door journeys by alternative modes (US Department of Transportation, 1994; US Federal Transit Administration, 1996). This confirmed that door-to-door times by auto and transit are similar in such corridors. One notable result, from New York, showed that where a road route was toll free, the journey times by auto and transit were similar, but where an alternative road route was tolled, the journey time by auto was much less, confirming that people trade off time and money.

A study from Oslo has also been reported which examines the before-and-after situation in a congested corridor to the central city which has had an upgrade of its public transport from bus to light rail (Tombre, 1997; Naess and Sandberg, 1998). The study showed that improving public transport trunk haul speeds is not sufficient by itself to improve journey times without complementary policies restraining car traffic. The latter study was done while the light rail route was still suffering from implementation problems, that is, signal failures and delays.

In order to explore the consequences of using marginal costs, and to attempt to define the optimum balance between public transport and car use, London Transport developed a new model called SESAME (Strategic Evaluation of Sectorally Aggregated Modal Equilibrium) (Abraham et al., 1993, Abraham and Maroney, 1994). Like the SCENARIO model, this was a market-share model, but limited to radial travel to central London, and thus effectively to the equilibrium between rail and car. Aggregate user costs are set equal for car and rail users at equilibrium, calibrated to the 1989 values. Average and marginal cost curves for rail and car were estimated; average costs decrease with increasing demand for rail and increase for car. A total demand curve was also estimated, decreasing as the price increases. This is shown in Figure 11.2.

The number of users on each mode is divided into 'switchers' who can change modes in addition to changing their volume of travel in response to a change in travel costs, and a 'tied' group who can only change their volume of travel but not mode in the same situation. This is reminiscent of both

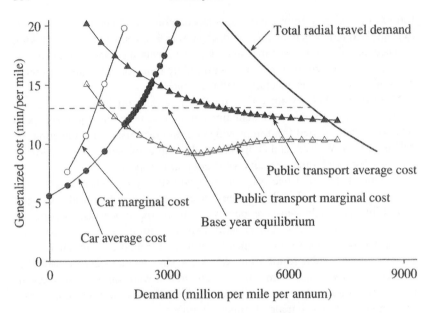

Figure 11.2   Demand and supply relationships in the SESAME model

SCENARIO and CRISTAL techniques. The 'tied' group do not have the same costs as the 'switcher' group, since they are not in the same equilibrium. Public transport is subject to a financial constraint.

The following scenarios were evaluated.

1. *Setting road prices so that car users paid their social marginal costs*   In this scenario, although there is a substantial net benefit to society, there are considerable net losses to 'tied' car users.
2. *Setting rail fare subsidies so that rail users paid their social marginal cost*   In this scenario, while all groups of travellers benefit, it is at the price of a substantial subsidy from the taxpayer. With a benefit to cost ratio of about 1.6, it is unlikely to be better than other uses of tax money and thus politically infeasible.
3. *Combining the two scenarios*   In this scenario, there is a slightly higher equilibrium generalized travel cost than in the previous scenario, though a higher demand. The revenue collected from car pricing partially offsets the rail fare subsidy, giving a higher net social benefit, and a higher benefit/cost ratio of over 2. It is still likely to be unattractive politically.
4. *Using road-pricing revenue (where car users paid their social marginal costs) to improve rail services*   Although equilibrium generalized travel

costs are higher in this scenario, the net social value is still high (at over £500 million, or about €800 million, per year); more importantly, all user groups benefit, though 'tied' car users the least, and the revenue stream is neutral, making the policy potentially politically attractive.

This was the first study in London to use marginal costs and variable demand, and clearly demonstrated that in the new equilibrium situation, taken to be several years ahead after the system had settled down again, substantial increases in net benefit could be achieved by a joint road-pricing/public transport improvement policy.

Finally, Glaister (1998) has proposed a simple method of licensing cars in London. Car users would have to buy and display a Travelcard valid for the zone in which they wish to travel or park on street. Travelcards were first introduced in London in 1983 for travel on public transport. They are valid for a given number of zones (in bands around the centre) and for a given time period (a day, a week and so on). This suggestion has the advantage that all revenues would go directly to the transport operators, and the retail network is already in place. The Travelcard becomes in effect a Supplementary Licence. A dual card would enable the car user to travel on public transport if they so chose for part of their journey. A variant of this suggestion has also been assessed in an updated series of tests using the APRIL model.

7 FUTURE DEVELOPMENTS: POPULATION AND EMPLOYMENT, ENVIRONMENT, ACCIDENTS

Clark's (1958) observation that decreasing transport cost causes cities to expand, with central densities falling and densities on the periphery rising, has been exemplified by Mogridge and Parr (1997). They examined the way in which the areal extent, and the population density at each distance from the centre of London, has changed over the last two hundred years, that is, from 1801 to 1991. They used a negative exponential model like Clark (1951) and Mogridge (1985) for the urban area up to 22 km radius from the centre, and a lognormal model like Parr (1985) for the region out to 75 km from the centre.

They likened the process to a pile of sand on a vibrating plate, with grains of sand moving at random for short distances in all directions, but overall the pile of sand subsiding. The further from the city centre, the faster the rate of growth. Obviously, the analogy cannot be taken too far, since there are births and deaths of people, and migration in and out of the urban/regional area. 'London', it should be noted, has spread well beyond the regional boundary, at approximately 100 km, from the centre, since the fastest rates of growth of population are now in the regions surrounding South-east England at about 150 km from the centre.

Since 1961, however, the inner area of London has been rejuvenated by a tremendous influx of young adults from abroad, from the European Union, the Eastern European countries and much further, due to the rapidly falling costs of air transport, and the attractions of London as a centre of employment (Mogridge, 1997b). This is, to extend the sand-pile analogy, as if an additional stream of sand were being added at the centre. The current UK government forecast is that this influx will continue into the indefinite future; Mogridge and Hollis (1999) have shown how this will affect the population of the London area. This can be seen by examining Figure 11.3.

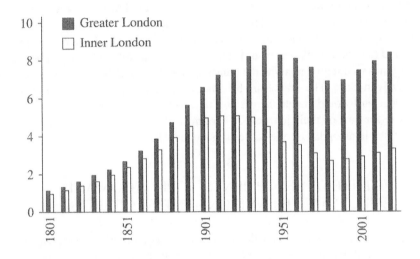

(UK) Crown copyright

Figure 11.3   London population 1801–2021 (million)

The inner London population age structure for the last four censuses can be seen in Figure 11.4. The population has changed from a mature age structure, where the population in each age group is roughly constant until people start to die off, to one in which there is a substantial peak in the 20–34 age groups, with a smaller peak developing as childbirth increases, that is, as the immigrants have children.

This shift towards a younger population, a large part of whom are coming from much denser cities than London, and who, as migrants, will tend to be much more entrepreneurial and radical than the existing population, will no

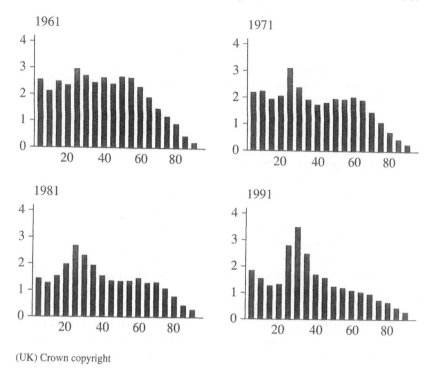

(UK) Crown copyright

Figure 11.4   Inner London population by 5-year age group (100 000s)

doubt have substantial implications for the development of public transport in inner London. This has yet to be addressed in transport/land-use models in London. In particular, the car ownership levels in inner London are already growing much less rapidly than in other urban areas in the UK. Since the current transport models do not have age structure in the basic description of households, they cannot as yet model this change and its implications.

Similar changes have been occurring in the employment structure of London over the last 35 years, with a massive loss of manufacturing industry and a growth of services of all types, especially of the new technologies connected with computing. While changes of this magnitude and direction are exceptional, economists in all urban areas are aware that population and employment changes are of vital importance in assessing future transport demands and supplies. Much work needs to be done on attempting to provide better estimates of how fast cities will expand (or decline) and the resulting spatial distributions.

Attempts are also now being made to include the costs of environmental externalities of transport into urban transport models but much of this work is as yet highly contentious, since such costs are extremely difficult to assess (on this subject, see Chapter 4). The base of this work is the *London Energy Study* (Chell and Hutchinson, 1993), one of nearly forty urban energy planning studies in cities in all the then twelve member states of the European Community. This study estimated transport use by each mode in each of the km squares of London, and calculated the emission of pollutants by vehicles in each such square. This study, and that of Wootton Jeffreys Consultants (1989) into road use, was then used by Mogridge et al. (1994) to estimate the effect of raising public transport fares on the level of pollutants in London, using elasticities of demand to calculate the changes. This could be extended into the assessment of the costs of increasing pollutants.

It is more typical that urban authorities act by using standards of pollution, for example, in Athens and Paris where, if pollution of certain vehicle emissions exceeds a stated level, then cars of particular number plates are banned from the city centre. In London, substantial reductions in traffic in the City of London have been achieved by the imposition of a 'Ring of Steel' or controlled entry to the financial district in 1993, with an extension in 1997, but the initial rationale for this was the improvement of security following a series of bomb attacks by terrorists, rather than the environmental improvement for which it had been designed. Moreover, the City of London Police Force (1998) are now using Automatic Number Plate Recognition (ANPR) technology. This has been in operation at each entry point since 1997. It allows them to check every vehicle entering the restricted area (over 100 000 per working day) against their records in seconds. The potential for using this technology to control access is now being explored by the City, whereby only those vehicles with pre-bought (or free) licences would be allowed to enter the controlled area.

The costs of road accidents in London, and the effects of transport policy on them, have also been assessed by Allsop (1983), Downes (1987) and Allsop and Robertson (1994). In the last paper, changes in public transport fares and petrol prices over a period from 1975–90 have been statistically compared with the changes in road accidents by type, and the resulting change in costs of accidents of a given change in transport price calculated.

The reduction of road accidents is, however, being addressed by the imposition of speed-limited zones in residential areas, following the example of the highly successful '*woonerven*' (residential yards) in the Netherlands, and by pedestrianization schemes in shopping centres, following the example of Germany, rather than by such transport price increases or by increasing the costs of travel insurance to ensure that drivers are fully aware of the risks they take in driving. The latter policy would require that drivers, particularly the young who are the most likely to have accidents, pay much larger insurance premiums to cover the costs of all the economic damage caused by an accident, including hospital and other health charges and the compensation for loss of earnings and so on.

Another strand of work is that of attempting to assess the effect of transport on the productivity of an urban area. The initial comparative study of London and Paris (London Research Centre/Institut d'Aménagement et d'Urbanisme de la Région d'Île de France, 1992) showed that the transport systems of the two cities are remarkably similar in the journey speeds in comparable areas. Drawing on this and other sources, the study by the Centre for Economics and Business Research/Observatoire de l'Economie et des Institutions Locales (1997) concluded that Paris, with a much more concentrated population, had a much higher accessibility for labour and thus a much higher productivity per worker than London. Although this conclusion is contentious, it raises interesting questions about the influence of transport on the shape, size and function of cities and their change over time.

8   CONCLUSION

Starting from the four-stage transport model as described by Fischer in Chapter 3, work in London over the last few decades has exemplified the developing ideas about how an optimum urban transport and land-use policy can be derived, incorporating economic theory into the basic engineering and planning techniques which dominated the early work. The separation of the track and operating costs of the national railways in 1996, with the London Underground railways to come, following the example of Sweden, suggests that it will now be possible to begin a more rational debate about investment in road and railway infrastructure on a comparable cost/benefit basis. The two track authorities, the Highways Agency and Railtrack, are now beginning to work together on this. The White Paper on integrated transport policy (UK Department of the Environment, 1998, paragraph 4.94) accepts, for the first time in the UK, the hypothecation of transport charges, that is, that the revenue from road pricing, parking charges and so on can be spent on public transport improvements. Legislation was introduced in the Parliamentary Session 1998/99 to allow this to be implemented in London. The removal of this major stumbling block to the introduction of road pricing in the UK may then allow economic rationality to be applied to urban transport policy, 35 years after the pathbreaking report by the Smeed Committee.

ABBREVIATIONS

ANPR   Automatic Number Plate Recognition
APRIL   Assessment of Pricing Restraint In London

CRISTAL   Circumferential and Radial Investigation of Strategic Transport
           Alternatives in London
DTM   District Test Model
GLTS   Greater London Transportation Study
LAM   London Area Model
LASER   London And South East Region model
LATS   London Area Transportation Survey
LILT   Leeds Integrated Land-use Transportation model
LPAC   London Planning Advisory Committee
LTS   London Traffic Study
SESAME   Strategic Evaluation of Sectorally Aggregated Modal Equilibrium
STEM   Strategic Transport Evaluation Model
STM   Strategic Transport Model
TASTE   Transportation Strategic Advice: Scenario Testing Exercise
URGENT   Union Railways General Evaluation Network Tool

NOTES

1. London can be thought of as three successively larger areas: Inner London with a population of about 3 million and a radius of about 10 km; the contiguous built-up area of Greater London (population 7 million, radius 25 km); and the London and South-east Region (population 17 million, radius 100 km).
2. Two separate sample frames were thus used to measure the travel patterns of car-owning and non-car-owning households. The grossing-up procedures were simply against the early estimates of population from the 1961 census (which were somewhat lower than the final estimates by some 5 per cent).
3. A substantial amount of upgrading to dual-carriageway status was, however, included when the Development Plan was finally approved (GLC, 1976). Crucially, the inner motorway box was scrapped, although its equivalent in Paris, the Boulevard Périphérique was to be built. An orbital motorway around Greater London, and almost entirely outside its boundaries, was, however, included in the statement as part of the national motorway plan (the M25); this was completed in 1986. Likewise the upgrading of the North Circular Road was kept in as part of the national plan.
4. Webster (1968) and Lyons (1969) reported calculations for different sizes of buses and demonstrated that small buses were more efficient in certain circumstances.
5. The 1971–72 survey used a single sample frame for its household sample, but sampled at different rates in different boroughs (or administrative districts). The grossing-up procedures used household structure (that is, not just total population, but also the number of residents per household and the number of employees per household), at Borough level. The zonal system and the network were both recast, in line with the new administrative boundaries formed in 1965.
6. The study used the 1966 census 10 per cent sample of journeys to work and the TRANSITNET assignment programme to assess a number of alternative schemes for rail improvements.
7. The acronym stood for 'Circumferential and Radial Investigation of Strategic Transport Alternatives in London'.
8. The model is calibrated on short-term elasticities and cross-elasticities of fare/price and service-level changes, especially those given by Lewis (1977).

9. There was essentially no redistributive element in the model, although some element of redistribution of traffic 'demand' among modes may well be incorporated into the calibration of the modal split parameters (GLC, 1983).
10. The results of the evaluation were produced just before the then Labour administration was defeated (GLC, 1977; Prestwood Smith and May, 1977) and were shelved by the incoming Conservative administration.
11. It should be noted that the Greater London Council's budget only covered London Transport's bus and rail services, and metropolitan road capital and maintenance expenditure – the national trunk roads and the national railways were excluded. The forecasts of population, employment, income, car ownership and so on were exogenous inputs to the process.
12. The Conservative GLC administration rejected the proposals in 1979 and the Labour administration of 1981 was unable to proceed with them as the GLC was abolished by the Conservative UK government in 1986.
13. By 1983 the Frank–Wolfe algorithm, for partitioning flows between road links on successive iterations to ensure a true equilibrium is approached (van Vliet and Dow, 1979), had also been incorporated. This can give problems in congested areas, but by starting from known speeds and flows (for junction delay calculations) the problem can be ameliorated.
14. The demand forecasts were still, however, limited by the fixed origins and destinations.
15. The interesting feature about the calibration of the model was that household size, car ownership and trip generation rates were all estimated using time trends. This means that no verification procedure could be used since all the data available were used in calibration. In particular, since the estimates of trip rates are made during a period of a particular change in trip costs, the estimates of future trip rates during different changes in trip costs may well be biased. Trip rates were, however, not estimated to change linearly with time, but logistically. In particular, there is no mechanism to change trip rates if trip costs change.
16. In the case of a 'doubly constrained' model, it is ensured that both of the following conditions are satisfied:

    1. the total number of trips from a given area of origin that is distributed over a network does not exceed the total number of trips from that area of origin; and
    2. the number of trips to a given area of destination does not exceed the total number of trips to that area of destination.

    In a 'singly constrained' model only one of these conditions will be satisfied.
17. These included the peak/off-peak split which was altered so that the proportions for each trip purpose conformed to that observed in the 1981 Greater London Transportation Survey; and the speed/flow relations which were altered to make them more sensitive to higher flows and to represent new road capacity where appropriate. Rail travel times were altered to represent new rail capacity where appropriate, and bus costs were changed to represent changes in unit costs after deregulation (which began in London in 1990). Various other features were also altered and sensitivity tests done on some of these to find the effects.
18. The LTS model actually has an odd side-effect; with constant trip ends and because it is doubly constrained, the increase in rail travel to central London causes an increase in road traffic on orbital routes.
19. This study had the specific objective of assessing the case for and against, and the practical feasibility of, implementing congestion charging within the M25, the London orbital motorway at about 20–30 km from the centre. This new study was apparently set up in response to the report to the LPAC described above, and to a series of other reports from professional and other interested bodies supporting road pricing, for example, by the author (Mogridge, 1990).
20. Calibration was essentially against a set of elasticities for public transport fares and petrol costs, for each trip purpose, as well as reproducing the known data from 1991. Again, these are short-term elasticities, and thus underestimate long-term effects. The LASER model was, however, used to assess these latter.
21. Some early applications are described in Baxter et al. (1975). The LASER model is described in Williams (1994) and the report for the government in MEP (1995). The work by MEP was also used in the next road-pricing study, commissioned by the government in 1991.

22. The assignment on the railways was done by a model called Union Railways General Evaluation Network Tool (URGENT). The report is given in Union Railways (1993) and further details of a comparison between the two land-use/transport models is given in Mackett (1993) (together with another built by Wegener, 1985, for Dortmund using microeconomic theory) and more generally in Mackett (1995).
23. Work started at last on the UK Channel Tunnel Rail Link in 1998.
24. This was based on the same survey procedures as before, but controlled by the London Research Centre, the successor to the GLC research unit. The grossing-up procedures were, however, different; in consequence, some of the time trends over the decades (for example, of car ownership) are no longer compatible. This has caused some problems in forecasting models.

REFERENCES

Abraham, H. and O. Maroney (1994), 'Road pricing and public transport provision in London', *Traffic Engineering and Control*, **35**, 666–70.

Abraham, H., O. Maroney and M.J.H. Mogridge (1993), 'A strategic review of the demand implications of alternative transport policies in London', in *Transport Policy and its Implementation*, London: Planning and Transportation Research and Computation (PTRC) Education and Research Services, P368, pp. 77–89.

Allsop, R.E. (1983), *Fares and Road Casualties in London*, London: Greater London Council.

Allsop, R.E. and S.A. Robertson (1994), 'Road casualties in London in relation to public transport pricing'. *Journal of Transport Economics and Policy*, **28**, 61–82.

Baxter, R., M. Echeniqué and J. Owers (eds) (1975), *Urban development models*, Hornby, Lancaster: Construction Press, Land Use and Built Form Studies (LUBFS) Conference Proceedings No. 3.

Bayliss, D. (1979), 'Area licensing in Central London', in European Conference of Ministers of Transport, *Proceedings of Conference on Urban Transport and the Environment*, II, Paris: Organization for European Cooperation and Development, 253–78.

Blase, J. (1980), *The 1980 Recalibration of the GLTS Model*, Transport Studies Note 97, London: Department of Planning and Transportation, Greater London Council.

Bly, P.H. and R.H. Oldfield (1986a), 'An analytic assessment of subsidies to bus services', *Transportation Science*, **20**, 200–212.

Bly, P.H. and R.H. Oldfield (1986b), 'Structure and calibration of the London Area Model' (Unpublished working paper), Special Research Branch, Crowthorne, Berks: Transport and Road Research Laboratory.

Buchanan, J.M. (1952), 'The pricing of highway services', *National Tax Journal*, **5**, 97–106.

Central London Rail Study (1989), A joint study by the Department of Transport, British Rail Network SouthEast, London Regional Transport and London Underground Ltd, London: Department of Transport.

Centre for Economics and Business Research/Observatoire de l'Economie et des Institutions Locales (1997), *Two Great Cities: A Comparison of the Economies of London and Paris*, London: Corporation of London.

Chell, M. and D. Hutchinson (1993), *London Energy Study: energy use and the environment*, London Research Centre, Environment and Transport Studies, London: London Research Centre.

City of London Police Force (1998), *Annual Report*.

Clark, C. (1951), 'Urban population densities', *Journal of the Royal Statistical Society A*, **114**, 490–96.

Clark, C. (1958), 'Transport; maker and breaker of cities', *Town Planning Review*, **28**, 237–50.

Dawson, J. (1983), 'Electronic road pricing in Hong Kong; the pilot stage', *Traffic Engineering and Control*, **24**, 372–4.

Dawson, J. (1986), 'Electronic road pricing in Hong Kong, (4) conclusions', *Traffic Engineering and Control*, **27**, 79–83.

Downs, A. (1962), 'The Law of Peak-hour Expressway Congestion', *Traffic Quarterly*, **16**, 393–409.

Downes, J.D. (1987), *Road Casualty Rates and Costs for London*, Research Report 126, Crowthorne, Berks: Transport and Road Research Laboratory.

Echeniqué, M.H., D. Crowther and W. Lindsay (1969), 'A spatial model of urban stock and activity', *Regional Studies*, **3**, 281–312.

Fairhurst, M.H. and R.S. Smith (1976), *Development and calibration of London Transport's SCENARIO model*, Economic Research Report R229, London: London Transport Executive.

Freeman Fox, Wilbur Smith & Associates (1968), *London Transportation Study Phase III*, 4 vols, London: FFWS&A for Greater London Council.

Glaister, S. (1982), *Urban Public Transport Subsidies: An Economic Assessment of Value for Money*, Summary report and technical report, London: UK Department of Transport.

Glaister, S. (1998), *Virtue out of Necessity: Practical Pricing of Traffic in Towns*, London: Social Market Foundation.

Greater London Council (GLC) (1966), *London Traffic Survey Volume Two: Future Traffic and Travel Characteristics in Greater London*, London: GLC.

Greater London Council (GLC) (1969), *The Greater London Development Plan: Statement*, London: GLC

Greater London Council (GLC) (1974a), *The London Rail Study* (Barran Report), London: GLC/UK Department of the Environment.

Greater London Council (GLC) (1974b), *A Study of Supplementary Licensing*, London: GLC.

Greater London Council (GLC) (1976), *The Greater London Development Plan: Notice of Approval; Written Statement etc.*, London: GLC.

Greater London Council (GLC) (1977), *Transport in London – a Longer Range View*, Joint Report of the Transport Committee and the Policy and Resources Committee, Minutes of the Council, 29th March 1977, London: GLC.

Greater London Council (GLC) (1983), *Area Control: A Scheme for Reducing Car Traffic Through Central London to Limit Congestion and Improve the Environment*, London: GLC.

Greater London Council (GLC) (1985), *Public Transport in London – the Next Ten Years*, London: GLC.

Harrison, W.J., C. Pell, P.M. Jones and M. Ashton (1986), 'Some advances in model design developed for the practical assessment of road pricing in Hong Kong', *Transportation Research A*, **20**, 135–43.

Holroyd, E.M. and J.C. Tanner (1974), *A Simplified Form of the CRISTAL Transport Planning Model*, Supplementary Report SR55UC, Crowthorne, Berks: Transport and Road Research Laboratory.

Lewis, D.L. (1977), 'Public policy and road traffic levels in Greater London', *Journal of Transport Economics and Policy*, **11**, 155–68.

London County Council (1964), *London Traffic Survey Volume One: Traffic and Travel Characteristics in Greater London*, London: London County Council.

London Research Centre/Institute d'Aménagement et d'Urbanisme de la Région d'Île de France (1992), *Paris: London; A Comparison of Transport Systems*, London: HMSO.

Lynam, D.A. (1974), *The Application of CRISTAL to Evaluate Changes in Travel Charges in London*, Supplementary Report SR40UC, Crowthorne, Berks: Transport and Road Research Laboratory.

Lyons, D.J. (1969), 'Bus travel in town centres', *Traffic Engineering and Control*, **6**, 20–23, 35.

Mackett, R.L. (1983), *The Leeds Integrated Land-use Transport Model (LILT)*, Supplementary Report 805, Crowthorne, Berks: Transport and Road Research Laboratory.

Mackett, R.L. (1993), 'Structure of linkages between transport and land use', *Transportation Research B*, **27**, 189–206.

Mackett, R.L. (1995), 'Land use transportation models for policy analysis', in *Issues in Land Use and Transportation Planning, Models and Applications*, Transportation Research Record 1466, Washington, DC: National Academy Press, pp. 71–8.

MEP (1995), *LASER Scenario Tests for London: Final Report for the Government Office for London*, Cambridge: MEP.

Ministry of Transport (1964), *Road Pricing: The Economic and Technical Possibilities* (Smeed Report), London: HMSO.

Mogridge, M.J.H. (1977), 'Traffic forecasting', *Highways and Road Construction International*, Part 1, No. 1811, 5–10; Part 2, No. 1812, 5–9.

Mogridge, M.J.H. (1985), 'Strategic population forecasting for a conurbation using the negative exponential density model', *Transportation Research A*, **19**, 189–206.

Mogridge, M.J.H. (1990), *Travel in Towns: Jam Yesterday, Jam Today and Jam Tomorrow?*, London: Macmillan.

Mogridge, M.J.H. (1997a), 'The self-defeating nature of urban road capacity policy: a review of theories, disputes and available evidence', *Transport Policy*, **4**, 5–23.

Mogridge, M.J.H. (1997b), 'Urban influx – the rejuvenation of inner London', *Town and Country Planning*, **66**, 104–5.

Mogridge M.J.H. and J. Hollis (1999), 'London's population looks set to grow still more rapidly', *Planning in London*, **28**, 6–7.

Mogridge, M.J.H. and J.B. Parr (1997), 'Metropolis or region: on the development and Mogridge, M.J.H., M. Fergusson and D. Taylor (1994), *Higher Fares? You must be Choking!*, London: Transport 2000 Trust.

structure of London', *Regional Studies*, **31**, 97–115.

MVA (1989) *Summary of LTS Model Forecasts*, London Assessment Studies Stage 2B, LTS Technical Note 114, London: MVA for the Department of Transport.

MVA (1990), *Transportation Strategic Advice; Scenario Testing Exercise (3), Evaluation of Options Using the LTS Model*, Prepared for London Planning Advisory Committee. London: MVA Consultancy.

MVA (1995), *The London Congestion Charging Research Programme: Principal Findings*, London: HMSO.

MVA and CBP (1989), *Transportation Strategic Advice; Scenario Testing Exercise (2), Desk Studies of Transportation Topics*, London: MVA and CBP for London Planning Advisory Committee.

MVA, CBP and Transport and Road Research Laboratory (1988), *Transportation Strategic Advice; Scenario Testing Exercise (1), Evaluation of options using the London Area Model*, London: MVA, CBP and Transport and Road Research Laboratory for London Planning Advisory Committee.

Naess P. and S.L. Sandberg (1998), *Choosing the Fastest Mode? Travel Time and Modal Choice in Two Transport Corridors of Oslo*, Report 1998: 15, Oslo: Norwegian Institute for Urban and Regional Research.

Oldfield, R.H. (1993), *A Strategic Transport Model for the London Area*, Research Report 376, Crowthorne, Berks: Transport Research Laboratory.

Parr, J.B. (1985), 'The form of the regional density function', *Regional Studies*, **19**, 535–46.

Paulley, N.J. and R.H. Oldfield (1989), 'Users' guide for the London Area Model (LAM)' (Unpublished paper), Crowthorne, Berks: Transport and Road Research Laboratory.

Prestwood Smith, P. (1979), 'Area control', in *Traffic and Environmental Management*, P180, London: Planning and Transportation Research and Computation (PTRC) Education and Research Services Ltd, pp. 37–49.

Prestwood Smith, P. and A.D. May (1977), 'The assessment of transport programme options', in *Transportation Planning Practice*, P155, London: Planning and Transportation Research and Computation (PTRC) Education and Research Services Ltd, pp. 43–60.

Richards, M., C. Gilliam and J. Larkinson (1996), 'The London congestion charging research programme; (1) the programme in overview', *Traffic Engineering and Control*, **37**, 66–71.

Smeed, R.J. (1961), *The Traffic Problem in Towns*, Cheetham, Manchester: Norbury, Lockwood for Manchester Statistical Society, revised (1964) as 'The traffic problem in towns – a review of possible long-term solutions', *Town Planning Review*, **35**, 133–58.

Smeed, R.J. and J.G. Wardrop (1964), 'An exploratory comparison of the advantages of cars and buses for travel in urban areas', *Journal of the Institute of Transport*, **30**, 301–15.

Tanner, J.C., L. Gyenes, D.A. Lynam, S.V. Magee and A.H. Tulpule (1973), *Development and Calibration of the CRISTAL Transport Planning Model*, Laboratory Report LR574, Crowthorne, Berks: Transport and Road Research Laboratory.

Thomson, J.M. (1967), 'An evaluation of two proposals for traffic restraint in Central London (with discussion)', *Journal of the Royal Statistical Society A*, **130**, 327–77.

Thomson, J.M. (1969), *Motorways in London*, Report of a working party, London: Duckworth for the London Amenity and Transport Association.

Tombre, E. (1997), *Public Response to Changes in the Oslo–Akershus Transport Infrastructure 1978–1997; Historical Data in View of the Theory Proposed by Downs and Thomson*, Working Paper 1997:110, Oslo: Norwegian Institute for Urban and Regional Research.

Traffic Engineering and Control (1979), News, **20**, 366.

Train, K. (1977), 'Optimal transit prices under increasing returns to scale and a loss constraint', *Journal of Transport Economics and Policy*, **11**, 185–94.

UK Department of the Environment, Transport and the Regions (1998), *A New Deal for Transport: Better for Everyone. The Government's White Paper on the Future of Transport*, Cm. 3950.

UK Department of Transport (1978), *Report of the Advisory Committee on Trunk Road Assessment* (Leitch Report), London: HMSO.

UK Department of Transport (1994), *Journey Times Survey; Inner and Central London*, London: HMSO.

Union Railways (1993), *Report on the Union Railway*, London: British Rail Board.

US Department of Transportation (1994), *Unsticking Traffic: When Transit Works and Why*, Federal Transit Administration (FTA) Policy Paper prepared by Hickling-Lewis-Brod Inc., Washington, DC: US Department of Transportation.

US Federal Transit Administration (1996), *The Role of Transit in Congestion Management*, prepared by Hickling-Lewis-Brod Inc., Washington, DC: US FTA.

van Vliet, D. and P.D.C. Dow (1979), 'Capacity-restrained road assignment', *Traffic Engineering and Control*, **20**, 296–305.

Walters, A.A. (1954), 'Track costs and motor taxation', *Journal of Industrial Economics*, **12**, 135–46.

Webster, F.V. (1968), *A Theoretical Estimate of the Effect of London Car Commuters Transferring to Bus Travel*, Laboratory Report LR165, Crowthorne, Berks: Transport and Road Research Laboratory.

Webster, F.V. and R.H. Oldfield (1972), *A Theoretical Study of Bus and Car Travel in Central London*, Laboratory Report LR541, Crowthorne, Berks: Transport and Road Research Laboratory.

Wegener, M. (1985), 'The Dortmund housing market model: a Monte Carlo simulation of a regional housing market', in K. Stahl (ed.), *Microeconomic Models of Housing Markets*, Lecture Notes in Economic and Mathematical Systems 239, Berlin: Springer Verlag, pp. 144–91.

Williams, I.N. (1994), 'A model of London and the South East', *Environment and Planning B*, **21**, pp. 535–53.

Wootton Jeffreys Consultants (1989), *A Study to Show Patterns of Vehicle Use in the London Area*, Contractor Reports 131 and 132 (Supplement), Crowthorne, Berks: Transport and Road Research Laboratory.

12. Transport in economies in transition

Jan Burnewicz and Monika Bąk

1 INTRODUCTION

The concept of 'transitional economy' appeared as a result of the collapse of the economic social and political systems in the former CMEA (Council for Mutual Economic Assistance) countries in the late 1980s. It also resulted from a universal aspiration of those countries for a market economy system. Such a situation seems to be unparalleled during the past development of industrial civilization. Moreover, it was an opportunity to observe a rare case of the transition from one economic system to another. Any conclusions from the observations will, however, have little value for future use, as there is a minimal likelihood that a similar situation in a different place and at a different time will occur. The evolution of the economy in such countries as China, Cuba or North Korea towards a different system does not have to be based upon the experiences of Central European countries in the process of transition.

It is hard to envisage the future creation of a similar system transformation, because even an outline of another economic model as perfect as the market economy – including the process of international integration – is as yet unknown.

From the viewpoint of European experience with the phenomenon of a transitional economy, these transformations are of great practical significance. Based on them, the following criteria can be assessed: what kind of valuable elements of the 'planned' system can be preserved and what kind of errors can be avoided in the course of the creation of market economies?

It has never been the case that an old economic system should be reduced to naught while a new system should start from scratch. Besides, the very term 'economy in transition' denotes transformation, not elimination of the former economic system. A simplified diagram of this transformation within the time system is presented in Figure 12.1.

The economy in transition tends to be ephemeral. Its rules are neither strictly defined nor put into effect according to a standard scenario. The transitional character of an economy can be maintained for a limited period, most likely not longer than ten to fifteen years.

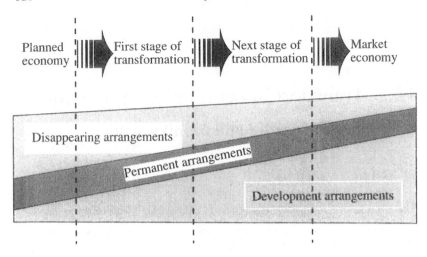

Figure 12.1   Evolution of components in economic systems in the transition period

A distinctive feature of this kind of economy should be a growth of the part of development arrangements in it. These are elements stimulating development of the whole system. Two categories of such elements may be distinguished: those of a 'material' and those of a 'functional' character.

- Material elements include: raw materials, machines, technical equipment as well as infrastructure for modern production and for new services, products with growing attractiveness and appreciation with customers and so on.
- Functional elements are, for instance, technical solutions inducing further progress, regulations stimulating competition, structures making firms save and reduce costs and so on.

In terms of a strategy of transition from the old to the new system, big differences can be observed in such formerly planned economies as Poland, the Czech Republic, Hungary, Bulgaria or Romania (within the years 1989–97). Which national strategy of transformation has turned out to be the most efficient will be evident in a few years' time. There are no standard methods and ways of privatization and restructuring in Central Europe; the character of economic legislation in specific countries is different; and the structure of political and social powers setting directions of those transformations differs as well. The analysis of these complex and specific ways of transformation is a difficult research task from which too hasty conclusions cannot be drawn.

2   FEATURES OF THE ECONOMY IN TRANSITION

2.1   The Concept of Transformation

In the world economy at the turn of the twentieth century the concept of trans-formation has appeared in a new, hitherto unknown dimension. All countries are carrying out economic, social and political changes, yet, the concept of transformation commonly is not applied to all of them. Transformation is usually defined as a process of profound system changes on all the planes of state functioning. In this understanding of transformation one can single out a few groups of countries in which these processes are being carried out at a different rate (Hübner, 1992).

The first group is composed of centrally planned economies in which reform processes began most recently and their present scope and rate are the least far-reaching. These countries include Albania, North Korea and Cuba. A second group consists of the countries in which some changes took place in an earlier period (before the late 1980s). These changes did not, however, upset the fundamental dogmas of a centrally planned economy, while the present changes are being carried out only slowly (for example, in China). The third group is made up of the countries where changes are of a fundamental nature. To this group belong the Central and Eastern European (CEE) countries. Some of them, particularly the former Soviet Union republics, fall between the second and third groups.

During the period of the socialist economy certain reform attempts had taken place in CEE countries. However, the reforms were selective, partial and to a large extent burdened with non-economic objectives which mostly made it impossible for activities to be carried out efficiently. An example of such reforms in some countries, especially in Poland, was granting more autonomy to enterprises, without simultaneous power limitation of the central administration.

The division into the specific groups shown above is not absolute. Taking into consideration real processes of system changes, almost all CEE countries can join in the transformation process.

2.2   Characteristics of Transformation in CEE Countries

The system existing before 1989 in the CEE countries was characterized by certain common features:

1. domination of a ruling communist party as a monopolistic political power;
2. domination of real socialism and its apparatus over all the forms of economic activity;
3. centralization of economic administration; and

4. closed character of the economy and society (Gołębiowski, 1995).

The transformation process in all the CEE countries is a departure from the principles and institutional forms referred to above. A number of common features of the transformation process can be identified:

1. in the sphere of politics – a transition from an authoritarian system to a multiparty system of parliamentary democracy;
2. in the sphere of the economy – a transition from a system of planned economy based on state-owned domination to a market economy based on private ownership, free competition, a universal financial economy and direct ties with the world market; and
3. in the social sphere – a change in the idea of civil liberty, a transition from a division of the population into large social groups (farmers, manual and office workers) into a division relating to ownership (owners of means of production, hired workers), a change of the system of values towards personal benefits, tolerance for different viewpoints and, finally, social dialogue.

The current stage of the transformation process deeply influenced the existing arrangement in international relations, despite the fact that none of the CEE countries has yet completed this process. As regards the time period for the transformation process (that is, a transition from centrally planned to market economy), the notion of a transition period has been widely used. The particular countries have been passing through different stages of that period. Some of the countries have carried out the most significant reforms, while others are trying to counteract a growing crisis.

It is hard to tell when an economy is leaving the transition period: is it at the moment when basic macroeconomic rates are beginning to improve (for example, growth of GDP, drop in inflation and unemployment), or when there is progress in a long-term process of restructuration (that is, improvement in the balance of payments, reduction of external debts, change of social behaviour, growth of business initiative and political stability)?

It is difficult to discuss at present a fully formed and coherent theory of transformation of systems, especially in the realm of economic changes. Although, as already mentioned, the processes of changes and reforms are also occurring in highly developed countries, in the case of the transformation process in CEE countries standard Western theoretical models of economic policy can be used only to a limited extent since the historical background and groundwork of the changes are quite different.

Restructuring of the economy is considered to be a key element of the transformation in CEE countries. Restructuring processes are positively taking place in almost all the countries, both developed and still developing, since the market economy is of an evolutionary character. Moreover, these processes are aiming at the formation of an optimal structure encompassing ownership, branch and organizational make-up of the economy. On the other hand, in the CEE countries restructuring is of a specific character and it resolves into a number of basic processes:

1. privatization (as opposed to the domination of a state-owned economy in a socialist economy);
2. demonopolization (as opposed to a central role of monopolies in a socialist economy); and
3. branch and sector transformations and company modernization.

2.3 Transformation and Economic Crisis

Although at present it is difficult to create a real theoretical model, a series of theses have appeared which show that in a process of transformation sooner or later there is an economic crisis. This economic breakdown in the majority of the formerly socialist countries has assumed a long-term character and routine means to stabilize it have failed. There is no doubt that the elimination of existing economic arrangements has to result in a temporary decrease in production and in exports, and a growth of unemployment. If new developments of an economic system cannot be created rapidly, then a periodical crisis can become a chronic state which will restrain the whole transformation process.

An answer to the question to what extent the depth of an economic crisis depends on an initial situation in an economy and to what extent on accepted ways and methods of transformation has not yet been found. Experts have been debating in which conditions in specific economic domains it would be advantageous to use so-called 'shock therapy' in a process of transformation, and in which situations and with reference to which areas of economic life an evolutionary approach should be applied. If the reform procedures of companies with financial difficulties were followed, then formulas for breaking the vicious circle of transformation within the whole macroeconomic system would have a very limited efficiency.

In practice, the transformation process has been far more difficult, longer and more expensive than was expected at the beginning. The first stage of its realization has brought such phenomena as a wide disruption of industrial production and loss of national income, increasing unemployment and inflation, and decreasing real incomes and consumption. Initially, it was thought that the transformation process would have been completed after about five years. Yet at present it is clear that a period of ten years is more likely, while for the countries where the transformation barriers were the biggest and where a deep economic crisis has taken place, a period of fifteen or even twenty years is more realistic (see Table 12.1).

Table 12.1   *Macroeconomic indicators (GDP and wholesale prices) in CEE countries, 1990–95*

Country	1990	1991	1992	1993	1994	1995
GDP growth						
Belorussia	–	–1	–9	–10	–16	–10
Bulgaria	–10	–13	–6	–5	1	2
Czech Republic	–1	–14	–6	–1	3	5
Estonia	–	–11	–26	–9	–2	4
Latvia	–	–10	–35	–15	1	–2
Poland	–13	–7	3	4	5	7
Romania	–7	–13	–9	1	4	7
Slovakia	–	–15	–7	–4	5	7
Slovenia	–	–9	–6	3	5	4
Hungary	–3	–12	–3	–1	3	2
Increase in wholesale prices						
Belorussia	–	4	96	975	1190	–
Bulgaria	24	339	80	56	87	62
Czech Republic	10	57	11	21	10	9
Estonia	–	–	1076	90	47	29
Latvia	11	172	951	109	36	25
Poland	586	70	43	35	32	28
Romania	4	165	210	256	137	32
Slovakia	10	61	10	23	13	10
Slovenia	550	117	201	32	20	13
Hungary	29	35	23	23	19	28

Sources: Data of statistical offices in Bulgaria, the Czech Republic, Hungary, Latvia and Poland available on Internet; Central Statistical Office of Poland (1991–97); Hungarian Central Statistical Office (1996); European Commission and Statistical Office of the EC (1997); Gaspard (1996).

The current situation in the Czech and Slovak Republics proves that there are now models of transformation, and therefore experts' predictions from the early 1990s have not come true. Even a few years ago it was expected that transformation in the former Czechoslovakia would be achieved quickly and at relatively low cost. Such a prognosis was justified by Czechoslovakia's democratic tradition and its relatively good economic situation. None the less, it was in the Czech Republic and also in Slovakia where a profound economic crisis occurred, which deepened sharply in 1997.

A trend of economic recession could be observed at the beginning of the transformation process in all the CEE countries while the largest decrease was noticed in the former Soviet Union republics. Likewise, the inflation rate was the biggest there. It was also noticed that the depression was stronger in the southern part of the CEE region (excluding the former Soviet Union republics): Bulgaria, Romania and the countries of the former Yugoslavia. However, since 1994 almost all the CEE countries have recorded a positive rate of GDP growth, which is a good indicator for the further process of economic transformation.

3 FORMS AND SCOPE OF ECONOMIC TRANSFORMATION IN TRANSPORT

3.1 Types of Changes in Economic Macrosystems

The restructuring of transport systems in the EU countries is being carried out within the framework of forms which derive from changes in the economic microsystems as a whole; for example, ownership, structural, functional, technical, organizational, economic, fiscal, spatial and social changes. Some forms of restructuring in transport are almost a precise representation of those existing on a macroeconomic scale (for example, ownership and social changes). Others are, to a greater extent, of a specific character for this sector (for example, structural or technical changes). Changes which are not applicable to the transport sector will not be considered here. The reorientation of policies on a macroeconomic scale, which has a clear influence on the transport sector, concerns those relating to market conditions, the budget, anti-inflation, credit, the energy industry, employment, and ecology or defence. Another feature of great significance for transport systems is purely political changes, in the form of such phenomena as widespread democratic procedures, legal status, protection of civil rights and the evolution of the relative power within political parties and social movements.

The domains of activities formerly reserved to the state sector – for ideological reasons – are beginning to disappear in transport. In particular, the principle of democratic election of supervisory or administrative board members is being applied. Also, those areas in the transport sector which were in a privileged position (that is, to a great extent enjoying a right of budget subsidies, or having a monopoly in some sections of the market) are being abolished.

Quite frequently, the disappearance of authoritarian power in the CEE countries has an unexpectedly negative significance for transport: democratic authorities – specifically those in which liberal parties are dominant – are on the one hand increasingly unconcerned about the development of a transport infrastructure which creates high budget charges and on the other hand they focus their attention on the development of firms which are suppliers of transport services. This is because the infrastructure lobby is smaller and less influential than the carriers' lobby.[1]

3.2 Disappearing Arrangements in the Economies in Transition

'Disappearing arrangements' consist of the elements and functional solutions in the transport sector which are:

1. incompatible with the market economy system;
2. aggravating the efficiency and performance of the system;
3. technically outdated; and
4. not compatible with international norms.

Solutions which are of a disappearing character tend to be functional rather than material.

Typical examples of functional solutions which are incompatible with the market economy system include:

1. guarantees for a monopoly position in a certain field;
2. a preference for state ownership;
3. discrimination of private ownership;
4. regulation of dimensions and structures of transport activity by administration;
5. the use of rigid fixed prices for services;
6. the incorporation of expenditure for fixed assets of transport firms in the state budget;
7. central planning of investments in infrastructure and transport rolling stock;
8. the treatment of mass transport as a 'public service';
9. the granting of exploitation subsidies to unprofitable transport services (cargo as well as passenger);
10. the wide use of reduced tariffs in passenger transport;
11. a legal commitment of exporters and importers to use the services of the national carrier as far as possible; and
12. a ban on access of foreign capital to transport property.

The whole system based on this kind of regulation was inefficient. In the 1980s it caused a visible collapse of the dynamics of development in transport as well as a financial decline of transport enterprises in all the CEE countries.

Along with the collapse of the former political system in the years 1989–90 it was necessary to abandon solutions like those mentioned above. However, for a number of years there was some ambiguity concerning how and when this should be done. There was also the question of what would replace them. It was hard to find a kind of univocal European model in this sphere or a model taken from a country with the best operating transport system (Germany, the Netherlands?).

A feature of the economy in transition is the fact that some functional solutions from the former system remain for a certain period of time. As far as transport within the CEE countries is concerned, a number of the functional solutions which originated in the system of central planning could be abolished from the very beginning of the transformation.

On the other hand, some functional solutions remained in existence, requiring evolutive changes, for a period of 10 to 15 years. These solutions include:

1. regulations on privatization and restructuring of the state transport firms;
2. central planning of investments in transport infrastructure;
3. a reduction in the scope of 'public service' in transport;
4. a reduction in exploitation subsidies to unprofitable passenger transport services; and
5. a definition of the scope of application of reduced tariffs in passenger transport.

These latter solutions are likely to remain, at least in a fragmentary form, in the market economy system.

Among the material elements of the CEE countries' transport systems inherited from the past, those which resulted from investment errors and a limited accessibility to advanced technical solutions will be disposed of. However, there are only a small number of such errors.

In the planned economies, an analysis of the financial profitability of investments, as is customary in most of the Western world, was not carried out. Surprising though this may seem, the strictly political decision making rarely resulted in cases where investments in infrastructure were redundant or unprofitable. Given the large-scale lack of infrastructural facilities, even an intuitive or political choice of investment brought advantages. Among the infrastructural investments which were economically unsuccessful are:

1. wide gauge railway lines for the carriage of large quantities of raw materials between the former Soviet Union and such countries as Poland, the former Czechoslovakia and Hungary;
2. terminals for the trans-shipment of crude oil and iron ore at some seaports; and
3. some stretches of electrified railway lines.

Purchases of aircraft produced in the former Soviet Union as well as vehicle
and inland navigation stock of domestic production can be included in the list
of failed technical investments. This limited negative assessment may seem
surprising in the light of critical opinions on the condition of transport infrastructure inherited by the CEE countries after the breakdown of the former
political system. However, one has to differentiate between qualitative
drawbacks of the infrastructure and cases of unnecessary or abortive
investments. Perhaps financial resources could have been better used in the
1980s by constructing, for example, fewer yet more modern and longlasting
means of transport. Undoubtedly, it would have been better if the purchase of
domestically produced vehicles that were energy consuming, expensive and
not very durable had been abandoned earlier.

Of course, the possibility of transforming transport stock depended first on
available resources and on the prices for these goods. Besides this, the existing
ban on imports (for instance, on aircraft for civil aviation) was also a limiting
factor.

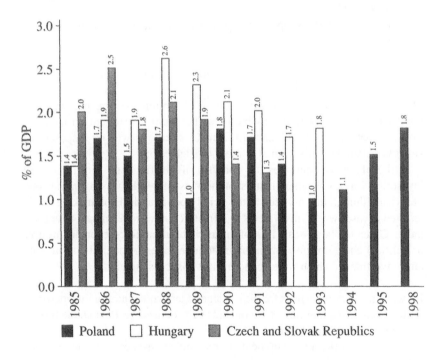

*Figure 12.2   Investment in transport in Poland, Hungary, and the Czech
              and Slovak Republics (% GDP)*

In the period preceding the economic transformation of transport in the CEE countries, capital expenditure in this sector was relatively high. This can be seen from data for the years 1985–96, which express the share of this expenditure in GDP (Figure 12.2). The unsatisfactory state of transport infrastructure in the CEE countries is not only the result of the level of expenditure, as this has fluctuated between 1.0 and 2.5 per cent of GDP in the last ten years (infrastructural investments in the EU were at about the same level, constituting 1.2 per cent of GDP in 1995; European Commission, 1997b).

The reasons for the shortcomings in infrastructure also lie in the generally low standard of wealth in CEE countries, which is reflected in per capita GDP. In Poland, an investment expenditure of 1.5 per cent of GDP (1995) represents an amount of about €1500 million, while a parallel percentage in Spain represented €5500 million.

3.3 Permanent Arrangements in Economies in Transition

Permanent arrangements are much more in the material domain of transport than in the functional one, as was the case for disappearing arrangements, discussed above. For transport infrastructure, a valuable inheritance from the past is a widely developed railway network, new or modernized airports, container terminals in seaports and a network of pipelines for the transport of oil and natural gas. Only a limited stretch of roads, on the other hand, is suitable for further exploitation without any major repairs of the surface and rebuilding of the layout of many stretches. In a similar way, only a limited part of the transport fleet constituted a permanent arrangement in the 1990s. In most cases, the domestic production of rolling stock for road and for rail transport has had to be abandoned. In certain cases the shipyard industry (for example, Szczecin, Gdynia in Poland) has been maintained on a relatively good level.

Among functional solutions, a significant part of technical standards in transport is permanent. These standards are based on the regulations of the Economic Commission for Europe of the United Nations or on conventions and international agreements. As a rule, technical standards for road, air and sea transport in the CEE countries were no different from the world's solutions. Furthermore, a fundamental framework of a system for financing transport infrastructure based on state and local budgets survives. A similar situation exists in the matter of transport companies' resources and bank credits. In addition, the principle of subsidizing public passenger transport – limited to slow trains and ordinary long-distance bus services – is secure. However, there is almost a total lack of permanent system solutions in such areas as the formation of companies, the regulation of the supply of transport services on the markets, competition control and price fixing.

3.4   Development Arrangements in Economies in Transition

The necessity for development arrangements within the transport sector of the CEE countries arose very strongly in the areas of company functioning and of market regulation. In order to restore an economically viable situation in the sector, the following legal solutions became indispensable: stimulating the establishment of new enterprises, accelerating the liquidation or restructuring of unprofitable firms, stimulating competition on the markets, attracting private and foreign investment (including for infrastructure) and facilitating the transfer of modern transport technologies.

The main ideas concerning the further development of the transport system involve improving competitiveness in international markets, restoring financial norms in companies, improving safety standards and reducing ecological noxiousness. Such ideas can be found in official papers on transport policy (for example: Ministry of Transport and Maritime Economy, 1995; Ministry of Transport, Communication and Water Management, 1996).

4   INTERNAL REQUIREMENTS OF SYSTEM CHANGES IN TRANSPORT

4.1   General Characteristics

The rate of the creation of a market system in transport in the CEE countries depends on the structure of economic and social factors. Both factors favouring transformation and those hindering it can be distinguished. These factors differ in nature, being, for example, of a political, financial, technical, administrational, managerial, sociological and cultural character.

An impediment to changes in transport is more often caused by human attitudes than by a shortage of financial or material resources. At times, there is a conflict between transport users' expectations on the one hand and aspirations of the workers in this sector on the other. This may be illustrated as follows. Wage demands on the part of railway employees or the workers in urban public transport make it difficult for companies to improve their own financial condition as well as to undertake investments that will offer their clients services that are more attractive. A strong aspiration to own a car reduces the demand for public transport services and limits the income of transport companies. The desire to own a transport company as a way of protecting oneself from unemployment leads to an excessive expansion of the sector and also to the emergence of an excessive number of companies that are unable to function longer than the lifetime of their re-purchased used stock.

The progress of privatization encounters barriers raised by the politicians and also those resulting from staff resistance.

4.2 Financial Factors

An economy in transition is not a situation favouring qualitative changes in transport systems. Intensive investments, active structural changes and profound amendments in transport legislation all require a temporary increase in expenditure for transport. Meanwhile, the crisis of public finances and the aggravation of economic conditions in the private sector that accompany the system transformations in practice generate a reduction in accessible funds. Therefore, an external financial support for technical transformation is necessary. This support can be in the form of foreign loans (for example, from the European Bank for Reconstruction and Development) or non-returnable aid (especially PHARE funds).[2]

Contrary to expectations, the creation of a legal framework for the commitment of private and foreign capital to transport does not necessarily attract a flood of new investors to the sector. This is because of the low efficiency of infrastructural undertakings. The absence of new investment has been even more visible in the case of tenders for the construction of toll motorways in Poland, Hungary and other CEE countries. If private capital is attracted to transport, then it is in the field of carriage activities rather than in the creation of new infrastructure.

4.3 Legal Aspects

A rapid amendment of legislation seems to be one of the fundamental factors that can stimulate the transformation of the transport system. Meanwhile, the number of laws to be passed by parliaments is so large in the transitory period that even urgent transport legislation has to take its turn before it is debated by legislators (Burnewicz, 1998). It is regarded as a success if two to three new transport acts are passed within a year. The debates on some of the acts are long drawn-out and even then their final contents sometimes not only differ considerably from the original draft but also are so much of a political compromise that they contribute very little to the system changes.[3]

4.4 Social Problems

As mentioned above, the process of economic transformation in transport within the CEE countries is being delayed as a result of resistance by employees of large transport enterprises, who fear redundancy. This is particularly noticeable in the case of railway companies as well as in that of the state interurban bus transport companies. In both these categories of transport there is heavy over-employment, causing real costs to be overestimated and leading to chronic financial difficulties. An untimely attempt to privatize the Czech railways, in 1995, had to be renounced because of a railwaymen's strike. Polish attempts in 1994–97 to privatize a large number (174) of state-owned bus companies had no noticeable effects. In many cases, it is the employees who are interested in the privatization of state-owned bus companies, but they do not have at their disposal any financial means necessary for the modernization of rolling stock.

The employees in the transport sector in the CEE countries are unfavourably inclined towards the process of integration with the EU and to liberalization of the access to the transport markets. They are afraid that the cancellation of the present system of bilateral permits may result in an instant sharpening of competition and in an increased number of bankruptcies of the national companies. It is the employees who urge a delay in the liberalization of the transport market and the protection of national companies against foreign competition.

The main motive power of structural changes in transport within the CEE countries in the 1990s has been small businesspeople establishing small firms, with one to three vehicles, which have been bought from state-owned companies. Because of their activity, the share of the private sector in bus transport has increased. On the other hand, this is not a financially strong sector and it requires a rapid modernization of its property.

5 ADAPTATION OF TRANSPORT IN THE CEE COUNTRIES TO THE EU SYSTEM

5.1 The Adaptation to the EU System as an Element of Economic Transformation

A fundamental challenge facing transport policy of the countries in transition is the transformation of transport into a system functioning on the basis of a free market. The process of transformation is carried out in a certain international context that influences its progress quite naturally. This is manifested in the adoption by the CEE countries of some of the existing patterns and experiences of other countries. Furthermore, it is natural for the transformation to move towards a transport system that has already adapted to that of West European countries. Political, historical and social reasons make it possible, after the collapse of the socialist bloc, to spatially enlarge the EU to the East. Both the EU and the majority of the CEE countries approve of such an enlargement.

Just as no model of economic transformation exists, so also no pattern has been formed for the adaptation of transport to the EU. The experiences of EU member states that have gone through an adaptation process can be applied to a limited extent only, because the starting-point of those countries was quite different from that of the CEE countries. Furthermore, it is hard to create an adaptation model based on the experiences of CEE countries, because the patterns and methods accepted in specific countries differ and the process itself has not yet been completed. Undoubtedly, in the future analyses will be carried out which will allow the creation of such a model as well as a definition of which aspects of transport development are, and which are not, the result of an adaptation policy and of adaptation to market economy conditions.

5.2 Approach in CEE Countries

The objectives of transport policy in CEE countries should in principle be the same, because the activities of the central authorities are directed towards overcoming similar difficulties, which are the result of a longstanding transport system in an economy administered centrally. Disparities can result from different priorities and strategies.

The hypothetical objectives of transport policy in CEE countries can be divided into the following categories:

1. *Market operations* Setting the principles of market regulation and fair competition in a market economy.
2. *Market organization* Changing organizational structures and encouraging privatization processes of transport undertakings.
3. *Infrastructure issues* Modernization of infrastructure and the creation of highly advanced transport infrastructure, especially in road and rail transport.
4. *Adapting to the European transport system* Adjustment to the EU, legal adaptation to the Single Market, and approval of international conventions.
5. *Social aspects of transport functioning* Improvement in the quality of service and a decrease in the harmful influence of transport on the environment.

The strategic aims of transport policies in CEE countries can be identified in cases where government documents exist which contain the whole policy. In some countries, however, no such documents exist. In addition, some of those which do exist often do not detail the long-term strategy. Nevertheless, in most CEE countries the basis for the activity of authorities in the transport sector had already been worked out during the first half of the 1990s (see Table 12.2).

Table 12.2   *Strategic priorities of transport policy in selected CEE countries*

Selected countries	Strategic priorities of transport policy
Czech Republic	Structural changes in the transport sector, privatization. Support for environmental protection by reduction of harmful influence of transport. Harmonization of the transport sector with the EU system

Estonia	Selected priorities:
	  demonopolization and privatization in the transport sector;
	  prioritized development of public transport to prevent its decrease in the general transport structure;
	  maintenance and development of transport infrastructure;
	  establishment of conditions that would enable the country better to fulfil the role of gateway between East and West;
	  harmonization with EU legislation.

Hungary	Promoting integration with the EU by development of infrastructure network, fleet modernization and harmonization of conditions of competition. Improvement of conditions for cooperation with neighbour countries. Encouraging a more balanced territorial development of the country. Protection of sustainable regional development. Efficient, market-orientated transport regulation (such issues as: financing, competitivity, payment for the usage of transport infrastructure).

Latvia	Selected priorities:
	  maintenance and development of transport infrastructure;
	  support and promotion of harmonized and complex development of the transport system;
	  improving and supporting a high level of traffic safety;
	  ensuring the development of an environmentally friendly transport system;
	  working out a transport legislation system according to EU rules.

Poland	Acceleration of privatization, restructuration of large transport undertakings and overcoming of monopoly. Adjustment of transport system to the EU. Technological and organizational changes.
Romania	Rehabilitation of transport infrastructures. Promoting competition between the transport modes and reorganization of the transport services. Harmonization of the quality of the transport services with that of the EU countries.

Sources: Ministry of Transport and Maritime Economy (1995); Ministry of Transport, Communication and Water Management (1996); Ministry of Transport (1993); ECE (1997a, b, c).

After analysing the priorities of transport policies in CEE countries as set out in the table, their similarity to and analogy with the above list of hypothesized aims of transport policy can be noted. The element of organizational changes has appeared in most countries. Also infrastructure improvement proved to be a very important issue. Further, in every official policy document it is stated that adapting to the European transport system will be essential. Finally, social aspects of transport functioning appeared as a postulate for high-quality services as well as protection of the human life environment.

5.3 EU Approach

In the 1990s, EU policy has been extended with an additional aspect, that is, an adaptation to spatial enlargement. Besides the changes in its own integration strategy, the EU has enacted guidelines for countries competing for EU membership. A general direction for the adaptation of transport in CEE countries to the EU is marked by such documents as association agreements and the White Paper of the EU Commission on the preparation of CEE-associated countries for integration with the EU internal market (European Commission, 1995).

The association agreements have been negotiated separately with each country competing for membership and they contain, among other things, resolutions on transport.

Transport issues are also mentioned in the White Paper of 1995. It contains EU legislation that is part of the so-called *acquis communautaire* (the body of common rights and obligations which bind all the member states together within the European Union) and that has to be taken into account by the countries aspiring to EU membership. It is worth remarking that the White Paper does not contain any desiderata on transport restructuring in CEE countries.

Another step in EU policy is 'Agenda 2000' (European Commission, 1997b), dedicated to the preparations of EU and CEE countries to EU spatial enlargement. The document deals with various issues, starting from EU internal policy, through some organizational aspects (for example, formation of special institutions), financial aspects (the PHARE programme, pre-accession aid for agriculture, structural funds on the regional level), legal aspects (European agreements, participation in the EU programme) and finally to the adaptation of specific countries to the EU.

5.4 Dynamics

The adaptation of transport in CEE countries is a dynamic process. It consists not only in putting certain laws into practice (that is, legal adjustment), but also in an adaptation regarding organization, function and space. Hence, it is a long-term process. The process of adaptation to the EU also has to take account of evaluations of the strategy of integration and of changes in EU transport policy. Every year new transport legal documents are automatically included in the *acquis communautaire*. Therefore, they constitute an adaptation applicable to CEE countries.

The integration processes of the countries in transition are being carried out at all levels of the economy. It is likely that the level of adjustment in transport will actively affect the rate and the scope of adaptation processes in other sectors of the economy. Some analyses have proved that delays in the integration of transport in the EU caused negative consequences to the macroeconomic features of transport, as well as to other economic and social sectors (Bąk, 1997). Therefore, the creation of a transport system is in the interest of the whole of Europe, regardless of whether and when spatial EU enlargement will take place.

5.5   Dilemmas

Although the objective of EU spatial enlargement is meeting with political and social acceptance, nevertheless there are different dilemmas in the adaptation process. The adaptation of transport in CEE countries to the EU system is very expensive. In the long run, costs should be covered by benefits arising from the integration of transport systems. Otherwise, one could hardly say that the integration process would be successful. In the adaptation process, the costs are borne both by CEE countries and by the EU member states. It is important to balance the costs so as not to cause any political and social tensions for either of the parties. Transport is an exceptionally difficult domain – next to agriculture and heavy industry – that requires capital-consuming modernization and trans- formation. The realization of the process cannot be carried out exclusively at the cost of the private sector. An important part of these costs has to be borne by the state, which can and should seek financial assistance from the EU. Moreover, it has to be taken into account that initially expenditures and costs of the adaptation process will exceed additional benefits.

The adaptation of transport in CEE countries will bring about various, quite frequently contrary, effects for different groups in society: companies, transport users, the public administration and social organizations. The adjustment of fiscal liabilities of transport companies may cause a decrease in competitivity of transport firms and eventually their bankruptcy. Structural changes may also result in higher unemployment or the elimination of professional privileges. These expectations cause resistance in transport enterprises and from trade unions, which are strong in many of the CEE countries, especially in Poland. Pro-ecological circles are opposed to an adaptation of the structure of the sector to the EU, in so far as it is motorized transport that predominates, with its degrading effects on the environment. In the CEE countries the position of rail transport, despite its decrease since the beginning of the transformation period, has continued to be more important than is the case in the EU.

In effect, it will be the transport users, with their greater opportunities for using cheaper and better-quality services, who will benefit most from the adjustment to the EU. The public administration will have to fulfil new and more difficult tasks, related to the control of fairness in competition, of technical and ecological standards, of recording infrastructural expenditures and of enforcing social regulations.

5.6 Expected Effects

It is not a foregone conclusion that the economic and social effects of the integration of transport in the countries with a transitional economy with the EU system will be positive. It is not known precisely when the cost–benefit balance will be advantageous. It seems certain that in the pre-accession period and at an early stage of membership the cost of the adaptation of transport will be higher than additional (positive) micro- and macroeconomic effects. In the long run, no country in Europe will be a loser because of transport integration, in an economic, social or political sense. However, it is illusory to expect that throughout the whole period preceding accession to the EU the effect of integration will be equally positive for all countries desiring EU membership. The existing differences in the level of economic development in a given country at the beginning of the integration process to a large extent are a factor determining a bigger growth dynamics in poorly developed countries compared with the countries on a higher level of development.

Theoretically, CEE countries will have the opportunity to accelerate their economic and social development at an early stage of EU membership. Paradoxically, it could happen, however, that the high rate of economic growth taking place in the pre-accession period (2–7 per cent annually) cannot be maintained at the same high level after obtaining full membership in the years 2002–5. Yet, it should be remembered that in an integrated structure, not only is growth – in a quantitative sense – of vital importance, but above all a general economic and social development – in a qualitative sense.

Incorporation of a country in a group of countries in a process of integration will in general involve drastic changes, both quantitative and qualitative, for the whole of that country. As far as the transport market is concerned, this is at present characterized by an oversupply of transport potential. It means that the integration of transport markets of CEE countries with those of the EU will lead to strong competition, especially in road transport. Differences in transport costs between Western and Eastern Europe still exist, which will make transport firms from the CEE countries fear competition. The spatial enlargement also carries with it certain risks, in most cases of a temporary character. For the countries with a longer period of membership in the Community it will mean the necessity of a certain reduction in their share of the expenditures from the common budget, submitting their firms to stricter competition from the new countries, strengthening of market control (fairness of competition, respecting norms and standards), enlargement of investments abroad, employing a greater number of foreign workers and a larger flow of relatively inexpensive commodities and services from new member countries. For the new member countries the threats are connected with the possibility of a collapse of technically outdated sectors of the economy and companies, a temporary increase in unemployment, and in the short run the necessity of concentrated expenditures for adaptation processes (more intensive legislation, restructuring, modernization).

In an early stage of membership of a given country, one can distinguish areas of accordance and contradictions of its interests and the interests of those countries that were integrated earlier. From the point of view of the transport sector, the areas of accordance can cover:

1. an increase in the efficiency of transport systems, as a result of the elimination of formalities at borders and ports;
2. a decrease in empty vehicle runs, resulting from free access to forwarding orders;
3. an acceleration of modernization of the transport infrastructure network, as a result of an enlargement in the range of its joint planning and financing;
4. a better use of resources and of qualifications of the transport staff, due to the introduction of a free flow of labour;
5. a quality improvement in transport services, due to a deeper organizational integration of the transport chain and the development of the logistic network on the European level; and
6. a reduction in transport service costs, as a result of bigger possibilities of canvassing of transport orders and intensified rationalization of carriage and handling operations.

On the other hand, in the transport sector, areas of contradiction of national interests still remain concerning:

1. changes in the existing division of the market between domestic and foreign carriers, as a result of symmetric lifting of restrictions to the access to markets (Burnewicz, 1996);
2. a limit to public aid given to transport companies;
3. changes in fiscal systems referring directly or indirectly to transport activity;

4. an introduction of uniform systems of concession and licence granting as regards activities connected with the provision of transport services and transport infrastructure exploitation;
5. the tightening of norms and technical standards as well as ecological restrictions;
6. the systematization of norms and work conditions in transport companies;
7. the establishment of principles of access to transport infrastructure – both of a point ('terminals') and of a line character – and payment for the access;
8. procedures and criteria of granting resources from the EU's budget for infrastructural investments or for modernization of transport rolling stock; and
9. a standardization of the system of prices and tariffs for transport services.

It is essential for the CEE countries to achieve additional economic benefits of an integration with the EU during the first stage of membership, rather than at the advanced stage. In the case of transport, meeting this requirement is not easy, because the adaptation period and the early membership stage are the years when the previous gross negligence and an investment backlog in transport infrastructure will have to be made up for. The first decade of the twenty-first century will see an intensification of those investments. The costs of terminating legislative regulation and of restructuring transport activity will also have to be taken into account. This course of events will be accompanied by a growth in the revenues of international transport services that will most likely be slower than in the 1990s. The latter will result from the liberalization of the access to markets and the consequent tightening of competition.

6 CHANGES IN THE SPHERE OF DEMAND FOR TRANSPORT

6.1 General Character of the Changes

The creation of a market economy system in the CEE countries affects changes in the scale of global volume and demand structure of transport considerably. As a rule, the directions of the changes are the following:

1. the demand for various kinds of freight transport services is increasing more slowly than GDP;
2. the rate of growth of demand for freight transport for hire and reward is higher than that for transport on own account;
3. the demand for various kinds of passenger transport services is increasing at least as fast as – at times even faster than – people's real income;

4. the demand for individual motorization is developing strongly at the cost of collective transport, which, except for aviation, is showing a strong decreasing trend;
5. the demand for international transport is increasing considerably faster than the demand for national and regional transport.

Table 12.3 shows the dynamics of freight and passenger transport and GDP growth in CEE and EU countries. The table gives the average figures for all EU countries and for four CEE countries (the Czech Republic, Hungary, Poland

Table 12.3   Dynamics of passenger and freight transport and of GDP growth in CEE and EU countries

Years	1985	1986	1987	1988	1989	1990	1991	1992	1993	1994	1995
Dynamics of passenger transport volume (passenger-km)											
Poland	100.0	99.7	102.4	110.8	117.4	107.9	101.4	95.9	111.3	132.2	163.3
Czech Republic	100.0	103.5	107.4	107.4	110.0	116.6	121.4	128.1	132.0	138.0	143.2
Slovakia	100.0	102.6	105.7	108.5	108.9	116.0	113.4	109.4	106.9	107.6	109.4
Hungary	100.0	105.5	110.2	111.8	116.8	124.7	121.2	126.7	127.0	138.3	145.9
Total CEE-4	100.0	101.9	105.3	109.9	114.7	113.8	110.9	110.3	118.5	132.1	150.0
Spain	100.0	104.8	110.6	117.7	123.9	131.4	138.3	146.1	148.6	150.3	155.9
Germany	100.0	103.4	107.0	110.6	114.2	118.2	120.6	123.5	125.5	124.9	127.6
EU-15	100.0	103.8	108.1	113.2	118.3	123.5	126.0	130.4	132.3	134.2	137.6
Dynamics of freight transport volume (tonne-km)											
Poland	100.0	101.7	101.7	103.3	95.9	79.0	65.9	64.0	67.1	71.9	76.7
Czech Republic	100.0	95.1	95.7	104.2	92.6	86.4	79.1	79.9	77.7	84.1	84.1
Slovakia	100.0	95.1	95.7	104.2	92.6	100.4	84.0	67.6	63.0	56.7	63.7
Hungary	100.0	101.5	98.9	96.4	98.5	91.6	77.8	68.6	63.1	61.0	62.3
Total CEE-4	100.0	99.5	99.4	102.7	95.2	84.6	72.3	68.4	68.4	71.4	74.9
Spain	100.0	102.8	106.5	110.4	121.3	131.8	137.4	140.0	141.9	149.0	156.2
Germany	100.0	99.4	101.4	106.3	108.7	106.9	106.6	108.2	104.9	124.9	126.2
EU-15	100.0	100.7	103.7	109.7	112.3	116.2	117.3	117.8	116.7	127.4	130.6
Dynamics of GDP (constant prices – 1995)											
Poland	100.0	103.3	108.8	119.2	130.9	127.1	118.2	121.3	125.9	132.4	141.7
Czech Republic	100.0	102.0	103.0	105.1	110.3	109.9	94.3	88.3	87.5	89.7	94.2
Slovakia	100.0	104.0	107.1	109.3	110.4	107.0	91.5	85.7	82.2	86.1	92.1
Hungary	100.0	102.0	107.1	106.0	106.0	102.3	90.1	87.4	86.7	89.3	91.0
Total CEE-4	100.0	102.7	106.8	111.5	117.8	114.9	102.9	101.5	102.7	106.9	112.9
Spain	100.0	103.0	109.2	114.6	120.4	125.2	127.7	129.0	127.7	130.2	134.1
Germany	100.0	102.0	104.0	108.2	112.5	119.3	125.2	127.8	126.5	130.3	132.9
EU-15	100.0	102.6	105.4	109.7	113.7	117.1	119.1	120.2	119.7	123.1	126.2

Sources: Burnewicz et al. (1996), Central Statistical Office of Poland (1986–97), European Commission and Statistical Office of the EC (1997), Ruppert (1999).

and Slovakia). Also, separate figures for each of these four CEE countries and for two EU countries have been included (figures for other CEE countries were not available to a sufficient extent; Germany and Spain have been chosen for comparison because these countries are similar in population size to the four CEE countries).

Evidence for the expectations just formulated may be obtained from an analysis of the rates of growth of transport volume and of changes in transport intensity. These findings are presented in Table 12.3 and in Figures 12.3 and 12.4, respectively. It appears that in the years 1985–95 all CEE countries went through a period of a sharp drop of GDP, which escalated dramatically in 1991 and 1992. This drop was accompanied by a periodic decrease in the volume of both passenger and freight transport (as expressed in passenger- and in tonne-km, respectively). However, from 1993 onwards, the volume of passenger transport tended to increase, accelerating rapidly as from 1994. Freight transport has begun to increase, but its volume in 1995 made up merely 75 per cent of the level in 1985, while in the 15 EU member states there was a slight yet steady growth.

6.2 Transport Intensity

The rationalization of transport operations in terms of lowering costs of production and distribution was an active factor in bringing about changes in freight transport in the CEE countries. Thus, ineffective transport services provided in the former centrally planned economies are being eliminated and average distances and traffic volumes rationalized. The effect of this may be seen from the evolution of the number of tonne-km per € of GDP ('transport intensity'). The trend of the changes in transport intensity in selected countries in the years 1985–95 is shown in Figure 12.3.

In the four CEE countries analysed, the intensity of freight transport (taken as the sum of transport by rail, road, inland waterway and through pipelines) decreased in the period mentioned from over 2 to below 1.5 tonne-km per € of GDP (in Hungary even to about 0.7 tonne-km/€). However, the intensity is still many times higher than in the 15 EU countries (about 0.24 tonne-km/€). The intensity of passenger transport (number of passenger-km per euro of GDP) in the CEE countries on the other hand is of a strongly increasing tendency. This is illustrated in Figure 12.4.

It may seem strange that the intensities of freight and of passenger transport in CEE countries have moved in opposite directions. This phenomenon may be explained by assuming that the previously existing communist regimes were more of an obstacle to the free movement of persons than to that of goods. Furthermore, given the increased possibility of movement, the transport cost factor in all likelihood has less weight in passenger transport than in freight transport.

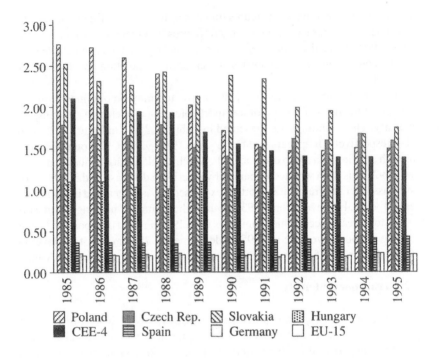

Figure 12.3   Intensity of freight transport in Europe (tonne-km per euro of GDP)

While in 1995 in the EU the intensity of passenger transport (passenger-km by passenger car, non-urban buses, rail, and air transport) amounted to an average of about 0.7, in the four CEE countries this rate reached an average of more than 2.5.[4]

6.3   Modal Structure of Demand

Some marked changes in modal structure are characteristic for the evolution of demand for transport in the CEE countries. The structural changes in this field are illustrated by Figures 12.5 and 12.6.

The political changes in CEE countries and the break-up of the former Czechoslovakia have broken the continuity of statistical data. It can be determined, however, first – as shown in both figures – that transport by road, both in freight and in passenger transport, has been growing very dynamically.

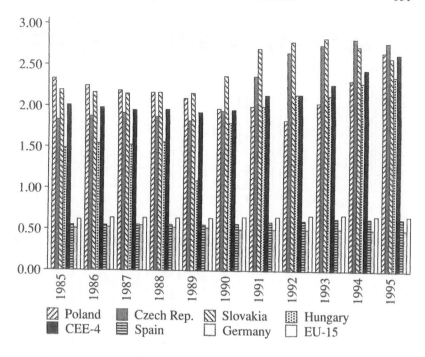

Figure 12.4   Intensity of passenger transport in Europe (passenger-km per euro of GDP)

The concomitant decrease in demand for rail transport services has been strongest in Hungary (from about 50 to about 30 per cent of total tonne-km). In Poland, railways have remained relatively significant (about 50 per cent), which is an advantageous phenomenon from the viewpoint of the ecology. Inland waterway transport, which has a remarkable ecological value, has been only slightly attractive for shippers, and most of this is in Hungary (about 5 per cent of demand).

A comparison of the changes in demand structure in passenger transport of the four CEE countries indicates a substantial growth of the importance of private motorization (in Poland more than 73 per cent of the number of passenger-km) with a significant decrease in carriage by non-urban buses and with a slightly lower but steady decrease in demand for rail transport. The significance of air transport has been growing, but in the number of passenger-km it does not exceed 2–3 per cent (see Figure 12.6).

Some special cases

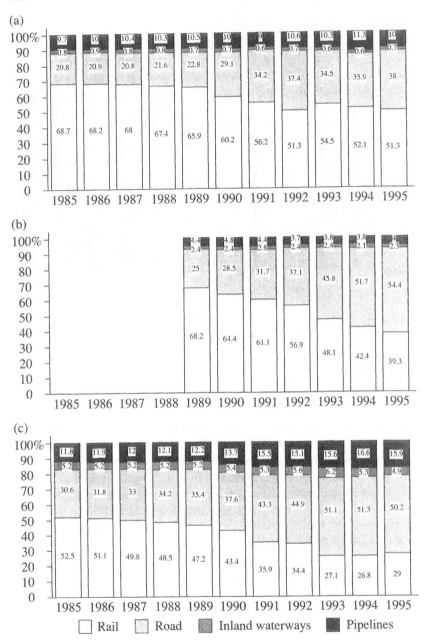

*Figure 12.5 Modal structure of freight transport in (a) Poland, (b) the Czech
        Republic and (c) Hungary (according to number of tonne-km)*

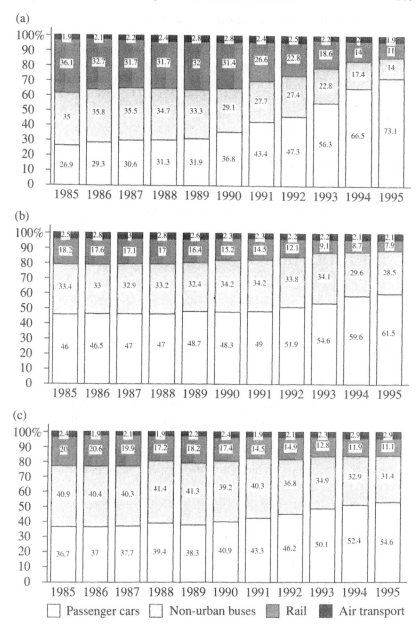

Figure 12.6   Modal structure of passenger transport in (a) Poland, (b) the Czech Republic and (c) Hungary (according to number of passenger-km)

6.4 Trends in the Forms of Transport Services

For the CEE countries, a characteristic relic from the past is the high share of own-account road transport (45–60 per cent of the number of tonne-km), resulting from the demand for a more elastic own fleet. An expansion of hire and reward services, performed professionally, cheaply and reliably, diminishes the role of own-account transport but this still exceeds that in EU countries (23–35 per cent) significantly.

The association with the EU had a greater effect on the development of international rather than national transport. As an example, in Poland the volume of road freight transport – both national and local – decreased by about 500 million tonnes annually, while the volume of international transport increased from about 0.9 million tonnes to more than 22 million tonnes.

7 THE EVOLUTION OF ENTERPRISES IN THE TRANSPORT SECTOR

7.1 Growth

It is difficult to imagine the case of a market economy in which the transport sector is composed entirely of large state-owned enterprises. In fact even in the 'planned economy' period in most of the former CMEA countries there was a limited sector of road transport occupied by private firms. Indeed, in the case of Poland, in absolute terms this sector was relatively large (more than 8000 enterprises), but even so it did not cover more than 5 per cent of the total fleet number. It had connections with a substantial private sector in the construction industry (about 10 per cent), in trade (more than 15 per cent) and in agriculture (more than 75 per cent). In the rest of the former CMEA countries, private ownership in transport was marginal.

The creation of the market economy system necessitated profound changes in the structure of ownership in transport. Thus, in the whole economy a need has arisen for a large number of small- and medium-sized enterprises. There were even attempts to define their minimal number, which would guarantee a sufficiently intensive level of competition (most frequently the given rate is one firm per 20 inhabitants).

The years 1990–96 in the CEE countries were further characterized by a very intensive process of new enterprise establishment, especially in trade and in the construction industry. In addition, in transport the process was very dynamic. It was, however, limited mainly to road transport. On the other hand, the growth in road transport did not take place at the expense of rail transport, which remained at a constant level.

7.2 Structure

Changes in the structure of transport enterprises have taken place in a number of respects:

1. *Ownership* Establishing different types of enterprises: joint-stock companies, limited liability companies, companies with shares owned by the state, companies with foreign capital.
2. *Size* The creation either of small, medium-sized or large firms or of groups of enterprises.
3. *Economic character* Hire and reward firms or firms with transport on own account.

In specific transport modes, the intensity of changes on these three planes is different. The biggest diversity of new forms of enterprises will occur in road transport, while rail transport will have the lowest diversity.

The establishment of small road transport enterprises in all the CEE countries has a leading role in the restructuring process. On the whole, they are not established as a result of the restructuring process and the privatization of the state-owned enterprises, but rather as a result of their creation at the same time as the big state-owned enterprises are being reduced.

7.3 Legal Regulation

Poland, the Czech Republic (the former Czechoslovakia) and Hungary were the first countries to introduce legislation allowing for the liquidation of the monopoly of large road transport enterprises (PKS, CSAD, VOLAN and HUN-GAROCAMION). In these countries as early as 1988–90 the first laws were enacted concerning transport demonopolization, its restructuring and privatization.[5] Although the Czech Republic was the last to introduce legal regulations concerning privatization, it was the first to put into effect the privatization process in the whole of road transport. The situation was similar in Slovenia, but in the other CEE countries, legislation concerning privatization was either introduced later or did not promote privatization processes to a large extent.[6]

7.4 Intensity of Privatization Processes

The form and speed of privatization processes being undertaken in CEE countries do not have to be and cannot be identical. They depend on national traditions, employees' opinions, the role of trade unions and private capital resources. Some countries give priority to 'mass privatization' (the Czech Republic, Poland, Romania, Bulgaria, Latvia, Estonia), others to selling shares to the workers (this is the most popular method in Slovenia and it has also gained some popularity in Poland). The 'royal' way of privatization is a direct sell-off, which is the most popular method in Hungary and is finding strong support in Poland, Romania and Bulgaria (Chatelus, 1995).

In Hungary, practically all major state-owned road haulage enterprises were converted – mostly after having been split up – into undertakings that are owned and run by the same private persons or into limited liability companies with, in the case of HUNGAROCAMION, the state retaining a 25 per cent share.

In the Czech Republic, privatization of the road transport sector was completed in 1995 and there are now 35 000 road transport operators in the market. In Latvia some 40 state-owned transport undertakings had been privatized by 1994. In Romania about 70 have been earmarked as suitable for privatization (Diaconu, 1996) and in 1993 approximately 14 per cent of Romania's state-owned operations were privatized. Lithuania has privatized 63 per cent of its road haulage firms (Economic Commission for Europe, 1997a).[7] In 1995, Bulgarian undertakings were being considered for privatization and 100 were actually privatized (Economic Commission for Europe, 1995).

In the Czech Republic, Hungary and Poland the percentage of privatized road transport companies is about 99 per cent. In other CEE countries it is more than 70 per cent. However, the percentage of employees and vehicles in private firms is slightly lower at 50–60 per cent in leading countries (the Czech Republic, Hungary, Poland) and 10–15 per cent in other CEE countries.

In the Czech Republic the privatization of the state-owned enterprise CSAD (the Czech road transport undertaking) was predicted by late 1995; however it was still not completed in 2000. None the less, the country is the most advanced in the sphere of privatization in the CEE countries.

In the countries of the former Soviet Union, the dissolution of the gigantic SOVTRANSAVTO created new opportunities for a bus transport market. In Latvia, in turn, up to the end of 1994 about 500 private bus enterprises were created, involving the use of about 1100 vehicles (Olants, 1995).

7.5   Other Changes

Statistical data on the progress of road freight transport privatization in CEE countries are very scarce. Therefore, it is difficult to make a comparison between the situation in those countries. Significant differences exist between CEE countries as regards the role of own-account road transport. This is illustrated in Table 12.4. In the years 1990–94 in these five CEE countries the share of own-account road transport decreased, namely from 78 to 69 per cent in tonnes and in tonne-km from 56 to 46 per cent. This may be considered a normal and expected tendency (see above, Section 6.1 under 2).

Table 12.4   Ratio of own-account to hire and reward road transport

Country	Tonne	Tonne-km
Czech Republic	36:64	64:34
Hungary	80:20	88:12
Poland	29:71	53:47
Romania	27:73	27:73
Slovakia	8:92	41:59

Source: Burnewicz et al. (1996).

During the first stage (1989–92) of liberalization of the economy in the CEE countries the number of small enterprises (almost entirely in road transport) grew dramatically. In this period a highly advanced diffusion of the market occurred, which at present requires a policy to encourage the fusion of

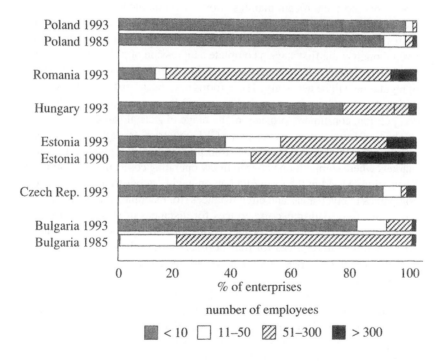

Figure 12.7   Structure of road transport enterprises according to number of employees

enterprises and the formation of group alliances. The scale of the diffusion, however, was different in individual countries, as shown in Figure 12.7. The biggest diffusion took place in Poland (more than 95 per cent of road enterprises employ fewer than ten persons), the smallest in Romania (predominantly by enterprises employing 51–300 persons).

New legislation concerning access to the carrier profession will harmonize the various transport enterprise structures in the CEE countries. The number of transport enterprises has not grown since 1997, rather it has been dropping. New types of enterprises have appeared: those which are holders of licences for the exploitation of road, rail, air and inland waterway infrastructure, in contrast to licences for transporting goods and persons.

8　NEW MARKET RELATIONS

8.1　Transformation as a Change in Market Relations

One of the most significant manifestations of economic transformation is the formation of new market relations. This does not seem to be a simple transition from a situation of direct decision making by the state to one of free competition. Even though at the first stage a complete suppression of old supply regulation instruments is undertaken, in the course of time a reintroduction of certain forms of regulation will be necessary. These forms have been verified in the countries with a developed market economy (carriers' licences, control of fairness of competition, consumers' protection, the range of state aid and so on).

The transformation processes of the CEE countries' transport sector consist, among other things, in a transition from predominantly regulated markets to markets where competition between freely operating companies predominates. Regulation existed in the form of a ban on having goods transported by some companies in given areas and circumstances (for example, in Poland there was a ban on cargo road transport services for distances of more than 100 km), instructions for the purchase of means of transport from specific producers, fixed administrative prices for transport services, obligatory organizational structures (for example, central associations created by the Ministry of Transport) and the like.

It is, of course, governments that decide on the replacement of central regulations. However, at present, associations of enterprises, including those of transport firms (for example, the National Economic House in Poland) can also influence parliament in order to change certain laws.[8] Government in CEE countries mostly having a liberal political orientation, they are not interested in preserving the old regulatory legal instruments. Delays in the liberalization of market relations are arising more as a result of pressure from the employees of large state-owned companies, unwilling to remove the state protective umbrella. As an example, the attempts in Poland to introduce the principle of universal access to bus station infrastructure by all companies in the market were treated by the staff of the state-owned bus company (PKS) as an attack on their property, which they had been developing for decades. In return, small private bus companies tried to organize services in the vicinity of those bus stations shortly before the scheduled departures of the buses. Thereby, a new form of unfair competition arose which had to be regulated according to the spirit of liberal market relations.

8.2 The Change in Market Relations during the Transition Period

In the CEE countries, before the beginning of the transformation process, the fundamental elements of the market mechanism in the transport sector either did not function at all or they functioned on a limited scale only, for example, rates were fixed. In addition, independent companies existed, acting on their own account in small market sectors. It was only in these sectors that the beginnings of competition could be discerned. Application of rates unrealistic to the market situation led to economic chaos, and caused chronic loss making in a number of companies, which, in turn, required that state subsidies be applied.

Soon enough, in almost all CEE countries, it became commonly accepted that it would be necessary to change the relations in the transport markets. The centralized structures of the management of transport organizations caused a lowering of the efficiency of the production of transport; moreover, they presented a strong barrier to the formation of new market relations based on economic criteria.

Thus, the task for the transition period has been to bring about changes in the behaviour of transport companies – which for the most part were state-owned – including monopolistic ones, as well as their adaptation to market conditions. The shaping of rules for the free market economy will be possible at the time when characteristics such as freedom of decision making, the development of a private sector, a partial deregulation of the market, price liberalization and a limitation of state subsidies have become widespread.

8.3 Experiences in the Shaping of New Market Relations

Looking for patterns of market relations in transport in the EU countries has often resulted in disappointments for the proponents of liberalized markets. The transport sector in the CEE countries was usually not aware of the real state of and the substantial delays in transport integration in the EU or of the existence of significant differences in the approach to regulation of the transport market in particular member countries (from strong regulation in Germany and France to liberalism in the UK and the Netherlands).

In some CEE countries deregulation in road transport was carried out very early (for example, in Poland in 1989). Yet, after a few years the difficult process of the introduction of certain – unpopular – restrictions in the form of licensing had to be initiated. It is both surprising and incomprehensible to many economic activists that the sudden liberalization of access to the trade was not accompanied by the liberalization of access to international markets. The existing contingents of bilateral licences for road transport between specific EU countries and CEE countries were at times treated as the work of officials from the transport ministry, not as an objectively existing form of international market relations for EU transport to and from third countries.

The principles of transport subsidization did not require very radical reforms. In the majority of the countries in the 1980s, they were already being shaped in accordance with EU principles. Subsidies have been maintained in the field of (national) passenger transport for slow trains and scheduled long-distance buses. In addition, lower-level public authorities have maintained subsidies for urban and suburban rail transport as well as for public bus transport services. All forms of subsidies from the state budget for international transport services as well as for national express passenger transport have, however, been abolished.

The issues of the control of fairness of competition were not dealt with at the initial stage of the transition period. Only later did regulations concerning fairness of competition appear, yet these related to the economy as a whole. It is worth stressing that the specific Community regulations on the principles of fairness of competition in road, air and sea transport, having the nature of a decree, will automatically be put into effect after the new candidates' accession to the EU.

9   RESTRUCTURING OF THE INFRASTRUCTURE SYSTEM

9.1   Specific Characteristics of Transport Infrastructure in the CEE Countries

The concepts and definitions related to transport infrastructure have been presented in Part III of this book (Chapters 6, 7 and 8). The objective of the present section is to emphasize a peculiarity of the process of infrastructure restructuring in the CEE countries.

Transport infrastructure in the CEE countries is, largely, a relic of the former system of a socialist economy. That infrastructure was developed for the needs of the system, with such industries as heavy mining, heavy chemical, and building materials predominating. In order to secure an efficient transport of large quantities of raw materials, railway lines and bulk transhipment terminals at seaports were being expanded as a priority.

Although the agricultural sector contributed substantially to the economy, an appropriate road infrastructure in agricultural regions was not created. These regions were doomed to using simple forms of transport on own account (in particular, farm tractors). The limited significance of the time factor and the low level of the development of individual motorization did not provide the state with the justification for undertaking a programme for the construction of motorways and expressways.

The policy of separation of CEE countries from the outside (Western) world was the cause of underdevelopment in air transport, the scope of which was generally limited to the airport near the capital and a few regional cities.

None the less, the development of transport infrastructure was more visible in a quantitative rather than a qualitative aspect (Burnewicz and Wojewódzka-Król, 1993). Specifically, in rail transport the network was being expanded as long ago as the early 1980s. This meant that after the beginning of the restructuring of the industry the uselessness of a significant part of the lines, which were of local importance only, was disclosed. Even trunk lines (double-track lines, electrified lines) only allowed for traffic at a technical speed of less than 100–110 km/h. Hard-surfaced public roads were constructed of poor-quality materials and were damaged prematurely. Yet, in the years 1970–85 in the whole of the CEE countries their length increased by 8–9 per cent. The biggest infrastructure development occurred in the oil pipeline network, the length of which was more than doubled in the period mentioned. The most neglected investment in infrastructure was for inland navigation. The navigable waterway network was even reduced in size and degraded in terms of depth. The state of infrastructure at the starting-point of economic transformation can be summed up as in Table 12.5.

A quantitative analysis of the infrastructural networks in the table shows that the situation in the CEE countries does not differ from the average infrastructural condition in the EU. However, quite different findings result from a qualitative analysis. Such an analysis indicates that the quality of infrastructure in CEE countries differs considerably from West European conditions. Furthermore, this quality is such that it does not suit the needs of the development of transport, especially road transport, in CEE countries.

9.2 CEE Transport Infrastructure and Trans-European Networks

The new political situation in Europe has made real the plans for the creation of a uniform transport infrastructure on the continent. Hence, the restructuring

Table 12.5   Characteristics of road and rail infrastructure in CEE countries

Positive	Negative
Road infrastructure	
Sufficient density of the total network of public roads, slightly departing from the average density in the EU	Poor condition of the road network, gross negligence in maintenance work
	Lack of motorways, making non-collisional transit traffic impossible
	Low share of motorways and expressways in the total network of hard-surfaced roads (in particular in Poland and the republics of the former Soviet Union)
	Large share of soil-surfaced roads, particularly as regards non-urban roads
	Insufficient number of urban ring roads within the interregional road network
	Insufficient capacity of border crossings towards the routes of heavy passenger and freight traffic
Rail infrastructure	
High density of lines – equal to or higher than the average in the EU (for example, in Poland: 7.5 km/100 km$^{2)}$ Higher than average density of lines in the EU (6.2 km/100 km^2) Large extent of electrified lines in severalCEE countries (for example, Poland, Hungary)	Low share of railway lines with single and double tracks in the total length of standard railways Outdated type of electric traction Insignificant scope of specialization according to lines exclusively for passenger or for freight transport – limits the speed of passenger trains as well as quality and comfort of rail travel Lack of fast railway networks

of the transport infrastructure system in CEE countries is not limited to modernization and qualitative improvement of already existing networks. It also means that CEE countries will join in the design of a trans-European network, that is, in the creation of new structures of a highly advanced technology. The prospect of spatial enlargement of the European Union and of growing transit traffic makes the adaptation of transport infrastructure in CEE countries to the EU system, as well as its further development, in the interest of Western Europe. Therefore, since the beginning of the transformation period, CEE countries and the EU have been cooperating in the field of infrastructure development. This cooperation consists in determining directions and necessities for infrastructure development (Transport Infrastructure Needs Assessment – TINA – process), as well as in giving financial aid, in the case of priority projects as seen from the EU viewpoint.[9]

One of the fundamental objectives of European transport policy is the creation of trans-European transport networks (TENs). The pan-European conferences held in Crete in 1994 and in Helsinki, Finland in 1997 proved that a common challenge for Eastern and Western Europe is the creation of a uniform network throughout Europe, by the realization of a programme to construct ten pan-European transport corridors.[10]

9.3 The Transformation of the Financing System of Transport Infrastructure

Transport infrastructure in CEE countries in the past was financed almost entirely from the state budget. The economic transformation opened new opportunities for non-traditional financing (for example, public–private partnerships) besides the use of EU aid funds, credits, and other external funds. Therefore, the financing issues of transport infrastructure in CEE countries parallel those in Western Europe. On the other hand, both the budgetary possibilities of the CEE countries and private resources are significantly lower. The global needs for investment in transport infrastructure in the CEE countries are estimated at a minimum of 1 per cent of GDP. This sum does not allow for the finance of big investment projects – which amount to more than 2.5 per cent of GDP. It will be realistic to take into account both that economic growth will most likely stay at a higher level and that the real value of investments will increase.

The motorway stretches which have been built in a number of CEE countries were financed in a non-traditional way, for example, in Poland through the granting of a licence. The licensee finances about 85 per cent of the project, while he can obtain government guarantees of up to 50 per cent of the project.

The first experiences of infrastructure investment financing coming from new sources have raised new problems. The involvement of private capital is not as high as was expected. The reasons for this include the following:

1. the limited existence of private capital (Wojewódzka-Król and Rydzkowski, 1997);
2. problems with obtaining suitable credits from national and international banks by private investors;
3. EBRD (European Bank for Reconstruction and Development) and EIB (European Investment Bank) credits are limited to up to 50 per cent of the costs and are subject to government guarantees.[11]

The CEE countries expect to obtain substantial project financing from their respective state budgets, from aid funds and from preferential credits from banks and international institutions. However, investment needs in transport in Western European countries are relatively high and the financial resources are limited. Therefore, it is not realistic for CEE countries to expect easy access to new investment funds. The transformation of the transport system taking place, especially the introduction of the private sector on a much larger scale, does not absolve the state budgets from their responsibility and does not allow for a reduction of financial means from these resources. On the contrary, it is necessary to revive the role of finance from public sources and to allocate bigger budget resources to infrastructural investment in transport.

10   CONCLUSIONS

The transport sector in CEE countries is one of the most difficult fields of economic transformation. It may be that its restructuring is not as difficult as in agriculture, and in the mining and metallurgical industries, but the latter do not proceed at such a quick rate as could be expected. Above all, in the transport sector the effects are visible of the birth of a large number of new companies, together with changes in ownership, in modal structure and in the forms of services carried out.

In some countries, the non-effective state-owned sector has been retained, in the privatization of which neither national nor international capital is interested, while labour generally is opposed to privatization.

The transformation of the transport sector has been greatly influenced by the integration with the EU. The effect of this integration is expressed in the rapid enactment of new legislation (in Poland, Hungary and the Czech Republic to date about 50–60 per cent of EU transport regulations and directives have already been adopted). It is also expressed in a highly advanced technical transformation of both infrastructure and the transport fleet. The transformation of employees' attitudes such that there will be complete acceptance of free competition on transport markets will require a longer time.

NOTES

1. Infrastructure lobbies consist of enterprises of the construction industry, the public roads administration and sea- and airports' managing boards.
2. PHARE = 'Poland Hungary Aid for the Reconstruction of the Economy'. The goals of the PHARE programme are the reorientation of the economies, the support for the establishment of market economies and the development of pluralistic political systems – at first (1989) only of Hungary and Poland and later on of all applicants for EU membership.
3. An example is a case of licence granting for national road transport to persons in Poland: in 1996 a draft on licence granting for this kind of transport was elaborated, and in 1997 the Sejm – the Lower House of the Polish parliament – passed an act from which the notion of 'licence' was entirely omitted (it was replaced by the notion of 'permit').
4. Both rates of transport intensity are undoubtedly distorted, due to the use of the official exchange rate in converting GDP into euros. This exchange rate seems to be unnaturally low.

In fact, the national currency value of Poland, the Czech Republic, Slovakia and Hungary should be about twice as high. If one adopts this figure, the divergence between transport intensity rates in CEE and EU countries would be within the limits of 20–50 per cent. The evidence of this is the fact that by expressing passenger transport intensity in the number of passenger-km per inhabitant higher rates are obtained for the EU than for CEE countries, even though the difference has been decreasing radically since 1995.

5. Hungary: Act No. 1 of 1988 on road transport and Government Decree No. 89 of 1989 on putting into effect of Act No. 1/1988 (Molnár, 1996); Poland: Act of 23 December 1988 on economic activity and on the economic activity with foreign partnership; Czech Republic: 1990 – small privatization; 1991 – large privatization (Opletal and Ryba, 1996).

6. Romania introduced legislation stimulating the process of demonopolization and transport privatization in 1990 (Act No. 31/1990) and 1991 (Act No. 58/1991), amending these in 1995 with an act on accelerated privatization. In Romania, 223 enterprises out of 252 still existing large state-owned motor-car enterprises were in the process of privatization in 1996 (Diaconu, 1996).

   The privatization process in Bulgaria – Act of May 1992 (Ivanova, 1996) – and in Estonia – Act on privatization of state-owned enterprises of 17 February 1994 (Puntaks, 1996) – began with a slight delay and the process has still advanced only a little.

7. For 1997 the data did not fully equal 100.

8. The National Economic House ('Krajowa Izba Gospodarcza') is the most important economic self-governing institution in Poland. It is the main representation of businessmen and entrepreneurs in relation to the state and local authorities ('voivodhips'). Among other such institutions, the Confederation of Polish Employers ('Konfederacja Pracodawcow Polskich') may be mentioned.

9. Transport Infrastructure Needs Assessment – TINA – was launched by the European Commission, with respect to the candidate countries for accession to the EU, as a result of the joint ministerial meeting in September 1995. TINA should help to identify the broad measures regarding trans-European networks necessary in the candidate countries. The TINA initiative has subdivided its work into three geographically orientated subgroups, namely for the Baltic Sea area, Central Europe and South-eastern Europe. The subgroups have analysed regional needs in detail.

10. Nine corridors were agreed at the Crete conference, and the tenth one in Helsinki.

11. The EBRD exists to foster the transition towards open market-orientated economies and to promote private and entrepreneurial initiative in the countries of Central and Eastern Europe and the Commonwealth of Independent States (the former Soviet Union) committed to and applying the principles of multiparty democracy, pluralism and market economics. The EIB is the financing institution of the European Union.

REFERENCES

Bąk, M. (1997), *Transport jako przedmiot i czynnik integracjhi europejskiej* (Transport as an object and determinant in European integration), Sopot: University of Gdansk.

Burnewicz, J. (1996), 'Overview of main issues and problems', in European Conference of Ministers of Transport, *Access to European Transport Markets*, Seminar on the Integration of Central and Eastern European Operators in European Transport Markets, Paris: OECD, pp. 25–44.

Burnewicz, J. (1998), 'Transformation of inter-urban transport structures in countries in transition (a. goods, b. passenger)', in European Conference of Ministers of Transport, *Intercity Transport Markets in Countries in Transition*, Round Table 106, Paris: OECD, pp. 221–65.

Burnewicz, J. and K. Wojewódzka-Król (1993), *Europejska polityka transportowa* (European transport policy), Sopot: University of Gdansk.

Burnewicz, J., M. Bąk, E. Adamowicz and A. Kozlak (1996), *Transport routier de marchandises pour compte propre dans les pays d'Europe Centrale et Orientale* (Road transport for own account in Central and Eastern Europe), Geneva: International Road Transport Union.

Central Statistical Office of Poland (1987–97), *Statistical Yearbooks 1986–1995*, Warsaw.

Chatelus, G. (1995), 'Indicateurs économiques et transport dans les principaux pays d'Europe Centrale' (Economic indicators and transport in the principal countries of Central Europe), in Séminaire de Barbizon, *De la transition à l'intégration: quelles conditions pour les transports?*, Paris: Paradigme, pp. 15–38.

Diaconu, P. (1996), 'Privatisation and deregulation of road freight transport: lessons learnt, mistakes made. Case study: Romania', in European Conference of Ministers of Transport, *Privatisation and Regulation of Road Freight Transport*, Seminar, Paris, 5 September, Paris: OECD, pp. 6–7, 10–11, 15.

Economic Commission for Europe (ECE) (1995), *Transport Policy Trends. Bulgaria's Replies to the Questionnaire Issued by the Inland Transport Committee*, Geneva: United Nations.

Economic Commission for Europe (ECE), Inland Transport Committee (1997a), *Development Regarding Transport Policies. Replies to the Questionnaire on Transport Development. Transmitted by the Governments of the Czech Republic, Hungary and Lithuania*, Trans/WP.5/1997/1, Geneva: United Nations.

Economic Commission for Europe (ECE), Inland Transport Committee (1997b), *Development Regarding Transport Policies. Replies to the Questionnaire on Transport Development. Transmitted by the Governments of Estonia and Latvia*, Trans/WP.5/1/Add.1, Geneva: United Nations.

Economic Commission for Europe (ECE), Inland Transport Committee (1997c), *Development Regarding Transport Policies. Replies to the Questionnaire on Transport Development. Transmitted by the Government of Romania*, Trans/WP.5/1/Add.10, Geneva: United Nations.

European Commission (1995), *White Paper on the Preparation of the Associated Countries of Central and Eastern Europe for Integration into the Internal Market of the Union*, COM(95)163/FIN/2, Brussels.

European Commission (1997a), 'Agenda 2000. Commission opinion on the Czech Republic's/Hungary's/Poland's/Slovakia's application for membership of the European Union', *Bulletin of the European Union*, Supplement 14/97, 91–2; Supplement 6/97, 87–8; Supplement 7/97, 99–100; Supplement 9/97, 85–8.

European Commission (1997b), 'Agenda 2000. For a stronger and wider union', *Bulletin of the European Union*, Supplement 5/97, 7–76.

European Commission, DG Transport, and Statistical Office of the European Communities (1997), *EU Transport in Figures: Statistical Pocketbook*, Luxemburg: Office for Official Publications of the European Communities.

Gaspard, M. (1996), *Transport Infrastructure Financing in Central and Eastern Europe*, Paris: Presses de l'école nationale des Ponts et Chaussées.

Gołębiowski, J. (1995), 'Transformacja' (Transformation), in W. Pomykało (ed.), *Encyklopedia biznesu*, Vols I, II, Praca zbiorowa pod, Warsaw: Fundacja Innowacji, p. 993.

Hübner, D. (1992), 'Transformacja w Europie Srodkowo – Wschodniej' (Transformation in Central and Eastern Europe), in L. Ciamaga, *Polskie przemiany. Transformacja rynkowa* (Polish transformations. Market transformation), Warsaw: Polish Scientific Publishing House, pp. 50–89.

Hungarian Central Statistical Office (1996), *Statistical Yearbook of Hungary 1995*, Budapest.

Ivanova, A. (1996), 'Privatisation and deregulation of road freight transport: lessons learnt, mistakes made. Case study: Bulgaria', in European Conference of Ministers of Transport, *Privatisation and Regulation of Road Freight Transport*, Seminar, Paris, 5 September, Paris: OECD, pp. 2–7.

Ministry of Transport (1993), *Transport Policy in the Czech Republic*, Prague.

Ministry of Transport, Communication and Water Management (1996), *Transport Policy of the Government of the Republic of Hungary*, Budapest.

Ministry of Transport and Maritime Economy (1995), *Transport Policy in Poland. Action Program to Transform Transport into a System in Line with Market Economy Requirements and the New Conditions for Economic Co-operation in Europe*, Warsaw.

Molnár, É. (1996), 'Privatisation and deregulation of road freight transport: lessons learnt, mistakes made. Case study: Hungary', in European Conference of Ministers of Transport, *Privatisation and Regulation of Road Freight Transport*, Seminar, Paris, 5 September, Paris: OECD, pp. 11, 18–22.

Olants, A. (1995), 'International road carriage policy in Latvia and integration into the European market', in European Conference of Ministers of Transport, *Seminar on the Integration of Central and Eastern European Operators in European Transport Markets*, Paris: OECD, pp. 141–5.

Opletal, J. and J. Ryba (1996), 'Privatisation and deregulation of road freight transport: lessons learnt, mistakes made. Case study: Czech Republic', in European Conference of Ministers of Transport, *Privatisation and Regulation of Road Freight Transport*, Seminar, Paris, 5 September, Paris: OECD, pp. 5, 9.

Puntaks, J. (1996), 'Privatisation and deregulation of road freight transport: lessons learnt, mistakes made. Case study: Latvia', in European Conference of Ministers of Transport, *Privatisation and Regulation of Road Freight Transport*, Seminar, Paris, 5 September, Paris: OECD, pp. 12–13.

Ruppert, L. (1999), 'Which new markets (CEECs)?', in European Conference of Ministers of Transport, *Which Changes for Transport in the Next Century?*, 14th International Symposium on Theory and Practice in Transport Economics, Innsbruck, 21–23 October 1997, Topic 1: 'What is the future for transport?', Paris: OECD, pp. 109–34.

Wojewódzka-Król, K. and W. Rydzkowski (1997), *Współczesne problemy polityki transportowej* (Present problems of transport policy in Poland), Warsaw: Polish Scientific Publishing House.

13. The new economics of sustainable transport in developing countries: incentives and institutions

Ken Gwilliam

1 THE CONCEPT OF SUSTAINABLE TRANSPORT

A recent World Bank transport policy review (World Bank, 1996) identified the major strategic challenges facing the developing and transitional economies. These included the longstanding problems of inadequate accessibility in some of the very poorest countries and regions and the worldwide crisis in asset maintenance in the sector, as well as the relatively new problems associated with motorization, the globalization of trade and the increased attention to consumer demands and service quality which that requires.

Sustainability is proposed as the philosophical framework for addressing all of these problems. While focusing on sustainability is now commonplace, the World Bank interpretation of the concept for policy purposes is less conventional. In the context of development, the report referred to gives equal emphasis to the economic and social dimensions of sustainability on the one hand and to the environmental and ecological issues which are normally associated with the sustainability concept on the other. The report highlights several respects in which there is a close synergy between the dimensions of sustainability (for example, improving technical efficiency contributes simultaneously to improvements in all dimensions), so that social and environmental objectives cannot sensibly be pursued in isolation from the economic and financial viability of transport systems (Figure 13.1). In those respects it would appear that traditional economic prescriptions, particularly in respect of getting the prices right (charging all costs, including external costs, to those that cause these costs to occur), still remain as appropriate as ever (see the more detailed treatment of this topic in Chapter 7 of this book).

The World Bank report also observes a number of respects in which there are tensions between objectives which requires political judgements to be made (Figure 13.2). By implication this means that there can be no simple 'one size fits all' policy for sustainability. Expressed in conventional economic terms,

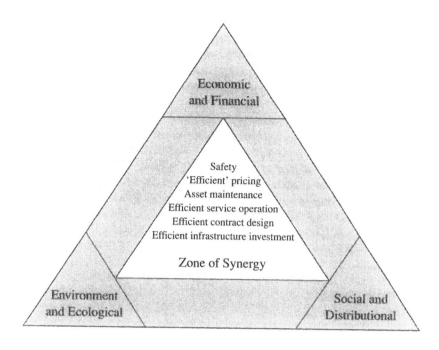

Economic
and Financial

Safety
'Efficient' pricing
Asset maintenance
Efficient service operation
Efficient contract design
Efficient infrastructure investment

Zone of Synergy

Environment
and Ecological

Social and
Distributional

Figure 13.1   Synergy of sustainability objectives

differences in these fundamental judgements may be interpreted to imply that
there are no universally applicable prices which can be employed in the internalization of external effects. This suggests more care in the international
transfer of evaluation conventions, and, by implication, emphasis on the need
for even more behavioural studies to derive implicit valuations.

If that were the full extent of the challenge to conventional economic analysis,
the profession could rest easy. Unfortunately, even in respect of the economic
externality of road congestion, effective internalization of external effects
through pricing has hardly been achieved anywhere in the world (despite the
much vaunted experience of Singapore – see Chapter 11, Section 4, also for
some other cities). Furthermore, the 'second-best' economic solution of compensatory subsidization of non-polluting or non-congesting public transport is
becoming less rather than more politically feasible as fiscal systems fail and as
direct government provision of transport service to handle externalities is
discredited. Those same failures have also undermined the traditional means
of pursuing distributional objectives through subsidy of transport services for
the poor.

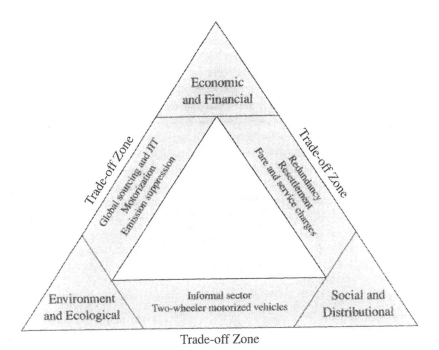

Figure 13.2   Conflict of sustainability objectives

In respect of environmental objectives, the political judgements often take forms (such as the specification of minimum acceptable performance levels) which cannot readily be converted into price equivalents for internalization. Particularly in relation to internationally distributed effects such as global warming, the issues concerning the international distribution of responsibility for costs and benefits may actually dominate all other considerations in determining national policies. While tradable pollution permits have already enabled economic processes to have scope in some markets (for example, sulphur in the USA), the international dimensions of such schemes, particularly the initial determination of standards and distribution of rights which are fundamental to the development of the market, are relatively poorly developed areas.

The worldwide response to these failures of traditional mechanisms – both in developed and in developing economies – has been to attempt to separate the 'political' elements of political economy (including questions of welfare distribution and environmental protection) from the economic. This has usually involved attempts to create a more commercial basis for provision of transport infrastructure and services, mobilizing increased private participation in supply

(Meyer and Gómez-Ibáñez, 1993). Even in the industrialized economies, with well-developed capital markets and commercial institutions, this has not been easy. In developing and transitional economies lacking such experience and institutions it is even more difficult.

The role of the private sector in transport is already great. At the global level, shipping, road haulage, taxi and paratransit services are almost exclusively privately supplied. About 80 per cent of air transport and bus services are privatized. Even in the rail sector, virtually all railways in Latin America are already privatized and private ownership is extending in both Europe and Africa. When it comes to infrastructure the story is different. Although private financing of transport infrastructure has increased greatly during the present decade, it is very heavily concentrated both modally – in ports, airports, freight railways and toll roads – and spatially – in Latin America and East Asia (Figure 13.3).

Both government and private sector have contributed to limiting private sector provision of transport infrastructure. Governments tend to be concerned that they will lose control over strategic infrastructure; that the private sector will exploit monopoly power and will not contribute to the traditional pursuit of social objectives in the sector. The private sector needs a secure revenue source to justify its involvement, and fears commercially damaging political intervention. The critical challenges in planning for private participation in the sector thus concern the way in which a more commercial transport sector can be structured to handle the perennial problems of traditional market failure such

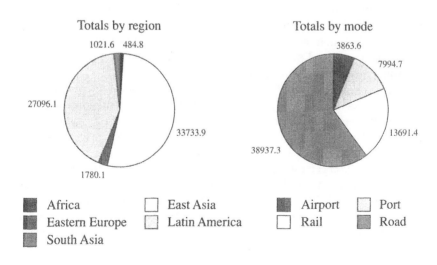

Figure 13.3   Distribution of private investment in transport infrastructure by mode and by region (US$m)

as intersectoral resource allocation, natural monopoly, externalities, and social and distributional impacts. The rest of this chapter considers, in four selected areas, the economic issues confronted in trying to avoid the classical features of market failure while at the same time avoiding the wastes of monopoly exploitation or severe regulatory failure (commercialization of road maintenance finance, highway concessions and tolls, private participation in rail transport, and competitive franchising of urban public transport services).

2   COMMERCIALIZATION OF ROAD MAINTENANCE FINANCE

During the two decades up to 1990, it was estimated that US$45 billion worth of road assets were lost in 85 developing countries due to inadequate funding of road maintenance. This was almost exactly equal to the amount invested by the World Bank in new roads over the same period (World Bank, 1988). While awareness of this problem has increased in the 1990s, the problem of inadequate maintenance, primarily of roads but also of other publicly provided transport infrastructure, remains the most serious transport policy issue not only in Africa but also in Latin America and some parts of Asia.

In the short term, deferral of road maintenance is very tempting as road deterioration reveals its consequences rather late in the process of decay. Thus, at the political level, expenditure on timely maintenance does not yield such obvious benefits as new investment, despite the fact that in the long term, investment expenditure undertaken at the expense of optimum maintenance is demonstrably counterproductive. The consequence is a tendency for myopic underfunding of road maintenance in developing countries, particularly in immature democracies with short electoral cycles.

At the simplistic level of government financing, deferral may even seem rational. Certainly, deferring maintenance until roads need major reconstruction results in total road agency costs which can, in total, be up to three times those involved in a policy of effective current maintenance. Even using a discount rate of 12 per cent the net present cost of a policy of deferring maintenance has been estimated to be more than one-third in excess of that of a timely maintenance policy. But in many developing countries the fiscal position is so weak that there may be many potential uses of public funds which can yield economic (and even financial) rates of return well in excess of the conventional 10–12 per cent rate of return cut-off for public investments. Hence for the government it may appear perfectly rational to defer expenditures on road maintenance (World Bank, 1996).

The policies pursued by many national aid agencies, as well as by some of the multilateral agencies and development banks, may have contributed to this sense of rationality. For, if soft funding is available for new investment or major reconstruction, but not for current maintenance expenditures, the calculations are shifted even further in the direction of postponing maintenance. The more favourable the terms for funding reconstruction compared with funding routine maintenance, the greater the incentive to the recipient governments to defer maintenance.

But even that does not make deferral of road maintenance truly economically rational. The essential problem is that vehicle operating costs are a high proportion of total costs of transport, and increase progressively as road conditions deteriorate. It has been estimated that for a road carrying 500 vehicles per day, which is already in poor condition, every dollar saved in the annual expenditure on road maintenance will increase the total operating costs of vehicles on that road by between 3 and 6 dollars in the same yearly period. What may appear to be rational politically (because votes can be more easily won by highly visible new investments than by timely maintenance) or even fiscally (because external funding is more cheaply obtained for reconstruction than for maintenance) is therefore not economically rational, however low the discount rate (World Bank, 1996).

Unfortunately, road users, and particularly commercial road users, are often in a relatively weak position to affect decisions concerning the allocation of government resources. Those who vote may have little understanding of the harm that inadequate road maintenance does to them, while those understanding commercial road users on whom the impact immediately falls (but who eventually pass the cost impacts on to others) may have low voting strength. The problem of underfunding for road maintenance is thus a problem of inadequacy of the existing institutions and the incentive structures that those institutions provide.

In some countries this problem has been addressed by the establishment of a single-purpose *Road Fund* as an institutional device through which a selected stream of tax revenues is earmarked for a government road department or agency without being subjected to general budget procedures and reviews. In the 1960s and 1970s, such Road Funds were established in Africa, Latin America and Asia, and several of the Road Funds established more recently in Eastern Europe (Russia, Georgia) are based on this model.

The empirical evidence on the effect of earmarking on resource allocation is relatively weak. Wherever the government retains control over the level of the user charges or over the allocation of complementary funds, the total level of funding may be just as vulnerable with a Road Fund as without one. In Colombia, for example, although the 'earmarked funds' for the National Road Fund grew at the same rate as GDP between 1979 and 1987, total funding for roads grew more slowly than GDP as supplementary budget funding declined and the road network continued to deteriorate (McCleary and Tobin, 1990).

Such 'earmarked' budgetary arrangements have also been criticized on the grounds that they limit macro flexibility and undermine stabilization programmes. For these macroeconomic reasons, the World Bank and the International Monetary Fund have traditionally opposed them (Potter, 1997). The critical issue is thus how to reconcile macro and micro efficiency considerations.

In an attempt to secure this reconciliation the emphasis has shifted from the establishment of earmarked taxation arrangements to a new agenda to commercialize the road sector (Heggie and Vickers, 1998). So-called 'second-generation Road Funds' are characterized by being funded by levies or surcharges designated as 'user charges' and identified separately from general taxation. Revenues are paid directly into a fund managed by a Road Board whose membership is chosen to represent users. The Board determines both the level of charges and the allocation of expenditures.

2.1   Road Funds

The introduction of Road Funds will improve the efficiency of resource allocation if users are more willing to pay for maintenance because payments are seen to be channelled more directly to the provision of a service of value to the users. Many countries in sub-Saharan Africa have experienced such a crisis of maintenance for the main trunk road network. Commercial road vehicle users have demonstrated a willingness to levy an additional charge on fuel so long as the revenues are devoted to maintaining the 'core' network. In Kenya and Tanzania, where only about one-third of the paved roads were in good condition, it was estimated that savings to users in the form of lower vehicle operating costs due to improved road maintenance would be between three to four times the costs of eliminating the underfunding of road maintenance.

The introduction of 'road-user charges' payable directly to a Road Fund can also improve operational efficiency within the road agencies if it facilitates a larger degree of autonomy from 'unwarranted' political interference. There is already some relevant empirical evidence. Budget approval and disbursement in many countries is delayed as a result of political wrangling. Studies in Latin America show part of the reason for low equipment utilization rates and low number of kilometres maintained per employee is the insecurity or untimely availability of the funding to maintain regular work schedules and to buy fuel and supplies (Gyamfi, 1992). Even if the 'total level' of road funding is open to competition from other demands, a Road Fund may enable the executing agency to perform more efficiently by guaranteeing the availability of a secure 'core of funding'. In Ghana, the establishment of a Road Fund has substantially reduced the problems of disruption to the planning and execution of maintenance work. These disruptions were caused by delays in budget approval, delays in release of budget allocations, and lack of synchronization between the budget year (the calendar year) and the construction season (September to May). These delays necessitated the awarding of small continuation contracts to contractors to whom the administration was already committed. With the establishment of Road Funds payment, delays have been eliminated, giving a significant boost to contractor cash flow, and enabling unit costs to be reduced by 15 to 20 per cent. The guarantee of a core of finance may also allow road agencies to extend and improve contracting-out arrangements with the private sector. In Ghana, the greater certainty of funding associated with earmarking allowed effective competitive bidding to be introduced.

2.2 The Institutional Requirements for Effective Road-user Charging

Introducing explicit 'road-user charges' is not without problems of course. Unless there is complete independence between the ability to raise specific 'road-user charges' and general taxes, there is an opportunity cost in other sectors for securing funding for roads. In developing countries with low taxable capacity, fuel taxes may account for 7 to 30 per cent of total tax revenues, and between 1 and 3.5 per cent of GDP (Gupta and Mahler, 1995). Introducing an indirect 'road-user charge', in the form of a surcharge on fuel taxes, will limit the extent to which taxes on fuel can be increased for general tax purposes and increase the gearing effect of any instability of remaining tax revenue on social expenditures such as health or education. The independence of general taxing capacity from the level of road-user charges is likely to be greatest to the extent that 'second-generation Road Funds' generate revenues through the use of vehicle licence fees, axle loading or distance fees and toll revenues.

The achievement of the benefits of second-generation Road Funds has some demanding institutional requirements. There must be a strong legal basis for users to be assured that extra charges will actually be devoted to improved maintenance. To that end an independent executive must be managed by a strong user-controlled board of management. And there must be credible external review processes to ensure that management has not been captured by limited factional interests. Second-generation Road Funds with these general characteristics were established in several African countries during the 1980s and 1990s. Similar arrangements are being considered for countries as diverse as El Salvador, Guatemala, Jordan, Lebanon and Pakistan.

Most of these arrangements are relatively new, and were established in times of crisis. Whether they will survive and continue to perform effectively is yet to be seen. In particular, there are some difficult problems of governance still to confront. In circumstances where the decay of the primary road network is the critical problem and both the costs and benefits of improved maintenance are immediately incident on commercial road users, there may be a homogeneity of interest which supersedes all differences. But where a wider diversity of facilities (including urban and rural access roads) and a wider range of interests (including private road users and frontagers) are concerned, that homogeneity of interest may diminish. Allocation of resources may then again become a major political problem as rent-seeking behaviour arises. The challenge then is not so much one of simple economic principles as one of institutional arrangements (Gwilliam and Shalizi, 1997).

3   HIGHWAY CONCESSIONS AND TOLLS

The commercialization of road agencies brings users into the management of publicly provided infrastructure, and establishes better incentive structures for the performance of maintenance and system management functions. But it still does not involve any private capital, or involve any assumption of risk by the private sector. The potential re-emergence of governance problems within the commercialized road agencies is in part due to the limitations on the nature and scope of truly private financial responsibility. Partly for that reason, and partly as a means of securing greater investment in times of scarcity of public sector investment funding, increased attention is now being given to the possibilities of private financing through the concessioning of major road facilities for tolled operation (Engel et al., 1997).

Some trunk road links, both existing and new, are capable of yielding a commercially attractive revenue if operated as tolled facilities. Major programmes of concessioning of toll roads have already been undertaken in Mexico, Malaysia and Argentina. Thailand has a more limited experience while China has extensive plans for infrastructure expansion employing various forms of public–private participation. Not all of these have been successful as purely commercial propositions. In both Argentina and Mexico, contracts have had to be renegotiated to avoid collapse (Estache and Carbajo, 1996). In both Mexico and Malaysia, much of the debt finance came from state-owned banks. In Thailand, the opening of a privately financed urban expressway in Bangkok was delayed pending resolution of conflict between government and concessionaire over the level of tolls to be charged. This experience raises questions concerning (i) optimum toll levels, and (ii) the desirability of privately financed toll roads.

3.1   Toll Setting: Profit Maximization and Welfare Maximization

Appraisals of toll road projects have suggested that the economic rate of return would be maximized at a toll which is not commercially viable and certainly substantially less than the profit-maximizing toll. The typical outcome is shown in Figure 13.4. The profit-maximizing price is determined by equating the marginal revenue of the operator (the first derivative of the revenue function) with the marginal costs of operation. The welfare-maximizing price is determined by equating marginal benefit with marginal cost. With high initial capital cost and (for uncongested facilities) very low short-run marginal costs of use, the traditional economic argument for short-run marginal cost pricing for use of sunk assets is inevitably incompatible with commercial profitability.

The discrepancy between profit- and welfare-maximizing prices arises because, even for uncongested situations, the costs are assumed to be constant, irrespective of traffic levels, while the gross benefit is a function of the amount of traffic attracted. The lower the price charged the greater the traffic, and, so long as the price covers the short-run marginal cost, the greater the benefit. Where existing alternative facilities are congested the effect is even more pronounced as benefits also accrue from reduced congestion for traffic on the alternative roads which are greater the greater the extent of diversion to the new road.

The conventional response to the basic anomaly is to argue that in order to ensure that short-run marginal cost pricing does not lead to inefficient use of investment resources it must also be accompanied by an investment criterion which compares the total welfare benefit of use of the facility with the total cost of provision – including capital cost. That is the conventional ERR

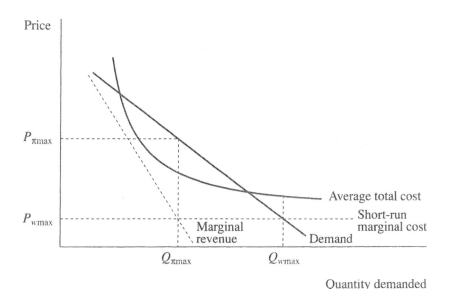

Figure 13.4   Profit- and welfare-maximizing prices

(economic rate of return) test. The equivalent pricing convention would be a requirement for the toll to cover the long-run marginal cost of extra capacity provision. If long-run average costs of extra road capacity are constant, the long-run average cost price will yield a revenue sufficient to cover capital and operating costs. Moreover, a surrogate price implemented through fuel taxation might be a reasonably efficient way of recouping that cost. But this still does not give continuous incentive to efficient use as would a short-run marginal cost price. It would also have to be supplemented by some other charge related to vehicle type to adjust for the imprecision of the relationship between fuel use and long-run marginal costs of road use.

3.2 The Case for Private Participation in Road Investment Finance

It is frequently the case that new facilities are tolled in networks in which most roads are free. In the case of the Mexican toll road programme, it was a condition that untolled alternatives should be available (Ruster, 1997). This raises two problems. First, there is a danger that the distribution of traffic between tolled and untolled roads will be both inefficient and commercially unattractive. Second, toll road operators may argue that users of toll roads are paying twice – in tolls and in fuel taxes. The implication is that it is the effective price (direct toll plus any mileage-related vehicle taxation) and not the toll itself that should equal the long-run marginal cost of provision. This appears, *prima facie*, to be an argument against private participation in road finance. In practice, in developed countries most construction is undertaken by the private sector, and in many countries the detailed design is also left to the private sector. This often works well, and it may be argued that most of the benefits of private participation can be achieved by this degree of private involvement, without relying on private sector finance. But there are two strong arguments against this in developing countries.

3.3 Efficiency Benefits of Private Supply

In many countries public sector procurement arrangements are cumbersome, slow, inefficient, and possibly corrupt. Private financial participation is assumed to lead to better control of construction time and costs, as well as more efficient operation and maintenance so that the total costs of projects are less than they would be if implemented in the public sector. Reducing the capital costs of a new facility in this way does not affect the profit-maximizing toll. However, it does lower the level of toll necessary to cover costs. Hence, reductions in capital cost can make it easier to find a toll which reconciles the need for private profitability with the needs of efficient capacity utilization. In addressing the issue of whether a project should be in the private or public sector, the benefits of any difference in costs of construction or maintenance associated with private financing should be offset against any welfare losses due to sub-optimum pricing. It is therefore desirable for an estimate of the magnitude of this cost difference to be made.

One contrary consideration is that the costs of financing may be higher in the private sector than in the public sector. In so far as this is a real cost difference it is probably due to the greater capacity of the public sector to spread and absorb risk and reflects the difference between programme financing and project financing as much as real differences in public and private sector finance.

3.4   The Shadow Price of Public Funds

In many countries, the justification for seeking private sector participation is that public sector funds are more scarce and constrained in the short run than they will be in the longer term as growth accrues. The preference for public sector funding, arising from the fact that the conventionally calculated ERR on an investment increases continuously as toll decreases to the level of short-run marginal cost, ignores the scarcity of such funds, as the conventional calculation implicitly assumes that a dollar of public expenditure has the same value as a dollar of private consumption benefit (Devarajan et al., 1997). If, instead, a premium was put on any public expenditure (whether it be a public subsidy or a capital cost contribution to the toll operator) the calculation would be altered.

3.5   The Possibility of Welfare Maximization under Private Supply

The implications of taking the differential supply efficiency of public and private sectors and the shadow price of public funds into account can be demonstrated in a simple numerical example. Consider a newly built toll road for which there is an untolled alternative. Assume that the variable road cost incurred by the toll road operator (vehicle-related road maintenance) is 1 dollar per vehicle and that the capital charges associated with the investment are \$800 per day. Assume that the demand for the road can be expressed as:

$$Q = 200 - 10P$$

(where Q is the number of vehicles per day and P is the toll per vehicle in dollars).

As revenue is equal to the toll multiplied by traffic volume, and cost is the sum of daily capital and maintenance cost, the daily net revenue – which may be a surplus or a deficit – R_N of the public sector toll road operator may be expressed as:

$$R_N = [P \cdot (200 - 10P)] - [800 + (200 - 10P)]$$

or

$$R_N = 190P - 10P^2 - 1000.$$

The net revenue of the same facility provided privately can be estimated by applying the appropriate cost deflator. Aggregate net welfare can be simply measured as the area under the demand curve less total costs at any price. However, if the infrastructure is supplied by the public sector we may consider any cost not covered by tolls as requiring some form of public subsidy. The deflation of the value of any surplus or deficit by a shadow price of public funds which is achieved through such implicit public subsidy changes the shape of the relationship between tolls and welfare, and changes the value of the optimum price. This is shown in Figure 13.5 for a shadow price of public funds of 1.5 and a 10 per cent cost advantage for construction and maintenance undertaken in the private as compared to the public sector. The price yielding the maximum net welfare is shown to increase under these assumptions from US$1 to about US$6. While this is less than the profit-maximizing price of

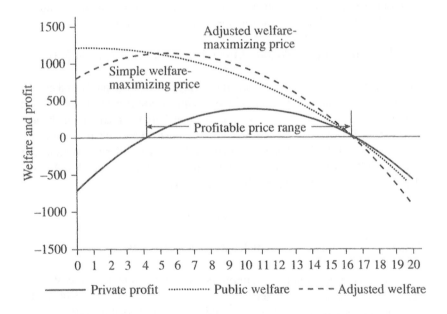

Figure 13.5   Welfare- and profit-maximizing prices adjusted for efficiency differences and the shadow price of public funds

about US$10 it does fall in the price range at which a private toll road operator could operate profitably.

3.6 Reconciling Private Finance with Optimal Pricing

If the welfare-maximizing price falls within the range of potentially profitable private supply prices, optimal pricing can be reconciled with private supply by putting a concession out to competitive tender on the condition that price is set at the calculated optimal level. Bidders should still be found for such a concession. Even if the optimal price does not fall within the profitable price range there may still be a net benefit achievable through private supply. This suggests the need for some additional methods of reconciling private sector participation with optimal pricing. Two possibilities have been tried.

3.7 Shadow Tolls

The first possibility is the use of 'shadow tolls'. In the case of recent British motorway constructions it has been shown that for private cars there is a sufficiently close relationship between the long-run marginal cost and the marginal rate of fuel tax to suggest that 'shadow toll' arrangements, involving payments from exchequer to road concessionaires based on the level of usage of facilities, might have attractive incentive characteristics (Newbery, 1994). Hence, if there is any efficiency advantage to be obtained from the incentives provided by the transfer of traffic risk to the private sector, private sector operation and finance can be reconciled with efficient resource allocation so long as the payments are in the form of competitively bid shadow tolls.

In discussing shadow tolls, it is important to note that private financibility of new roads based on the revenue stream offered on a shadow toll basis is not a sufficient test of their economic viability. Any investments so financed should also pass the economic tests applied to public sector investments. If that requirement is not enforced, the employment of shadow toll arrangements, in which there is a contractual commitment to a future flow of maintenance expenditures, may be a covert way of hypothecating tax revenues to the transport sector which would not be so allocated through the normal budgetary process.

3.8 Complementary Finance; Public–Private Partnership[1]

Government may secure private financing through concessioning the right to provide infrastructure to the private sector. The Build–Operate–Transfer (BOT) concession, in which the private sector invests and operates over a period of years before transferring ownership back to the government, is probably the most common form. Within such concessions, toll levels or structures may be limited by the contract. Where they are, it will inevitably affect the price that government can obtain for the concession. If the constraints are substantial, it will require payments from the government.

Public sector participation may take a number of forms. Direct financing of part of the construction is the most direct method. A less direct method is that of 'back-to-back' finance involving the commitment of some existing road (currently untolled) to form part of a new private facility as in the case of the M1 motorway in Hungary. In that case, users of the previously untolled section are now being subject to toll and the public purse is contributing (and hence loses) the potential toll revenues forgone. Where the financial outcome is less certain the public support may take the form of guarantees. Revenue or traffic guarantees are the most common, and were used extensively to stimulate rapid implementation in the Mexican toll road programme. Administrative devices to force traffic on to the toll road, as employed in the Hungarian case, should only be employed if there is a demonstrable congestion, safety or environmental benefit from the policy exceeding the real costs of the diversion. Otherwise the toll revenues so generated represent an earmarked tax on specific categories of users. Construction risk sharing is a more novel arrangement being implemented in a major new toll road in mountainous terrain in Colombia.

All of these arrangements are forms of subsidy which should be subject to test to demonstrate the net benefit that accrues as a result of the choice of private sector funding for the project. The appropriate cost–benefit test would compare the net benefits to users, net of any toll payments made, with the cost to the public purse of the support given. Only if that yields a positive net present value greater than that achieved by direct public financing (making appropriate allowance for a realistic shadow price of public funds) is the public–private participation scheme justified.

3.9   Welfare Distribution and Efficiency

One of the considerations that typically affects the level of toll that a private sector operator is allowed to charge is the welfare distributional impact of the proposed tolling arrangements. For example, in both Mexico and Hungary, governments insisted that tolls were only introduced on roads for which an untolled alternative was, or could be made, available.

Where a new completely private facility duplicates an existing free facility, this creates relatively little tension between efficiency and distributional objectives. In this kind of case those who have the highest values of time may be willing to pay a sufficiently high price to fund the new alternative. In practice, this represents a form of price discrimination which has improved welfare substantially, both for richer and poorer users of facilities in many other sectors (air transport, telecommunications and so on). Users of the existing facility lose nothing (and may actually gain if diversion reduces congestion on the existing road). The only possible adverse spin-off effect would be if the new road generated enough new traffic to congest some feeder facilities used jointly by new and old road users, the avoidance of which may involve some contingent public sector cost. While that may normally be a second-order effect, there may be circumstances (as, for example, in the need for new feeder facilities to deal with traffic from the Skyway toll road in Manila) where the contingent costs are unexplored but potentially very large.

Where no reasonable alternative exists, the government may actually undertake construction or improvement of untolled alternatives as part of the strategy for making privately financed toll roads acceptable, as in Mexico. Unless traffic volumes are very high indeed, this is likely to be an economically inefficient strategy.

Two important conclusions arise from the above analysis of tolling.

1. In addressing the issue of whether a project should be in the private or public sector a direct comparison should be made of the net welfare benefit of the alternatives, taking into account differences in cost, effects of any suboptimality of prices and the shadow price of public funds.
2. In assessing the appropriateness of any proposed toll levels the calculation should take into account the long-run marginal costs rather than the short-run marginal costs of road use, and should also incorporate a shadow price of public funds in comparison between alternatives with different fiscal impact.

4 PRIVATE PARTICIPATION IN RAIL TRANSPORT SYSTEMS

In most countries rail transport has been provided by a single parastatal company, ostensibly on the grounds that rail transport is a natural monopoly, and that state ownership was necessary to avoid exploitation of economic power. These countries have often had separate ministries to administer their railways (for example, in China, India and Russia) and have established strong political powerbases. In practice many state railway companies in developing countries have used resources, particularly labour, very inefficiently and have incurred deficits which have become a serious drain on the public purse (equal to nearly 1 per cent of GDP in the case of Argentine railways). This has eventually, despite the strong political position of the railway companies, led to calls for their transfer to private sector ownership or management (Tynan, 1999).

The private sector operates major freight railways in many countries including the United States, the UK and New Zealand among OECD countries and Argentina, Brazil, Bolivia, Chile, Mexico, and some African countries in the developing world. The form of private participation varies, however. Outright sale has occurred in the USA and New Zealand, and in a rather convoluted way in the UK (Van de Velde, 1999).

In the developing world, concessioning is the most common arrangement, leaving the ownership of at least the basic right of way and infrastructure reverting to the state in the long term. Concessioning of rail operations to the private sector, *per se*, is not novel, even in developing countries. For example, the only part of the Jamaican rail system to survive is that part which was concessioned to a large bauxite exporter.

Concessioning has been adopted as the channel for private participation in Argentina, Bolivia, Brazil, Chile, Mexico, and also for a number of smaller African systems. In all cases it has been possible to find a private party willing to pay for the concession. Because of the strong competition from the dominant road haulage sector (which carried 92 per cent of freight tonnage in Argentina prior to rail concessioning) it has usually been unnecessary to impose any constraints on the commercial freedom of the concessionaires. In one case in West Africa, a joint concession has been granted by the governments of Côte d'Ivoire and Burkina Faso for the operation of their national railways services.

The nature of a concession is that the right to develop a specified system or service is granted to a private party, under terms and conditions which are clearly set out in the concession contract. For example, the Argentine passenger rail concessions fix the rates in real terms and contain detailed provisions covering conditions under which these can be adjusted. Even if ownership of the assets remains public (as in the Côte d'Ivoire/Burkina Faso rail concession), or investment is financed by the government (as in Argentina), the implementation of works and maintenance of assets must be the clear responsibility of the concessionaire.

The defining difference between concessioning and privatization is that the contract is for a finite period of time. This limitation of period can create difficulties concerned both with the start of the concession and its termination.

At the outset, existing operators are likely to lose interest in system maintenance as soon as the intention to concession is announced. The experience of rapid decline in the Argentine freight railways in the two years prior to concessioning emphasizes the need for speed of process. In Mexico, this danger was confronted by immediately reconstituting the company as a joint-stock company and then bringing in private participation through the sale of stock.

A different initial problem concerns the encouragement of real investment to overcome what is often a serious backlog. The attempt to address this in

Argentina, by making a commitment to invest one of the criteria for award, does not appear to have been effective as concessionaires who, once in place, are in a strong position to ignore what they consider to be obsolete conditions of constraint. A different approach has therefore been adopted in Bolivia by using a procedure of 'recapitalization' in which the private sector buys in to a controlling road in the railway through capital payments not to the government but to the company itself.

The disincentive to invest because of the prospect of termination creates its own problems. The need to overcome this is the main reason for long concession periods – 30 years in the cases of Argentina and Brazil. But it also creates a need to supervise the concessionaire in the latter years of the concession to ensure that he maintains the value of the assets for reversion. This can also be assisted by careful initial contract design, particularly in the specification of conditions for renegotiation, extension and terms of transfer of assets to a succeeding concessionaire.

Most national rail monopolies have been restructured prior to private sector involvement, with the focus falling primarily on the degree of vertical and horizontal integration thought most likely to reconcile the desire for competition with the desire for operational efficiency.

As far as vertical integration is concerned, the OECD experience is widely polarized. US and New Zealand private railways retain the complete vertical integration which was characteristic of state railways. This is based on a belief that there is sufficient external competition for rail management to be driven to outsource functions to whatever extent is most economic, and that no structural adjustment is necessary to achieve this. In Europe, it is increasingly common to separate infrastructure from operations in order to allow competing operators on a monopoly infrastructure (Thompson, 1997) (see also Chapter 9, Section 4). The extreme case of vertical separation has been that of the UK, where track investment and management, track maintenance, rolling-stock supply, rolling-stock maintenance and train operations have been vertically separated, with different forms of competition (from regulated private monopoly in track provision, through pure market competition in the maintenance and rolling-stock leasing markets, to competitively tendered franchising in passenger service provision).

Developing countries have generally followed the vertically integrated model. Argentina, Brazil, Bolivia and Mexico are all totally integrated, with the main exception being the requirements for access for other train operators as, for example, for passenger trains under regulated charging arrangements in Argentina. But there are exceptions. In Chile, the government initially concessioned only the freight services on the broad gauge network, while keeping infrastructure and passenger services in the public sector. It is now moving, however, to concessioning the infrastructure in one piece and passenger operations in one intercity and two suburban concessions. The bi-national railway of Côte d'Ivoire and Burkino Faso, which is an unusually short period concession of fifteen years, also separates the ownership of track and equipment, which remains in the hands of two national companies, from operations which are concessioned as a whole (including both freight and passenger services). Even in India, a privately funded container operation, CONCOR, is engaged in hauling containers over the national railways network.

Horizontal separation for concessioning is the norm. Argentina and Brazil both adopted six freight packages, Mexico three and Bolivia two. This was often made very easy by the fact that the national railways had originated from regional private companies which had little interconnection or through traffic, and were often of different gauge. The primary advantage of having several different concessions is that it attracts a wider variety of bidding interest. Only in small systems, such as the Côte d'Ivoire/Burkino Faso railway, is it impracticable to create separate concessions.

Award criteria for freight concessions have also varied considerably. For the Argentinian concessions, there were seven criteria (including such qualitative items as bidder qualification, nature of the investment proposal, access changes proposed) each ranked on a scale from 1 to 10, with the award going to the bidder with the highest weighted average ranking. Curiously, the fee to be paid to government for the concession carried only 12 per cent of the total weight. Brazil adopted a different approach, specifying most of the Argentinian variables as conditions or terms of contract, and using the payment to government as the sole choice criterion. That approach has subsequently been adopted in Mexico and Bolivia, and for passenger concessions in both Argentina and Brazil.

Probably the most critical impediment to concessioning is the problem of labour redundancy. In most publicly owned railway systems, the combination of public sector employment conditions and secular decline of demand has resulted in severe overstaffing. The concessioning of railways reduced the required workforce by 80 per cent in Argentina, 60 per cent in Brazil and about half in Chile, without reducing output. Especially where governments impose obligations on enterprises in respect of forced severance, potential concessionaires will typically require the government in one way or another to accept financial responsibility for all redundancies. This needs careful design to combine the government responsibility for 'clearing the decks' with the concessionaires' ability to decide what staff to keep and what to sever. Although the returns to the fisc may be large and rapid, where the initial severance payments are large the immediate burden on the fisc may be offset by covering them through borrowing (for example, World Bank loans have facilitated railway restructuring in this way in both Argentina and Brazil).

4.1 Performance Improvement

In both Brazil and Argentina rail freight carryings have increased despite the abandonment of substantial mileages of little used track. Rates have not increased. Above all, a heavy fiscal burden has been eliminated. The main source of contention is that in some cases companies are not achieving the increases in traffic that they had reckoned on, and are in consequence unwilling to undertake investments which were promised as part of the concessioning contract. Given the absence of any realistic course of action, government is forced to tolerate that default. In a subsequent exercise in Bolivia, the form of private participation was modified to attempt to pre-empt that problem. Instead of making an up-front payment to government for the concession, the concessionaire was given a managing share in a recapitalized company, with payment for that share taking the form of resource inputs into the company.

The preliminary results of rail freight concessioning are thus generally impressive (Thompson and Budin, 1997). This is to a very large extent due to the fact that, because freight railways are viewed essentially as a normal commercial enterprise, and not a strong monopoly at that, governments have felt comfortable in relying on market competition both as the stimulus to efficiency and as the ultimate determinant of what services should be provided.

4.2 Rail Passenger Service Concessions

What is new in the rail sector is the recognition that negative concessions, in which the government pays the concessionaire for the provision of service, may make as much sense as positive concessions (Rebelo, 1999). That may require some constitutional preparation. For example, one of the problems that has slowed down the concessioning of the suburban railways and metro in Rio de Janeiro, Brazil, was the uncertain status of such long-term public sector commitments under the existing law. Again, the initial experience in Argentina has been that, with fares at levels specified by government, concessioning can improve service and patronage while at the same time reducing the burden on the fisc. That experience has led even governments with such a Marxist background as the African National Congress (ANC) in South Africa to the point of adopting a policy of regionalization and eventually concessioning of urban rail services to the private sector.

Private sector involvement in the financing of new passenger rail facilities under BOT or other similar arrangements is less common (Fouracre et al., 1990). Two large concessions have been awarded in Bangkok, and the first line, BERTS, has been operating since 1999. A third LRT (light rapid transit) line in Manila, which is mainly an elevated construction in the central reservation of the largest and busiest thoroughfare in the city, is in construction under a concession arrangement. In both of those cases, the concerns about financing appear to have dominated concerns about the integration of the new facilities within the overall urban transport system. Moreover, in both cases the absence of an effective metropolitan transport planning agency has inhibited the efficiency with which new private sector initiatives can be incorporated into the total urban transport network.

A different approach to private financing of urban transport infrastructure was attempted in Bogota, Colombia, where the government identified a corridor for which mass transit service was required but indicated its willingness to entertain proposals embodying a range of different technologies. The selection of a busway proposal, similar to that of Curitiba, Brazil, was the beginning of a story which has not yet ended. But one lesson is already clear from that experience. The broader and less precisely specified the product being procured, the greater the scope for post-award renegotiation or litigation. That is particularly troublesome in countries like Brazil where legal challenge of public contract awards is rife. Where private financing is contingent on the prior completion of works by the public sector, as in the proposed BOT for metro Line 3 in Manila, the scope for conflict is also very high.

4.3   Why do Forms of Rail Privatization Differ?

The different approaches to private participation partly reflect a learning process. The Brazilian difficulties with multicriteria ranking led subsequent privatizations to adopt a different method. The treatment of labour redundancy and of investment requirements has also become more sophisticated on the basis of experience. But there are some other more pervasive reasons for differences.

Differences in the geographic and historical structure of the railways have largely driven the degree of horizontal integration. Differences in rail market share have largely determined the extent to which it has been considered necessary to set investment or price constraints on freight railways. But the most important determinant has probably been the differences in objectives. This is exemplified particularly in the difference between freight services, which are generally viewed as inherently commercial and, therefore, requiring control only to prevent private monopoly exploitation, and passenger services, for which social objectives, both of fare and service levels, apply. Even within the passenger sector, intercity service has more generally been viewed as commercial, while urban and suburban services have an explicitly social dimension. A number of important lessons have emerged from this experience. Despite the long history of railways as a non-commercial sector, the private sector can be attracted into the market on a commercial basis if the relations between the state and the private operator are clearly set out in contractual form.

Moreover, the concession contract is a flexible instrument which can involve negative or positive payments, so that loss-making but socially necessary services can also be successfully concessioned to reduce the cost to the state of its social obligations. There is a growing number of international groups willing to enter into consortia to provide rail services under concession, so that genuine competition can be mobilized for well-designed concessions. This means that a genuine willingness to restructure and to invest in the design of a proper contractual and institutional basis for private participation in rail supply can have a large pay-off so that rail service becomes sustainable, and able to make its best contribution to the achievement of social and environmental, as well as economic, objectives (Mitric, 1998).

5 COMPETITIVE FRANCHISING OF URBAN TRANSPORT SERVICE PROVISION

In most industrialized countries, the public transport revolution of the last decade has taken the form of conscious decisions by governments to seek to reduce the fiscal burden of maintaining subsidy to existing – and usually quite high-quality – public sector passenger transport provision. Outside the industrialized countries the search for new approaches to public transport is more typically associated with progressive operational failure of conventional public transport supply whether from the public or private sector.

5.1 Overspecified Regulation

At any given level of supply efficiency, the financial outcome is determined by the quantity of service provided (frequency), its quality (vehicle type, crowding and so on) and its price. Simultaneous regulation of quantity, quality and price determines the financial outcome. The combination of high aspirations in all these dimensions in the absence of any mechanism to increase supply efficiency or to reconcile them financially is the most common reason for the failure of conventional public transport in developing countries.

The most common process by which this inconsistency affects service is that enterprises starved of funds defer vehicle maintenance. Eventually this causes vehicles to be taken off the road. Reduced service increases waiting times and on-vehicle crowding, often making it increasingly difficult even to collect fares from those who do travel. This has been the common process in West Africa where traditional services have often been replaced by informal sector services outside any effective regulatory regime.

Even competitively tendered franchising cannot solve the problem where the fundamental incompatibility of very low fares and absence of direct subsidy is not recognized. For example, in December 1994, the Jamaican government after years of decline of public transport under tight price regulation put out to competitive tender exclusive franchises for the operations of five segments of the city of Kingston for a period of ten years. Unfortunately, the franchising process was critically flawed (Gwilliam, 1996). The franchises were awarded to the bidders offering to provide the best service without subsidy under a controlled fare regime. While ostensibly recognizing that increased fares were necessary to achieve the desired level of service without subsidy, the government was unwilling to increase prices, offering instead the promise of a future fare rise and the payment of a compensating subsidy pending the introduction of a commercial fare table. Although the initial fares were adjusted for inflation in February 1996, the basic inadequacy of the fare level was not addressed, without any continuing subsidy being paid. In these circumstances, franchisees have been unable to provide the required capacity. By the end of 1997, no sustainable basis had been found for the operations and three of the franchises were in severe financial difficulties.

Outcomes can also be affected in other ways by fare regulation. In Dhaka, Bangladesh, both private and public sector vehicles have been shifted from the fare-regulated urban transport service to the unregulated intercity bus business. The public sector operator Bangladesh Road Transport Corporation, under instructions from government to improve its financial outcome, is even renovating old urban buses and leasing them to private operators to work in the interurban market. Urban passengers are increasingly forced to use smaller shared taxis at higher fares.

5.2   Unfunded Social Obligations

In the transitional economies, a common form of intervention is the imposition on the operators of obligations to offer free or reduced fares to a wide range of categories. Not only was this of dubious redistributional validity but it also made it much more difficult to enforce payment even from those who should be paying. With the disappearance of the fiscal basis for such subsidy in many transitional economies, the continuing legal commitment to widespread fare reductions has simply contributed to a financial crisis resulting in deterioration of assets and service. For example, in the Ukraine for the first four years after political liberalization 50 per cent of riders travelled free and the number of buses on the road declined at a rate of between 5 and 10 per cent per year. Similar problems affected most of the other former Soviet Union states, with cost recovery being as low as 10 per cent in some cases. Reforming these arrangements is often hindered by the fact that the concessions are embodied in national law, which central governments are loath to change, even though the financial burden falls on the municipalities.

Other unfunded public service obligations have similar, though sometimes less obvious, effects. For example, the state-owned Barbados Transport Board (BTB) is required to provide specified levels of service throughout the island at a fixed flat fare. Since 1980, however, permits have been granted to private operators for a number of 33-seat minibuses and 10-seat maxi taxis to operate primarily on shorter and more heavily patronized routes into and within the capital Bridgetown at the same flat fare. By 1992, BTB had lost most of its urban market to the new entrants. Despite a bold operational 'streamlining' in 1993 which reduced its staffing level from over ten per vehicle to under five, BTB has not recovered its position because so long as it has the obligation to provide the longer-distance services under a flat fare system the advantage of the smaller vehicles in frequency and flexibility will allow them to take the shorter-distance traffic, even if the larger vehicle could do the job at a lower unit cost and lower fare (Gwilliam, 1996). A similar distortion in the mix of vehicles has occurred in South Africa under apartheid, where the informal sector was legally prevented from operating large vehicles but nevertheless took over 50 per cent of the public passenger transport market from the state-subsidized large bus fleet operators.

5.3 Public Sector Supply and Fiscal Failure

The problem of inappropriate intervention has frequently been accentuated by state ownership to create a vicious circle of decline. As the financial condition of the parastatal services has declined it has become increasingly difficult to afford to maintain vehicles which have dropped out of service (for example, vehicle availability rate is only a little over 60 per cent in several of the central Asia republics that were part of the former Soviet Union). As services have declined, so has patronage and revenue, which has fuelled further decline. The problems of parastatal operators have been compounded by the protected status of public sector employment which could not be adjusted. In many countries the number of staff per vehicle of public sector bus operators – which should not exceed about five in any well-managed company – has exceeded twenty. In Caracas, Venezuela, the number of staff per bus reached 60 before public sector bus operations were discontinued.

In many of the transitional economies, the first impetus to liberalization comes when national governments transfer responsibility to regional or municipal governments. The motive for the transfer is usually to escape a drain on the national budget, and *ipso facto* the transfer is often unaccompanied by any intergovernmental fiscal transfer adequate to maintain traditional levels of service (Gwilliam, 1999). The ensuing local fiscal crisis typically sharpens the willingness of the local authorities to seek cost-cutting strategies. The same pressure is also likely to arise in South Africa with the devolution of responsibility from central to provincial government.

5.4 Competition in Service Supply

Developed and developing countries have a common desire to seek improvement in the performance of public transport through the introduction of stronger commercial incentives. But there is a spectrum of degrees of commercialization and private participation in supply associated with different degrees of transfer of responsibility and risk from the political level to operational management in either private or public sector (Table 13.1).

Table 13.1   Division of function between public sector (P) and private sector or concessionaires (C) under different supply arrangements

	Public monopoly	Performance agreement	Management contract	Gross cost franchise	Net cost franchise	Full concession	Free entry
Ownership of infrastructure	P	P	P	P	P	P/C	C
Ownership of rolling stock	P	P	P	P/C	P/C	C	C
Route service definition	P	P	P	P	P	P/C	C
Fares control	P	P	P	P	P	P/C	C
Revenue collection	P	P	C	P	C	C	C
Labour contract control	P	P	C/P	C	C	C	C
Operational management	P	C	C	C	C	C	C

The critical question is how to select a regime with characteristics that are appropriate to the local situation (Gwilliam and Scurfield, 1996). In the metropolitan areas of developed countries there seems to be an emerging consensus that competition for the market is likely to be preferable to competition in the market. Where multimodal integration and complicated concessionary fare arrangements are desired this is often seen to favour gross cost concessioning, involving secure means of fare collection and transfer to the concessioning authority. The achievement of the same objectives with net cost concessions requires sophisticated inter-operator venue transfer mechanisms. Both variants of franchising depend on the existence of a sophisticated, efficient and uncorrupt public administration. But many countries have no similar tradition of clean administrative competence or even of private enterprise in the supply of public services under a rule of law (Gwilliam et al., 1999). Immediate privatization of parastatals in these circumstances may simply be an invitation to mafia control, as appears to have happened in the taxi business in some Russian cities. The process of liberalization clearly needs careful adaptation to local conditions.

5.5 Commercializing Public Enterprises

The mildest, and often the first step, towards liberalization is a move from deficit financing of the publicly owned enterprise to a more arm's-length relationship formalized in a performance agreement. Such agreements are being designed in many Russian and other former Soviet Union cities (for example, Ashkabhad in Turkmenistan), as well as in cities accustomed to rather milder forms of etatism, such as Tunis. The general consensus on such agreements is that they involve only very weak incentives and penalties, and do not work very well (World Bank, 1995). But they may offer a necessary learning period, both for the enterprise and for the government, in the process of liberalization. The lesson would appear to be that performance agreements should only be introduced as part of a broader strategy involving some genuine introduction of competitive pressures and incentives.

5.6 Recognizing Social and Environmental Imperatives

It has been typical of the measures of liberalization in rich countries for reliance on cross-subsidy of social services (however defined) to be replaced by a much more explicit subsidy mechanism (often in the form of competitively tendered franchising of subsidized services). Even where some cross-subsidy has been retained, competitive tendering of balanced packages with defined service and price conditions has been used to reconcile competition with the maintenance of some unremunerative services. In many of the poorer countries which are seeking to liberalize, the essence of the problem is that there is neither any obvious market basis for internal cross-subsidy nor a fiscal basis for direct subsidy.

A common way of trying to reconcile the desire to have a cheap basic transport service for the poor with the need to maintain an adequate total supply is the introduction of multi-tier systems. For example, both in the bus and taxi markets in Korea the basic services at controlled fares are supplemented by superior services (the 'seat-bus' and the 'de-luxe taxi') allowed to charge higher prices. Capacity has been maintained simply by allowing suppliers to vary the mix of low-fare and high-fare services supplied so that the average fare rises. Air-conditioned or express services are permitted at premium prices in regimes as different as those of Jamaica (where basic services are area franchises), Buenos Aires, Argentina (where the basic services are overlapping route monopoly franchises) and even Shanghai, China (where the basic form of transport is the bicycle).

The long-term effects of relying on 'peripheral free entry' to maintain total supply are not always favourable. First, as is happening in Korea, the new entry tends to replace, rather than supplement, the basic service, so that at best waiting times increase for those dependent on the basic service. Second, the controlled fares often support such a sparse level of service that even the very poor are forced to use the peripheral services at many times the basic service cost, as in Dhaka. Third, the regulatory segmentation tends to distort the choice of technology. The fact that the public sector operators have often had a statutory monopoly in the provision of services by large vehicles has meant that their decline has artificially reduced average vehicle size (Barrett and Powell, 1999). The 16-seater minibus in South Africa and the similar sized 'jeepney' in the Philippines already serve 50 per cent of the commuting market despite the protected status given to the formal large-bus companies.

As with social objectives there is a commonly felt concern that private sector operators will be less concerned with environmental issues than the public sector. In respect of the more direct effects of vehicle emission standards, the empirical evidence hardly supports the concern. Public transport vehicles have been among the most polluting in many of the transitional economies, and there is an inherent unwillingness of government to take action against itself in such circumstances.

In respect of less direct effects there is a widespread concern that liberalization will lead to excessive supply, reduction of average vehicle size and adoption of environmentally damaging technologies. All are valid fears. But the Chilean experience in Santiago has shown that competitive franchising can be designed both to control the total amount of traffic in sensitive areas and to give high private incentives to operate in environmentally benign ways (Darbera, 1993). The beauty of embodying environmental standards within a contractual process is that there are strong incentives for both parties to ensure compliance.

5.7   The Role of the Informal Sector

A common feature of developing countries is the very large role played by the informal, non-corporate sector in the supply of public transport services. This comprises a wide range of technologies, from the rickshaw pullers of Bangladesh, through the peculiar indigenous 'jeepney' of the Philippines, to the air-conditioned special buses in Argentina. It also comprises a wide range of regulatory responses, from route licensing for the Manila jeepneys, through total vehicle stock constraints as in Bangladesh, to effective free entry (which often occurs despite formal regulatory requirements). For example, it is estimated that between 30 and 40 per cent of the minibus taxis in South Africa are currently operating illegally.

The perennial objection to the informal sector – and to free entry into the transport market more generally – is the lack of operating discipline that fragmentation engenders. Not only does this take the form of unsafe behaviour such as racing and overtaking on the road (which should in principle be controllable by the normal processes of law) but also in the development of patently uneconomic operating practices.

A common phenomenon in many countries is the development of the practice of controlling departures from terminals to secure full loads on departure. This may be enforced by associations (minibus/taxis in South Africa) or by terminal operators (Bangladesh). This has the effect of reducing the proportion of vehicle time spent in revenue-earning business, making it impossible to board buses outside terminals and hence adding walking distance to trip lengths, and undermining schedule reliability. The problem is that, once established, this practice represents a kind of prisoner's dilemma, with no individual having the incentive to break the practice even though it would be in the common interest if everyone were to do so.

Some constraints on such chaos are often self-imposed by 'operators' associations' which flourish particularly in Latin America and West and South Africa (Gwilliam, 1993). Such associations typically establish property rights – often over terminal positions or slots – by force of arms if necessary. Once entry is restricted by some means it becomes in the interests of members of the association to establish some stability and discipline in operations in order to protect the market value of the product and to distribute costs and revenues 'equitably' among members. The devices to achieve this (for example, holding vehicles in terminals until they are fully loaded) do not necessarily maximize consumer or total social welfare. However, in the context of a more regulated situation such as that in Buenos Aires, where overlapping route monopoly franchises are granted to individual associations, operators' associations may be effective in reconciling fragmented ownership with disciplined service management.

Some very special problems are arising in a number of East Asian countries such as China and Vietnam and South Asian countries such as Bangladesh, where the predominant form of mechanized personal transport has been the bicycle. In those countries there is very little motorized public transport, and what there is, is often more expensive and little quicker than the bicycle because of its relative inflexibility and inability to exercise its potential speed advantage due to (predominantly bicycle-caused) congestion. The most obvious trade-up as income increases is not into the bus but onto a motorcyle – and eventually into a car. Even completely free entry into the public transport industry seems unlikely to break that trend. Given the typical fiscal inability of municipal governments in developing countries to subsidize public transport and the continued resistance to internalization of externalities through road pricing, it remains critically important to the establishment of the proper role for public transport that there are some strongly pro-active surrogate policies of private vehicle restraint and public transport priority.

Infrastructure is also a problem for public road passenger transport. A major limitation to the effectiveness of bus transport in most countries lies in the difficulty of giving it sufficient separation from general traffic congestion to allow its full potential to be exploited. In a number of Latin American countries, but particularly in Brazil, completely separated busways have shown the capability of carrying peak single direction flows of 20 000 passengers per hour at effectively free flow speeds (Rebelo and Benevenuto, 1997). In the best-known (though not the largest) system, in Curitiba, Brazil, the busway forms the trunk haul section of a well-integrated trunk and feeder system. Both this system and the even more highly utilized busways in Bela Horizonte and São Paulo involve private sector buses using publicly provided infrastructure. Moves are now being made to secure private financing of busways in Brazil through private concessioning of construction and operation.

6   CONCLUSIONS

All of the four areas – road maintenance, highway construction, rail transport and urban bus transport – discussed in this chapter have traditionally been domains of public sector monopoly supply, considered essential for the achievement of social, environmental or economically strategic objectives.

In the case of urban public transport, rail transport and road maintenance these public sector monopolies have usually performed poorly, largely because the very existence of a secure supply monopoly generated incentives to look after the interests of the agency itself (including the staff of the agency) rather than those of the consumers of the product. The continued achievement of the social or economic objectives on which the monopoly was founded has been won only at the expense of progressively increasing subsidy.

In the case of trunk roads the use of competitive supply of design and construction has partly overcome the incentive problems but has not mobilized private capital to supplement public sources.

So all of the cases, for one reason or another, represent domains in which a public financing gap has been perceived, the magnitude of which is such that private sector financial participation is increasingly urgent.

The strategic objectives remain. But experience in a number of sectors and countries has shown the possibility of structuring private supply arrangements to reconcile the achievement of these objectives with financially viable private transport supply. The questions that are now being posed do not concern the desirability of the strategic objectives or whether private sector supply is possible, but how best to design institutions and incentive structures which reconcile efficient supply with social objective achievement.

Experience now suggests some important conditions for success in concessioning public transport infrastructure to the private sector.

First, there must be a favourable economic environment. The existence of experience of concessioning in other sectors, particularly in the context of a national law on concessions, is invaluable. A stable macroeconomic situation and undisputed rights to remit profit are particularly important if it is intended to attract foreign participation in the funding. The existence of a mature local capital market is also important.

Second, there must be a very clear commitment of government to the participation of the private sector. It must be willing to commit itself contractually to a long-term series of payments. Furthermore, for a concession contract to be a meaningful commitment – rather than an invitation to renegotiate – government must also be willing to accept constraints on its freedom to intervene in fares and service strategy outside the terms of the concession contract. The experience with the Bangkok urban expressway in Thailand (see Section 3, above) may seriously inhibit the willingness of the private sector to enter future agreements with government.

At the heart of the general reluctance of the private sector to invest in public transport infrastructure is often a lack of faith in governments to honour the terms of concession agreements over a long term and to abjure interventions which will damage the value of the investment. There are a number of ways in which the multilateral lending institutions can help to overcome this through guarantees to private sector lenders backed by counter-guarantees from the government to the institution. This can cover such things as the good faith of government, or lengthening the term of private financing. One of the major challenges to the multilaterals is to develop such guarantee instruments which can be mobilized sufficiently quickly and flexibly to match private financiers' requirements.

In all cases, the reconciliation of private and public sector interests is based on the development of competitive forms. In all cases this competition requires institutional restructuring. And in all cases, this involves some residual role for the state – as the source of investment in the case of most of the road sector, and as customer and/or regulator in cases where supply is concessioned to the private sector.

Traditional concerns about efficient pricing are not redundant in all this. They remain necessary. But they are not sufficient. What is needed in addition are:

- detailed attention to incentive structures for supply agencies;
- institutional reforms to put the effective incentive mechanisms in place; and
- careful attention to the location-specific characteristics which determine what will and what will not work in particular circumstances.

Those are the new economics of sustainable transport.

NOTE

1. About the involvement of the private sector in the provision of infrastructure services generally, see Chapter 9, Section 4 above and following.

REFERENCES

Barrett, I. and T. Powell (1999), 'Analysis of bus types for urban transport services in Central Asia and Russia', mimeo, Washington, DC: World Bank.

Darbera, R. (1993), 'Deregulation of urban transport in Chile: what have we learned in the decade 1979–1989?', *Transport Reviews*, **13** (1), 45–9.

Devarajan, S., L. Squire and S. Suthiwart-Narueput (1997), 'Beyond rate of return: reorienting project appraisal', *The World Bank Research Observer*, **12** (1), 35–46.

Engel, E., R. Fischer and A. Galetovic (1997), 'Highway franchising: pitfalls and opportunities', *American Economic Review*, **87** (2), 68–72.

Estache, A. and J. Carbajo (1996), 'Designing toll road concessions – lessons from Argentina', *Viewpoint*, Note No. 99, Washington, DC: World Bank Group Finance, Private Sector and Infrastructure Network.

Fouracre, P.R., R.J. Allport and J.M. Thompson (1990), *The Performance of Rail Mass Transit in Developing Countries*, Transport Research Laboratory Research Report 278, Crowthorne: TRL.

Gupta, S. and W. Mahler (1995), 'Taxation of petroleum products: theory and empirical evidence', *Energy Economy*, **17** (2), 101–6.

Gwilliam, K.M. (1993), *Urban Bus Operators Associations*, Infrastructure Note UT3, Washington, DC: World Bank.

Gwilliam, K.M. (1996), *Getting the Prices Wrong – A Tale of Two Islands*, Infrastructure Note UT6, Washington, DC: World Bank.

Gwilliam, K.M. (1999), 'Private participation in public transport in the FSU', Paper presented to Sixth International Conference on Privatization and Competition in Land Transport, Cape Town, South Africa.

Gwilliam, K.M. and R.G. Scurfield (1996), *Constructing a Competitive Environment in Public Road Passenger Transport*, Transport, Water and Urban (TWU) Discussion Paper TWU-24, Washington, DC: World Bank.

Gwilliam, K.M. and Z. Shalizi (1997), *Road Funds, User Charges and Taxes*, Transport, Water and Urban (TWU) Discussion Paper TWU-26, Washington, DC: World Bank.

Gwilliam, K.M., A.J. Kumar and R.T. Meakin (1999), 'Designing competition in urban bus passenger transport – lessons from Uzbekistan', Paper presented to Sixth International Conference on Privatization and Competition in Land Transport, Cape Town, South Africa.

Gyamfi, P. (1992), *Infrastructure Maintenance in Latin America and the Caribbean: The Costs of Neglect and Options for Improvement*, Latin America and the Caribbean (LAC) Regional Studies Program Report No. 17, Washington, DC: World Bank.

Heggie, I.G. and P. Vickers (1998), *Commercial Management and Financing of Roads*, World Bank Technical Paper No. 409, Washington, DC: World Bank.

Kessides, I.N. and R.D. Willig (1995), 'Restructuring regulation of the railroad industry', *Viewpoint*, Note No. 58, Washington, DC: World Bank.

McCleary, W.A. and E.U. Tobin (1990), *Earmarking Government Revenues in Colombia*, Policy, Research and External Affairs (PRE) Working Papers WPS 425, Washington, DC: World Bank.

Meyer, J.R. and A. Gómez-Ibáñez (1993), *Going Private: The International Experience with Transport Privatization*, Washington, DC: Brookings Institution.

Mitric, S. (1998), *Approaching Metros as Development Projects*, Transport, Water and Urban Development Department, Transport Division (TWUTD) Discussion Paper TWU-28, Washington, DC: World Bank.

Newbery, D.M. (1994), 'The case for a public road authority', *Journal of Transport Economics and Policy*, **28** (3), 235–54.

Potter, B. (1997), 'Dedicated road funds: a preliminary view on a World Bank initiative', *IMF Papers on Policy Analysis and Assessment*, WP/97/7, Washington, DC: International Monetary Fund Fiscal Affairs Department.

Rebelo, J. (1999), 'Rail and subway concessions in Rio de Janeiro', World Bank Group Finance, Private Sector and Infrastructure Network, *Viewpoint*, Note No. 183, also in *Public Policy for the Private Sector*, Finance, Private Sector and Infrastructure Network, Washington, DC: World Bank, 59–66.

Rebelo, J and P. Benevenuto (1997), *Lessons from São Paulo's Metropolitan Busways Concessions Program*, Latin America and the Caribbean Region Finance, Private Sector and Infrastructure Department Policy Research Working Paper 1859, Washington, DC: World Bank.

Ruster, J. (1997), 'A retrospective on the Mexican toll road program (1989–94)', *Viewpoint*, Note No. 125, Washington, DC: World Bank.

Thompson, L.S. (1997), 'The benefits of separating rail infrastructure from operations', *Public Policy for the Private Sector*, Finance, Private Sector and Infrastructure Network, Washington, DC: World Bank, pp. 49–52.

Thompson, L.S. and K.-J. Budin (1997), 'Global trend to railway concessioning delivering positive results', *Public Policy for the Private Sector*, Finance, Private Sector and Infrastructure Network, Washington, DC: World Bank, pp. 41–8.

Tynan, N. (1999), 'Private participation in the rail sector, recent trends', *Public Policy for the Private Sector*, Finance, Private Sector and Infrastructure Network, Washington, DC: World Bank, pp. 51–8.

Van de Velde, D. (ed.) (1999), *Changing Trains: Railway Reform and the Role of Competition – The Experience of Six Countries*, Aldershot: Ashgate.

World Bank (1988), *Road Deterioration in Developing Countries: Causes and Remedies*, A World Bank Policy Study, Washington, DC: World Bank.

World Bank (1995), *Bureaucrats in Business: The Economics and Politics of Government Ownership*, Washington, DC: Oxford University Press for the World Bank.

World Bank (1996), *Sustainable Transport: Priorities for Policy Reform*, Development in Practice Book, Washington, DC: World Bank.

Select bibliography

Ben-Akiva, M. and S.R. Lerman (1985), *Discrete Choice Analysis: Theory and Application to Travel Demand*, Cambridge, MA and London: MIT Press.

Blanco, L.O. and B. Van Houtte (1996), *EC Competition Law in the Transport Sector*, Oxford: Clarendon.

Brooks, M.R. and K.J. Button (1992), 'Shipping within the framework of a Single European Market', *Transport Reviews*, **12**, 237–52.

Button, K.J. (1993), 'East–West European transport: an overview', in D. Banister and J. Berechman (eds), *Transportation in a Unified Europe: Policies and Challenges*, Amsterdam: Elsevier, pp. 291–313.

Button, K.J., K. Haynes and K. Stough (1998), *Flying into the Future: Air Transport Policy in the European Union*, Cheltenham: Edward Elgar.

Ettema, D.F. and H.J.P. Timmermans (eds) (1997), *Activity-based Approaches to Travel Analysis*, Oxford: Pergamon.

European Conference of Ministers of Transport (1996a), *Access to European Transport Markets*, Seminar on the Integration of Central and Eastern European Operators in European Transport Markets, Paris: OECD.

European Conference of Ministers of Transport (1996b), *Privatisation and Regulation of Road Freight Transport*, Seminar, Paris, 5 September 1996, Paris: OECD.

European Conference of Ministers of Transport (1998), *Efficient Transport for Europe, Policies for Internalisation of External Costs*, Paris: OECD.

Gaspard, M. (1996), *Transport Infrastructure Financing in Central and Eastern Europe*, Paris: Presses de l'école nationale des Ponts et Chaussées.

Glaister, S. (1998), *Virtue out of Necessity: Practical Pricing of Traffic in Towns*, London: Social Market Foundation.

Heggie, I.G. and P. Vickers (1998), *Commercial Management and Financing of Roads*, World Bank Technical Paper No. 409, Washington, DC: World Bank.

INFRAS/IWW (1995), *External Effects of Transport*, Study for the Union Internationale des Chemins de Fer, Zürich and Karlsruhe: IWW.

Jansson, J.O. and G. Lindberg (1997), *Transport Pricing Principles in Detail*, European Commission, DG VII Project No: ST-96-SC.172, Brussels.

Jara-Díaz, S. and C. Cortés (1996), 'On the calculation of scale economies from transport cost functions', *Journal of Transport Economics and Policy*, **30**, 157–70.

McGowan, F. (1998), 'EU transport policy', in A.M. El-Agraa (ed.), *The European Union, History, Institutions, Economics and Policies*, London: Prentice-Hall, pp. 247–65.

Meyer, J.R. and A. Gómez-Ibáñez (1993), *Going Private: The International Experience with Transport Privatization*, Washington, DC: Brookings Institution.

Mogridge, M.J.H. (1990), *Travel in Towns: Jam Yesterday, Jam Today, Jam Tomorrow?*, London: Macmillan.

Nijkamp, P. and E. Blaas (1992), *Impact Assessment and Decision Support in Transportation Planning*, Boston: Kluwer.

Organization for Economic Cooperation and Development (OECD) (1995), *Urban Travel and Sustainable Development*, Paris: OECD.

Oum, T.H. and W.G. Waters II (1996), 'A survey of recent developments in transportation cost function research', *Logistics and Transportation Review*, **32**, 423–62.

Pearce, D., E. Barbier and A. Markandya (1993), *Blueprint. Measuring Sustainable Development*, London: Earthscan.

Quinet, E. (1994), 'The social costs of transport: evaluation and links with internalisation policies', in European Conference of Ministers of Transport, *Internalising the Social Costs of Transport*, Paris: OECD, pp. 31–75.

Rus, G. de and C. Nash (1997), *Recent Developments in Transport Economics*, Aldershot: Ashgate.

Small, K. (1992), *Urban Transportation Economics*, Chur: Harwood.

US Federal Transit Administration (1996), *The Role of Transit in Congestion Management*, prepared by Hickling-Lewis-Brod Inc., Washington, DC: US Federal Transit Administration.

van den Bergh, J.C.J.M., P. Nijkamp and P. Rietveld (1996), Spatial equilibrium models: a survey with special emphasis on transportation', in J.C.J.M. van den Bergh, P. Nijkamp and P. Rietveld (eds), *Recent Advances in Spatial Equilibrium Modelling: Methodology and Applications*, Berlin etc.: Springer, pp. 48–76.

Van de Velde, D. (ed.) (1999), *Changing Trains: Railway Reform and the Role of Competition – The Experience of Six Countries*, Aldershot: Ashgate.

Venables, A.J. and M. Gasiorek (1998), *The Welfare Implications of Transport Improvements in the Presence of Market Failure*, Report prepared for the Standing Advisory Committee on Trunk Road Assessment (SACTRA) Committee, London.

Vickerman, R.W. (1991), *Infrastructure and Regional Development*, Pion: London.

Wardman, M. (1997), *A Review of Evidence on the Value of Travel Time in Great Britain*, Working paper 495, Leeds: Leeds University, Institute of Transport Economics.

World Bank (1994), *Infrastructure for Development*, Washington, DC: World Bank.

World Bank (1996), *Sustainable Transport: Priorities for Policy Reform*, Development in Practice Book, Washington, DC: World Bank.

Index